INTO THE LIGHT

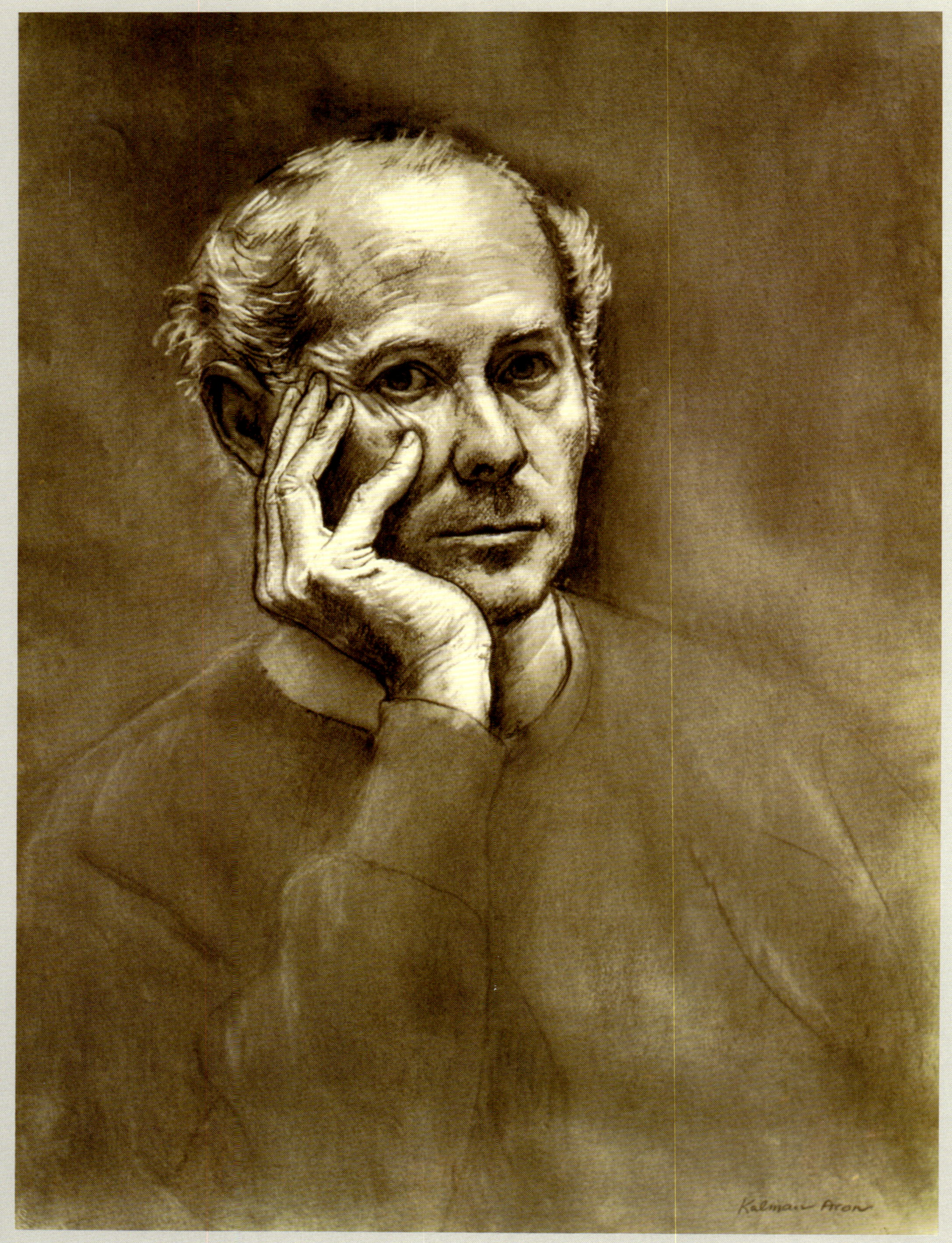
Kalman Aron

INTO THE LIGHT

The Healing Art of Kalman Aron

Susan Beilby Magee

Published by Hard Press Editions
and Posterity Press, Inc.
in association with Hudson Hills Press

Published by Hard Press Editions, Inc.
Stockbridge, Massachusetts
and Posterity Press, Inc.
Chevy Chase, Maryland
in association with
Hudson Hills Press LLC
New York, New York

www.IntotheLightKalmanAron.com
www.HardPressEditions.com
www.PosterityPress.com
www.HudsonHills.com

Distributed in the United States,
its territories and possessions, and Canada
by National Book Network, Inc.
Distributed outside North America
by Antique Collectors' Club, Ltd.

Printed and bound in the United States of America by
Capital Offset Company, Concord, New Hampshire

Library of Congress Cataloging-in-Publication Data

Magee, Susan Beilby.
Into the light : the healing art of Kalman Aron /
Susan Beilby Magee.
p. cm.
Includes index.
ISBN 978-1-55595-385-0 (alk. paper)
1. Aron, Kalman, 1924– . 2. Artists—California—Los Angeles—Biography. 3. Holocaust survivors—California—Los Angeles—Biography. 4. Holocaust, Jewish (1939–1945)—Latvia—Riga—Personal narratives. 5. Spiritual healing. I. Title.
ND237.A743M34 2012
759.13—dc23
[B]

2012023512

Art Photography Credits:

Except for the pages indicated below, all photography of Kalman Aron's artwork is by Dub Rogers

Richard Almada, p. 125

Kate Carr, pp. 74, 79, 103, 140, 141, 144, 206

Lindsay George, pp. 16, 27, 33, 36, 43, 44, 47, 83, 91, 93, 106 left, 107 left, 107 right, 109 top, 113, 117, 122, 133, 134, 135, 150, 163, 171, 179

Gregory R. Staley, pp. 12, 73, 102, 108, 143, 147

Brandon Webster, pp. 15, 17, 66, 70, 75, 98

Other Photograph Credits:

Bildarchiv Preussicher Kulturbesitz, 40 bottom

Todd Cheney, p. 204

Jono David/HaChayim HaYehudim Jewish Photo Library, p. 30

Gisling, p. 62

William G. Hanson, Jr., 172, 175

Dub Rogers, p. 19

Elena Spungina, p. 200 top

U.S. Holocaust Memorial Museum, pp. 39, 40 top and bottom, 46 (courtesy Staatsanwalt beim Landgericht Hamburg), 49 (courtesy American Jewish Joint Distribution Committee), 52 (courtesy Yad Vashem Photo Archives), 54 bottom (courtesy Terezin Memorial Museum), 55 (courtesy Yad Vashem Photo Archives), 199

Frontispiece:
Self-Portrait (mid 1960s), sepia stick on white paper, 24 × 18 in.

Page 220:
Self-Portrait (late 1960s–early 1970s), ink on paper, 14 × 11 in.

CONTENTS

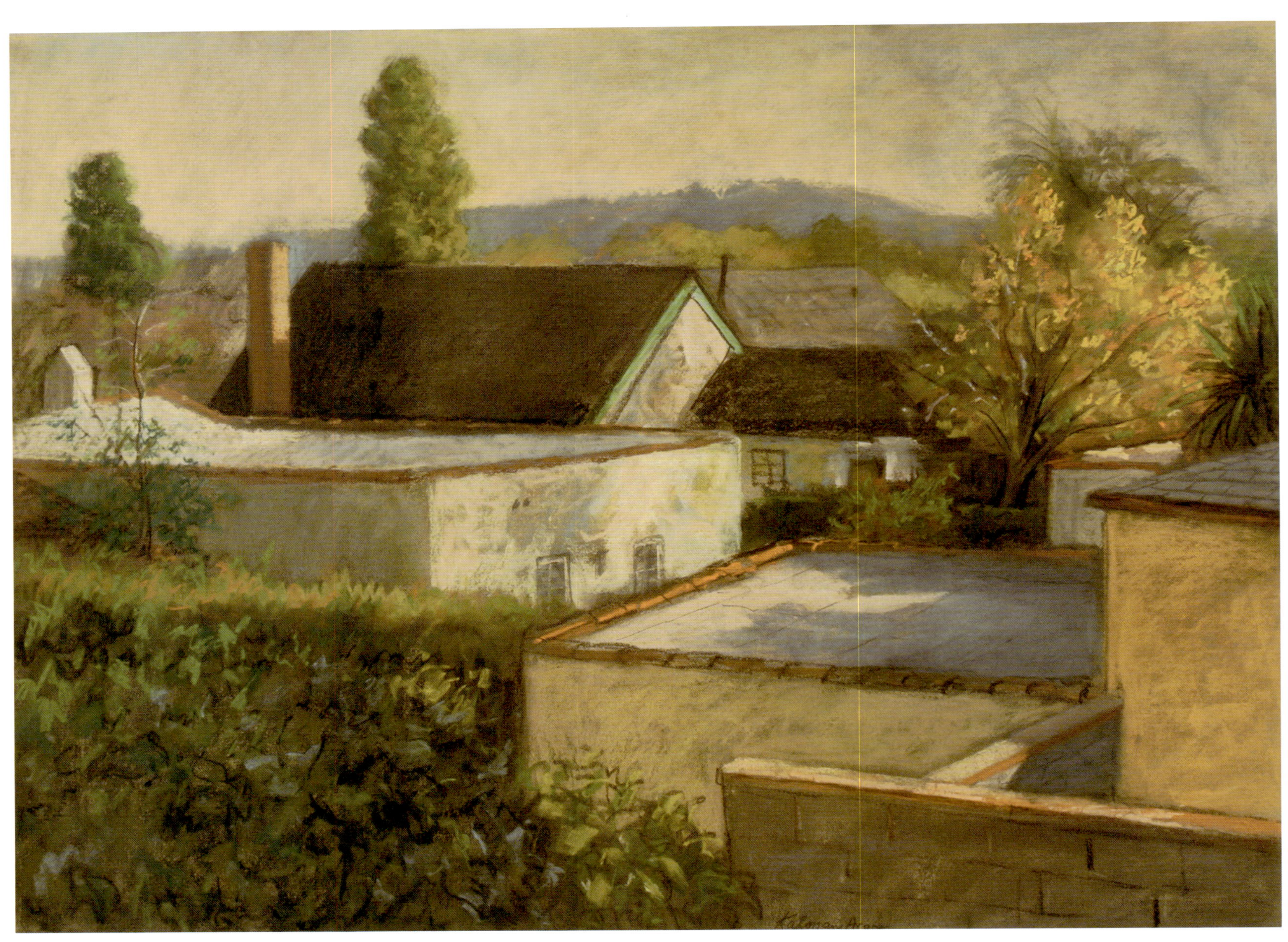

Rooftops Off My Balcony (1980s), pastel on paper, 12½ × 29½ in.

To John,

For the dreams manifest,
paths traveled,
ideas explored,
love and laughter shared,
I am forever grateful.

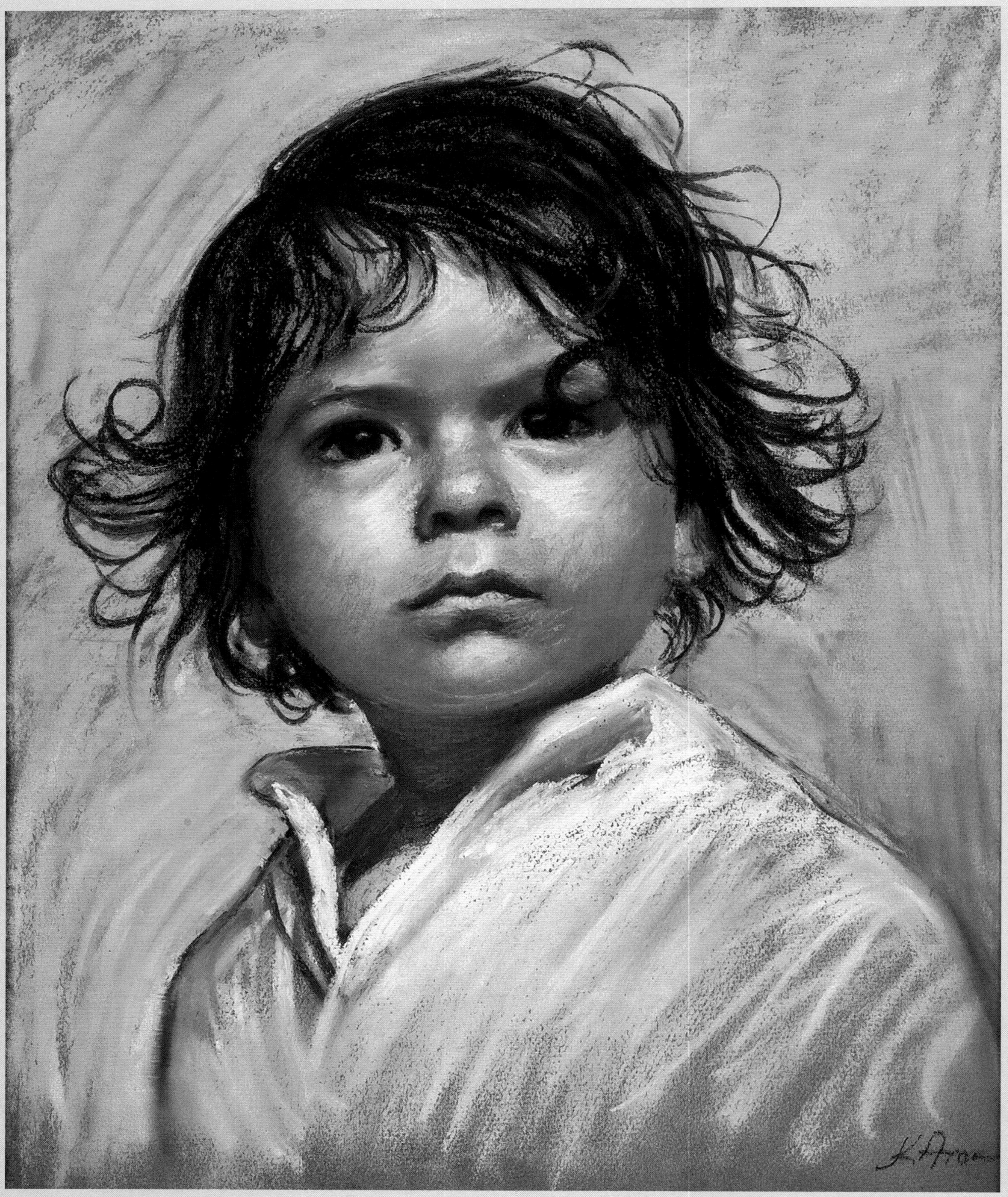

1

PROLOGUE

The Artist and the Healer

Each man's life represents a road toward himself.

Hermann Hesse

Child with Black Eyes (1951), pastel on paper, 17 × 13½ in.

This is a story of the heart and the alchemy of the soul.
It is about courage, evil and survival . . . love, loss and hope.
It is about remembering, healing and sanctuary.

Most of all, it is about choices:
How does one respond to the extremes of human brutality?
How does the experience of evil inform one's life,
relationships and work over a lifetime?
What happens to the rage, sorrow and despair?
Does one ever trust again?
Does one choose to remember, forgive and heal?

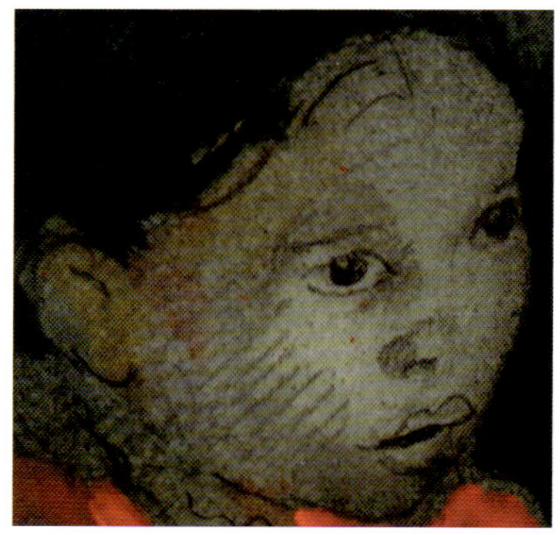
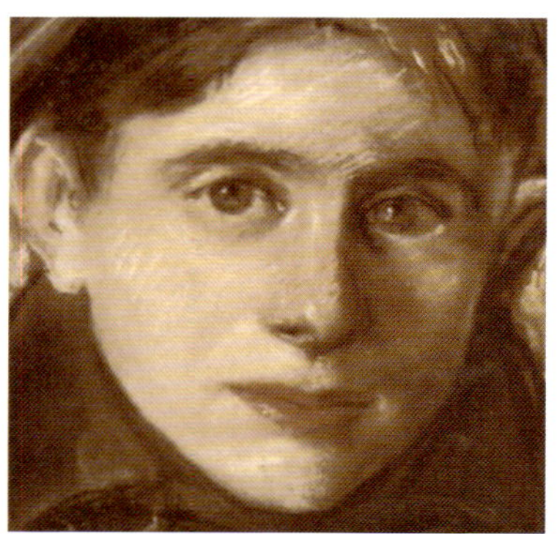
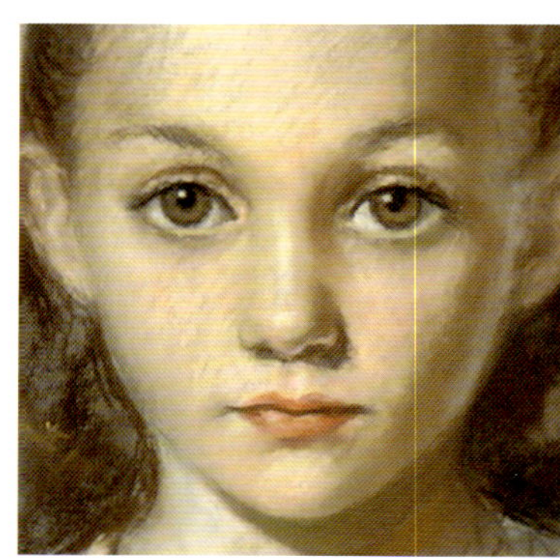
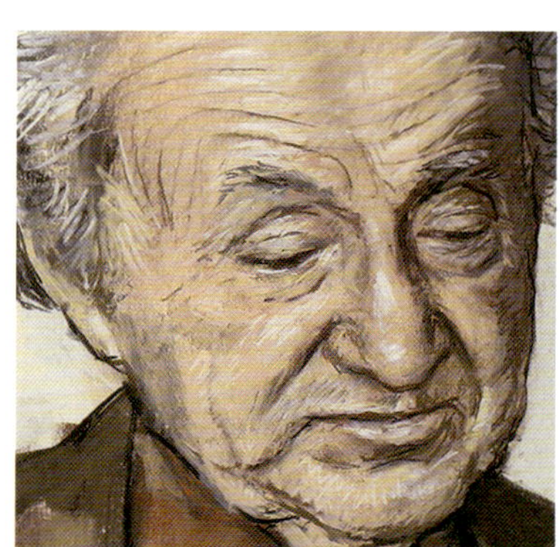

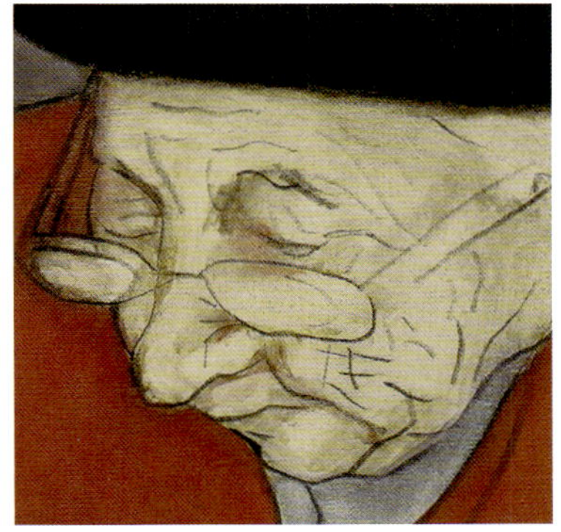

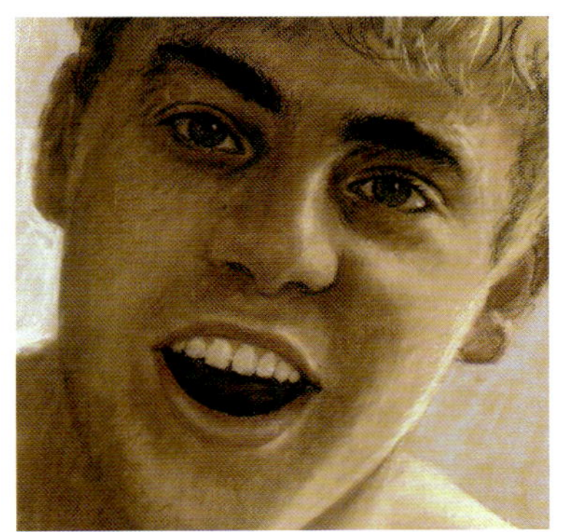

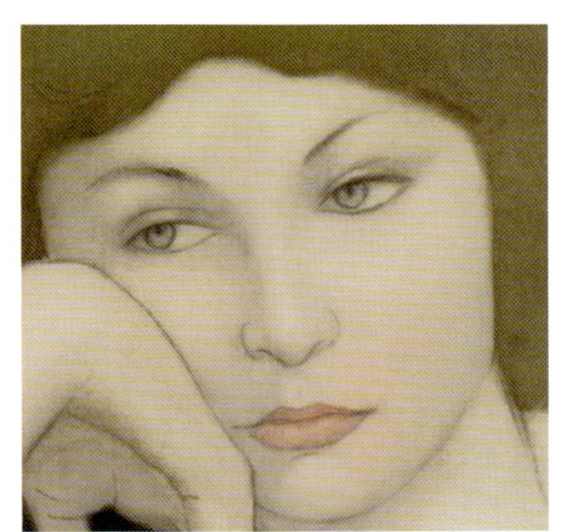

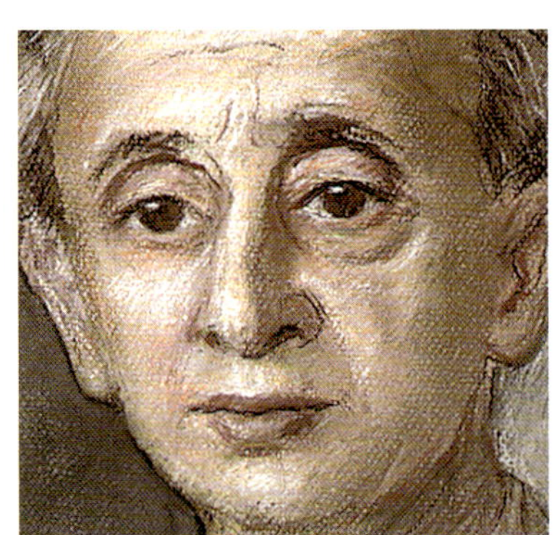

Join me on a journey that explores these questions. The life of artist Kalman Aron is one man's instinctive response in resolving these issues. He survived four years imprisoned in the Riga ghetto and in a series of Nazi death camps, and then spent a lifetime transforming the experience of the Holocaust's evil into truth, beauty and understanding—on canvas and on paper. In this process he recaptured his own light. His visual works of art testify to the triumph of the human spirit and reflect his journey from the dark to the light. This book, which melds both his memoir and my account of his life, is a universal story about healing. Its lessons relate to all who have suffered—whether physically or psychologically, whether collectively or individually. I hope it may guide all who seek to put their suffering aside and reclaim their light.

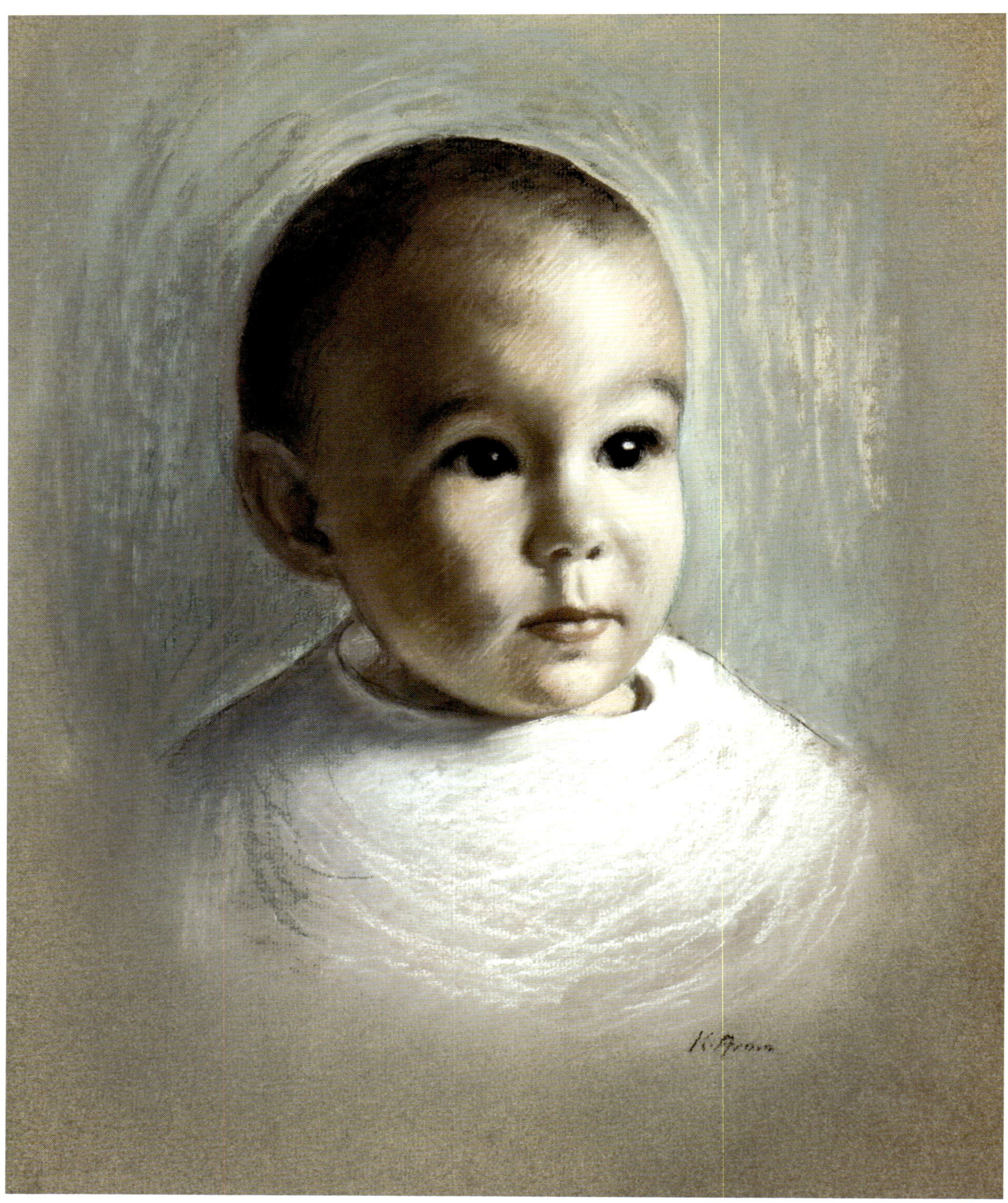

Portrait of Nonnie (1951), pastel on paper, 16 × 13 in.

The Invitation

Life is a mystery, full of surprises. We move along day by day, then an invitation of cosmic proportions drops into our world, shaking the ground of our being. The mind scrambles to understand its meaning. Our emotions yell: "No, don't accept it." The soul says: "Quiet; listen. You already know you will do this." One clear morning in the new millennium, I received such an invitation.

My plane circles over Palm Springs, California, a vastly different landscape from the rich greenery of my home in Washington, D.C. The palette is sandy; the air is clear; and the light foreshortens distance. I feel I could reach out and touch the San Jacinto Mountains looming in stark relief against the blue sky. Palm trees line the streets, recalling an era of glamour and romance. I feel refreshed as I leave the plane to visit my mother, Marichu Aurrecoechea Beilby.

Her garden is a crisp array of yellow, pink and red flowers: snapdragons, roses and daisies, all standing before a beige stucco wall. Over the top of the patio wall falls a brilliant fuchsia bougainvillea. My mother's love of gardening recalls her English heritage. She was born and raised in England. Her Spanish Basque father, Bernardo, lost his import businesses in the crash of 1929, and in 1930 her English mother, Laura, moved her family to Los Angeles to start a new life. At age sixteen Marichu arrived in America. She went to work in a fine furniture store, Barker Brothers, and after a year or two she talked her boss into letting her be an interior decorator. By 1951 she had developed her own successful decorating practice.

One day as she walked to a frame store on Seventh Street in Los Angeles, she saw a pastel hanging in the window of a boy, *Child with Black Eyes*. His head, slightly tilted, was crowned with wisps of black hair. His deep black eyes reached into Marichu's heart. A decade earlier she had lost her first child, a black-eyed girl, also named Marichu, whom my parents called Nonnie. Born a "blue baby" with a heart defect, the doctors said she would die in a few days. She lived for nine months.

Child with Black Eyes (detail); full image on page 8.

When my mother saw this pastel, she fell in love with it. She asked the store owner, "Who did the drawing?" He answered, "The artist is a refugee from Europe. He survived the camps in part by doing drawings of children of guards from photos they gave him." "Give him my phone number," said Marichu, "and ask him to call me." The owner protested: "He doesn't speak English." "I don't care," she responded. "Have him call me." She wanted him to paint a portrait from a photograph of the black-eyed baby she had lost and then to paint her two living daughters: my sister, Elena, and me.

When a tall, thin young man with sparkling blue eyes and wispy blonde hair came into our home, I liked him instantly. He set up his easel in the living room. I sat opposite in a chair and he asked me to sit still. I watched him. He looked at me. He held up his thumb to measure my features. He worked quickly, with pastels. He knew what he was doing.

When the portrait was done, I saw myself. I was amazed. My eyes were huge. He had captured their hazel color. When I moved around the room, the eyes followed me. My parents' friends looked at it, walking back and forth, fascinated by the movement of the eyes. This was our first glimpse of his artistic gifts in portraiture.

I believe that our eyes reveal our souls. Looking into my six-year-old eyes in that portrait, I realize that Kalman captured something that I have carried all my life. I have always been curious about who we are and why we are here. I have wondered why there is suffering, pain and cruelty. Kalman caught that curiosity in my eyes.

When we first met, my mother was thirty-eight, Kalman was twenty-seven, and I was six. The encounter with the portrait of the black-eyed boy sparked a lifelong friendship of respect and affection between Kalman and Marichu.

Portrait of Susan (1951), pastel on paper, 21 × 17½ in.

In Palm Springs I walk into my mother's living room and see her collection of Kalman's paintings hanging on the long wall. Among them is the boy with black eyes and a profile of my daughter, Elizabeth, at age five. Down the hall I find my mother sitting up in bed, a cigarette in hand. She flashes a smile. Her pure white hair is still thick, her blue eyes huge; they look even larger today on a face that has become so thin, with high cheek bones, a straight nose, a long Basque upper lip and strong chin. She too is a survivor. Having lost her home and opportunity for higher education, she went to work during the Depression and didn't quit until she was eighty. She was a successful entrepreneur who started five businesses and became the nation's top manufacturer of artificial flowers. A creative artist in her own right, no wonder she had found a kinship with the young Kalman Aron.

I remind her that Kalman is coming to show us his new paintings. When he arrives, his blue eyes still have that sparkle and curiosity I saw a lifetime ago. Wisps of sandy hair above his ears lighten his face. His skin is fair, his body tall. His hands are strong. The fingers of his right hand curl with arthritis after all these years of painting. Wearing a short-sleeved shirt and khaki trousers, Kalman is full of life and spirit. It is uplifting to be in his presence. He is so alive. . . . How, I wonder, after all he experienced?

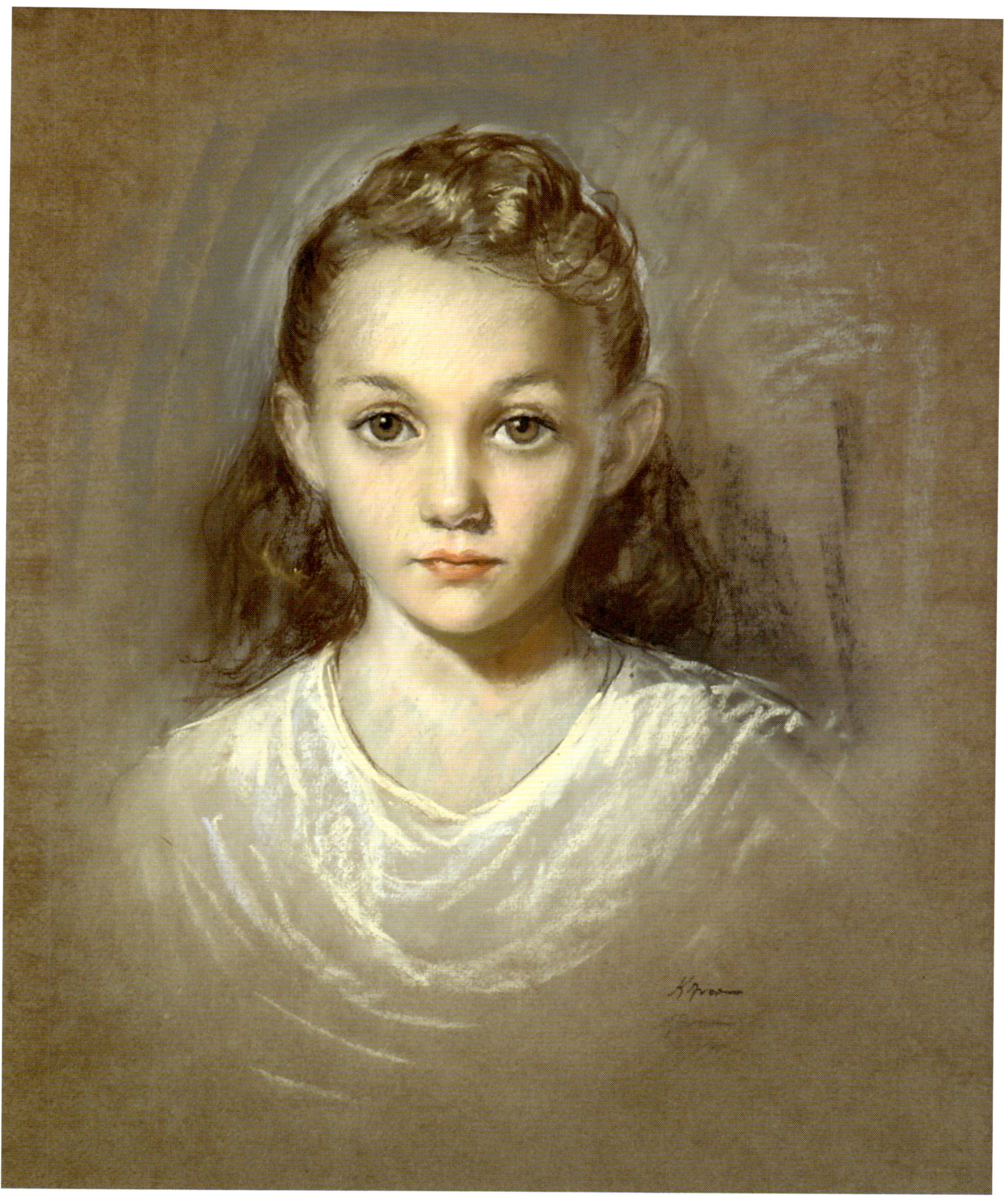

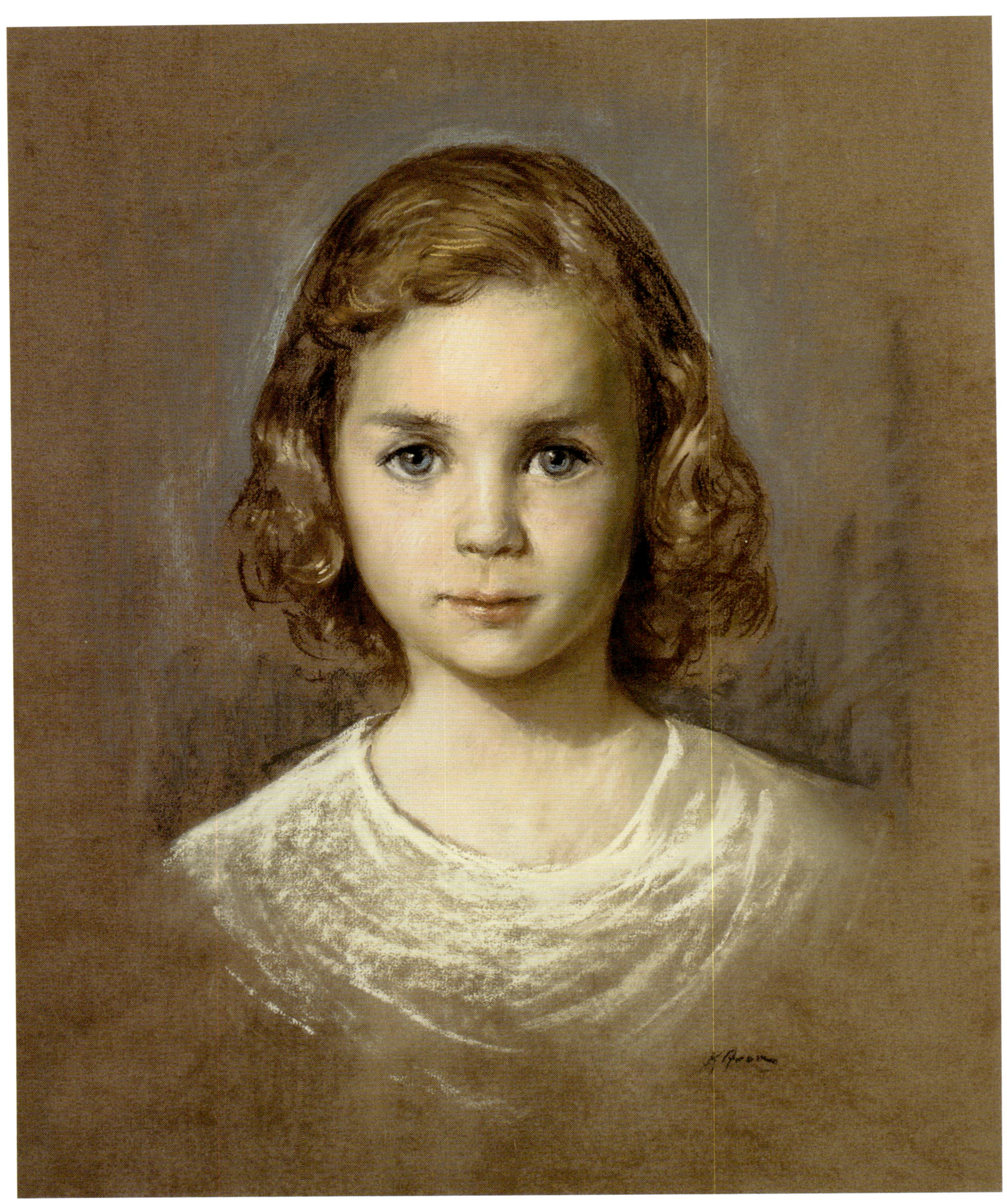

Portrait of Elena (1951), pastel on paper, 21 × 17½ in.

He sees his paintings, remembers this one and that. In the bedroom he greets this woman he has known for over fifty years. Above her headboard he sees his portraits of her three daughters, Nonnie, Elena and Susan. Outside, on this clear, sunny day, we sit at her patio table. Kalman begins to show us new paintings in acrylics—semiabstract drawings of trees in green and blue, yellow and orange—so much movement, so much life. He shows us abstracts with intricate patterns in black, red and white, some with pink, green and yellow. All seem to flow effortlessly from his mind. He gives Mom two.

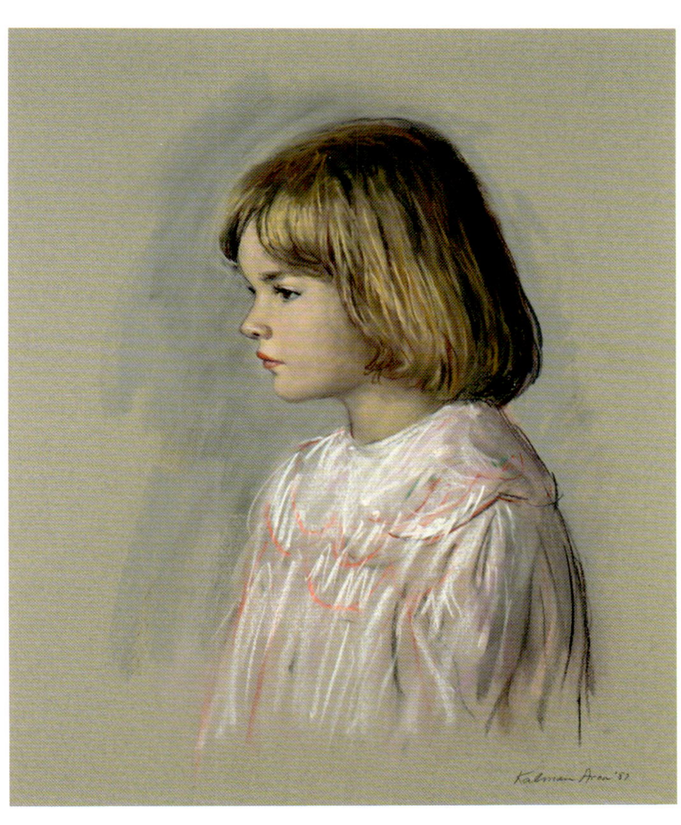

Profile of Elizabeth (1987), pastel on paper, 22 × 17½ in.

Kalman tells me he just saw the movie *The Pianist,* about a Polish Jew in the Holocaust. "Susan," he says, "I have never wanted to remember until I saw that movie. Seeing it has given me permission to tell my story. It is even more involved, with all kinds of twists and turns." I listen. I know he survived the Holocaust, but I also know he never talks about the details. He continues:"Several people have approached me to write my story and do a film. I don't know them. I don't trust them."

Suddenly, Kalman turns to face me. Looking at me intently with those clear blue eyes, he asks,"Will you write my story?" I look at him. My thoughts race. In high school I saw *The Diary of Anne Frank*. The images and siren sounds of the Gestapo cars still haunt me. In my twenties I read a book set in the Warsaw ghetto. It upset me so much I made a conscious decision never to read anything more about the Holocaust. What happened in the Holocaust was incomprehensible—evil incarnate.

I respond: "Kalman, give me time to think about it. A day."

Our conversation resumes. When he is ready to leave, I thank him for coming and tell him I will call in a day.

Later my mother asks, "Why don't you do it?" The idea swirls in my head. Why don't I do it? I have never written a book. I have written a lot of memos and papers over the years, and I knew I would write a book one day. In the late 1980s I had begun deep studies in spirituality, meditation and the spirit realms. In one of my early meditations I saw a big book rise out of my abdomen. I looked for the title; there was none. I opened the pages; they were blank. I asked: What is it about? "Good and evil," the answer came. It was such a powerful experience that I didn't question its truth. I knew one day I would write a book.

I understood instantly that it was an honor that Kalman had asked me. The question I had for myself: Was I strong enough to hear what happened? Could I hold the space for him to remember?

The next day I called and said, "Yes, Kalman, I will write your story. Thank you for asking me."

The Acceptance

Kalman had asked a person to write his story who had spent the last two and a half decades practicing the healing arts. Exhausted in 1986, I took a break from my career in government and business and planned to return in a year. Although I didn't know it at the time, my executive days were over. I began a profound spiritual journey that eventually led to writing this book.

Today I am an energy healer and certified hypnotherapist. I lead meditation healing circles, including one I founded in 2003, the Washington Circle of Master Healers. We meet monthly to address individual, community and global healing. I also participate in healing programs at the Center for Prayer and Pilgrimage at the Washington National Cathedral.

I have always been curious about the meaning of life. I studied world religions in high school and theology in college, and I have continued to explore the rich religious and spiritual traditions of the East and the West. I have been blessed with excellent teachers who have taught me various forms of meditation, visualization, hypnotherapy, past life regression and energy healing. Over time my psychic gifts unfolded.

One of my early teachers was a gifted woman who guided me in meditative visualizations. In an early session my father appeared before me on his knees, asking for forgiveness. He had committed suicide when I was nineteen. I thought I had forgiven him because I understood why he had done it: he was in a state of utter despair. But when he came on his knees and asked, I could not say the words. My heart had not forgiven him at all. Twenty-three years later, I was still furious. I adored him, and he had abandoned me. It took quite some time and several visits before I could genuinely forgive him.

This experience taught me that a vast realm of feelings lies deep in the unconscious and that there is a safe way to access it. Since then I have explored this realm and refined techniques to help myself and others discover true feelings, heal traumas and release old beliefs and patterns that no longer serve.

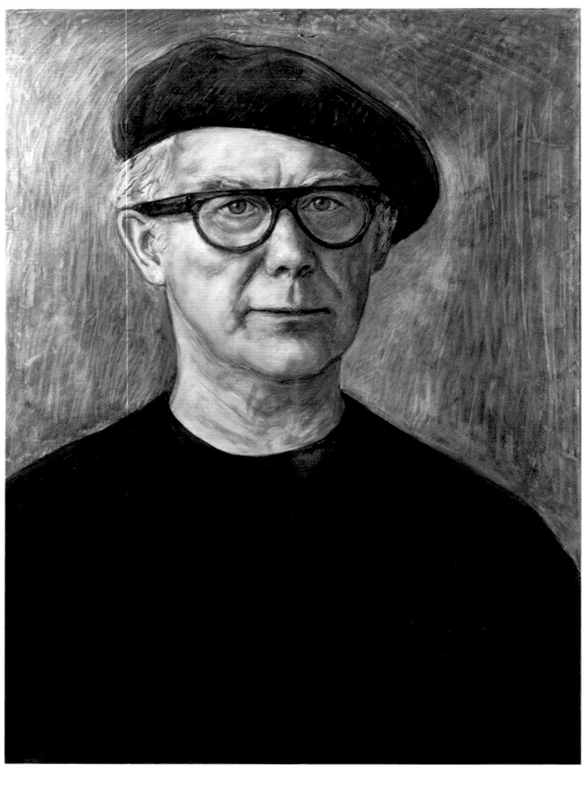

Self-Portrait (1994), charcoal on foam core, 40 × 30 in.

Developing psychic gifts was a surprise. They came slowly and grew organically, like the fruit on a tree. One day I was playing cards with my daughter, and I could see what cards she was holding. That's interesting, I thought. I told a friend, who said, "That is the tip of the iceberg. Do you want to open more fully to psychic phenomena?" I wasn't sure, but the visions were beautiful. Animals appeared with lessons about gentleness, courage and strength. I met aspects of myself I didn't know existed. I could track feelings back to scenes in my childhood and ask my father's spirit what was really happening.

I have learned that the body is a master teacher. The archive of our experiences, it remembers everything that has ever happened. It is also the repository of wisdom. My greatest teacher said, "Stop seeking answers from others. Go within, and you will find all that you seek." Over time I learned my interior landscape and began to recognize where my body held fears, sorrows and anger, as well as love, compassion and joy.

This background prepared me to work with an artist who expresses himself with paint on canvas rather than words. If I ask Kalman why he painted a certain subject a certain way, he responds, "I don't know. I just did it." I access the meaning of his life through his art by tuning into the energy of his paintings. I ask: Why did Kalman paint this? How does it reflect his experience and what he learned in the Holocaust? What does it reveal about his personal transformation?

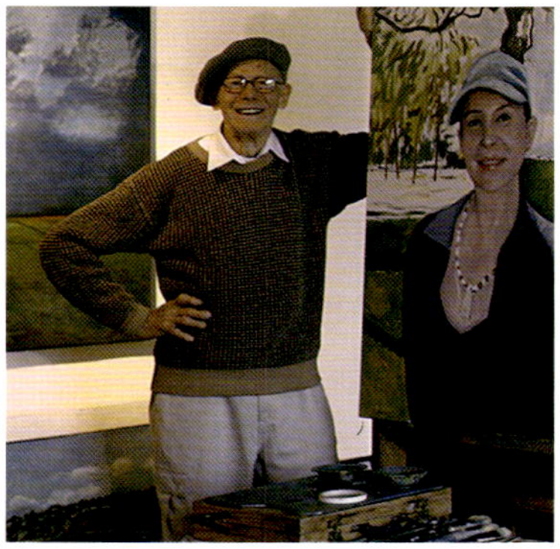

Kalman Aron in his studio (2008), with *Portrait of Miriam* (page 209).

Nor could I have written this book if I had not taken my own healing journey. I understand how challenging it is, and I recognize the milestones along the path. I can hold the space for Kalman to remember. I also do not believe in coincidences. There was no rational reason for Kalman to turn to me that day and ask me to write his story. It was an intuitive act. I believe our souls understood each other. They knew we could move beyond our wounds and limitations so that we may be free.

While my life is deeply embedded in the world of spirit, Kalman doesn't believe in any of it. For him life begins with birth and ends with death: "end of story," he says. This book is really two stories woven together: Kalman's narrative of his life as he tells it, and my perspective on his art as a reflection of personal transformation.

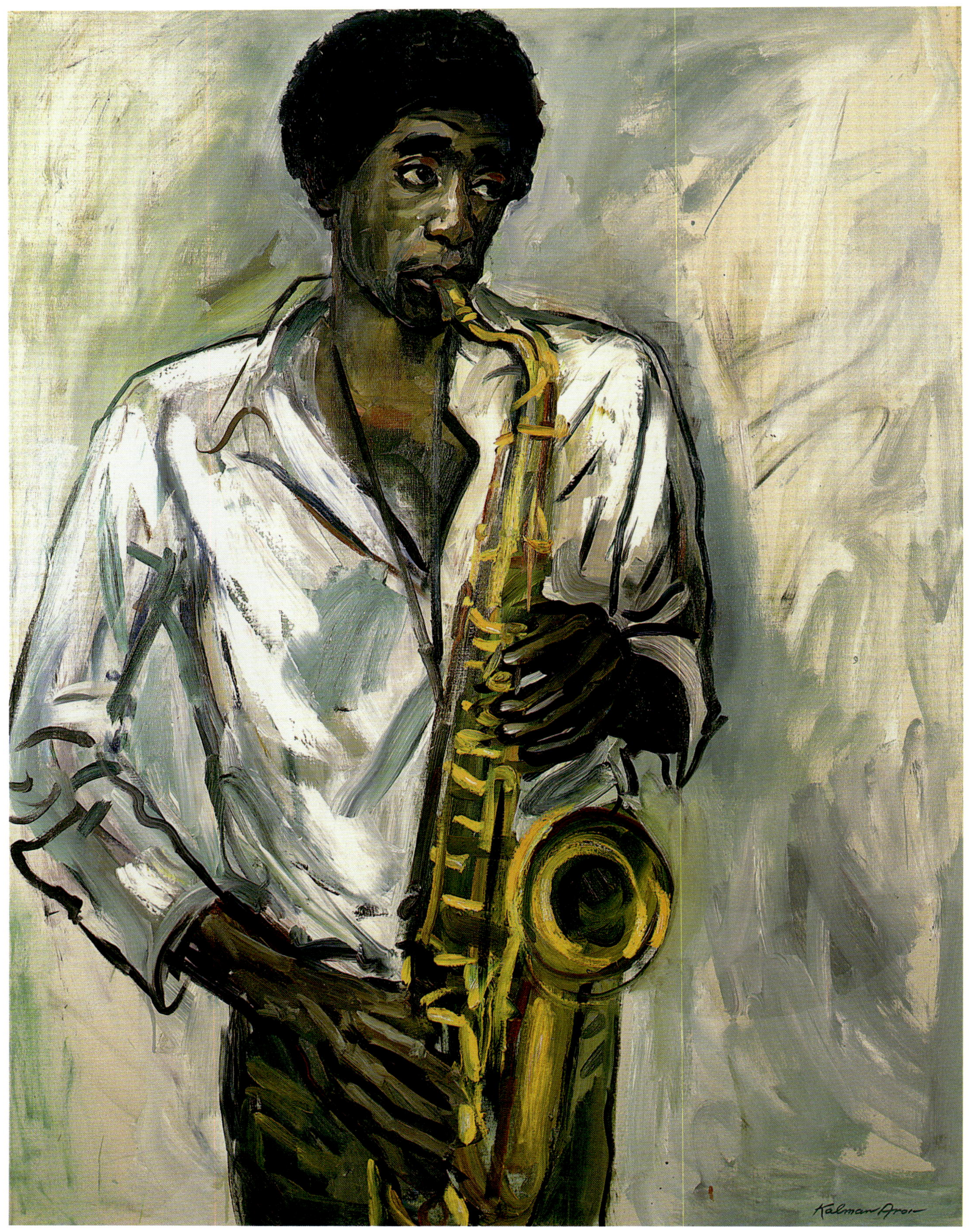
Kalman Aron

A Starting Point

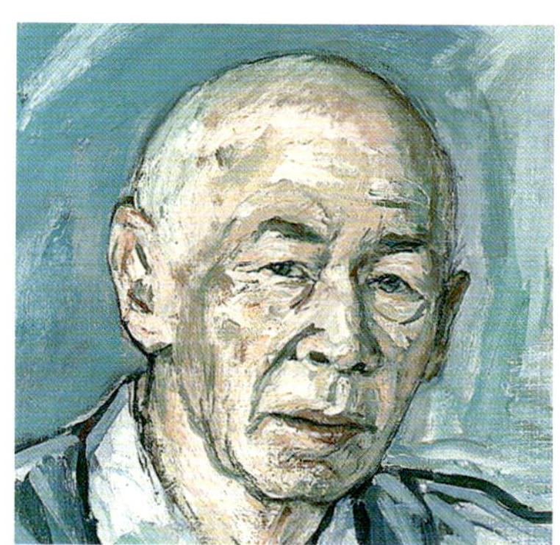

Portrait of Henry Miller (detail); full image on page 129.

Given my background, it is not surprising that the journey with Kalman begins with two visions. The first I have on my way to California to interview him. Sitting in the plane, I move into a timeless space and feel an uncomfortable churning in my stomach. *I see Kalman, a boy frozen in time . . . his eyes closed. He does not want to thaw, to remember. I see myself, a girl telling him that I am frightened to hear his story.* Something inside me feels ancient. I wonder whether every human has a deep familiarity with the fear and terror Kalman experienced.

After arriving in California, I check my messages at home and hear Kalman's voice: "Don't come. I'm sick. I have pneumonia. I am going to the hospital." He has checked into Cedar Sinai Hospital. I have a second vision. *I see him, wearing a thick black vest with sharp spikes jutting out. In a low, strong tone I hear: We do not tell our story. Stay invisible. Keep your head down and paint.* I realize this is the voice of survival from the camps, and the vision reveals a raging battle within Kalman. Part of him wants to tell his story, and part fears he will be killed if he does. Perhaps the pneumonia is a step in releasing the old belief.

After a few days Kalman recovers, and I can meet him for our first interview. Driving from Pasadena across Los Angeles, I remember our childhood home in Glendale, where I first met him over fifty years ago. I pass the back of Forest Lawn, where our little sister, Nonnie, is buried. In a way, she made this book happen. Were it not for her brief life and jet black eyes, my mother would have never met Kalman.

Kalman lives on the first floor at the back of a modest two-story building. His apartment has a large living room and balcony with views of downtown Los Angeles and the Hollywood Hills. His living room serves as his studio. Stunning oil paintings line the walls like old friends: the tall *Musician* with his saxophone and the seated *Henry Miller.* Leaning against another wall are three pastels: *Tractor in a Field* and *Oak Tree in the Poconos*, both painted during a trip in upstate New York, and *Indian House*, done on a visit to Taos.

Musician (mid 1970s), oil on canvas, 48 × 36 in.

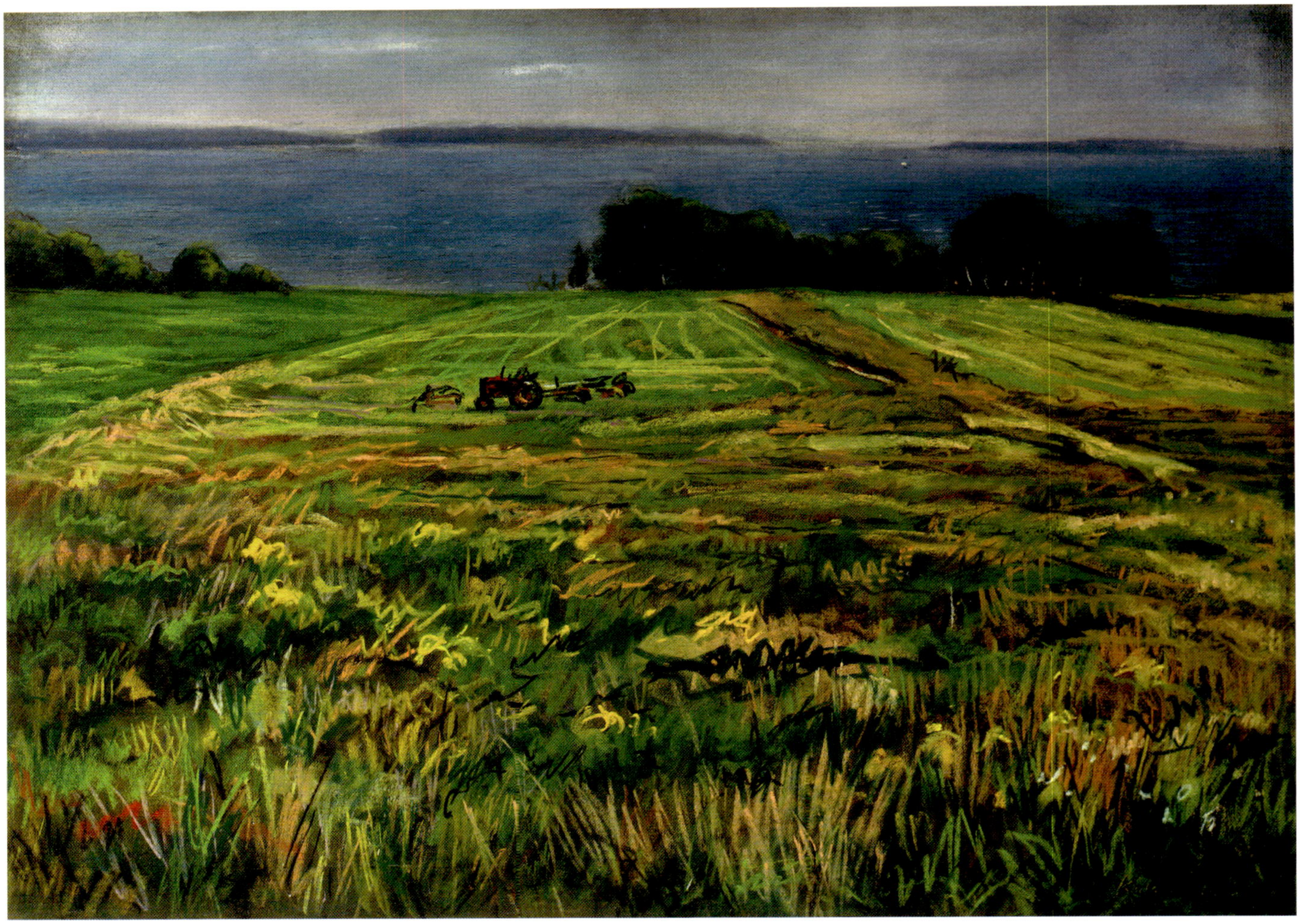

Tractor in a Field (1970s), pastel on paper, 21½ × 29½ in.

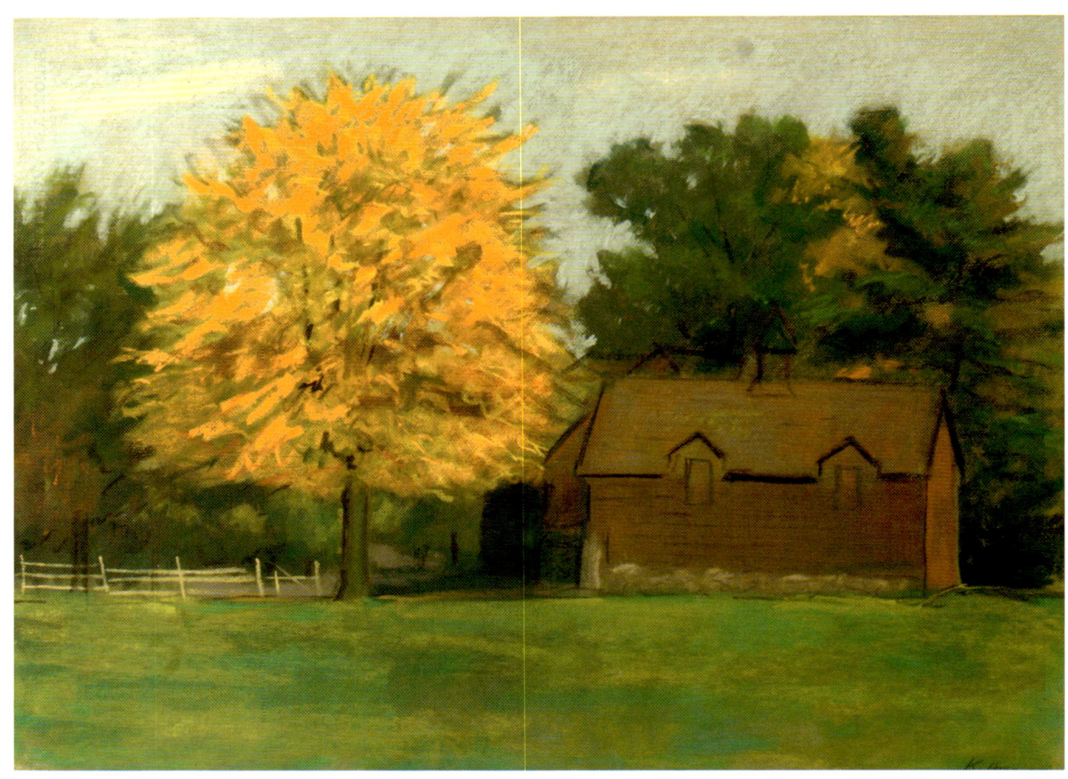

Oak Tree in the Poconos (1970s), pastel on paper, 22 × 30 in.

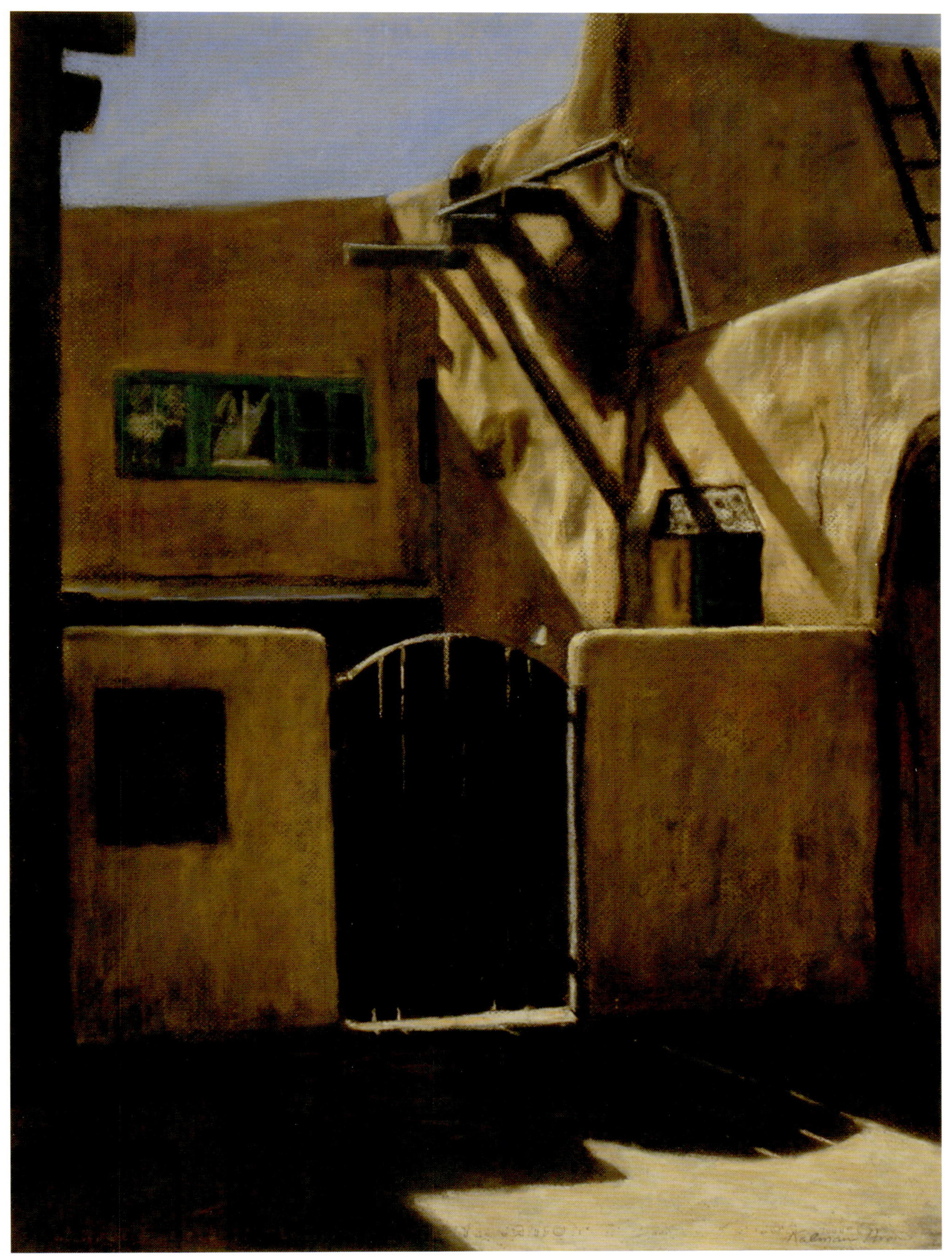

Indian House (1980s), pastel on paper, 29 × 22 in.

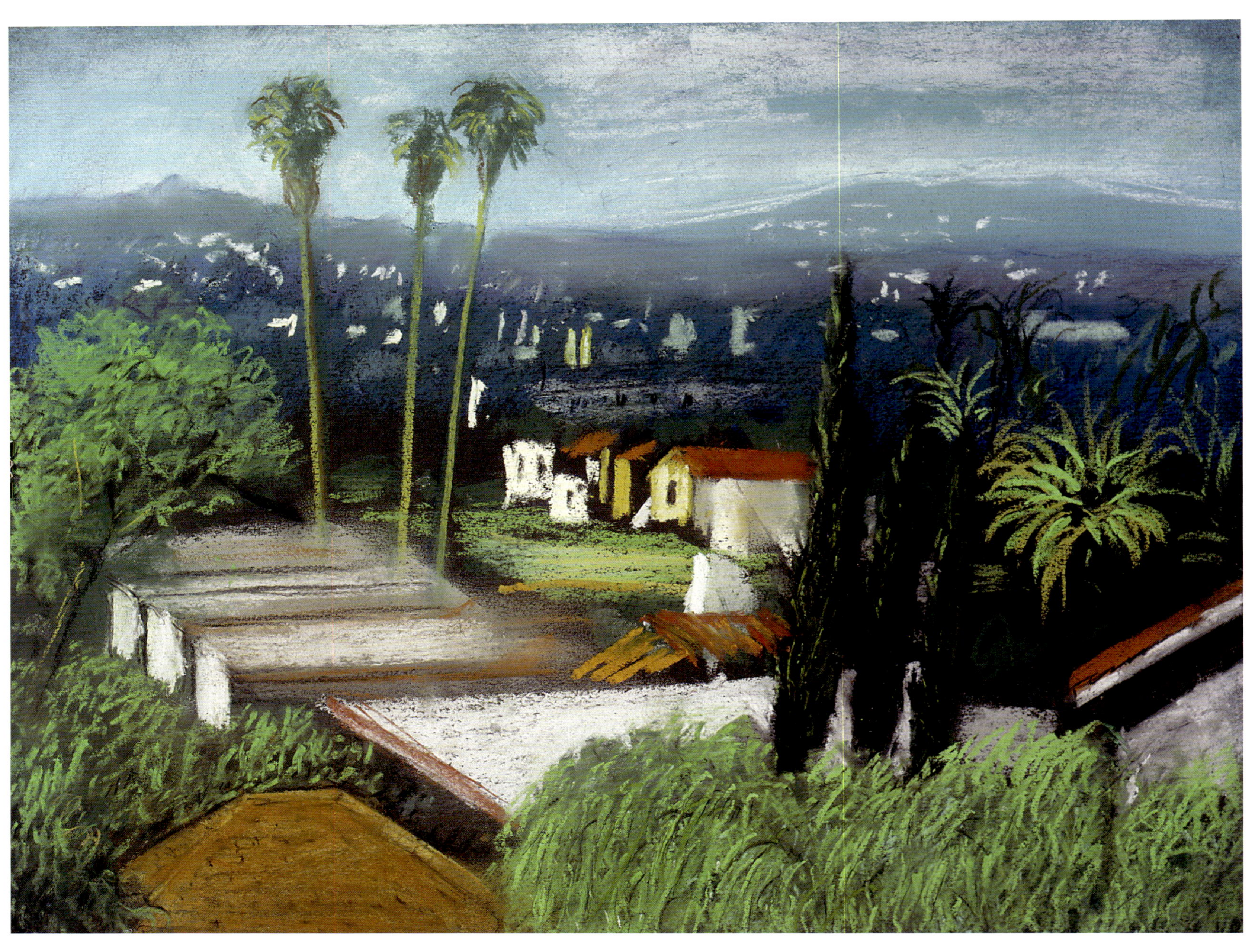

Hollywood Hills in Late Morning (2007), pastel on paper, 12 × 15½ in.

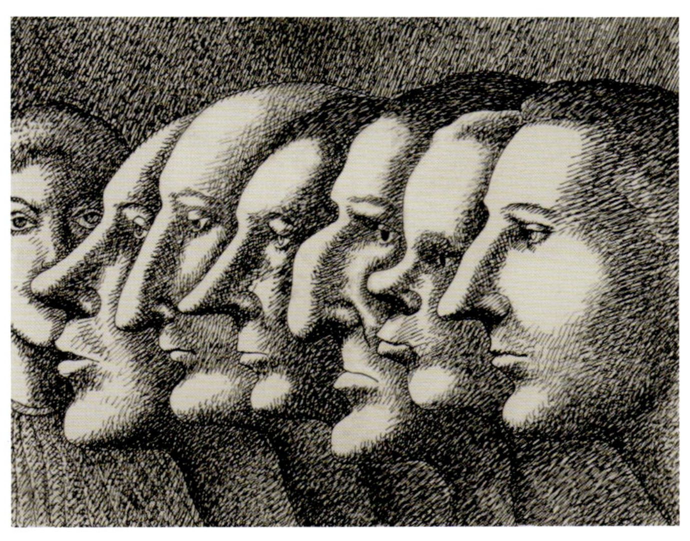

Profiles (late 1960s), black ink on paper, 11 × 14 in.

Kalman spends a lot of time on his balcony, painting visions of downtown Los Angeles and the distant Hollywood Hills, for example, *Hollywood Hills in Late Morning*. He has captured these rooftops and hills in all seasons. Clouds move across the sky, sometimes blocking the sun. The light changes constantly, and he works fast, as he learned to do when painting children playing in the street.

Portfolios of drawings rest on the table near his kitchen. What fun he has with ink on paper, drawing men's noses in *Profiles*. Nearby are two studies of people: *Man with Orange Hat* and *A Man from Lithuania*. Kalman captures a person's essence, revealing inner strengths, feelings and idiosyncrasies. These paintings show his use of rich colors and vivid combinations. He mixes his own colors, as he learned in art school as a boy.

Aron is not interested in painting anyone who does not have character. He once dated a woman who had been Miss Universe. His friends asked why he didn't paint her. "She didn't have enough depth," he replied.

After greeting his paintings—his children and my old friends—we sit down to begin.

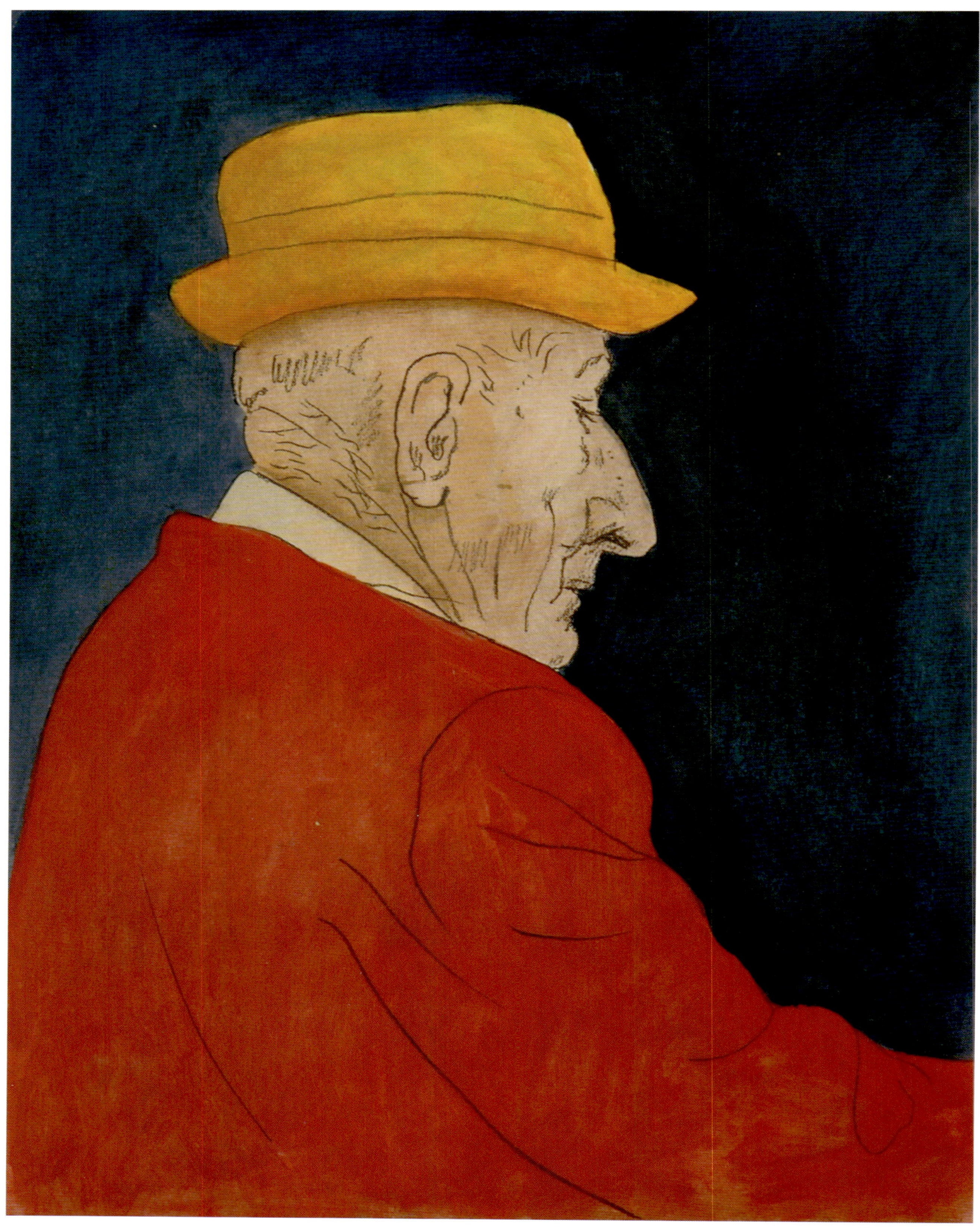

Man with Orange Hat (1970s), oil on paper, 14 × 11 in.

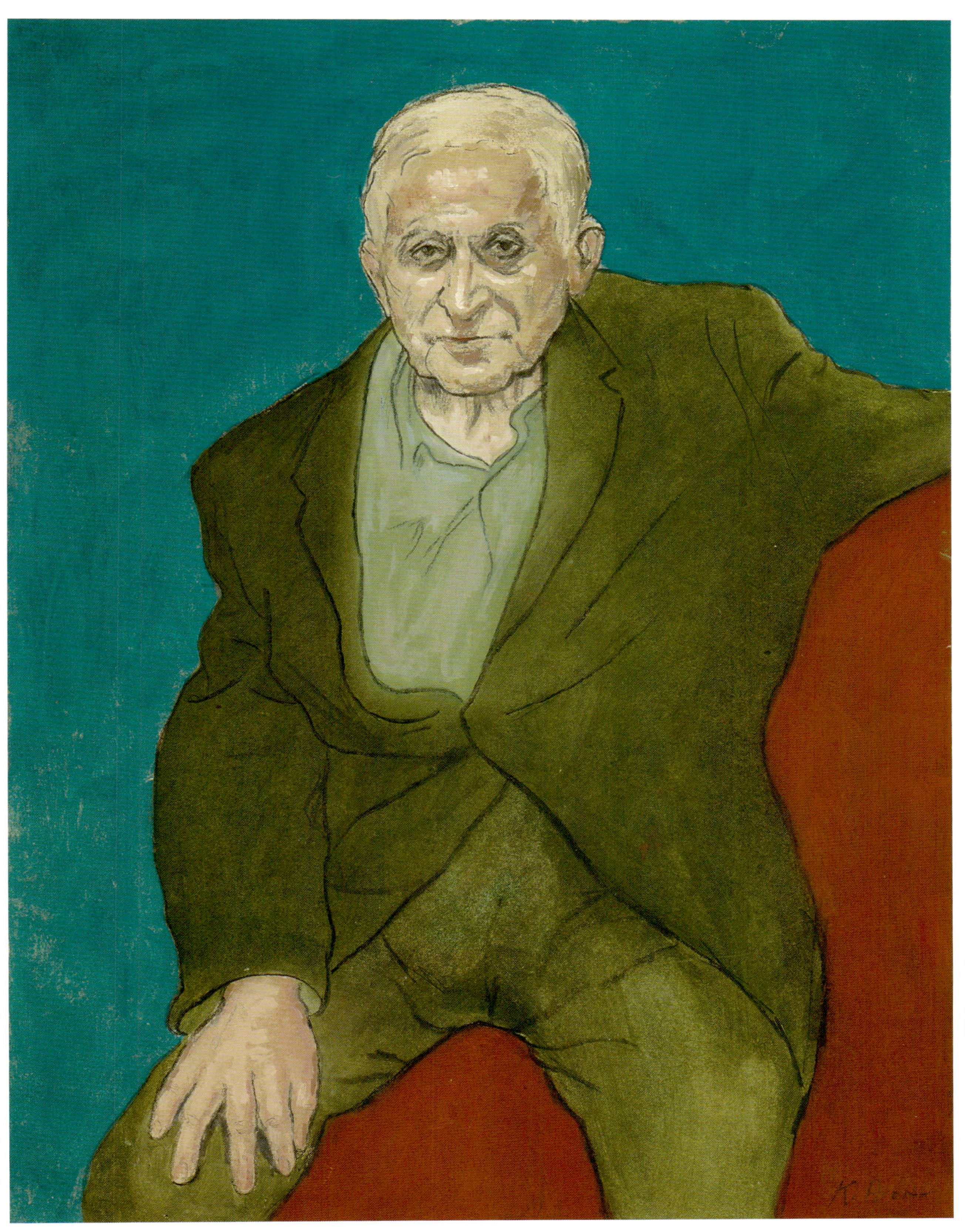

A Man from Lithuania (1958), oil on paper, 14 × 11 in.

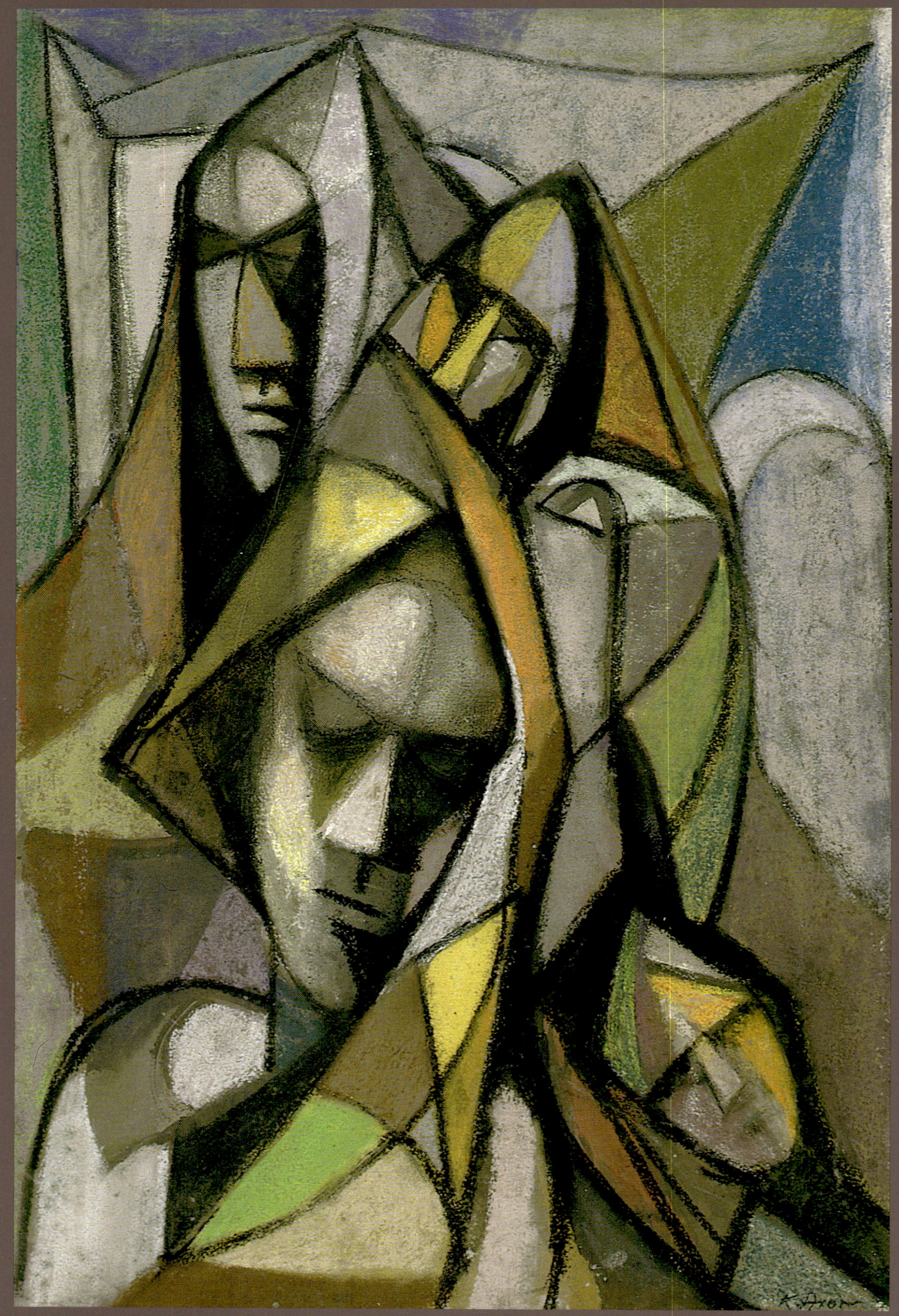

2

DARKNESS

Kalman Remembers

The Cubist Gathering of Women (early 1950s), pastel on paper, 18 × 11½ in.

Riga, Latvia, Summer 1941

They knew. They had talked about it for months. But now they knew. "Gather a bundle of clothes," my parents said. "The Germans are coming."

It was a gray day in Riga. Fear floated in the air like a cloud over our small neighborhood of wooden buildings. We were leaving our home. We were leaving our country. The Germans had entered Lithuania to the south, and they were moving north into Latvia. The Russian soldiers were already withdrawing. The only way out was by train east to Russia. We were going to the land where my father was born.

I lived with my mother, father and brother in a small house behind the shoe factory on Maskavas Iela (Moscow Street) along the River Daugava on the outskirts of the old medieval town of Riga. How I loved to look out my window at the small island in the middle of the river, where my first girlfriend lived. We met at the Fine Arts Academy. She was several years older than I, and she was studying dressmaking. I invited her to the big ball being held at the end of the school year, but she could not go because she didn't have a dress. Her father had died, her mother was working, and she had no money. Then one day she told me that she could go after all. She had taken the drapes down at home and made a smashing long white gown that set off her blue-green eyes, framed by her blondish brown hair. She was the most beautiful girl at the ball. How proud I was to escort her. After the Germans came, she disappeared. Sixty years later I have nightmares trying to remember her name.

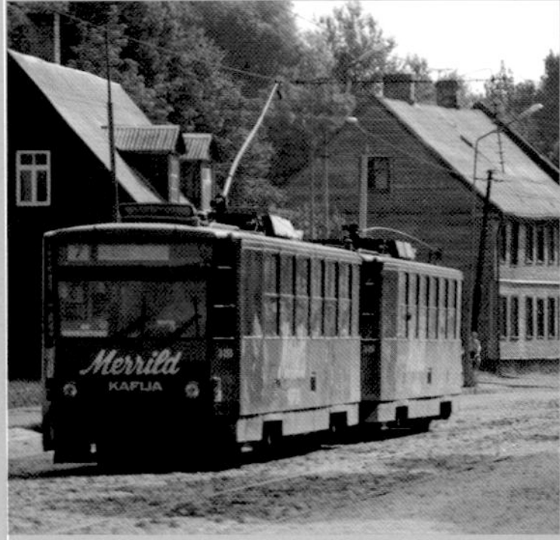

As in the 1930s, Moscow Street in Latvia's capital still features trolley cars—a half-century after World War II.

For months my father was trying to convince his brother to leave the country. But my Uncle David did not want to go. They had made their lives together in this poor Jewish neighborhood where they manufactured and sold shoes. My father designed and made the tops of the shoes. My uncle ran the factory in the building in front of our home, putting the shoes together. They purchased leather from Polish Jews. After the Germans occupied Poland in 1939, my father and uncle heard the whisperings about Germans moving Jews out of their homes into ghettos and forcing them to do slave labor. My parents knew.

During the Russian occupation in 1940, our lives didn't change much. They took over the whole country, there were soldiers, and we started learning Russian in school. During that winter I remember one very large Russian soldier who used to stand near the entrance to my home. Each day he would buy a bottle of vodka, hit it to pop the cork, stand and drink his vodka while eating salted herring. One morning as I went to school, I saw a big hole in the snow where this huge Russian had fallen asleep.

There was not a big change under the Russians. We were poor and we had nothing they wanted. They left us alone. Not so with other Jews. The Russians confiscated their businesses and property and sent five thousand into the Soviet Union to slave labor camps. One of my uncles was well off by our standards. The Russians took over his business and forced him to work for them. They sent another wealthy uncle to Siberia.

It was inconceivable to imagine what the Germans planned to do to us. Anti-Semitism was nothing new in Latvia. I remember a Latvian on the streetcar calling me "*Jid*," Jew. Sometimes on Sundays the Jewish store was open. They didn't want it open on Sundays. They would come and close it up. Throughout history, monarchs segregated Jews into ghettos and limited their commerce. They forced them to convert to Christianity or be exiled. But no one, including my parents, could imagine that the Germans intended to kill us all, to eliminate Jewry and make the race extinct.

That morning I left my home. With my mother, father, brother, uncle and cousin, I walked through the portal of the front factory building onto the street. The train station was not far. Carrying our bundles, we walked down Maskavas Iela, passing the old clapboard buildings of our neighborhood. Suddenly, as we neared the train station, shots rang out. We saw Latvians with machine guns, killing Jews who had gathered on the platform. Latvians were killing Jewish Latvians who were trying to leave the country. I saw them with my own eyes. I saw them dead and injured, lying on the train station platform.

We turned and ran back toward our home. Two Latvian men were standing on the roofs of buildings on Maskavas Iela with rifles. Shots kept ringing out. They were shooting at us. Latvians were shooting at us. The Germans had not even arrived in Riga.

My brother turned; a bullet ripped through his left shoulder. My father yelled, "Keep running. Keep running." We made it through the entrance of the factory building. We ran to the back of the courtyard to our home. My mother washed Henech's wound but could not stop the bleeding. We waited until it turned dark.

After nightfall my father told my mother and me to stay still in the house. He snuck out with my brother and went to a doctor to clean and bandage the wound. They returned home, exhausted. My father told us to sleep. The look in his eyes reflected his regret that he would carry to his death. He had not protected his family. He had not left Latvia in time. He knew we were trapped. We knew we were trapped.

That is how we got locked in there. We couldn't get out anywhere. Then the Germans came.

July 1, 1941. The knock came on the door. My parents knew. My mother hid my brother and me in the armoire in the main room. My father told her to move into the second room so she would not be heard. We heard them call my father by name: "Chaim Aron. Come with us." We waited until they were gone. Then we snuck out to find they had taken our Uncle David too. We never saw them again.

My brother was twenty-two, I was seventeen. That day our world changed forever. We entered a time warp that would last four years. How quickly the nightmare began. We were told to wear yellow stars.

What has always shocked me was Latvians killing Latvian Jews. Latvians shot at us, stopping us from getting on the train to Russia. It was Latvians who told the Germans who was Jewish and where they lived. Within two days of arriving in Riga, the Germans began the roundup, with the aid of the Latvians.

We do not know when or where my father and uncle were killed. They may have been among the early ones shot in the Bikernieki Forest, the first killing fields on the outskirts of Riga.

Camp Survivors (1952), ink on paper, 8½ × 4 in.

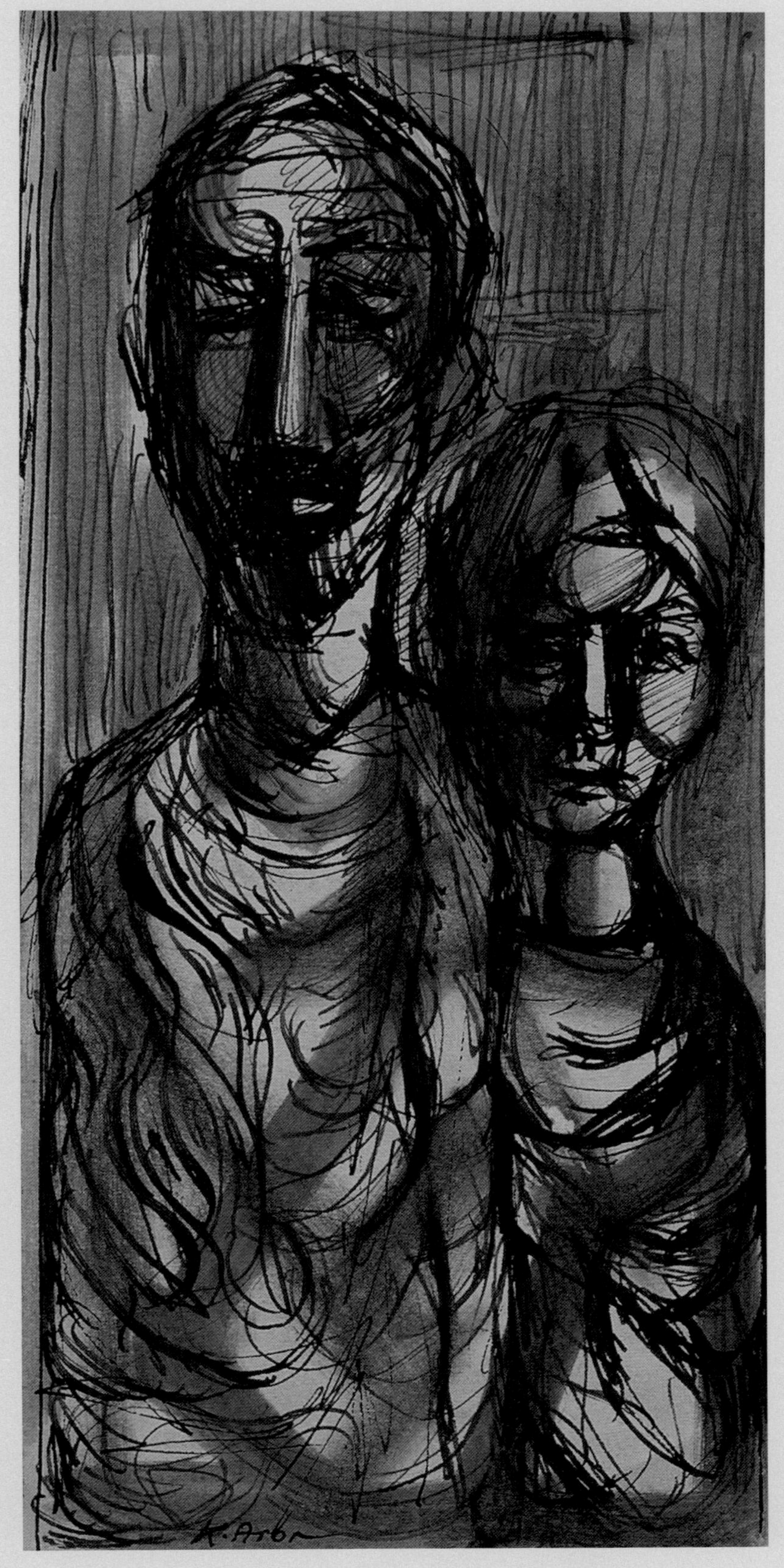

A Boy's Life

I lived with my mother, father and brother in a two-story house we shared with my Uncle David's family. David, his wife, son, and daughter, Ida, lived upstairs. We lived on the first floor. My brother slept in the living room. My mother, father and I shared the bedroom. There was a common room next to the kitchen where my father, uncle and friends gathered to talk politics.

Our house was in the backyard of a lot. In the front was a five-story building where my uncle had the shoe factory. In the yard we kept horses. Streetcar tracks ran down the center of our street leading to the railroad station and the rail crossing over the river. The neighborhood was full of craftsmen.

My parents were Orthodox Jews. My father went to synagogue and observed the Sabbath. My mother kept a kosher kitchen at all times. Before Passover she scrubbed everything clean. Neither of my parents was born in Latvia. My father, Chaim Aron, escaped from the Russian army and came to Latvia during the revolution around 1917. A quiet man, he was tall, with blonde hair and blue eyes. I look like him. When the Russians occupied Latvia in 1940, I never once heard him speak Russian. Nor could he speak Lettish. I guess he was born in a shtetl in Russia; we spoke Yiddish at home. He was interested in politics, and he loved classical music.

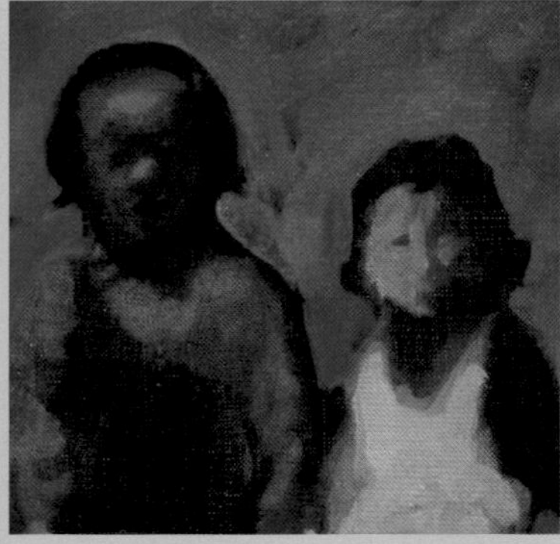

The Lost Children (detail); full image on page 73.

My mother was born in Lithuania. Her name was Sonia Gervis. People called her Sarah. She had dark hair and dark eyes. I heard stories that the people in her village considered her a great beauty when she was young. She loved singing to me when I was little, and every day except Saturday she used to take me to school, where I learned to read and write classical Hebrew.

We were just a regular family, not rich at all, though Riga was a prosperous city in the 1930s. My father worked all day, designing and making shoes, and then we had dinner together. After dinner he sat around the table and listened to the radio with his brother and friends. They listened to a German station, which he could understand but never speak.

My brother Henech had the dark eyes and hair of my mother. Born in Riga in 1919, he was five years older than I. He read the paper all the time; he was knowledgeable, and he was more involved in politics. When the Russians came, they could not pronounce the "H" properly, so they called Henech "Genech," and he was called that for the rest of his life. After the war he returned to Latvia and became a shoe designer like my father. Henech was also very musical.

I was born on September 14, 1924, in Riga. My full name is Kalman Aron—no middle name. I never had a nickname until the Russians came in 1940, and somehow I got the name Colia, perhaps from Nicholai. I had a couple of friends in school. They were always watching me draw, and they wanted me to help them in our art class with their drawings. One in particular was a good friend. He disappeared when the Germans came.

I was always in my own world and I loved to draw. My parents told their friends that I began drawing around age two, when I could first hold a pencil in my hand. They called me the little Mozart of art. Sometimes I would play with the kids outside, but mostly I watched them on the street. And I drew: the men walking down the street, the children playing. I was drawing all day long. I was kind of an outsider.

As religious Jews, my parents could have told me not to draw the human face—a graven image, a reflection of God. But even though they were religious, they never stopped me from drawing a person's face. They never discouraged me from being an artist. They always supported my art. I remember drawing in my parents' bedroom. By the time I was five or six, I was sketching and doing drawings of the people who came to our home. I would watch them and try to capture them. A designer by trade, my father had a good eye. He said to my mother, "Look at what he is drawing. It looks like our friend."

When I was outside, watching and drawing kids and adults around the street, at first I used pastel chalk and color pencil. I didn't draw any airplanes, like most kids. Sometimes I drew a house or backyard. But mostly I drew people.

There was a painter who was a big influence on me. He was called Irbe *meshugener*, which means "crazy one." He had been a philosophy professor at the university in Riga, but he gave that up. I saw him in the street doing landscapes in the snow. He looked very, very poor. He had a beard, and he bound his feet in rags. He ran around in the wintertime, wrapped in towels. He would sit right in the middle of the street on the streetcar tracks, sketching with his pastels. When a streetcar came, he moved and then immediately returned to the tracks after it passed. He was the image of the starving artist. I was a little kid, probably four or five. I watched him very carefully, and I learned from him. He didn't paint people at all, just landscapes. Later on he disappeared. But I remember him very well: the snow, the color, the beard and the chalk pastels. He was very interesting to me.

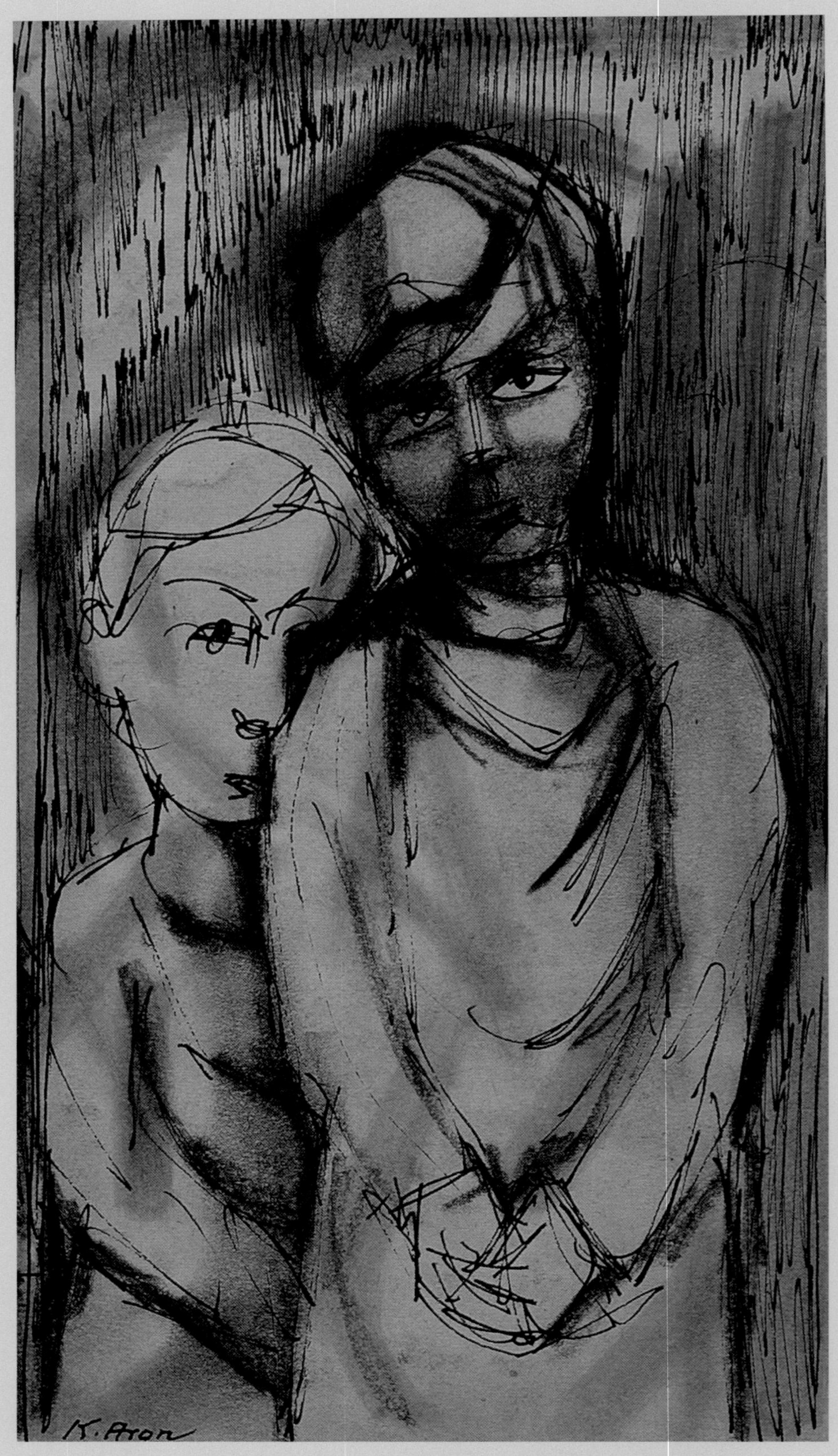
K. Aron

Two Children (1952), ink on paper, 8½ × 4½ in.

By age seven I had a collection of drawings of my parents' relatives and friends who came to our home. There were good resemblances. The head man at my school told a gallery owner about me. The gallery had never shown a kid's work, only art by older people. My parents agreed. Before I knew it, the gallery took about twenty of my drawings. My mother picked me up at school the next day and took me to the gallery. We walked in, and my mother was really upset. She asked, "What happened to his pictures?" There were only nails in the wall. The gallery owner said, "Don't worry, Mrs. Aron. Everybody bought his own picture." The drawings were gone, all sold the first day. I never got to see them hanging. The Latvian and Jewish newspapers carried articles about the show, calling me a little genius. I became a celebrity in my neighborhood.

Jews are not too proud of having a kid as a painter. Nobody wants a starving artist in his family. For some reason, my father didn't mind at all, maybe because he was a designer. He gave me paper; he gave me pencils. My mother didn't mind either. Everybody was surprised that they even let me do it. But they were very calm about it. They never discouraged me. I kept on drawing all the time.

When I was thirteen, the Latvian president, Karlis Ulmanis, chose me to paint his official portrait. Someone told him about this young man. I went to the Presidential Palace. I had about three sittings, maybe four, with him. I used pastels on paper. The portrait was about thirty-six by twenty-four or twenty-eight inches in size. There were articles in the Latvian and Jewish press about this young kid who painted the president's portrait. I never saw it again. When the Germans came in, they bombed the whole area. I don't know if it survived.

Years later, in the 1970s, I had a show in Sweden. The weather was terrible. It was snowing, and the temperature was fourteen degrees below zero. I said to the gallery man, "I don't think anybody is going to show." All of a sudden the place was full. Before the show, a big write-up reported that I had painted President Ulmanis when I was young. An old man who came from a great distance walked up to me and said in Lettish, "I was there when you were doing the portrait of Ulmanis. I helped you put up the easel to do it." He told me that when the Russians came in 1941 he escaped to Sweden.

I enjoyed doing the portrait, and it changed my life. President Ulmanis pulled me out of my local Jewish school and arranged for me to attend the Fine Arts Academy in the old medieval town. At age fourteen, I was the youngest student there. At art school you sit there for five days and draw a piece of sculpture. I learned perspective: to draw the hallway. Sometimes I sat for three or four days, drawing the hallway to get the right perspective.

The second year I was put into a life class because I was advanced in my drawings of people. Suddenly, I see this big, blonde Latvian woman, nude. I had never seen a nude before. Here I am faced with this huge woman with pink skin. I hid. I didn't want her to see me. I was shy. During the break, she called me to go into her little room to pull out a chair. She was teasing me. It was funny: a little kid who had never seen a nude.

I started doing nudes. I was getting better with it and less shy about it. Suddenly, before I knew it, I had a portfolio of nudes, and I didn't know what to do with it. I couldn't bring it home. A young kid in a religious family? No way. Finally, I did bring it home, and my brother enjoyed looking at it. Because we didn't want our parents to see it, we decided to hide it behind the armoire in the bedroom I shared with my parents. Passover came. Where would my mother look for bread? Not in the bedroom. Nobody ate in the bedroom. But you have to look everywhere for bread, just in case. I wasn't there at the time. My father must have pushed the armoire away, and they pulled out the portfolio with all the nudes. I came home, greeted by silence. Nobody talked to me. It was very strange.

The next morning when I went to school, I heard my mother yelling. She was in the room with the head of the school, behind the door with this frosted window. She was yelling loudly, and I knew it was my mother: "Don't let him do nudes." So I had to go back to the portrait class. Of course, my father saw the nudes. I am sure that he enjoyed them.

I spent three years in the art school, including the year when the Russians were there. The school was a good distance from where I lived. I used to go on bicycle, skates, or skis. No other kids from my neighborhood went there. I loved the school, and I made some friends. I helped them with their drawings. They liked me. They liked what I was doing. They were always checking on me. The art books we studied were printed in black and white. I would not see the masters, such as Rembrandt, in color until after the war.

I met my first young love there, the beautiful girl who made the lovely dress she wore when I took her to the ball. Soon after the Germans arrived, I snuck over to the island in the middle of the River Daugava where she lived. The house was empty. She and her mother vanished. For years I could not remember her name; the night after I told Susan about her for this book I had nightmares, and the next day I remembered: her name was Sima Rosenberg.

The Ghetto in Riga

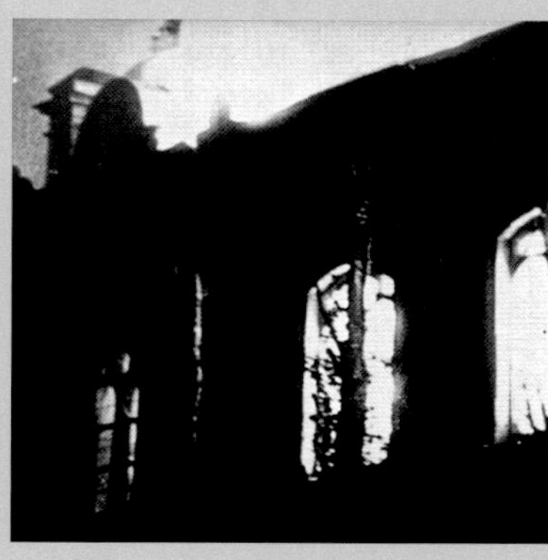

Chor Synagogue, the principal temple in Riga, burns on July 4, 1941 with the loss of many Jews trapped inside.

The Germans came. I was blond, and they didn't know I was Jewish. I walked out one day without the Star of David, and I saw smoke coming up from the synagogue I used to go to. The rabbi was a good friend of my father and uncle. I heard from a neighbor who lived across the street from the synagogue that he saw people trying to run out. They were burning. The Latvians and the Germans pushed them back inside. Everybody in there perished. I said to myself, Where is God?

I was never really religious. When I was a little kid, I would ask the rabbi in the *shul*, "You are talking about God *in himmel* [in the sky]. What does he look like? Does he look like us?" He didn't know what to say, so he said, "Don't ask stupid questions." I was asking *good* questions. But I was not popular for asking questions like that. My religion went out the window. It never came back.

We couldn't do anything. We were just there, waiting to see what was going to happen. Many people tried to be optimistic, thinking they weren't going to do anything to the Jews. But we knew what was happening in Poland, so we knew that it was going to happen to us.

At first we had to do menial jobs. We cleaned out houses that had been owned by Jews who had been sent to the ghetto or the camps. The German soldiers told us to do this or to do that. They decided what belongings they would keep, which ones to sell. These were homes of the rich Jewish people. The Germans went and lived in these houses and had us clean them.

Again, the knock on the door: German soldiers and Latvians yelling, "Get out! Get out! Bring whatever you can carry. You have to go." But this time only with my mother and brother, I packed a bundle of clothes and walked through the factory building portal onto Maskavas Iela. We marched down the street, following the river. We just kept walking and walking, to an area created as the Jewish ghetto. Barbed wire and post fencing greeted us. Guards were surrounding the place. Once inside you couldn't get out.

They told us to find an empty room. There were little houses. We moved into one room of two on the second floor of a small building. We shared this floor with two brothers. My brother and I had to go out every day to do slave labor.

I later learned that the Germans penned thirty thousand Jews—men, women and children—in an area of about ten streets and twenty blocks of old wood-slatted buildings. We didn't know who had lived there. The Germans liquidated a whole neighborhood on the outskirts of Riga to make room for us.

Early in the morning we lined up to go to the factories, and we returned at the end of the day. I was assigned to a clothing operation to sort winter coats for pilots in the Luftwaffe on the Russian front. In the back there was a guy with a gun. If you didn't do what you were told, you were gone.

I figured out early that if I did a sketch of a guard, he might give me some food. Once at the factory I carefully drew a sketch from a distance, because if I did it too close I was afraid they would see me doing it. When I finished, I tried to show it to the guard. He would show it to another guard, and then that guard would want me to do one of him. I wound up being given food for a drawing.

I remember one kind man. He was a German doctor, in charge of something at the factory. He saw a sketch I had given to someone else. He was a frustrated painter and liked my work. He got me a canvas, brushes and oil paint, and I did a very good portrait. I never forgot this guy.

Doing this was dangerous. If I got caught, the Germans might think I was trying to escape or to send notes out into the "normal" population. I could get killed. Anyone with a pencil and paper had to be very careful.

Sometimes I returned to the ghetto at the end of the day with food hidden. We formed a line to enter. The guards would pull some people out of the line and check their clothes and shoes for food or other goods. If they found something on the prisoner, they shot him dead in front of our eyes. You looked ahead and passed the checkpoint and returned to the hovel where you lived. Bringing in food was worth the risk, as there was not enough to eat in the ghetto. I was lucky to be working in the coat factory. They fed us lunch: some bread and a little soup.

The Germans gave us food that they couldn't give to other people: a little stinking fish or some horse meat when a horse would die. The pigs would not eat it. We had to eat very fast.

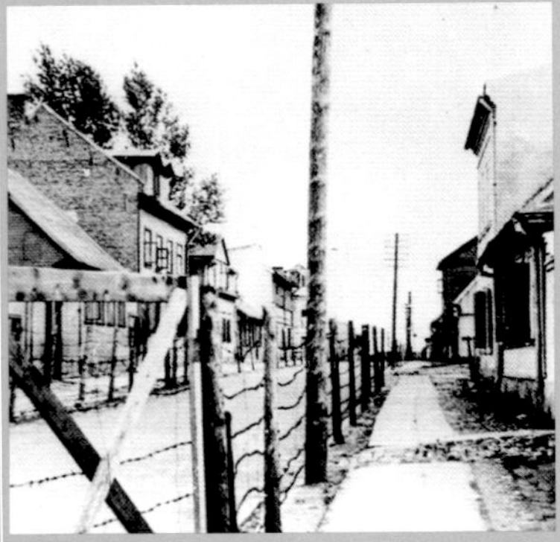

A barbed wire fence marks the boundary of the Riga ghetto along Sadowika Street, circa 1942.

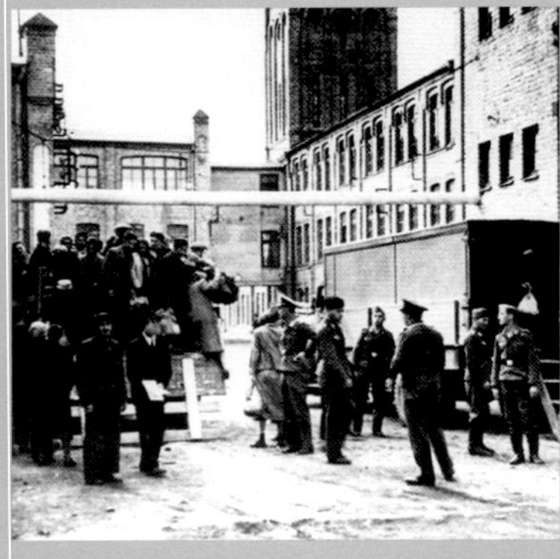

Forced labor in Riga: Jews trucked from the ghetto arrive to work at the Luftwaffe clothing depot on Moscow Street in 1942.

Aktions: The Killing of Jews at the Rumbula Forest

On a cold morning in late November, we lined up as usual at the gate to go to work. A truck picked up a group of us for the coat factory. When we returned that evening, I was stunned. Half of the population was gone. My mother was gone; the person who saw beauty in the world, the woman who always loved me was gone.

We heard what had happened. The guards, Latvian and German, came into the ghetto and told half of the residents to come into the streets and march as directed, out of the ghetto. They were resettling them in another place. If any refused, the guards shot them dead. If they didn't move fast enough, the guards shot them on the spot. Dead bodies lay about the streets. Blood colored the snow on the ground.

The people not ordered out of their buildings kept their curtains drawn. They heard the screams. They heard the orders. "Get out. Get out. March, march, march." They heard the shots. A few dared to look out their windows to watch the horror. All day and into the night, the guards rounded up people—men, women and children.

We did not know their fate at first. But one woman who had been taken to the Rumbula Forest played dead and came back to the ghetto. She told what she saw: killing, the cold-blooded execution of innocent people. The executioners were Germans.

Frida Michelson wrote a chilling account in her book *I Survived Rumbuli*. On November 30 the Germans took about fifteen thousand Jews from the ghetto to the Rumbula Forest. They were told to stay in line and put their shoes in a pile on the left. Then the German and Latvian guards told them to remove all of their clothes and put them in a pile on the right. In the November cold they forced them to walk to big rectangular pits that had been dug. The guards told each one to jump into the ditch and lie face down. The guards then shot each in the head. When that layer was full, the guards told the next people to lie down on top of the dead or dying people, and the guards once again shot the people in the head. They did this killing all day until the ditches were full. They executed fifteen thousand men, women and children. This would be known as the first *Aktion*. Some Jewish doctors who knew what was going to happen poisoned themselves before the *Aktion*.

On December 8 the German and Latvian guards repeated the procedure, killing another ten thousand in one day. The commanding officer, Friedrich Jeckeln, was proud of his work.

The day before the second *Aktion*, we were told to move into the "small ghetto." For my brother and me, this meant moving across the street. The Germans decided to move four thousand men between the ages of eighteen and forty—those healthy enough to work—into a small part of the ghetto. Henech and I were among them.

From time to time the Germans and Latvian guards took a small *Aktion* in the small ghetto. When we went to work, they would leave some people behind, put them on special buses and gas them. When we returned to the ghetto at night, people had simply vanished.

Jews from outside of Latvia started arriving, filling up the spaces where family and friends had lived in the big ghetto. Loads and loads arrived from Germany and Austria. We didn't know what the hell was going on. Nobody had a radio. Gradually we realized that the Germans had killed my mother and twenty-five thousand other Riga Jews to make room for Jews from other parts of Europe. A tall barbed-wire fence divided the large and small ghetto. The Germans kept us separate from the new arrivals.

Memory (1953), ink on paper, 10½ × 7 in.

There was a young man at the art school who was older than I. He used to come over to our house and watch me draw. We were friends. One day while walking to the factory, I managed to get out and find him. I don't know how the hell I did it. I found him and asked him to hide my brother and me. He refused to do it, but the one good thing was that he didn't give us away. He didn't go to the SS and tell them. He said he was sorry. I didn't blame him, because he could have been killed. I managed to sneak back into the factory without being caught.

Some people worked in ammunition factories, making guns. They managed to bring some weapons into the ghetto and hide them in the little house where we lived. They hid the guns in the cellar below the stove. Some men from the small ghetto jumped the fence at night to meet women in the big ghetto. News circulated. An Austrian Jew who was working with the Germans heard about the guns. He told the Germans. They rounded up seventeen Jewish policemen, just kids aged eighteen to twenty-four. They took them to a square in the big ghetto and machine-gunned them all. They made us all watch.

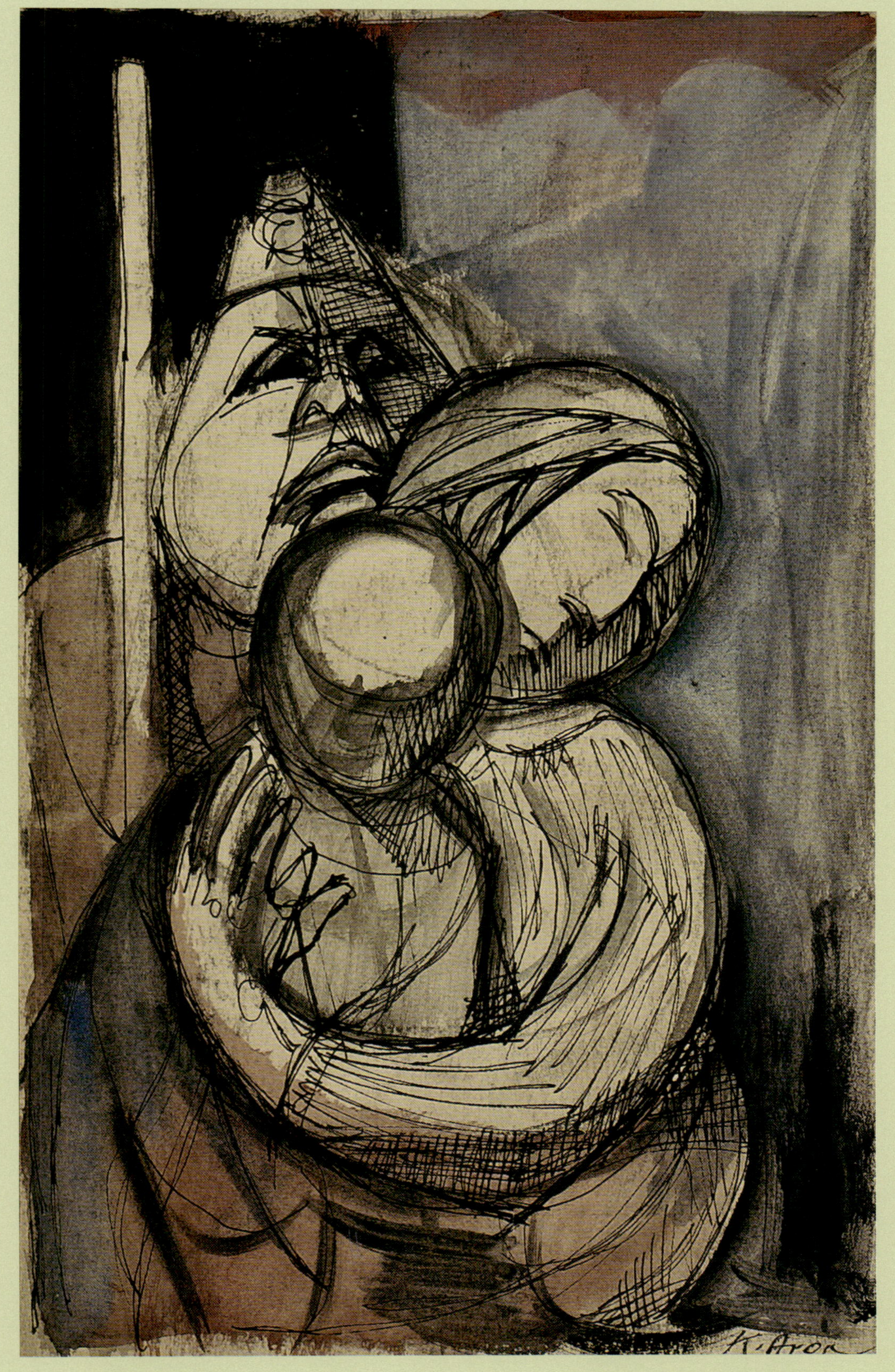
K. Aron

One tough Latvian Jew, Zalman Peretzman, quit being a Latvian police officer the day before. He was several years older than I and a boxer. That was a lucky decision for him and me, as we later became friends and helped each other escape at the end of the war.

That same day, the Germans took all of the Latvian Jews out and made us run and do push-ups. They decided who would live and who would die. The next day when we went to work, the Germans killed the weak, sick, or old Jews.

The men who had hidden the guns disappeared. We heard that the Germans took them to the forest and killed them. I later heard that prisoners at the concentration camp Kaiserwald on the outskirts of Riga killed the Austrian Jew, a tailor, who had betrayed those hiding the guns. They pushed his head into a latrine and killed him. His name was Vandt, I think.

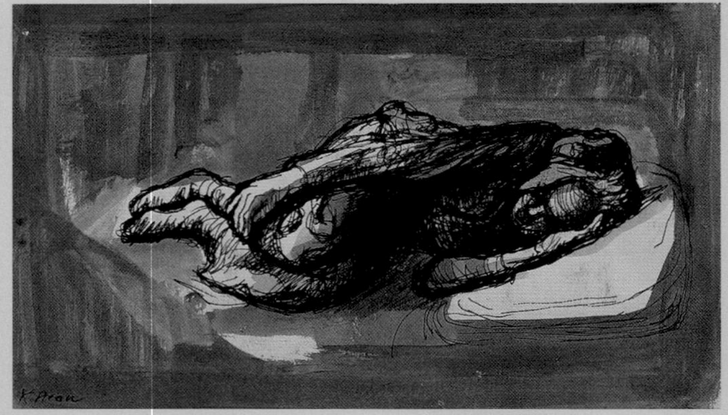

Homeless Man (1970s), ink on paper, 6⅜ × 10⅝ in.

The guards needed no excuse to kill. They killed indiscriminately; they killed with pleasure. People sometimes would bring in things to trade for food. The Germans caught a man who hid a watch in the heel of his shoe. They took him away and killed him. But you had to do this; you had to bring things into the ghetto to trade for food. Another day, when I was standing in line to go through the checkpoint to the ghetto, I watched a guard shoot the person standing in front of me. Dead.

I remember a time when we stood for the constant counting. A man I knew walked out of line. He couldn't stand any more. He was too weak. A German came and shot him right there, next to me. I did not comprehend. I do not understand how one human being can treat another like this. Again I asked: Where is the God of my father and mother? I saw too much to hold on to any belief in this God.

I saw Germans throw babies in the air and shoot them. I remember that. I saw it in the ghetto a few times, guards shooting children, throwing them in the air, using them like target practice. What do kids have to do with this—taking a mother's child and throwing him up and shooting him? After you have seen that . . . My religion went whoosh.

A rabbi did more damage to my beliefs after the war. He was in the American army in Salzburg. I couldn't speak English, but Zalman Peretzman could. I had him ask the rabbi, "Why would people that had never sinned or anything be killed?" He said to us, "You died for people that may have sinned two generations ago." This turned me off completely. There was no reason to come up with this kind of thing.

Still today, I go along with it. I go to Passover things. Friends invite me, but I don't pray. I just sit there, and I say "Amen." That is about it. If they want to be religious, that's fine with me. But as far as I was concerned, God, right then and there, was finished. It is interesting that some of my friends became very religious, because they were saved. They figured that God saved them, and some became really religious. I went the opposite way.

I survived because I was young, healthy and strong. You couldn't get too upset about what was happening because you wouldn't survive. We were just like zombies walking around. We didn't know what was going on. We didn't know what was going to happen an hour later or five minutes later. If you got upset, that didn't help. We lived from minute to minute, not from day to day. And you didn't know if you were going to get killed. That is how I handled it.

To lose hope was the death penalty. Suicide? I never thought of it. I worked; I kept to myself; I ate the food given to us. I sketched guards in hopes of getting extra bread for my brother and me. I slept. I thought about escaping. I watched the guards carefully. I made myself invisible.

I began learning how to do that in the ghetto. Living there was like having a nightmare, expecting to awaken and find myself in my safe home on Maskavas Iela. Life was moment to moment. These moments added up to two and a half years. Around November of 1943, the Germans closed the ghetto.

Three Camps in Latvia: Kaiserwald, Poperwahlen and Dundaga

One cold, icy day in 1943, the guards told us to line up to march out. They didn't tell us what was happening or where we were going. They took us to a camp they had built on the outskirts of Riga, Kaiserwald. When we arrived, the guards told us to strip to be checked for lice and to take a shower. Snow and ice covered the ground. I don't know what happened. Suddenly they took us out of there, and we stood naked in the snow, freezing, for hours. My toes were frozen. That is the main thing I remember about this camp.

I wasn't there long, a week or less. The Germans took our clothes and told us to wear black-and-white striped prisoner clothing. Whether the clothing fit did not concern them. We slept inside, but it was still freezing. There was no work. It was a big transit camp.

I stood in a line again. You go here. You go there. The Germans randomly assigned one prisoner here, another there, totally arbitrary. They put me with others on a truck. We had no idea where we were going or what was going to happen to us. I was separated from my brother.

I was sent to a little slave-labor camp, Poperwahlen, with about two hundred people in the Baltic forest in northwestern Latvia. One third were young women from Hungary. We were digging ditches, lifting out trees, shoveling dirt, cutting wood, planting things. It was freezing cold—snow on the ground and howling winds. They stuffed eight or nine of us into a flimsy hut in the middle of the forest. We slept on straw, no mattresses. It was difficult to sleep, crowded on this flimsy floor of straw. Survival was a miracle.

The camp commandant was a very bad guy. With no provocation the guards would beat and kill prisoners at will. I watched; I'm visual. In this cold green forestland in the northern Baltic peninsula of Latvia, it felt like a dark, evil force hovered, striking and killing prisoners at random. I learned how to be invisible. I learned how to watch the guards but not let them see me.

I lived minute to minute, from piece of bread to piece of bread. It was there that I decided never to smoke again. I would do a sketch of a guard, and he would give me cigarettes. I will never forget a man in the camp who wanted a cigarette; he wanted to give me his piece of bread for the whole day for a few cigarettes. I gave him the cigarettes, and I didn't take the bread. Every piece of bread was priceless.

I remember four things at this camp: drawing a miniature portrait for the commandant, falling in love with a beautiful Hungarian singer, watching a German guard's behavior change from bewilderment to cruelty, and seeing the Jewish Latvian overseer escape.

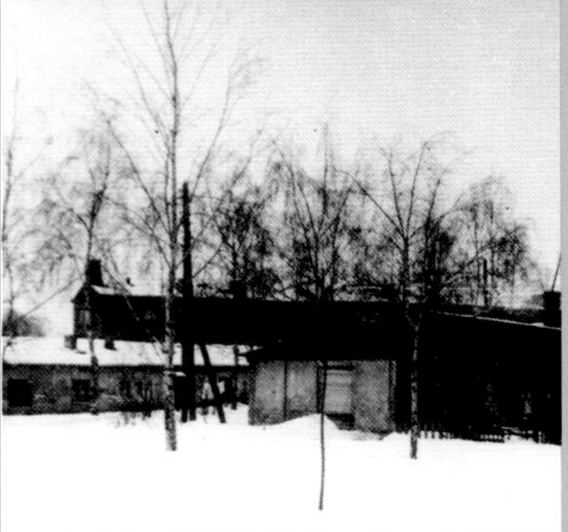

Kaiserwald concentration camp (after its liberation).

I did a sketch of a guard to get food. The Germans in the factory in Riga had given me a little paper and charcoal pencil. I had to be careful, having a pencil and paper, but I drew the guard. The head of the camp, this really bad guy, saw it. He locked me in his barracks room and shut the door. It was warm inside. He gave me a photograph of his mother and father. He wanted me to do a miniature portrait of them that could fit in a locket on the top of his ring. I was sharpening the pencil every minute. It had to be sharp like a needle. And I remember what the portrait looked like, sixty years ago. Half the size of my thumb, it had two people in it, heads and shoulders. He also gave me photographs of his parents for me to draw larger portraits, and he had me draw one of him. That is when I got a little bit more food.

I was in his barracks a couple of weeks. To stay warm and get some food, I took a week to draw something I could have done in two days. I had injured my shoulder before that, carrying a tree. There were six of us carrying it. If you let it go, you got shot. There was a rifleman at the back. I felt something was wrong; my shoulder hurt. To this day that shoulder is lower than the other. I was lucky that I could stop. The drawing got me out of doing hard labor for a while. Probably my survival is due to that. Occasionally I could get a sandwich or some bread. It helped a lot.

There were some prisoners of war from Copenhagen in the kitchen cooking food. I did a drawing of one of them; then another one wanted one. They would give me more food.

I met a beautiful Hungarian girl. I had never heard Hungarian before, but I am good with languages. She said something, I said something. She didn't understand a word of German. So she started singing. She was studying singing with a well-known singer named Karády in Budapest. They had shaved her head. She wore a scarf with a little bit of her blonde hair showing.

She was younger than I, probably seventeen. I was nineteen. She used to sing to me, and little by little I started learning Hungarian. Now when I say something in Hungarian, Hungarians think I am Hungarian. I learned the accent. I could sing some of her songs. She was part of a small group of women at the camp. We had to hide from the Germans who watched us from the watchtowers. You weren't supposed to talk with a woman, particularly. Our huts were segregated—a few huts there and a few huts here, with no fences between.

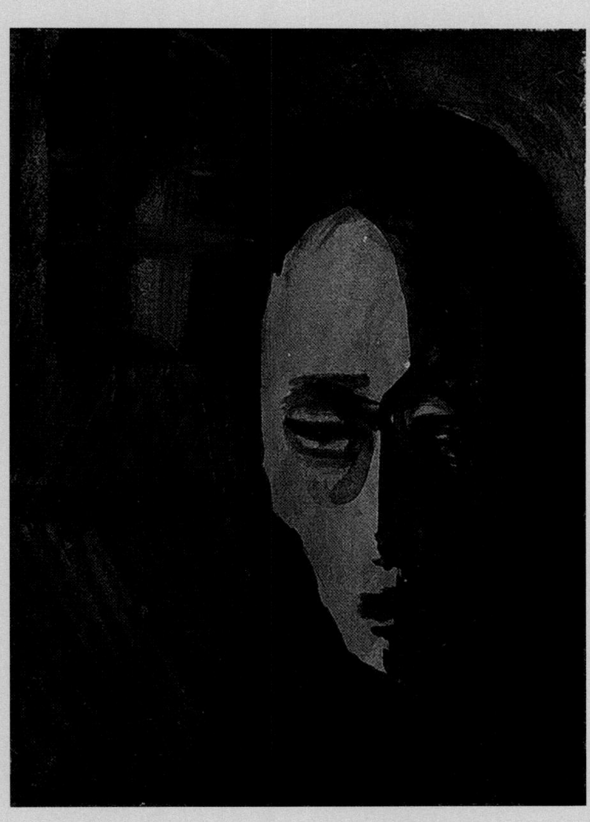

Haunted Visage (1950s), watercolor on cardboard, 5⅞ × 4$^{5}/_{16}$ in.

When I got the job working for the commandant in the barracks, I would bring her food. I was in love with this girl, but I couldn't save her. I tried to. I was getting food from this guy, the head of the camp, and I would bring it to her. I got a job for her to clean the barracks inside to get her out of the hard labor. Then, when the camp was dissolved, we were all walking toward another camp. I tried to get her close to me, to walk together. They somehow pushed her away, and I never saw her again. Her name was Kori Brown.

After the war I looked for her. I knew where she came from, a town sixty kilometers from Budapest. I couldn't find her. She is probably gone. I ask every Hungarian I meet, "Have you ever heard of a woman, Kori Brown?" No, she is not alive, I am sure, unless she reads this book and finds me. I understand that the Hungarian women were marched out of the camp and killed, as there is no record of them being transported to Stutthof with the men from the two camps, Poperwahlen and Dundaga.

In Poperwahlen there were Ukrainians in the German army. They were terrible, as bad as the Germans. Ukrainians were very anti-Semitic. So we got it from all sides—Germans, Latvians and Ukrainians. At any minute the guards beat us up. They didn't need excuses. If they didn't like you, they beat you. If you did not pick up the shovel the right way, they would beat you. I saw a lot of people being beaten up and killed in the camps. The smaller the camp, the worse it was, because there were more guards watching you. You couldn't hide in a small camp like Poperwahlen.

I will never forget one German soldier there, this little kid. I am always watching; I always look at people or at things. So I was watching this young German, who had probably never seen a Jew before in his village. He was shy, and he wouldn't touch anybody. I noticed that this one would not yell at anybody or beat anybody. He was kind of walking around, puzzled, wondering what the hell is going on. A few weeks later, he started beating up people. What happened, I am almost sure, is that if guards wouldn't do what they were told, the Germans would send them to the front line in Russia. So I think that is what happened to the young boy: suddenly he became violent. He became hateful to avoid being sent to the front line.

I remember a kind man at Poperwahlen, a Jew who used to be in the Latvian army. The Germans made him an overseer, the one who gathered everybody together and made the operational rules. One day we couldn't figure out where he was. He had decided to escape with his girlfriend. He had a woman staying with him, which was very unusual. We heard the dogs. They were after him. They found him and shot him. He was a nice man. After that they dissolved the camp, and the Germans took us to a nearby camp called Dundaga. I don't remember how, walking or by truck. It was terrible there too.

Our main concern in all these camps was to get food: a piece of bread, some soup. That was our main concern. And we were working all day long.

March to the Sea: Stutthof, Buchenwald and Rehmsdorf

I wasn't in Dundaga for long. In the summer of 1944 we started walking in long lines for days to the sea. By that time our heads were shaved down the middle on the top. Finally they were walking us toward a boat. I dropped back to the end of the line, and I sort of jumped off the road to hide in a stack of hay. They didn't know I was gone, because there were lots of people there. But this little kid saw me, and he went and said something. The Germans pulled me out, and this guy hit me with his fist and knocked out two teeth. That was the only time I was beaten.

The Germans loaded us onto the boat and took us down to the port city of Danzig, known today as Gdańsk in Poland. At the time it was in Germany. Then they transferred us to a barge that took us along the coast to a concentration camp called Stutthof. It was a big camp. It had the same barracks with people lying on top of each other and the same Germans yelling and screaming and pushing. The same things. There was no difference. The bosses were criminals. The food was bitter from a plant like nettles. It stank.

When I came there I found my brother, and we were very happy, of course. He had been there for some time before I arrived. But then they separated us again, and that was the last time I saw my brother. I had come in a later group, and my whole group was sent to another place. In August 1944 the Germans put us into cattle cars, and we spent several days traveling to who knew where, with no water or food. I wound up in Buchenwald. I didn't even know where I was.

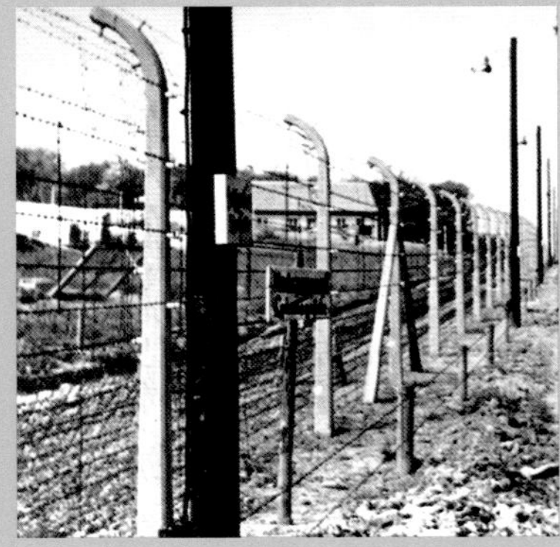

Electric fencing surrounds Buchenwald concentration camp in the early 1940s.

Buchenwald was a completely different situation. There was a crematorium there, with a chimney. When we got there, we could smell it right away. There was smoke coming out, and it smelled like flesh. It was a big, big camp with thirty thousand people, surrounded by an electrified fence. Lots of people got killed, or starved, or sickened and died. Some would get fed up and commit suicide by going to the fence to get electrocuted. I saw children being electrocuted. It was supposed to be the worst camp. The smell was terrible. We were there for quite a while, and the Allies bombed the camp.

We arrived late summer. It wasn't too cold, and it wasn't too hot. We still wore the striped clothes, and our heads were shaved down the middle. If you wanted to escape to a German village and ask a peasant to hide you, even if you got other clothes you were still identified by the bald line on top of your head. So there was no place to go. You didn't have any money. You had no passport. You had no identity. Most of us spoke German, but we had an accent, a Jewish accent. They could tell you were Jewish.

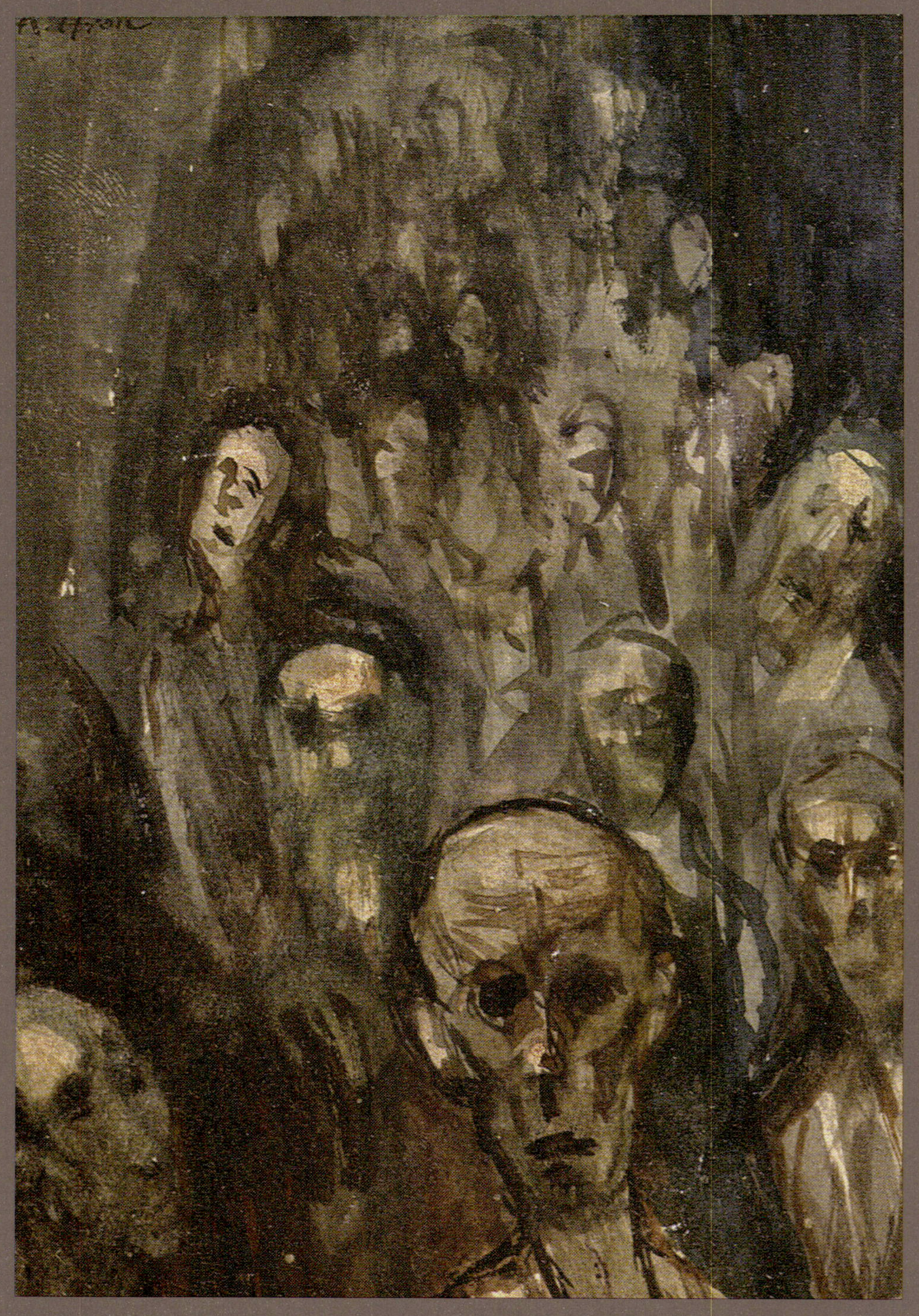

Because V-2 rockets were made underground at Buchenwald, Allied airplanes bombed us. The reconnaissance must have been tremendous, because when they bombed they managed to keep the bombs away from the main portion of the camp. You saw the bombs coming down. I guess a lot of Germans were killed underground. The bombings destroyed the water supply.

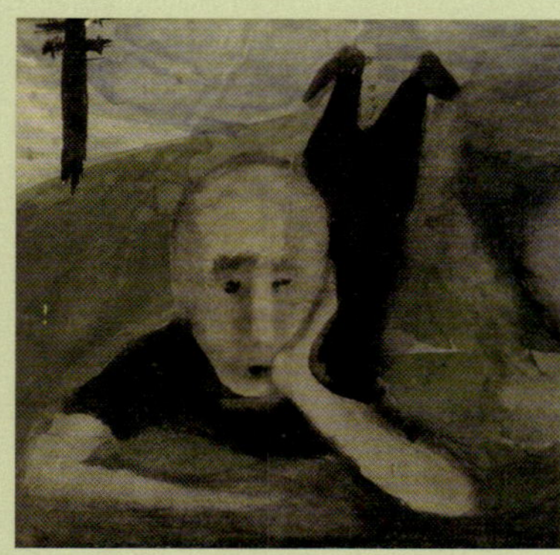

Sleeping Next to the Rock (detail); full image on page 86.

In Buchenwald they put us in the quarantine area, called the Little Camp. It was very crowded. The barracks were full. What outdoor tents they had were full of Jewish prisoners. We didn't have a place to sleep. So I slept outdoors on the ground with a rock as my pillow, the stars as my canopy, and the trees as my night sentinels. My connection to life was through nature, for the Germans could not remove the stars from the sky. They could not stop the sun from rising in the morning. They could not stop the trees from growing in the Little Camp. This was my connection to a world I had long since left. Every morning I awoke and saw the sun. I said to myself: Victory, I have survived to live one more day.

I remember a famous surgeon from Riga, Professor Mintz, who worked in the Jewish hospital there. He had gone to Russia to operate on Lenin. When he arrived at Buchenwald, the chief German doctor recognized him and shook his hand as he greeted him. A Nazi officer came and slapped the German doctor in the face. It was not permitted to treat a Jew respectfully. Professor Mintz was sick. He couldn't eat the food, got diarrhea and died in the hospital.

I survived by disappearing. I learned how not to be noticed by the SS and the guards, while I studied the guards and prisoners. I learned that prisoners who gave up hope died, whether they were hungry or not. This camp was a place of filth, terror, darkness, inhumanity and cruelty. It was not of this world. It was certainly not of the world where I lived before in Riga. And I had a very strong connection to the outer world and a desire to live in it once again, to be free to draw, to paint, to dream.

I was pretty solitary. As an artist I had always been in my own territory, if you will. In the camps we never knew when a friend might be struck down and die. So one way to protect yourself, to insulate yourself, was to be alone. A deep, stark place of loneliness is where I was.

Kalman Marching in the Camp (early 1950s), gouache on paper, 4½ × 3⅛ in.

This was an international camp, and I always remember the courage of the prisoners—not just Jews, but also the gypsies, Poles, Russians, French, Belgians. They had great courage not to go mad or lose their humanity. Being in the camps was not like being in the shadow. It was the dark void. It was a place beyond words or imagination.

I didn't do any art in Buchenwald because it was too chaotic after the bombing. But my concentration there and in the other camps changed my painting for the rest of my life. To not be noticed—to disappear—took intense concentration. I found myself studying other people, studying the traits that helped some to survive. I learned to draw people's faces—adults, children and models—in the art school in Riga. In the camps I studied emotions as people expressed them in their bodies and on their faces. When I drew later, I had the capability to see the feelings and moods of a person and draw them.

After the bombs they sent us to another camp. We were always going from one place to another. When the Russians, Americans and English were coming, the Germans tried to escape and they took us with them. We were their slave labor. I was sent to a camp called Rehmsdorf near Leipzig to work in a factory where they were making synthetic gasoline. I was a long time in this camp.

The Allies bombed this factory also. They seemed to do it every time the train was loaded with the gasoline. There was probably somebody there telling them. The airplanes could not see well because the Germans surrounded the factory with smoke pots. As soon as the siren came on, the guards took us out of the factory, and we all ran and hid. Ten minutes later the bombs would start coming down, and people from the camp were killed. One day a bomb exploded near us on a hill and buried us in the ground. I was buried up to my shoulder. After the bombing we had to clean up the mess.

We lived first in tents and then in barracks. We used to get up at four or five in the morning, and we worked very late. We had a piece of bread for breakfast. Then we would walk from the camp to the factory, a long walk. In the factory maybe we would get some soup. At night we dragged ourselves home in the dark to the barracks by the railroad tracks. Back at the barracks you ate some soup and bread and went to bed. The soup had a few carrots or kohlrabis, a hard green vegetable.

We didn't know if the planes were American, English, French, or even Russian. They would fly high because the Germans were shooting at them. The Germans built the camps right near a railway station so they could escape quickly. One day bombs were coming down on our barracks, this time huge time bombs. They would stick into the ground and explode ten minutes later. Can you imagine the panic? A lot of people got killed there too. The second time they bombed there were also smaller airplanes coming down, machine-gunning, and it was at night. We tried to escape. There were gates, but they weren't electrified so we ran out of the gates up the hill. While we were running, the Allied pilots machine-gunned us. They were so fast. A lot of people got killed. We were trying to get out of the barracks, in a stampede.

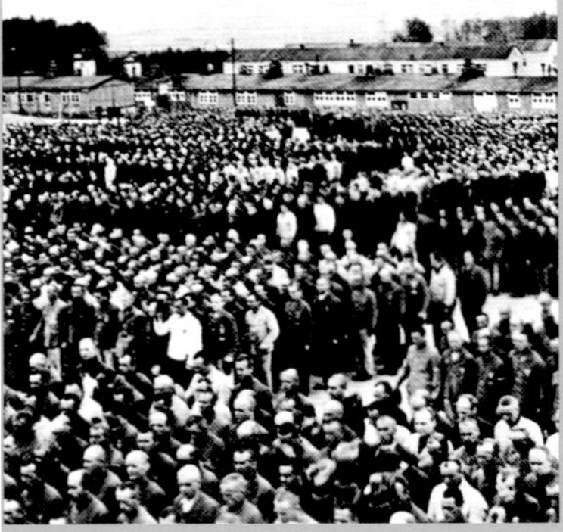

Prisoners mass for a roll call at Buchenwald (early 1940s).

One of those killed was my only real friend in the camps. He was a young man from Cologne, Germany. The bomb tore him apart. I had been in a barrack across from his. I saw parts of him flying in the air, pieces of flesh flying, parts of the body. I was told later on that they were 500-pound time bombs.

One day I saw my father's cousin at the camp. His name was Lezer. He was starving. A dead bird lay on the ground. As he picked it up to eat it, I ran and yelled, "No, no. Don't eat the bird!" I figured the bombs had poisoned it. But he ate it, and that night he fell ill and died. Remembering what happened upsets me to this day.

The son of my father's brother, my cousin, Leibe, also came to Rehmsdorf. We had been in the ghetto together. He was very sick. I tried to save him. I tried to get him help. We were together for probably a month or less. One night I got some of my food and went to take it to him in the barrack. His bunk was empty. I asked the capo where he was. They sent him away. He wound up in Buchenwald, killed, I'm sure.

There was one German guard in Rehmsdorf who was kind, an older man. I didn't know his name. I remember him walking around, talking to the capo, a Jewish man from Germany.

The capos ran the show inside the camp. They told people to get in line, to do this or that. They assigned work. The Germans stayed outside the gate. They used the capos to do all their dirty work. The capos wouldn't kill people, but they yelled and made sure that this or that was done. They became big shots.

One of the soldiers, a guard, sent to Leipzig to get some pencils and paper for me to draw. By that time I had nothing left. I remember a man from Lithuania was doing murals for the Germans in the kitchen, though I never saw one. He didn't do any portraiture or sketches. He is the only artist I remember in the camps.

There were "selections" at Rehmsdorf. We would run and scream our names and professions before the Germans. The officers would write something down. In the morning they would call numbers and take people away to kill them. Some people were just skin and bones. Some got swollen from starvation.

To Theresienstadt

One day in the spring of 1945, I heard the sound of cannons shooting. Right away we knew that the Allies were close. That was our hope right there. They put us like cattle into a car, but before they could start the train moving east, the Allies bombed the train tracks at the railway station. We were stuck in that cattle car with no food or water for four days. People died standing up. Once the Germans repaired the train tracks, we began a journey to we knew not where.

That's how we started on the way to Theresienstadt. The Allies continued bombing the train again and again on the way to that place. They thought there were Germans inside. The Germans were outside on the cars guarding us. We were inside, but the Allies didn't know that. Lots of fast planes were coming. Bombers were bombing the train. Other airplanes were machine-gunning us. A lot of us got killed.

Finally we got out of the train. People started running in every direction, some hiding in some burned-out building while others went up the hill. But where could you go? You couldn't get far. The farmers would give us away. They were not going to take a chance. They are going to get killed if the Germans found somebody hidden.

One German, a guard we knew in the camp, tried to escape. He was chasing after us, but he was shooting in the air. He would run, pretending he was chasing after us, and shoot not at us but in the air. He did it because other Germans would go after him. I guess a few of them escaped during that time. We let him escape.

There were a lot of people killed from the bombs. They took all the dead people and put them into an open cart, and they dumped them.

They finally found us. We were on foot. We walked the rest of the way—fifty-two miles over four days. If you couldn't keep going, the Germans simply killed you on the way. We wound up in Theresienstadt in Czechoslovakia.

There was an epidemic of typhus. I was one of the guys helping delouse and clean the prisoners in the shower, with the boxer Zalman "Zaltzy" Peretzman. We didn't get sick; we didn't catch it. I don't know how. This Czech camp was more like a ghetto, a village with buildings. They had an orchestra, and people were doing art; some paintings were found after we were liberated.

Within a few days the Russians liberated us. We didn't know that the Germans were going to kill us. One more day, and we would not have been there. The head of the camp was supposed to kill all the Jews before the Russians came. But he saved his own neck by not doing it, I heard afterward, because they let him go.

We still didn't know what the hell was going on. The Russians told us that we were all supposed to be dead.

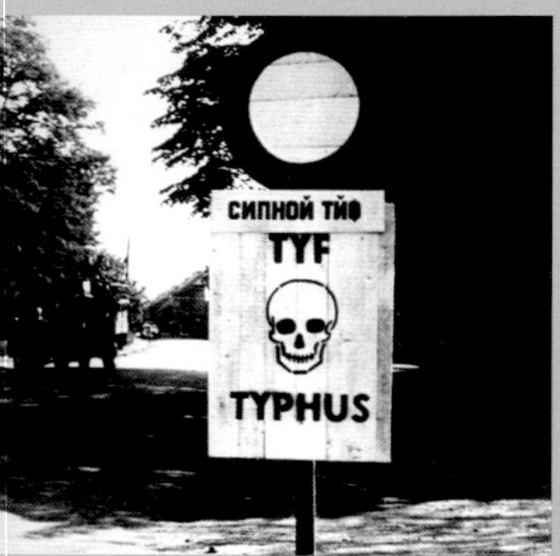

Signs in two languages warn of typhus at Theresienstadt in May, 1945.

Liberation and Escape

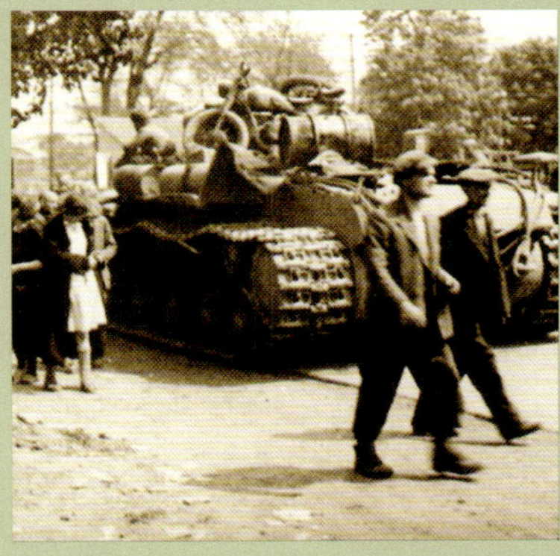

A Russian tank polices Theresienstadt after liberation, in May 1945.

The Russians separated a small group of us from the other prisoners, who were German Jews and Czech Jews. They put us, three Latvians and three Lithuanians, in a truck and drove away. The Russians had recaptured Latvia and Lithuania, so they considered us Russian citizens. They wanted to send us back to Latvia and Lithuania. They were talking about us being in the Soviet army. So that was it. We were not liberated.

After a while, the Russians stopped. We were led off the truck into a bombed-out house somewhere in Czechoslovakia. They dropped us off during the day and said they would come back in the evening. They were going to steal horses and sell them on the black market. They came back at night and gave us some clothes and a few things in little Red Cross packages. Then one Russian took two of us out into the woods, holding us up with a gun. He took away our two packages. Zaltzy and the other people didn't know what was going on. We told them they just robbed us, taking the toothpaste or whatever was in the little packages. That is when we decided to get out of there. We don't want to go back to Latvia to go into the army. We knew our parents were killed. I didn't know if my brother was alive. The Russians left again. They were coming back in the morning to pick us up. We decided to escape.

We didn't know where we were. We just decided to get out of there. Zaltzy was the leader. He said, "Let's get out and see if we wind up in Prague." We didn't know where Prague was, this way or that way. We just knew there was a Prague somewhere.

We walked along a road and jumped into the ditch when military trucks passed. Finally, we took a chance. We stopped a Russian truck, planning to say that we were German Jews. There were two soldiers in the truck, a driver and a young captain. We didn't know if they would arrest us. The young Russian captain asked, "*Amcho?*" which in Hebrew means "Are you our own?" He was about thirty-five. He didn't know much Yiddish, and we were afraid to speak Russian. We took a chance and asked in Yiddish for help getting to Prague. He threw us into the truck and drove us to Prague. Once in the truck he found out that we were Latvian and Lithuanian Jews, but he helped us anyway. He dropped us off on the outskirts of Prague, and that was that.

We arrived sick and starving, barely alive. We were like walking skeletons. We did not know where to find food. We went to the charity called Harit. We asked for food wherever we went. We were told that we needed papers that showed where we were born. We didn't have any papers. The Russians controlled Prague, so we said we were German Jews and didn't speak Yiddish. Zaltzy was a sharp guy.

Finally, we went into a place with Czech officers, an office where we could get a passport. It was a museum on a hill that had been bombed. I don't know how we found the office. All I know is that we arrived there, said we wanted papers and told them that we were German Jews. That was it. All of a sudden one of us spoke in Yiddish. Realizing that we were not German Jews, a Czech soldier got up and went into a back room. He returned with some Russian soldiers. We ran outside as fast as we could in our sick condition. Zaltzy and I jumped onto a cable car and took off.

The next thing I remember is waking up in a Catholic convent. I don't even know how I got there. I guess that Zaltzy and I collapsed on a street, and they picked us up. I don't even know how long we were there—a week, maybe two. They fed and took care of us. We were so sick that we probably couldn't talk. As soon as they let us out, we started talking: "We have to get out of here. They will find out that we are Russian Jews, and we will be in big trouble."

Of the six of us who escaped from the Russians, two wanted to go to Israel because they had relatives there. Yakob Basner and a guy named Weinberg chose to return to Riga to see if any relatives survived. I went with them on the streetcar to the train station in Prague, carrying my small case of paints. When I got there I decided: No, I don't want to go. I don't want to see the Latvians. I didn't know anybody in Latvia. Everybody I knew was dead. And the Russians would put me in the army. So why would I want to go to Riga?

I went back and found Zaltzy. He said that we had to get out of Prague. The Russians would find out that we were Latvian Jews. He heard that American soldiers were in a place called Pilzen where they make beer, a famous place. So we walked all night through the country and wound up in Pilzen.

The American soldiers did not know who we were. Refugees and Germans were wandering all around. So they put us in jail. One day a rabbi walked by. Perhaps he heard us talking. He stopped and talked to us. He told the soldiers in charge that we were not German soldiers on the run, that we were concentration camp survivors and should be freed. We moved on to Salzburg, where we went to a displaced persons camp.

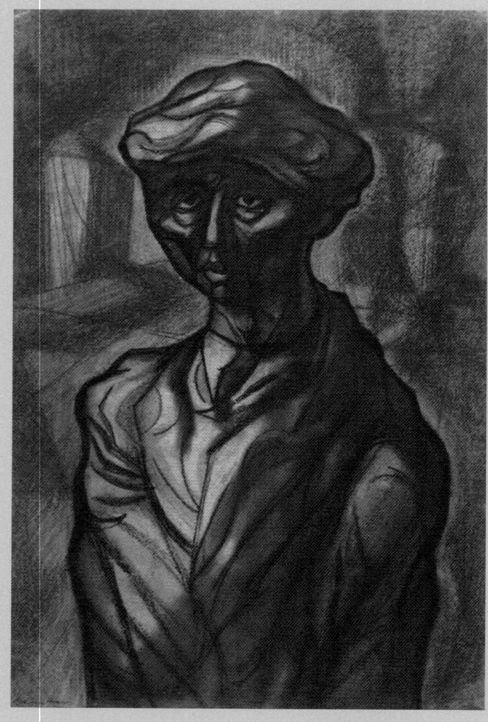

Man from the Camps (1990s), compressed charcoal on paper, 36 × 24 in.

Salzburg, Austria

The American government and the Jewish Federation set up a camp for displaced persons in Salzburg. They took five or six apartment buildings and offered rooms. I shared one room with a man from Poland. Zaltzy was in another building. There was a fairly new kitchen where they gave us food. Some wanted to go to Israel. Some wanted to go to Poland. No one knew what to do. Zaltzy knew a little English. He talked to the soldiers and told them I did portraits. I would then do a charcoal drawing. We would split the money the soldiers paid us. I did sketches like this all year long.

The head of the displaced persons camp was a Polish woman with the United Nations. She had a Jewish boyfriend who was in the U.S. Army. He had been a judge in the United States before the war. One day I received a letter from the Fine Arts Academy in Vienna. They offered me a full scholarship if I would go to their art school. I had done a drawing of the Polish woman and her friend, the American GI. Apparently, he took the two drawings to Vienna and showed them to the people at the academy. I was twenty-two. I was ready to go. Now I just had to get to Vienna.

When asked if I would return to Latvia, I have said I never will. Why would I? They killed my father and my mother.

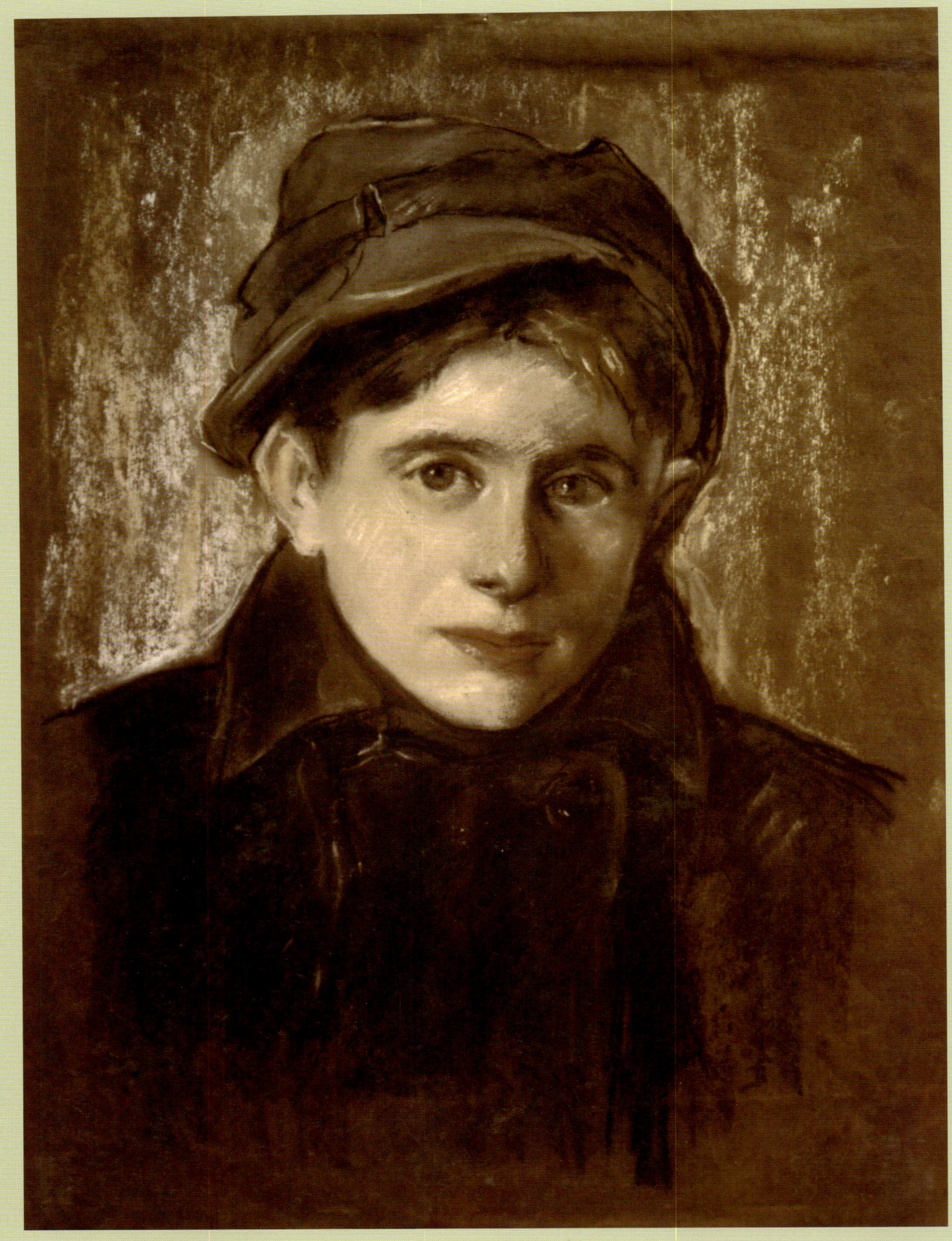

3

SHADOWS AND LIGHT

Vienna

Camp Survivor (1947), pastel on paper, 18 × 13 in.

On the train to Vienna I talked with a man I knew very well in the camp, Aaron Simkin. He too was a Latvian Jew, and he was going to Brussels. I told him I was supposed to go to Vienna and stay in a hospital there for displaced persons. He said "Go to my brother. He is in the English army outside of Vienna, and he has a little room that he rents. On Saturdays and Sundays he takes his girlfriend there, and then he goes back to the army. He'll let you stay there."

To get to Vienna, I had to take the train through the Russian zone. At one stop the Russians looked at my papers. They noticed that I was born in Latvia, and they pulled me off the train along with some Nazis they found. Maybe they thought I was a Russian army deserter.

The Russian soldiers marched us along the train platform in a row toward a truck. I carefully fell to the back of the line, and when I thought no Russian was looking, I dropped off the platform into a bush. I waited. They kept marching; they had not noticed. I escaped. Being in the camps all those years, I had learned how to hide and escape. Invisible again.

I had no idea where I was. I had a few schillings in my pocket, and I saw a truck. The driver was an Austrian, and I asked him in German if he would give me a ride to Vienna. I gave him the little money I had. He was hauling furniture. He opened the truck and removed some furniture to make room for me. He put me all the way at the front. I could see the back of his head when he was driving. We went through a series of checkpoints, and I wound up in Vienna.

When I arrived I went to the hospital; it used to be a school, and now it was crowded—twenty people sharing a room. I decided to look for my friend's brother and found him outside of Vienna. He told me to use his room in Vienna when he wasn't there. I only had to stay four days in the hospital.

I moved into his rented apartment on the top floor. It had a bed with sheets and a down pillow. I had not slept in a real bed in a long time. I will never forget how that felt. The owner was an opera singer, and the apartment building was in the Russian zone. Russian soldiers lived on the floors below. On the weekends I slept on a park bench.

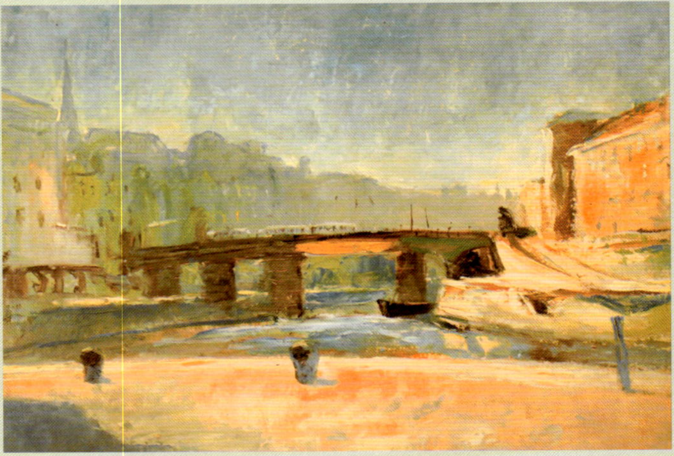

Donau Bridge (1949), oil, 24 × 29 in.

Vienna is one of the great cities in Europe. I saw styles of art I had never seen before. I loved the Academy of Fine Arts. I continued to avoid capture by the Russians, and I met my first wife.

I remember my first day at school. I walked through the Russian sector to get to it. It was in the American sector, not far from Gustav Klimt's Secession Gallery. The professor began his lecture by telling us a story about a strange young man who had come to the school years earlier. "We kicked him out," the professor said. "And then he came back again. And we kicked him out again. He was Adolf Hitler." Can you imagine that? He was telling us that if they had let him stay in school, there might not have been World War II. All these people might not have been killed. They kicked him out because he didn't know anatomy. Every day we had to learn anatomy. That school was very advanced.

I spent about three and years at the school. The professor who told us about Hitler was a portrait artist who tried to imitate Rembrandt. He was okay. He liked me. He used to bring me paper and pencils because I had no money. I couldn't buy anything at all. He would meet me outside in the mornings so that the other students couldn't see that he was favoring me. One time he went away for two weeks to do some portraits, and he put me in as his substitute. I was twenty-three years old, and I was an assistant professor. The students liked me better because I would tell them that their eyes in their portraits were a little too small, or to change the noses a bit.

This academy was not like the one in Latvia. Everybody did his own thing. The professor was neither an expressionist nor an impressionist. He would suggest that you darken something, like Rembrandt, who used dark and light. Some of the students did surrealistic figures. One student had things sticking out of the head, the brain coming out, that type of thing.

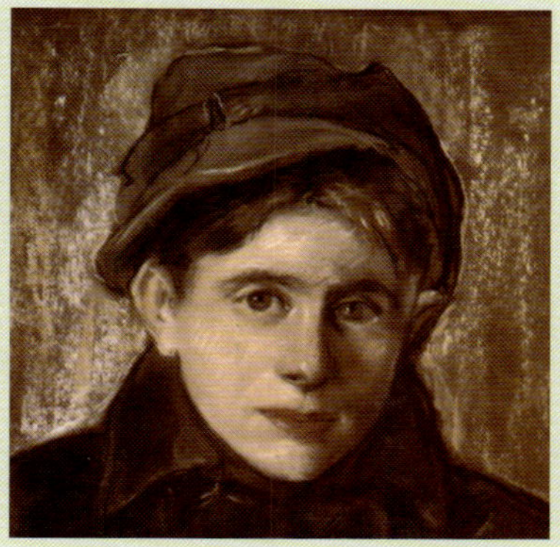

I drew a lot of models—nudes and clothed. I used pastels, oils, charcoal and pen. A lot of people did etchings and lithographs; I didn't. I used to go in the street and do landscapes. There is a nice one of the *Donau Bridge* in Vienna. I have another framed that I would never sell. It looks like early Monet. I hide those pieces because I don't want to sell them. I continued to draw people. One is a pastel on paper of a boy in Vienna who survived the Holocaust, *Camp Survivor*.

Camp Survivor (detail); full image on page 58.

I loved Vienna. I saw paintings by Egon Schiele, Gustav Klimt and Oskar Kokoschka. A group of Schiele drawings were for sale. I could have bought three for about eighty dollars. I had no money, so I asked to borrow some from my student friends. First, they wanted to see the drawings. They didn't like them. No way were they going to let me buy those. I wish I had them today!

Klimt painted in a way I had never seen before. As we entered the academy building every morning, we passed several of Klimt's paintings hanging on the walls. Most of us would say, "Too much gold." Klimt painted wealthy women with expensive jewelry. Kokoschka's painting was dark, brooding, powerful and colorful. I liked his self-portraits.

One day I go to art school and I see Russians stopping people to check their papers. I stop and hide around the corner until they are gone. Another evening I am returning to my apartment and Russian soldiers are checking everyone's papers at my apartment building. Of course, my papers show Riga, Latvia. They could pick me up and send me to Siberia.

I decide that I better find someplace to live outside the Russian quarter. I am getting worried about it. I came back one night and told Aaron Simkin's brother that I had to get out of there. He found me a place in the British zone, which was quite a distance.

It was on Radetzkystrasse near a lake. I told the landlady I was going to get a CARE package. She had six children. She was very nice. I couldn't give her any money, so once a month I gave her my CARE package in place of rent. I stayed there about a year. The nickname she called me was "Schenki," meaning "wavy hair." She had a pretty daughter who was a gymnast.

One day the mother went to the countryside and left her daughter, who had just broken up with her boyfriend. You can imagine the trouble we got into—both young. I did two nude paintings of her, which I submitted for my final exams at the art school. In 1961 I went back to Vienna to get these paintings, but they were gone.

It was easy to spot an anti-Semite in Vienna. They would tell you, "Oh, we hid a Jew in the cellar." So I said, "How many Austrians hid Jews in their cellars?" "Oh, a lot of them." Right away they would justify or try to hide the fact they were Nazis. They were not out-and-out anti-Semites. They didn't show it. But I speak German, and I could hear them talking to each other.

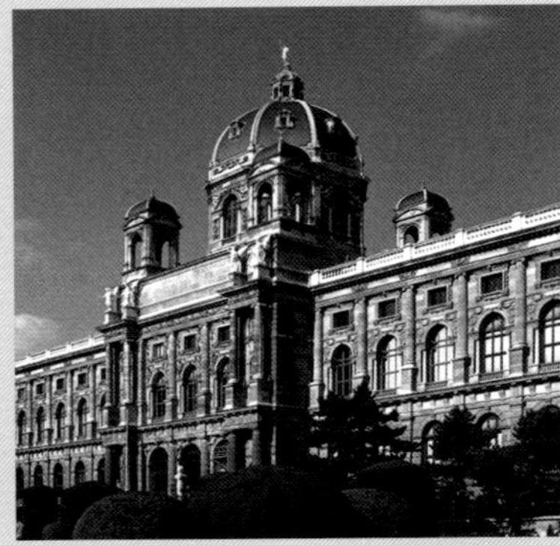

Vienna Academy of Fine Arts.

Some of my friends were angry at me for going to art school. They said I would starve for another four years. There was no food in Vienna. I didn't have any ration coupons; only Austrian citizens got coupons. But I am an artist, and I was determined to finish art school. I had a scholarship. I figured I'd never be able to afford to go to art school otherwise, so I went there through 1949. I did sketches occasionally if somebody would give me some money, bread or cigarettes. Things were getting a little better.

I had my one meal a day at a kitchen for displaced persons from the camps. That is where I met Trude, my first wife. She had brown hair, intelligent eyes, a sharp mind and a keen wit. Although her brother returned to Vienna from England after the war, Trude was on her own, like me. She had lost her parents and little brother in Riga also. They were among the Austrian Jews sent there to be killed in 1942. Her full name was Gertrude Schneider.

Trude had escaped Austria before the war under the auspices of Kindertransport, a Quaker program that moved children out of Europe. She went to England, where she was sent to a Quaker organization that placed her in foster homes. She moved around and finally got some jobs for the duration of the war. In 1946 she returned to Vienna and went to school to study philosophy and anthropology.

At the apartment on Radetzkystrasse the landlady's husband found out that a Jew lived upstairs. He would not come up to my floor where I lived, so I decided to move out as soon as I could. Trude and I looked together and rented part of an apartment in the British zone.

One day we went to the American Consulate. I had applied for visas to America, Canada, England and Australia. As there were very few Latvians in Vienna, my number came up. They told me that I could go to America in December 1949. Many people from Europe went to New York or Chicago because they had relatives there. I had none, so they sent me to Los Angeles. Trude pretended to be my wife, and they said that we could go together. Trude and I then married, and we prepared to leave Europe. I did my exams early and got my diploma three months before my classmates.

Trude remembers their coming this way:

People at the UN relief agency arranged for us to fly to Munich. Otherwise, we would have had to go through the Russian zone in Vienna, and the Russians would have picked Kalman up. From Munich we took a train to Hamburg, where we stayed in a camp for six weeks. Like in Vienna, everybody was dealing this for that on the black market. I never did; nor did Kalman. He was so honest.

From Hamburg we went on a boat to New Orleans. They didn't want us in New York. We then got on a train with about a thousand others. There were two hundred Jews, and the rest were ex-Nazis. They were bringing them into the country. The Nazis didn't want to sit with the Jews.

We arrived at Union Station in Los Angeles. They took us off the train to a Jewish organization located where the Chandler music center sits today. I was wearing the wine-red suit and white blouse that I had worn for our wedding. I saved the whole thing because I was going to arrive and look good. A lot of the people made themselves out to be poorer than they were. They wore babushkas and begged.

We sat around to be interviewed. I spoke perfect English. I had a really heavy British accent from years in England. It was phony, but I spoke English better than I do today. An American social worker interviewed us. She spoke in a pidgin English that combined Jewish, Yiddish and English. She would not recognize my English; she did not hear me. I was a refugee. She wanted to give me ten dollars to go to the May Company basement. I didn't want it. I kept saying, "Please speak English; I understand." I'll never forget this. For years I was rude to every social worker I met. She really infuriated me.

From there they sent us to the Himmelblau Hotel, owned by an old Jewish man, just off Soto Street. Because I spoke English, we got out of there in a hurry. I found us an apartment on Willowbrook, just off Vermont, two blocks south of Santa Monica in Los Angeles. We moved again briefly and finally moved onto Micheltorena Street at the edge of Silver Lake, where we lived together until 1956.

Kalman continues:

It was nice coming to America, because I was getting away from Europe. That was the main thing. I didn't want to stay in Europe.

Portrait of Gertrude Schneider (1949), oil, 29½ × 24 in.

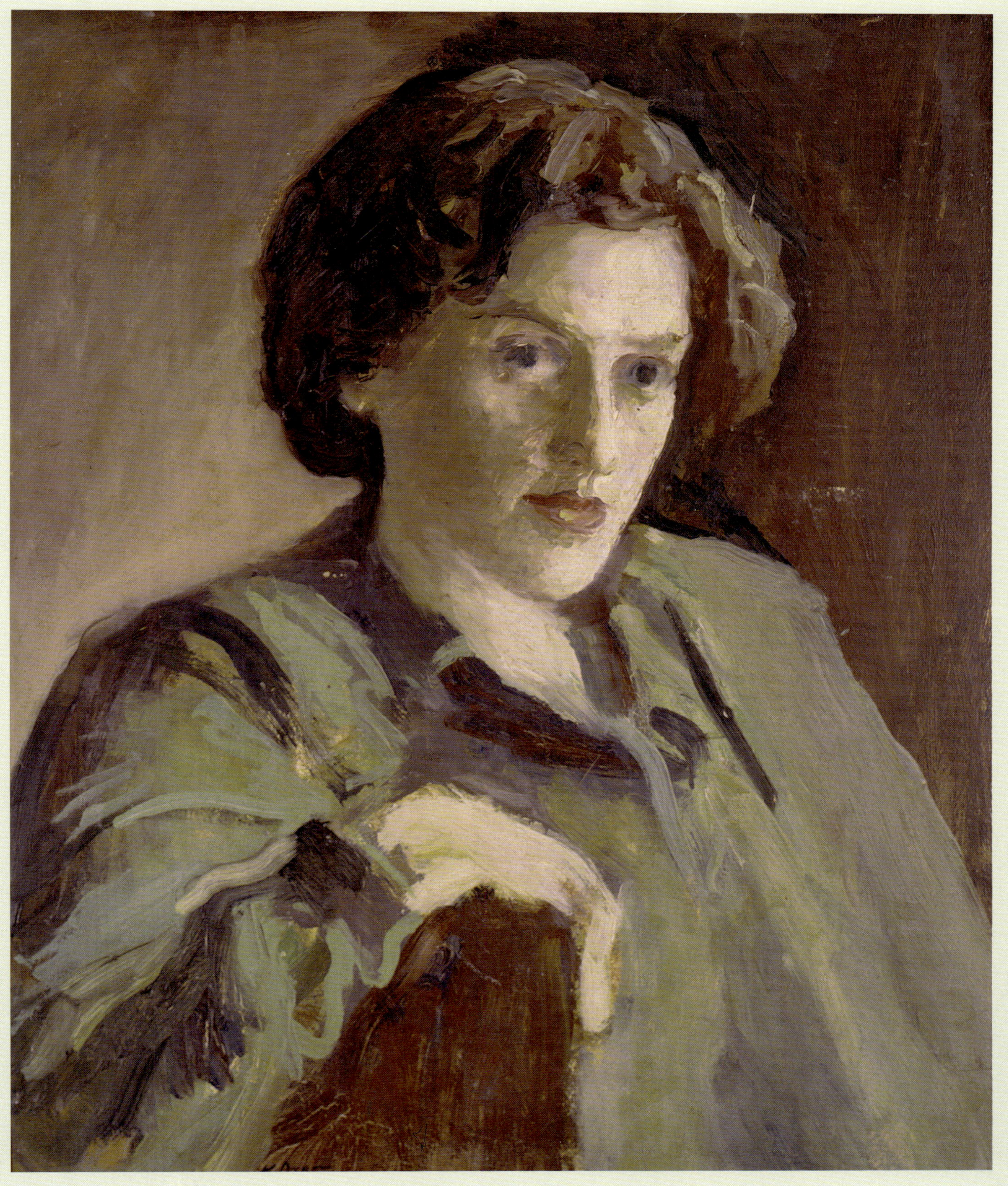

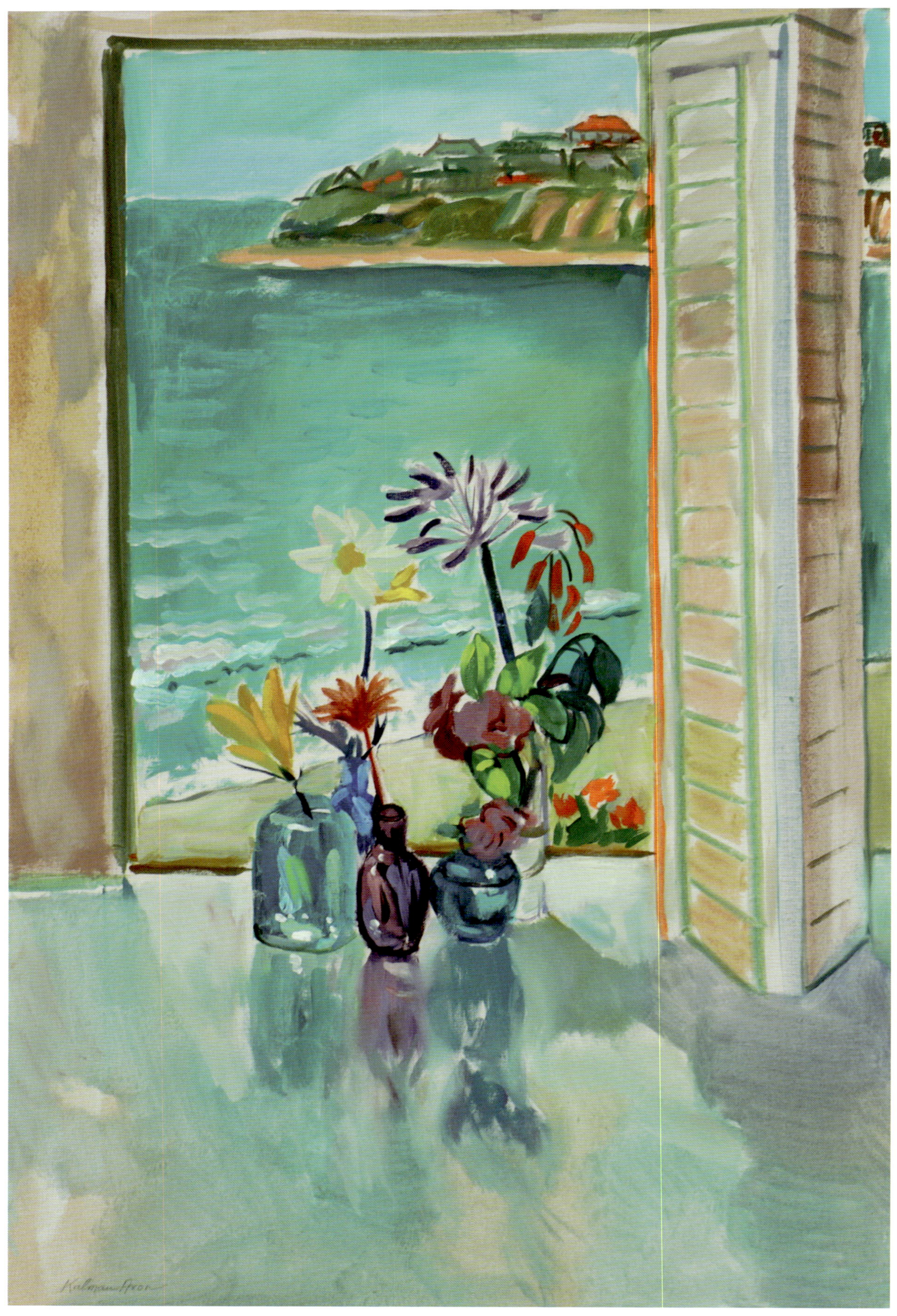

4

LIGHT AND WARMTH

California

View of Laguna Cove (1980s), oil on canvas, 36 × 24 in.

Aron remembers:

When I arrived in Los Angeles, I was twenty-five with a wife and four dollars in my pocket. I had done a sketch of the captain of the boat we took to New Orleans, and he gave me the four dollars. I don't remember how we started getting money. Trude didn't work until much later. She had completed her training to be a psychologist in Vienna, but she was not licensed here. I must have sold a few drawings or sketches. I remember it was a very hard time.

I found a job painting dishes. I sat all day long, painting flowers on ceramics in a factory near Glendale. Years later I saw one in somebody's house and said that I probably did this. Then somebody suggested a job making maps. So I went and saw them making maps, aerial cartography, using pen and ink to draw lines. I began doing it freehand. I was so fast that I had to wait for the other guys to finish. This gave me time to do sketches, so I had little drawings to take home each night. I would leave about five in the morning to ride two buses to get there at seven. I worked from seven to three and got home about five or six. Trude would make me dinner, and I would paint at night.

After a year, the manager called me in and said, "Mr. Aron, you have a great talent for making maps, and we want to give you a promotion." I was getting ninety cents an hour, and they were going to promote me to maybe a dollar and ten cents an hour. I said, "Mr. Johnson, thank you, but I went for six years to art school, and I don't want to become a mapmaker. I like doing it, but it is not the kind of job I had in mind." So I quit. Trude was very upset because we had no money. I said, "Look, I will do something else." She understood. That was one good thing about her. She respected what I was. After that I started selling paintings of children.

We also rented one of our two bedrooms to a young man. We had no furniture when we moved into the apartment. I watched for stuff thrown out on the street every Thursday afternoon. I picked up wood. Out of this I made my own furniture. I made a table; I made a chair; I made a lamp. People would say: "Hey, this is terrific." It was modern furniture.

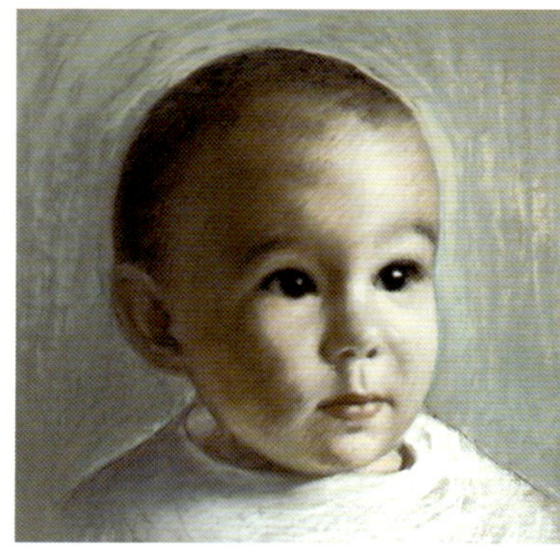

Portrait of Nonnie (detail); full image on page 12.

Trude and I met some interesting people. I did a portrait of Fanny Brice's son, Bill. He was a good artist, and he introduced us to his mother. She arranged a scholarship for me at the Jepson Art Institute in 1951 so I could get credentials to teach. I then could supplement my income from my paintings. I taught at the Hollywood School of Design on Highland Avenue in Los Angeles in 1956. I taught generals, veterans from the Korean War. I enjoyed that. Throughout my life I taught painting, including some years at the Pasadena Art Center College of Design, and I always enjoyed it.

I had more nightmares during those years. Trude told me I was yelling and screaming for a long time. Then I would wake up, sweating. I don't remember much about the nightmares—Germans chasing me, fire, things like that. But nightmares and dreaming don't necessarily correlate with what happened. After a while they lessened.

Today I don't remember what I dream. I guess I blocked out all those years. If somebody asks me, "What did you dream last night," I wouldn't know, because the next day it's gone.

Aron told me that when he arrived in Los Angeles, he straddled two worlds. He began exploring America's people, buildings and landscape. He learned that talking about his past was not productive. People who had never starved could not begin to understand. Some who survived the Holocaust could not stop talking about it, and he would find himself listening for hours, whether with a stranger in Beverly Hills or his friend Zaltzy Peretzman in Brooklyn. "I could not listen," he says. "It took me down."

Aron and Trude sought friends who had no history like theirs in Europe. Nonetheless, the experience of the Holocaust still haunted him. He expressed it in his painting even as he was moving ahead. In those early California years, his eye fell on three subjects: children and his new neighbors; the buildings and landscapes around him; and memories of the Holocaust.

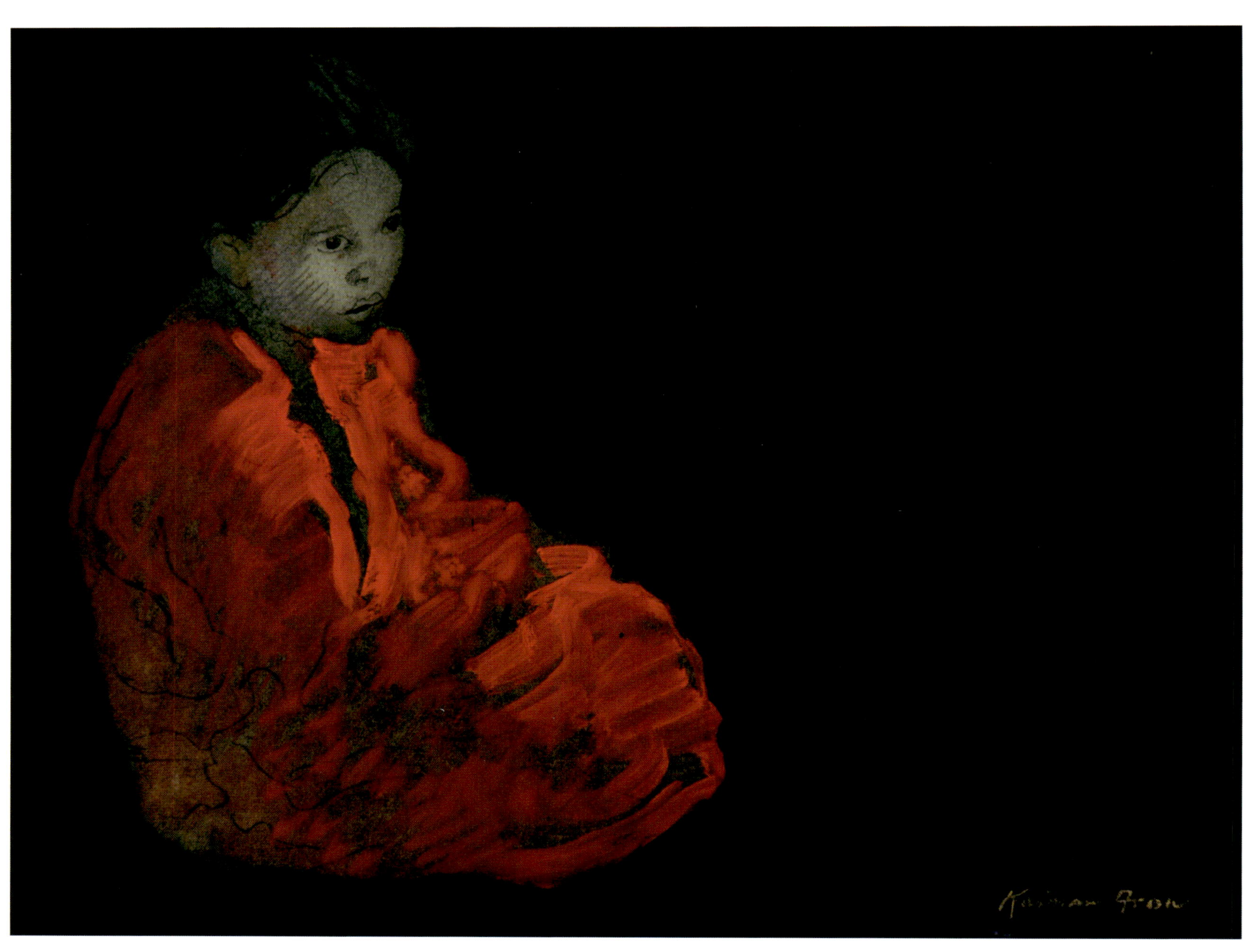

Girl in Red (1950s), gouache on paper, 10½ × 14 in.

The Children

A school for children with special problems was across the street from where they lived in Silver Lake, and Trude was studying the psychology of children with problems. Aron says:

I used to walk across the street and from a distance sketch them. I had to sketch quickly because the children never stayed still. Then I would go into the apartment to make paintings out of the sketches. I wound up doing a lot of children—paintings of them playing, talking, sitting on the curb. Before I knew it, the street was lined up with cars, and people were buying my paintings of the children. All of a sudden, I was also doing commissioned portraits of children. That boy with black eyes started the whole new ball game.

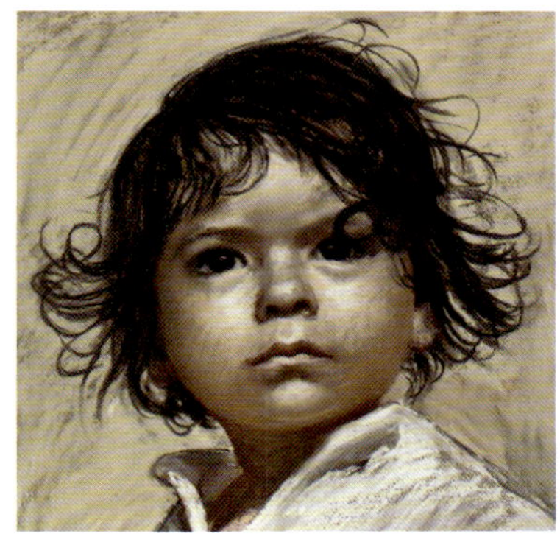

Child with Black Eyes (detail);
full image on page 8.

Child with Black Eyes was the first of Aron's paintings that my mother saw in 1951, the picture that compelled her to ask him to paint portraits of her daughters. Impressed by his work, she recommended Aron to her decorating clients. This kept him busy drawing portraits for the next decade. For years, Mom pestered him to sell her the *Child with Black Eyes*. Finally he agreed to draw a second pastel of this child, which he sold to her after writing the word "Copy" on the back. The original hangs in the bedroom of his apartment as a talisman, the composition that allowed him to work full-time as an artist in his adopted land.

What in this boy's countenance spoke to Aron? Life and power. There is strength and composure in his face and a deep knowing in his eyes. This child is alert and seems quite capable of handling life's challenges. Aron uses pastels in a rich palette to offset his dark eyes and wispy, black hair. He draws him with clear, bold, lively strokes to match the energy he found in this child. The boy reflects the determination that kept Aron alive, and he carries the vitality that Aron seeks to renew in his life.

Girl in Red, a small painting in oil, pastel and ink, shows a child huddled in a brilliant red wrap, alone against a black background. Her eyes show concern, her lips a touch of sadness. She appears disappointed, a bit frightened and disconnected from the world. She might be contemplating her life and what she has seen. How does one maintain life alone in such a void? Will she reengage in life? The contrast of the black background with her red wrap suggests that something remains vibrant in the darkest of times. How often did Aron find himself in the same circumstance? Suspended in time and space, surrounded by darkness, alone, watching and whispering: I still breathe; I live.

Aron painted *The Lost Children* from a sketch he made of two children in an orthodox Jewish neighborhood in Brooklyn. As though in a fog, the boy and girl hold hands as they stand together. Dressed like Europeans, they appear lost and alone. Aron said, "I painted the young girl with the face of an old woman. I don't know why." Throughout his ordeal he saw children starving, torn from their parents. Any child who survived this would lose innocence and age. In this painting he honors all the children who came through the fog.

Three Children Playing, done in pastels, shimmers with a circle of life. Aron uses soft pastels, yet the children still sit in the shadows. Where is the California sunlight? *The Family* recalls paintings Aron saw by Oskar Kokoschka in Vienna. He uses thick paint strokes and strong colors to define this family, and he outlines each person in black, a technique he used throughout his career. The mother's outstretched arm holds space for her children. Her eyes are sad. The young person holding the baby seems detached. The others are watching, waiting; all seem hesitant, not involved in life, as their emotions range from observation and sadness to fear and detachment.

Why did Aron spend so much time drawing children in the 1950s? On one hand, it gave him a chance to reconnect with the spontaneity and wonder of being young. On the other, he could express the trauma and fear he saw children suffer during the Holocaust. Aron is processing what he experienced—the loneliness, detachment and desolation. He is painting the impact of terror on children. He chose to paint these—for himself—while he painted portraits on commission during this period.

The Lost Children (1950s), oil on canvas, 13½ × 12½ in.

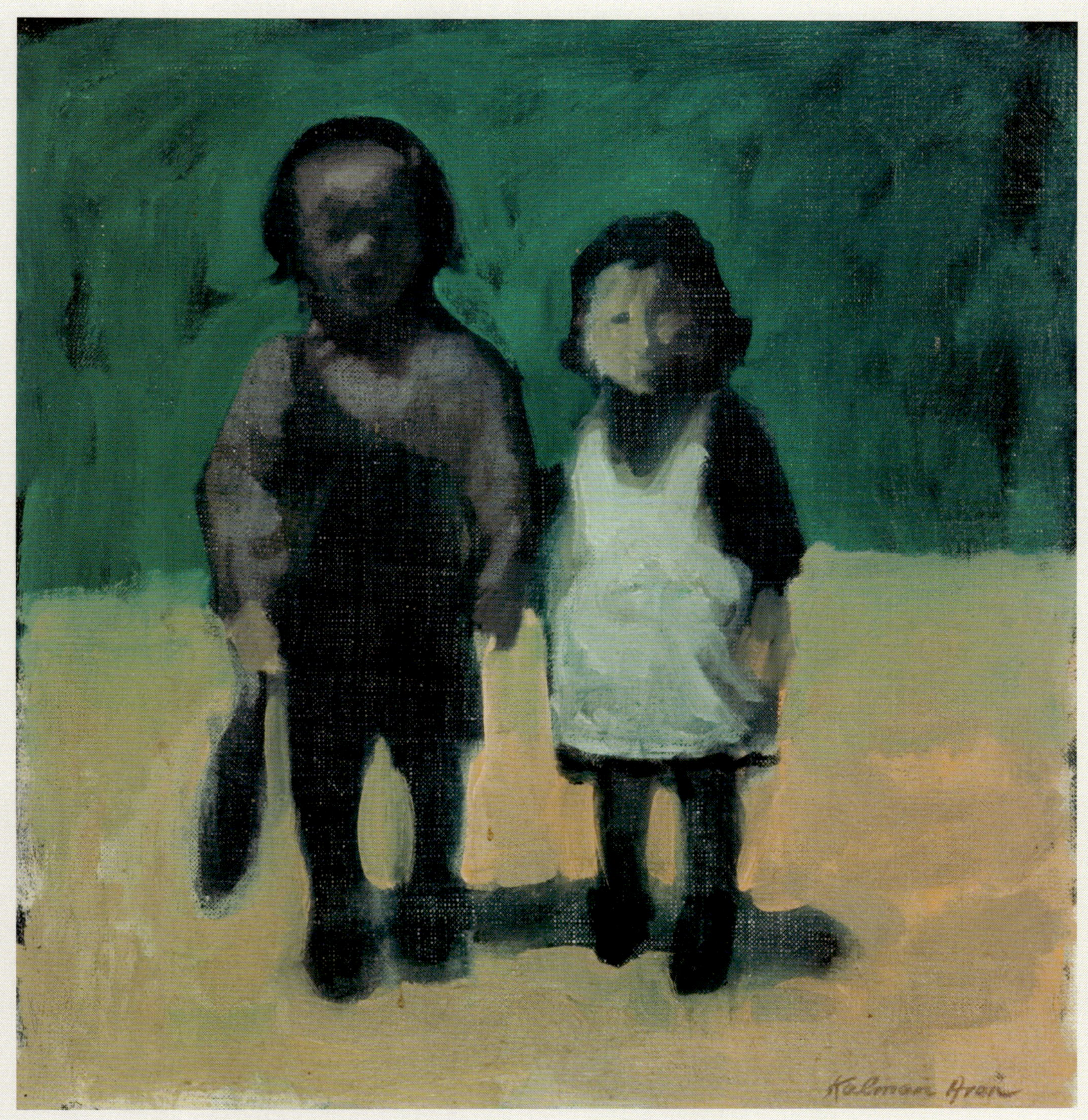
Kalman Aron

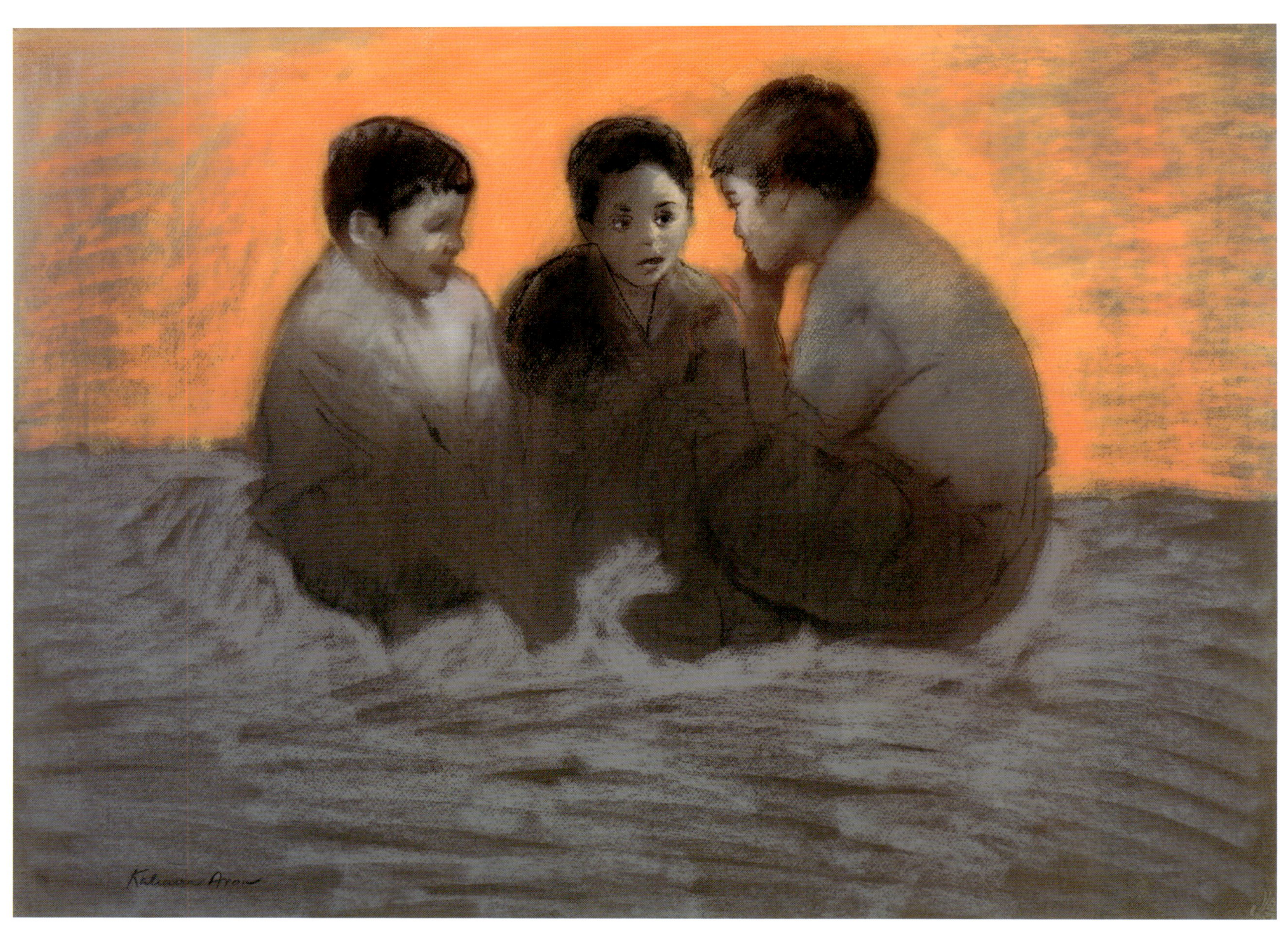

Three Children Playing (late 1950s), pastel on paper, 20¾ × 29 in.

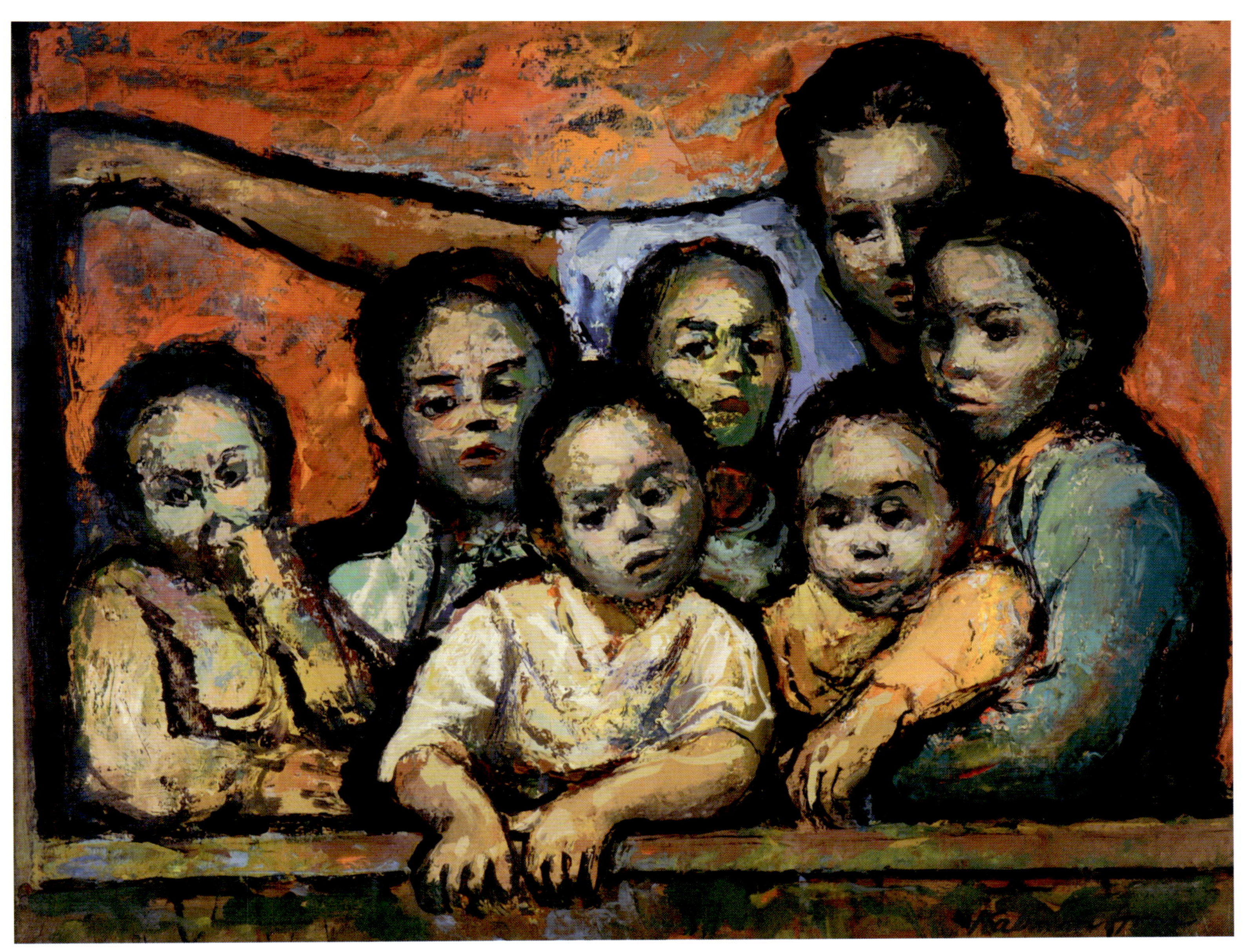

The Family (1950s), oil on paper, 18 × 23½ in.

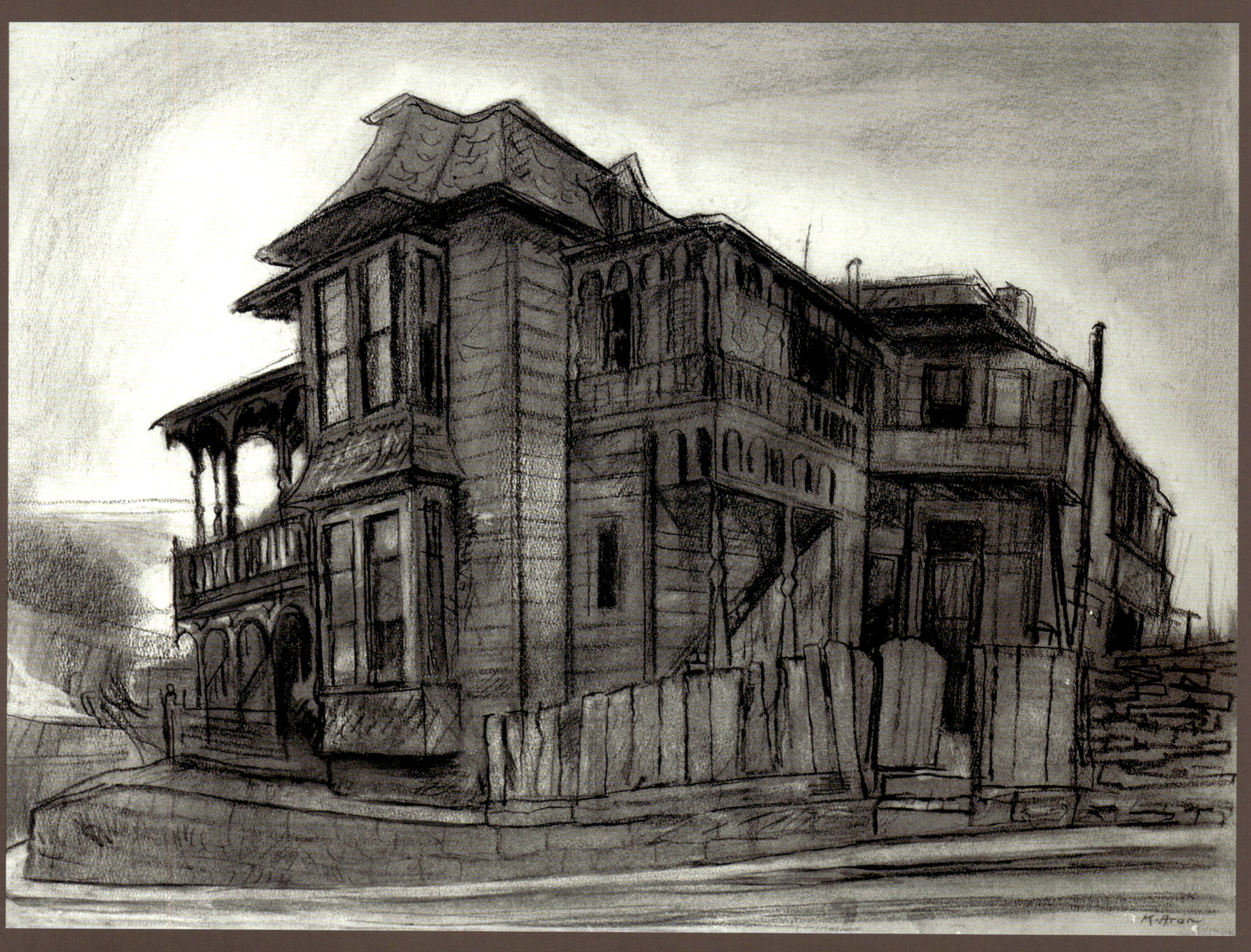
K. Aran

New Surroundings

Exploring his new surroundings, Aron used many media—oils, pastels, pen and ink, charcoal. His paintings of the new world carried echoes of his past.

The mapmaking company where he worked was close to Bunker Hill in Los Angeles. He would walk and sketch the Victorian homes, as in the charcoal *Old House on Bunker Hill*. In the late 1860s a developer had built grand two-story homes on this summit, which overlooks the Los Angeles basin. Bunker Hill became a wealthy enclave. When streetcars and later freeways enabled the elite to leave downtown, the neighborhood changed. By the 1950s, when Aron began drawing there, it was a slum.

Here Aron draws an old mansion, a grande dame full of life and movement with many stories to tell, a survivor. A bit down-at-the-heels, she stands alone in black and white, framed by a brilliant light in the sky. There are no signs of life. No dogs or cats walk the street; no bushes or trees. She has many rooms and balconies. Some windows are dark; some reflect the light. Is she one or two houses? What secrets does she hold? Does she know her time is almost over? A few years after Aron drew her, the city fathers tore her down to redevelop Bunker Hill with skyscrapers, museums and the music center.

Old House on Bunker Hill (1950s), charcoal on paper, 19¼ × 25½ in.

In the oil *Bunker Hill* Aron painted a neighborhood that could easily have been in Europe. He used thick, strong brush strokes reminiscent of Van Gogh and dark colors enlivened by touches of red and ochre. The sky is dull; no clear California sun here. Nor are there any people, animals or trees. If the neighborhood could speak, it might say: "We are old. We have seen the rich and the poor, the cycle of life and death. It weighs us down. While we have retained some of our color, we stand alone."

These two paintings recall Aron's old world in Latvia. In 2004 I visited his boyhood neighborhood and the area where he was imprisoned in the ghetto for two and a half years. Both had clapboard buildings. Walking the streets, I felt suspended in time. The buildings still carried the imprint of what happened around them. Like the houses in Bunker Hill, they felt old, tired and sad.

In 1952 Aron drew his new neighborhood in charcoal, *Silver Lake*. It reveals the changes occurring within him. There is more life—a new world of movement, structure and nature. There is light. Nature is alive in the plants, grass and trees growing on the hill behind the houses. But it is still void of human life. No children play on the lawns. No adults return from work. It is a neighborhood of light and dark, abandoned and suspended in time. What will it take to bring the landscape into the sunlight, revealing the rich colors of life? How will Aron reconcile the lifeless void in which he lived with the offerings of the new world?

In addition to painting his surroundings, including *Demolition,* Aron also painted people who lived in his neighborhood. In *A Neighbor* he uses pastels to draw a man peering out at the world, looking, thinking. The movement and power in Aron's strokes create the subject's shoulders, arms and chest, the rich color of his skin, the beautifully shaped lips and the movement in his hat. In the oil *Neighbor Seated* he captures an individual rapt in thought without showing his face.

Bunker Hill (1951), oil on canvas, 15½ × 19½ in.

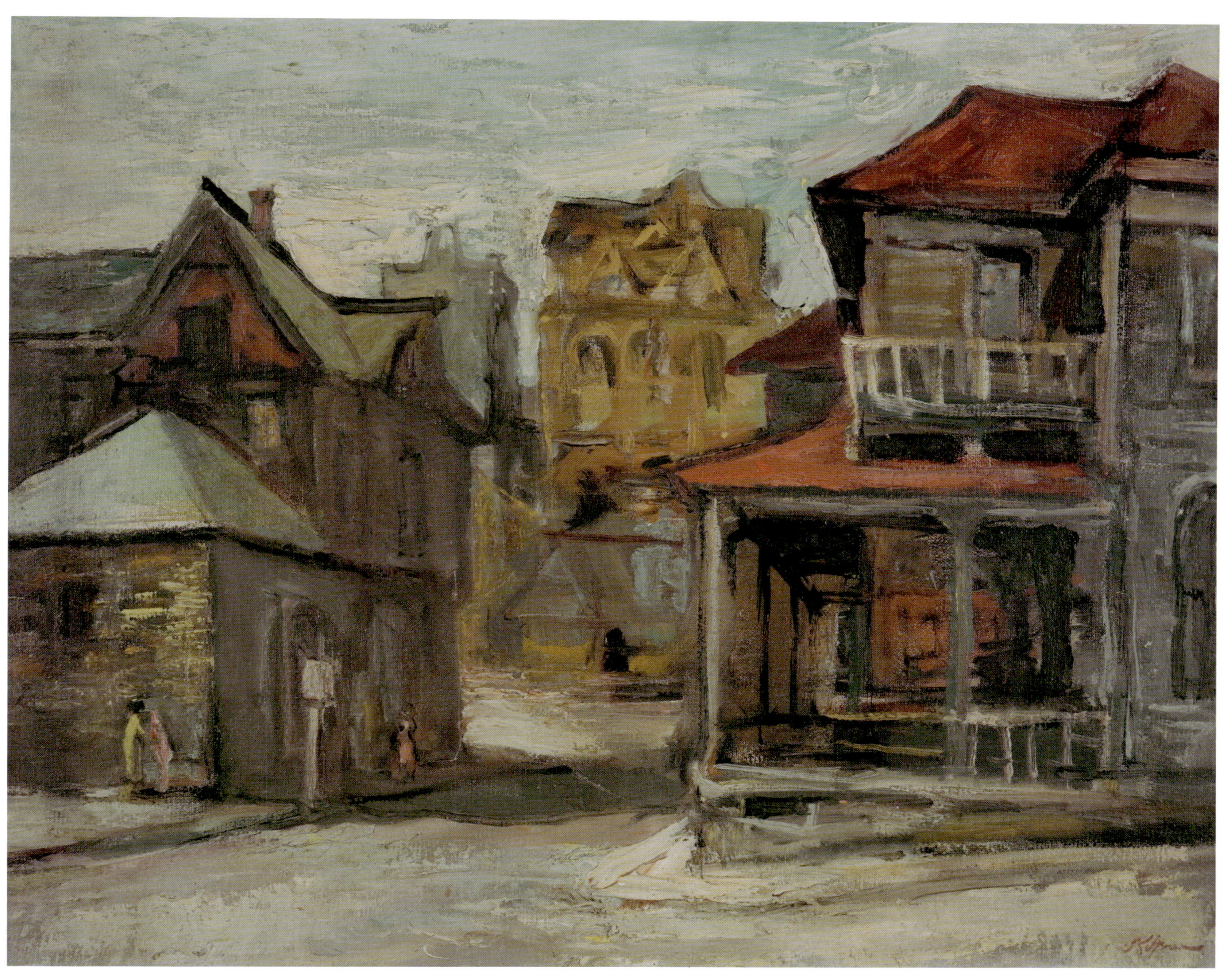

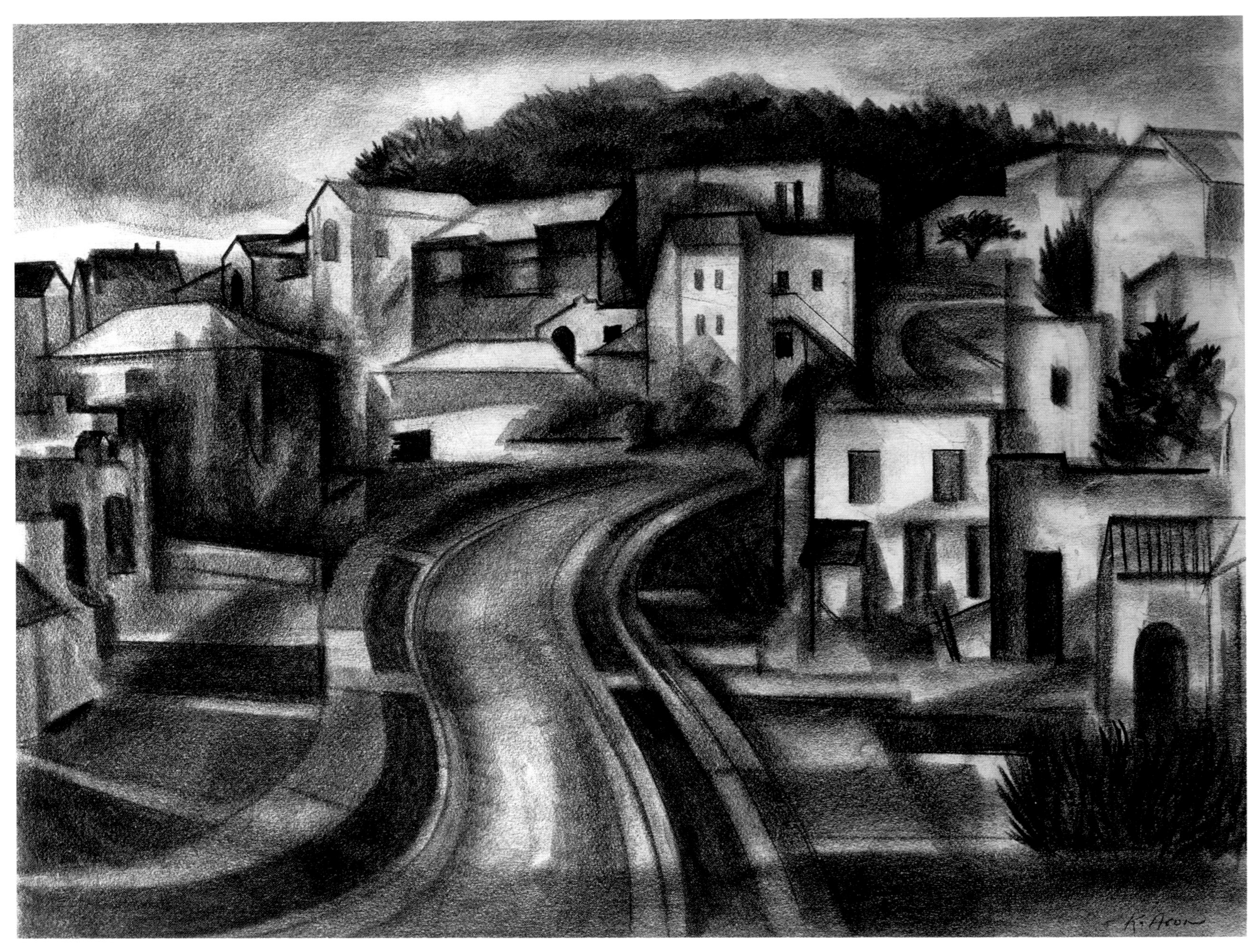

Silver Lake (1952), compressed charcoal on paper, 18 × 24 in.

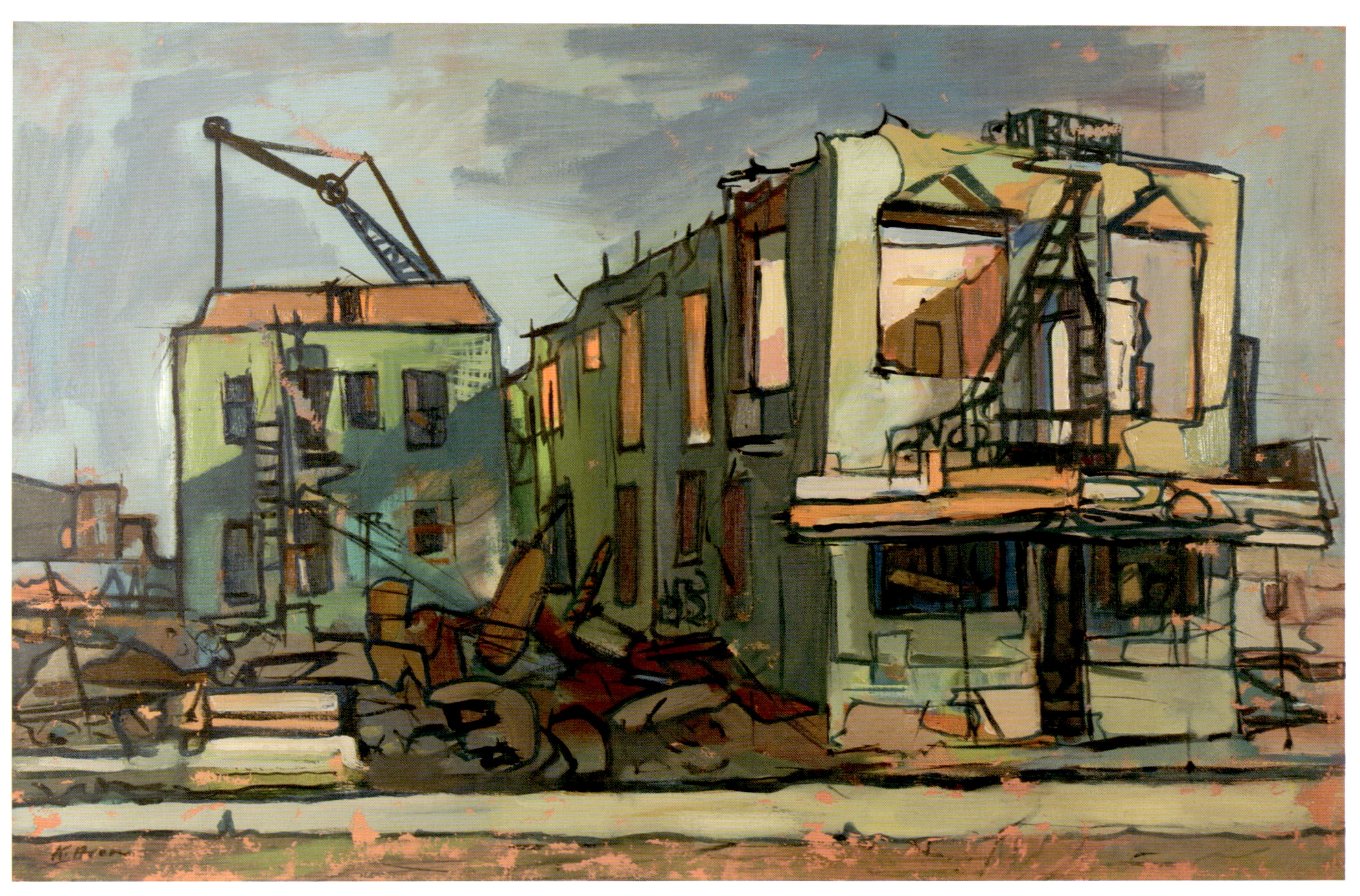

Demolition (1955), oil on canvas, 24 × 36 in.

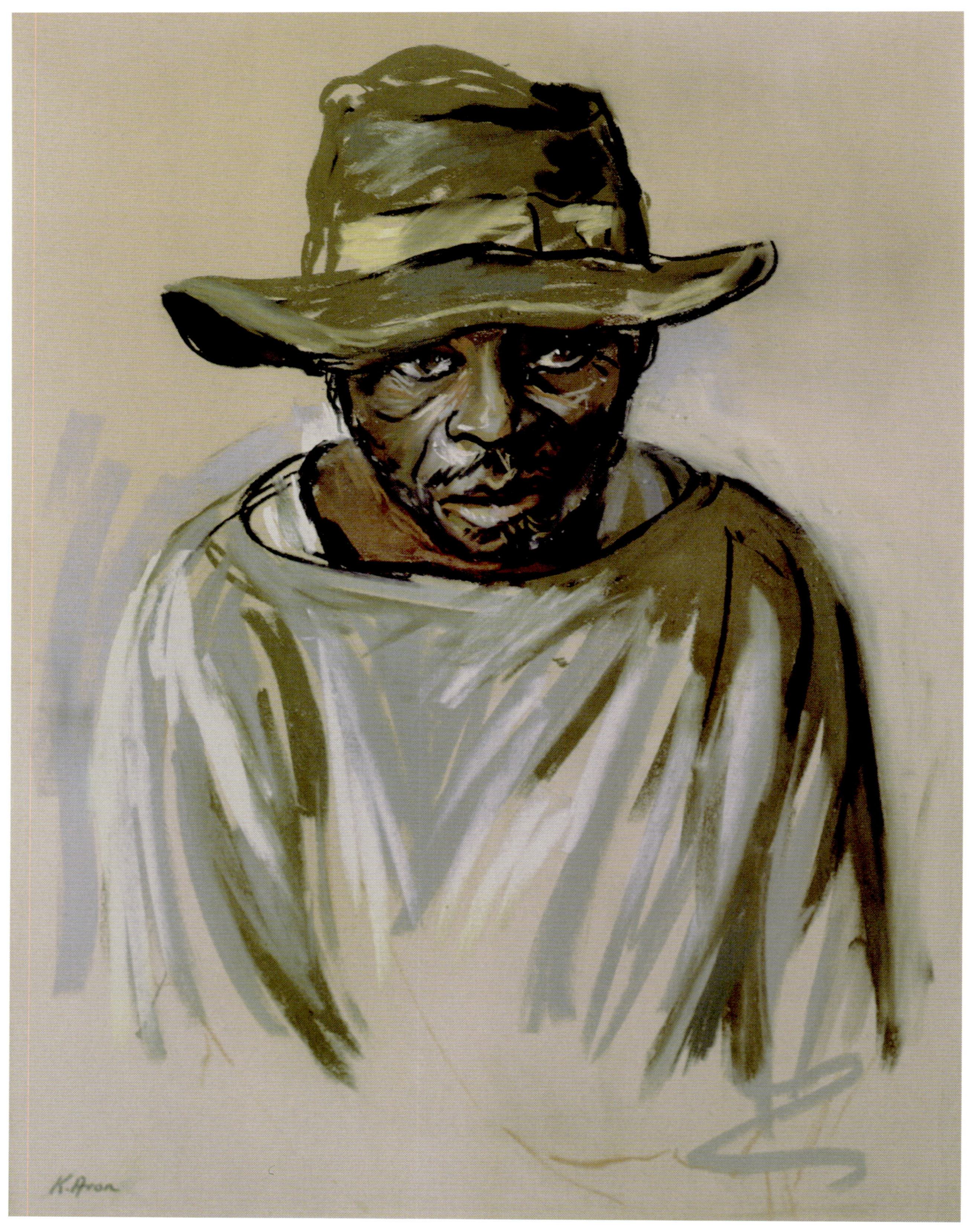

A Neighbor (1950s), pastel on paper, 32 × 25½ in.

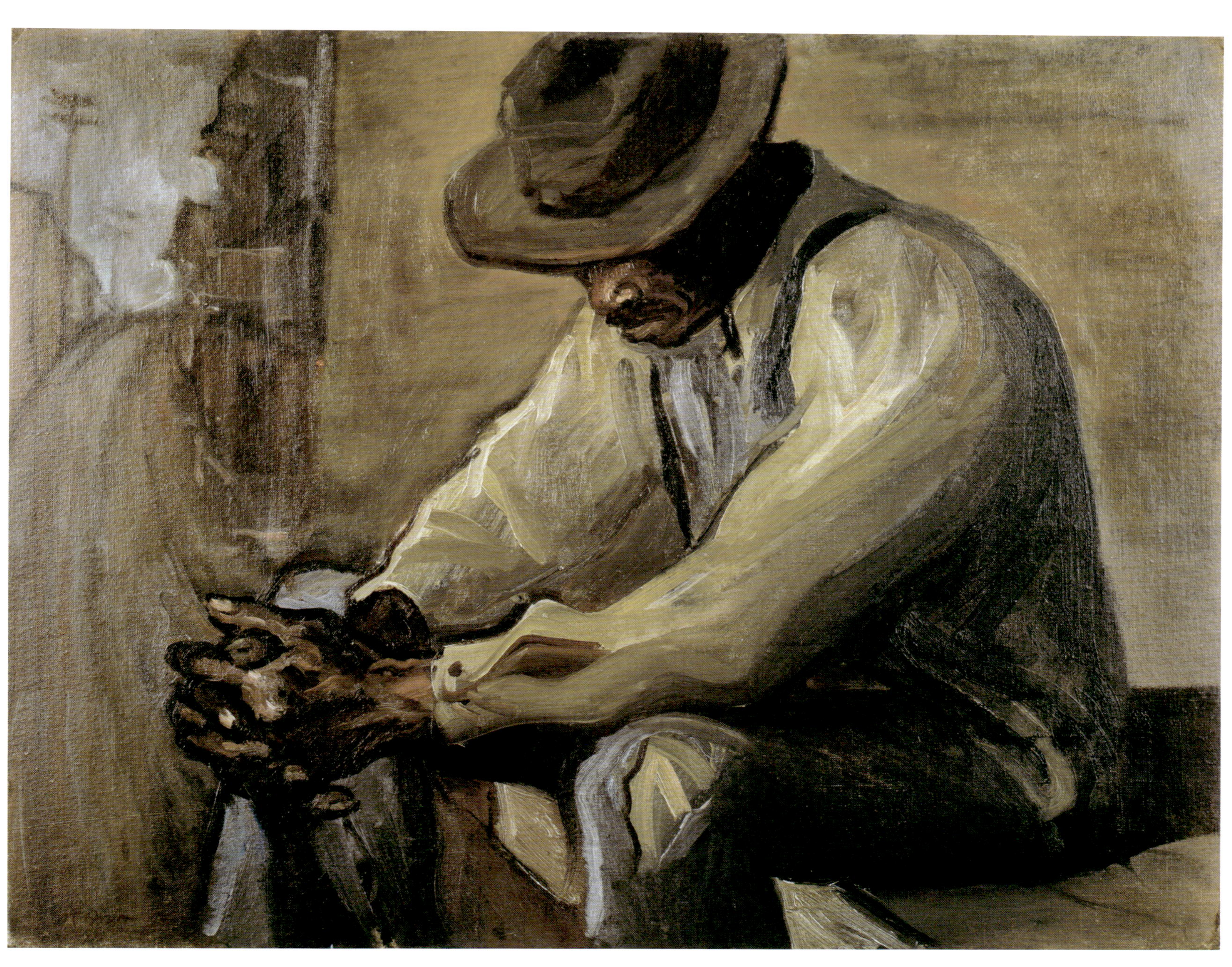

Neighbor Seated (1951–52), oil on board, 22 × 28 in.

Echoes of the Holocaust

Some of Aron's paintings directly echo his experiences during the war. He worked out on paper and canvas what he saw and felt. Some survivors talk about it; others write; Aron painted it. He searched for an answer to every survivor's question: why? He asks it in a small charcoal from 1950, *Searching for Answers*. A man draped in shadows sits alone in the dark, reading a book. One can hear him ask: why? Are there answers in a book to explain what happened? Aron finds no answers here.

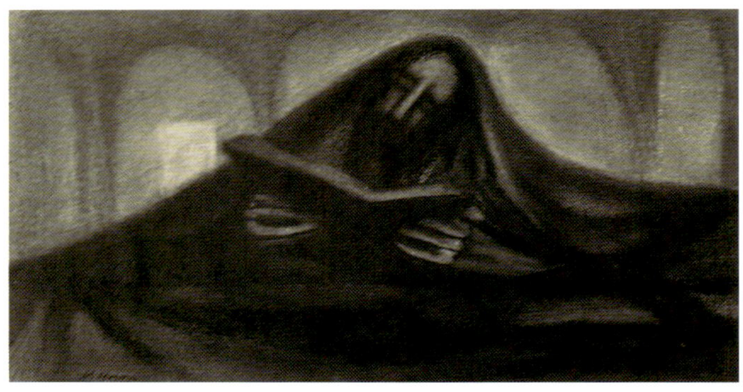

Searching for Answers (1950), compressed charcoal, 8 × 15½ in.

While he was making maps by day, he sketched and painted at night as well, starting work on what became the later masterpiece, *Mother and Child*:

I did several studies for the picture in pencil and watercolors. I came up with the idea of getting the two faces close together because of the bond between mother and child. The idea was to show the anxiety of the mother trying to run away from the ghetto or the camp. Glued together, she won't let go, no matter the punishment. That is what I saw. I added the moon in the upper corner. I don't know why.

As he says, the mother and child are bonded as one body, inseparable, with the child's body held next to the mother's heart. Their eyes are closed; the mother's defiantly so. They stand alone in gray isolation against a plane of sharp corners, echoed by the mother's pointed chin and elbow and the top of her scarf. The only softness is the round curves of the child's head and leg, the mother's shoulder and the moon in the upper corner. This mother and child exist in a colorless world. The only earthly context is suggested by the moon.

To paint this, he took two large maps of a city, turned them over and painted on the white side of the paper. He then glued them together onto a board. Over time the glue came through the paper to create a brownish tint on the face of the woman. It remained in his studio for almost sixty years. In 2010 it moved to its permanent home, the Los Angeles Museum of the Holocaust, where it now hangs at the entrance.

Mother and Child has a life of its own. It not only reflects Aron's experience during the Holocaust, but it also represents one of many explorations of the mother and child relationship. Aron says that his mother believed in a world of love and beauty. She cherished him and supported his artistic gifts. Although Aron disagrees with her view of the world, he never lost his connection to it. In later drawings he depicts with great tenderness the relationship between mother and child.

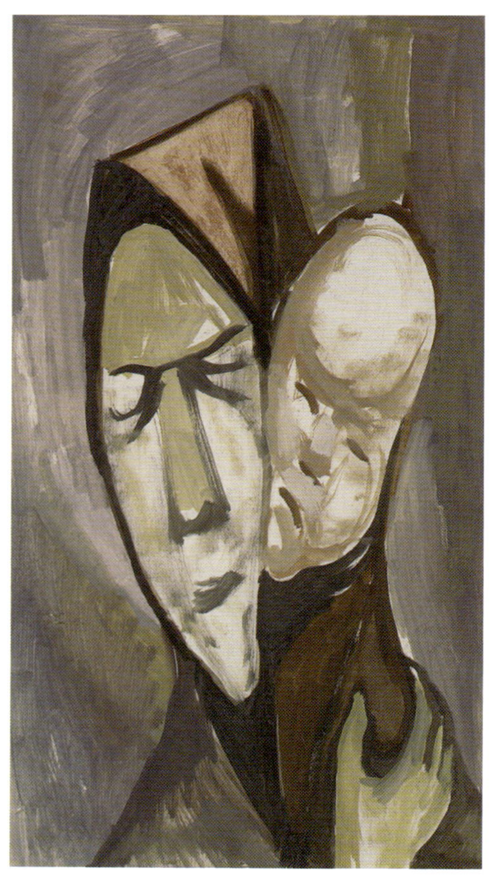

Sketch for Mother and Child (1951), oil on paper, 21 × 12 in.

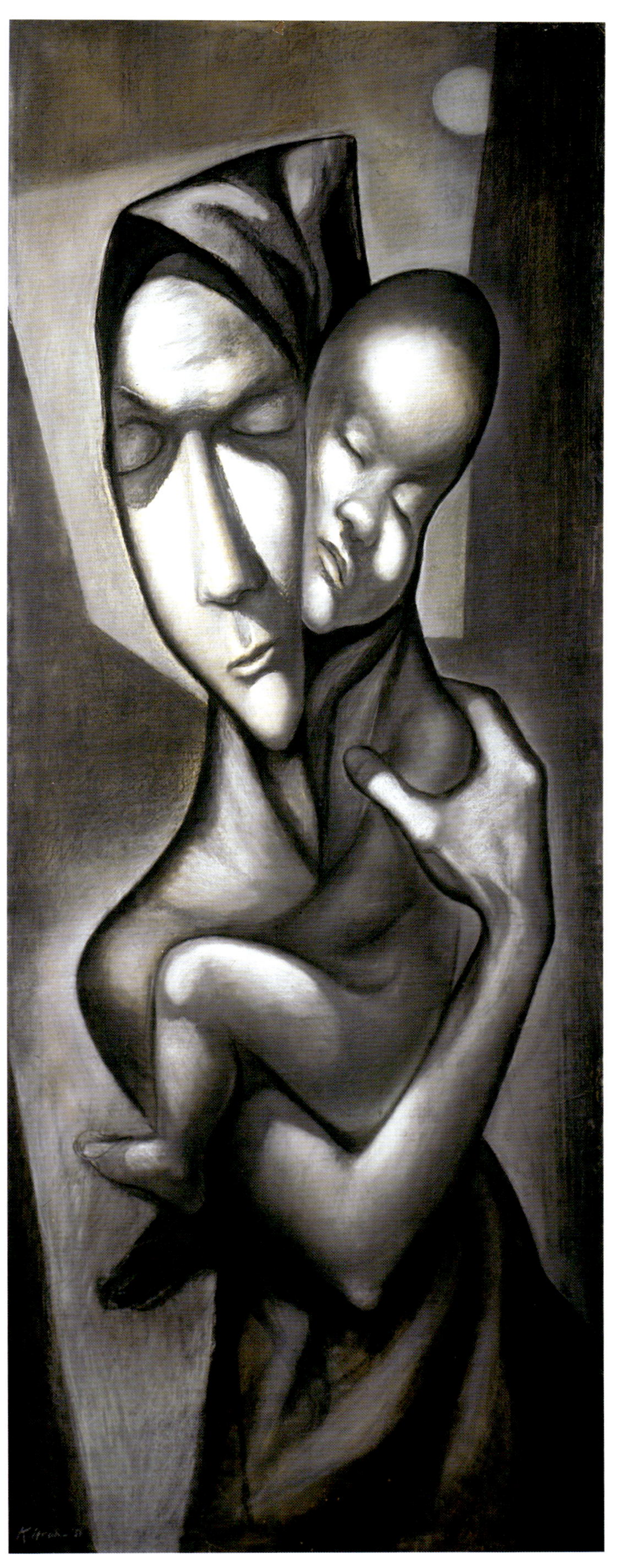

Mother and Child (1951),
pastel on paper on a board, 96 × 24 in.

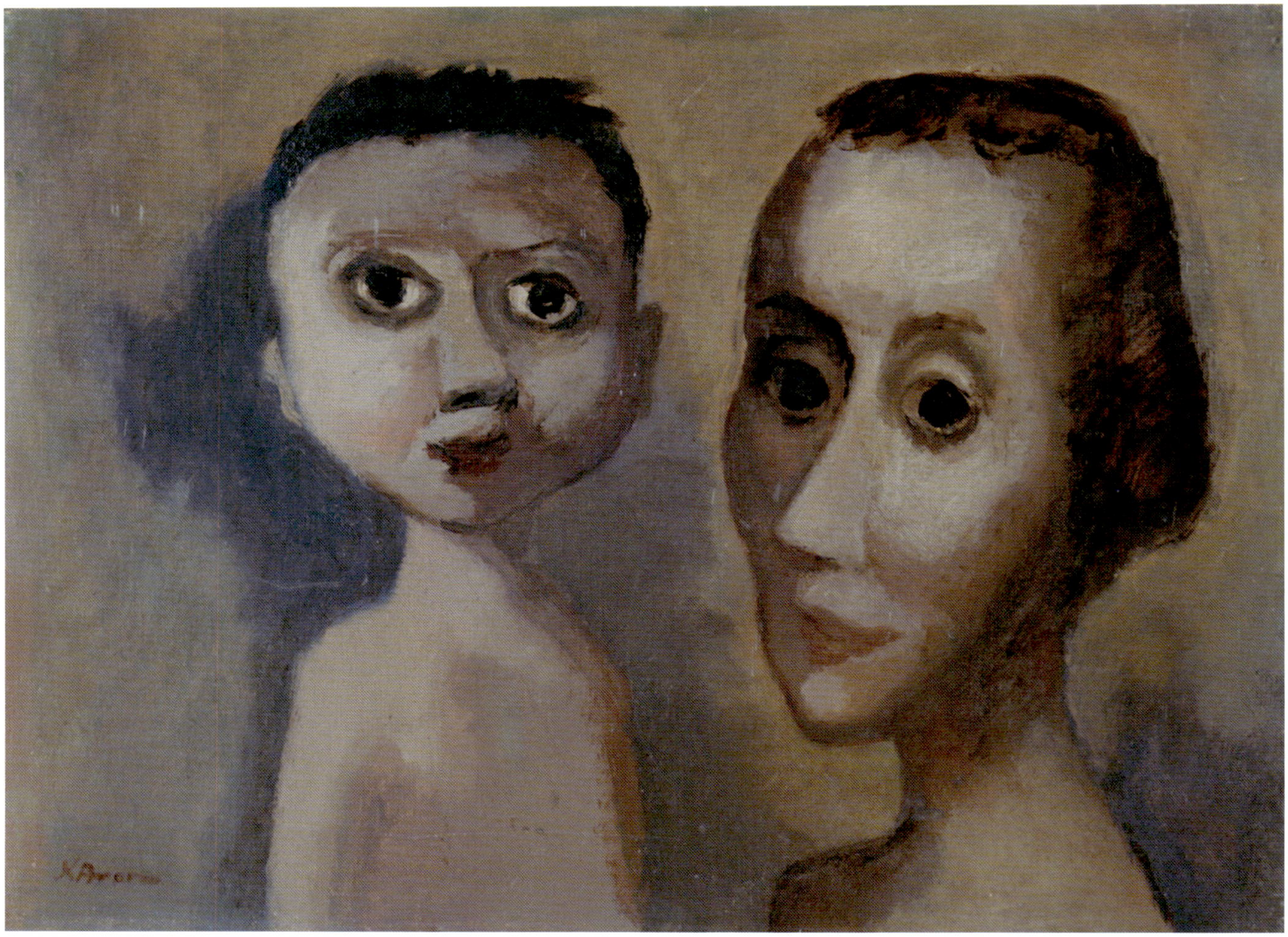

Mother and Child II (1951), oil on board, 12 × 16 in.

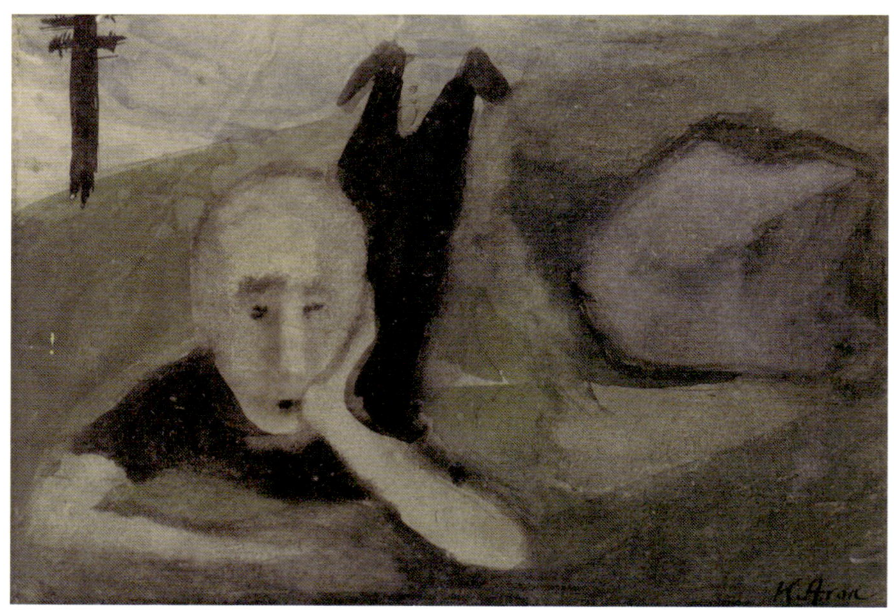

Sleeping Next to the Rock (1951), gouache on paper, 3½ × 5 in.

In 1952 Aron painted the oil, *Mother and Child II*. Here the child is thin but alive. His eyes are open and carry both light and life. The mother seems in a trance. While her eyes are open, they are hollow, reflecting a black abyss. Both appear naked. They have only each other in a barren world. These two survived the war but are no longer connected to each other or the larger world. They are not bonded, as the mother and child were in the earlier pastel.

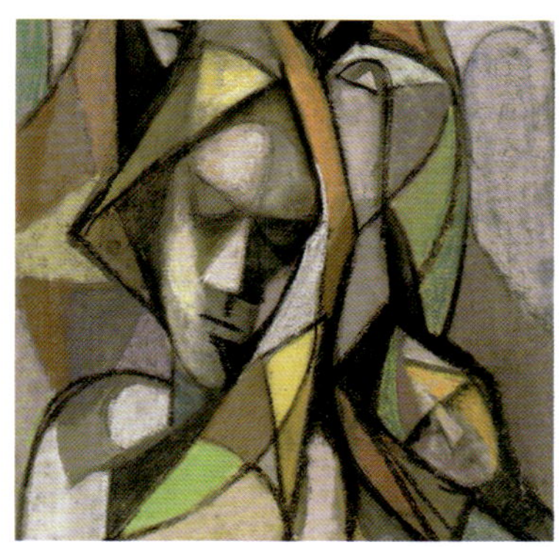

The Cubist Gathering of Women (detail); full image on page 28.

A pastel, *The Cubist Gathering of Women*, comes from the same period. It shows a gathering of mothers, cloaked, almost dead emotionally: eyes closed, shawls covering their heads, faces with no smile lines or expression. The one in the upper left seems withdrawn. The next one seems to be hiding. The woman in front looking down is sad. The older woman, exhausted, rests her head against the sad woman. There is indeed a cubist feel to this painting, and one wonders: Into how many pieces can a woman be broken? Is this a gathering of four women or does each depict facets of just one? There is no reference to nature.

About the same time Aron did two gouaches representing himself in the camps. In *Sleeping Next to the Rock* (1951), he lies on the ground next to the rock he used as a pillow in Buchenwald. When he arrived in August 1944, the camp was overflowing with thirty thousand prisoners. The Germans put the Jews at the farthest point from the main gates in the worst area, the Little Camp. Since the barracks were full, many slept on the ground. The night sky was Aron's canopy. In this gouache one eye is wide open. There is only a faint trace of his right ear. No fingers appear on his left hand. Aron has no lips, only an opening for a mouth, and no wisps of curly blonde hair on his head.

I asked why he painted this. He replied:

To remember. To remember I slept on the ground. I was alone with just myself, the ground, the rock and the dull sky. There is a Jewish saying that translates 'alone as a stone.' My eyes could still see, but they had become empty dark holes. My mouth was still there but only as an opening through which to eat, to survive. I am a man alone in a desolate landscape.

Why the pole? For perspective, he said. But it may be because this was a real place on earth created by people who walked, talked, ate, appearing normal. This time warp of darkness, shadows and terror was real. The Nazis had chosen a site on a hill near the city of Weimar, known for its golden age of Goethe and Schiller; what a juxtaposition of light and dark! Aron continued:

The Nazis could not remove the stars from the sky. I looked at them every night, and each morning I looked at the sun and said, 'Yes, I have survived one more day.'

In 1953 he painted a small gouache, *Kalman Marching in the Camp*:

The one in front is supposed to be me walking. You see the one man with a beard and all these people walking in from the camp. It's more symbolic. It doesn't show a particular situation.

This scene is reminiscent of medieval paintings of hell. Aron here is a far different man than the one sleeping by the rock in Buchenwald. He has a steely strength, a distinct presence and a determined look. He stands alone, one among many, yet solitary. He depends on no one else. No emotion is permitted, no softness of being. He has become a skeleton of bones with no light in his eyes. The darkness defines him: the black line around his body, the black holes of his eye sockets and the dark, firmly set mouth. This is what Aron has become. He has passed through shock, incomprehension, fear and terror. Now I hear his thoughts: *No one can touch me. I alone am responsible for my survival.*

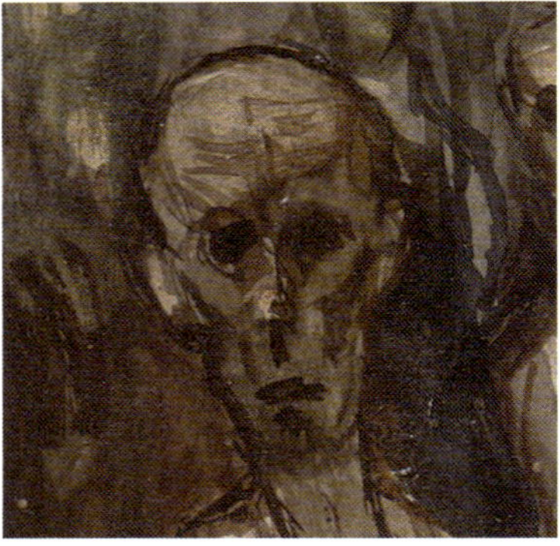

Kalman Marching in the Camp (detail); full image on page 50.

He had to detach from what was happening around him. In *Man's Search for Meaning* Viktor E. Frankl quotes the German philosopher Gotthold Lessing: "There are things which must cause you to lose your reason or you have none to lose." In this painting a man who delighted in creating art has become a skeleton, simply determined to survive to paint another day.

Aron's enduring connection to nature shows up in the rich dark blue field in the upper right-hand corner. Painted in the gray-blue dark mass are six other defined faces, aspects of Aron himself. Particularly interesting is the white face on the left side, a stark face in pure agony. While Aron clearly experienced this paralyzing agony, there is no room for that emotion in the man who stands at the head of this mass of humanity.

In this painting Aron illustrates what happens to a man treated brutally. Having survived, how does one recapture one's light? How does the phoenix rise from the ashes? Aron did it one painting at a time.

In 1954, when he was thirty, Aron drew a *Self-Portrait*. A handsome young man with all his features present, he has certainly changed. But his eyes do not look in the same direction. They are viewing two different realities. The right eye seems distant, perhaps still trapped in the dark void. His left eye is present with a bit of light, but his gaze feels sad, tired. There is no joy.

While definitely alive in this painting, Aron has not yet integrated the worlds he knows exist. His vision is not harmonized nor focused on what is before him. He straddles two realities, as though living simultaneously in two parallel universes.

Self-Portrait (1954), charcoal pencil, 31 × 21 in.

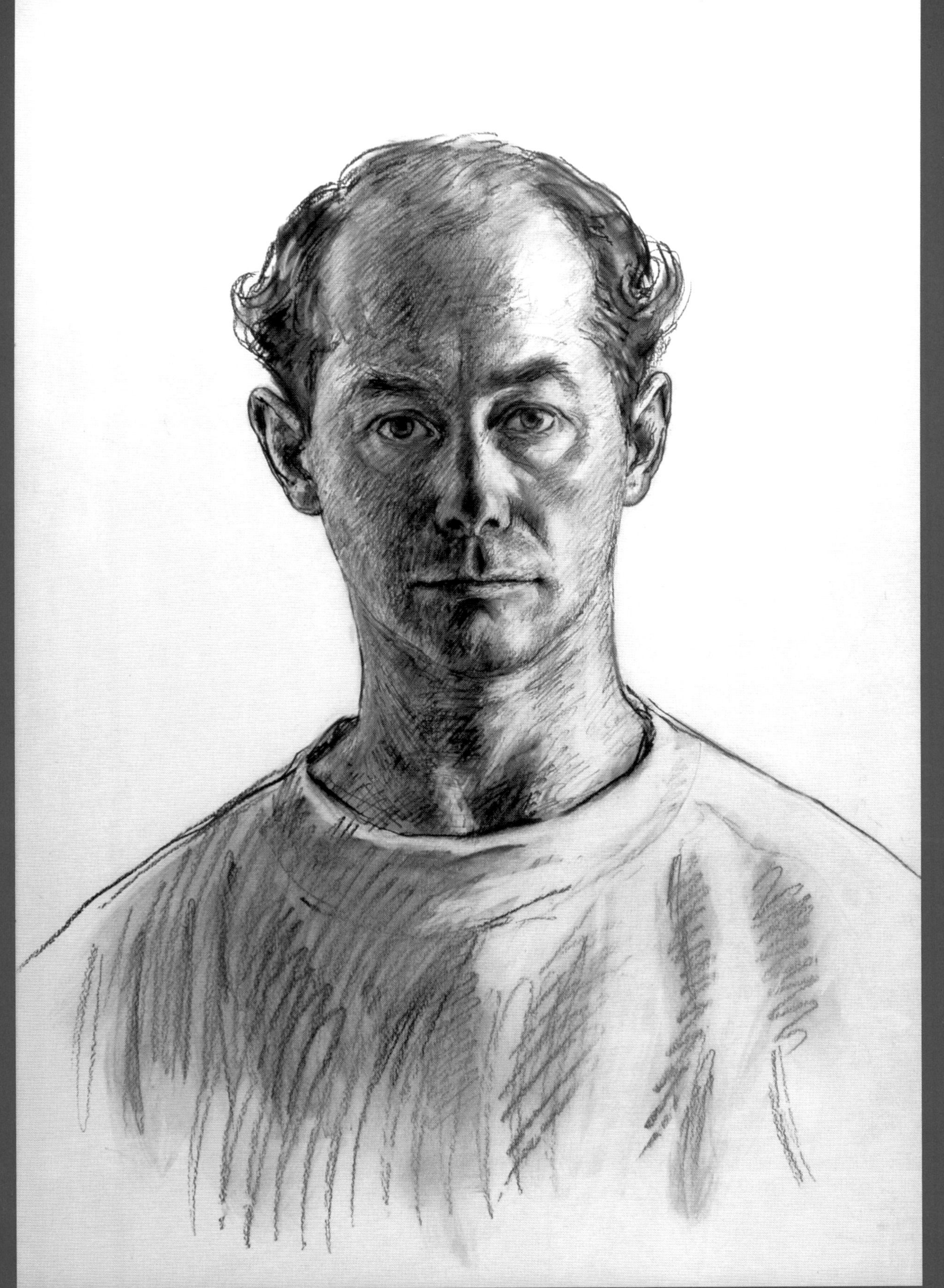

In 1956 Aron left Trude. They had no children. Aron says:

I decided to split up. She was very good, but I was too young to be married. I didn't want to divorce her, but I realized it was not good for her or for me. I didn't want to stay together and then both be sorry.

Trude recalls:

We were married for seven years. It was not a happy marriage, but I would not have left it. I couldn't give him what he needed. I wasn't equipped. In retrospect I was more like a mother than a wife. Aron shut out the experience in the Holocaust. That way of handling life doesn't lend itself well in a marriage. I needed more than he could give, and I'm sure he needed more than I could give. He is a good man, but he needed somebody else because he left me.

Trude moved out, and they have remained friends all these years.
As she told me:

We've always stayed in touch. If something good happens, he will call me. If something bad happens, he will call. I've never had bad feelings toward him. He's not had much luck with women.

During these years Aron met a number of people who loved his paintings and helped him with exhibits. One who became a lifelong friend and patron is Lou Lenart. An extraordinary man in his own right, Lou was born in Hungary, came to America as a boy before World War II, and flew as a Marine Corps fighter pilot. Called "the Chuck Yeager of the Israeli Air Force," in 1948 he helped Israel fight for its life, earning lasting fame when he led an Israeli flight of four Czech-built fighter planes against an Egyptian armored column, to repulse 10,000 troops within sixteen miles of Tel Aviv. Lou instantly liked Kalman—as my mother did—and appreciated his talent, character and gentle nature. Lou introduced him to others who bought his paintings. Aron recalls:

In 1957 a woman named Hilda Swarthe held my first one-man show in America at her gallery on Santa Monica Boulevard. It included children's portraits and portraits of people. She held several showings.

Around 1958 I wound up in a studio on Westmount Drive in West Hollywood. A woman friend who was a painter said, 'Aron, you'd better go quickly.' I went there, and they showed me the studio, and I took it right away. They had kicked out the well-known painter who was there after he drank, smoked a cigarette and caused a fire in the bedroom. I moved in right away. Twenty-two years I was there. With its high ceilings and abundant light, it was perfect for painting.

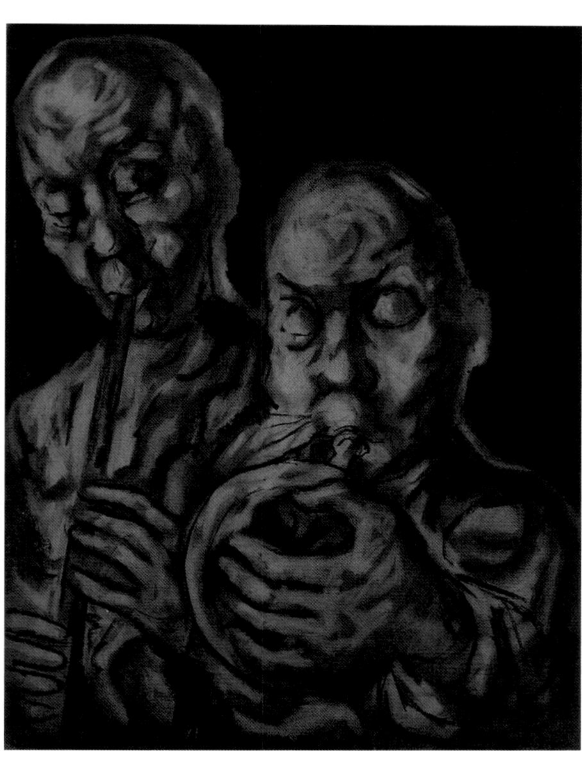

Night Club (1957), compressed charcoal, 22 × 17 in.

Oh, I had girlfriends from 1956 to 1961, and I had painting parties, big parties in my studio. It would get very late with dancing, drinking and eating. In the morning we would wake up; I would go outside and hear noise. What was going on? Three or four people would be sitting there eating breakfast. One time there must have been a hundred people there. I had never seen them before. 'Aron is having a party,' someone had said. It was parties all the time. But I never got involved in dope or pot. One woman asked for a knife to take cocaine. I told her to go home. I didn't want anything to do with it.

In the late fifties I began showing my paintings and drawings at an art gallery run by a countess. It was a nonprofit organization, the Los Angeles Art Association. She liked my work and often put one of my paintings in the window. The local art critic wrote about my paintings in the newspaper.

Aron's exhibitions received good notices and reviews. One writer called him a "master portrait artist," and another a "distinguished artist, one of the greats." Arthur Millier wrote in the *Los Angeles Times*: "Large pastel and portrait drawings by Kalman Aron bring to notice a consummate draftsman. His portraits of children are some of the best being done here . . . the absorption of children in their games, the attitudes of women and the personalities of people of all ages are portrayed by him with kindly sympathy and without artifice."

Painting children is a challenge because they do not sit still. Usually working in three sessions, Aron became adept at drawing quickly, and he knew anatomy, which helped him finish a child's hand or arm in the original position. Doing these portraits, however, made him anxious, as it forced him to contain his strokes and form in order to capture a likeness.

As Aron completed his first decade in California, he considered himself fortunate:

I guess I was lucky. People would look at my art and say, 'What is it, Aron?' I don't know, but here comes another one. I turn the page, and there is another drawing. The important thing is doing it. The outcome is not that important. It's doing it, and that may be why my situation may be a little bit better than some people who came out of the camps. They may have nothing else to do but watch television and think about those bad days of the camp. I did that in the beginning, but I got away from thinking about it by doing portraits, landscapes, traveling and painting. I think that kept me away from all this agony of 'How I did survive or why did I survive?' I did, and that's it. I'm here now, and if I start talking, thinking about the past all the time, I can't go forward. It's hard to go forward, in my opinion.

In America Aron clung to his freedom as an artist. He gave up security to be free to paint. He accomplished a great deal for someone who arrived with four dollars, a wife and no English. Art critic Janice Lovoos summed up his career during his first decade in America in an article in *American Artist* in March 1964:

Kalman Aron's love for people, and his ability to portray them with great tenderness on paper and canvas, reaches out to attract clients from all walks of life. Professional men, lawyers, doctors and their wives, seem particularly drawn to his work. He has had several one-man shows on the west coast, including one at the Hilda Swarthe Gallery in Beverly Hills. His work has been included in shows at the Los Angeles County Museum; Frye Museum, Seattle; Museum of Fine Arts, Houston, Texas. . . . His portraits are included in many private collections. In 1956 he was chosen as one of the "One Hundred Outstanding American Artists" in *Art in America*.

Over time Aron also showed in the Denver Fine Arts Museum, the San Francisco Museum of Art, the La Jolla Art Museum, the Long Beach Art Museum and the Santa Barbara Museum. His collectors live across the United States, in England, France, and in Israel. Those in California included well-known actors such as Vincent Price and William Powell.

Aron established himself as a portrait artist with sensitive works like *Rabbi Jacob Sonderling*. He also examined the innocence of children, explored his own interior landscape and remembered his experiences in the camps. He grappled with his past, trying to make some sense of it, while looking at his new world for signs of life, texture, color, perhaps safety. He reached for a new beginning.

Rabbi Jacob Sonderling (late 1950s–early 1960s), charcoal on paper, 40 × 30 in.

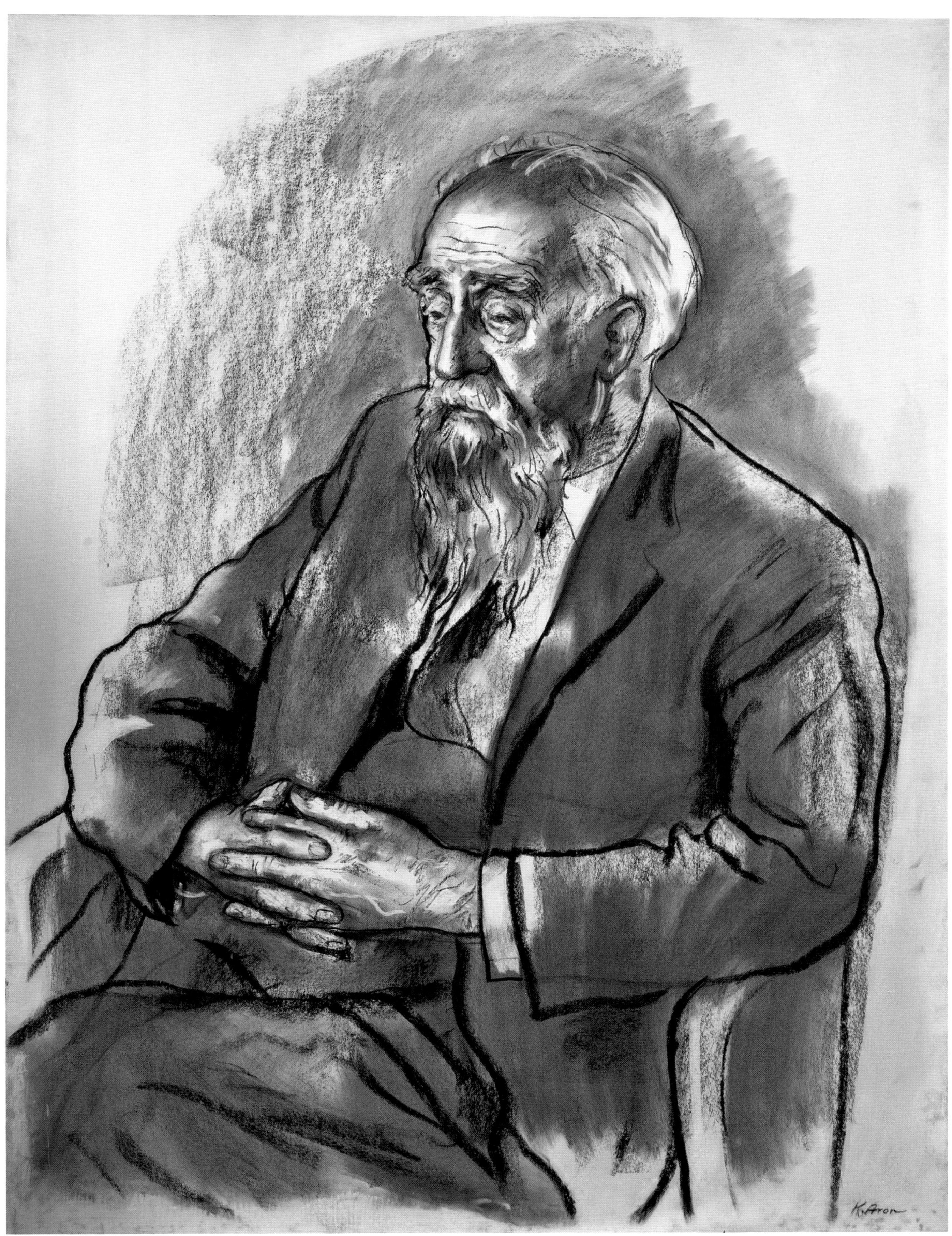

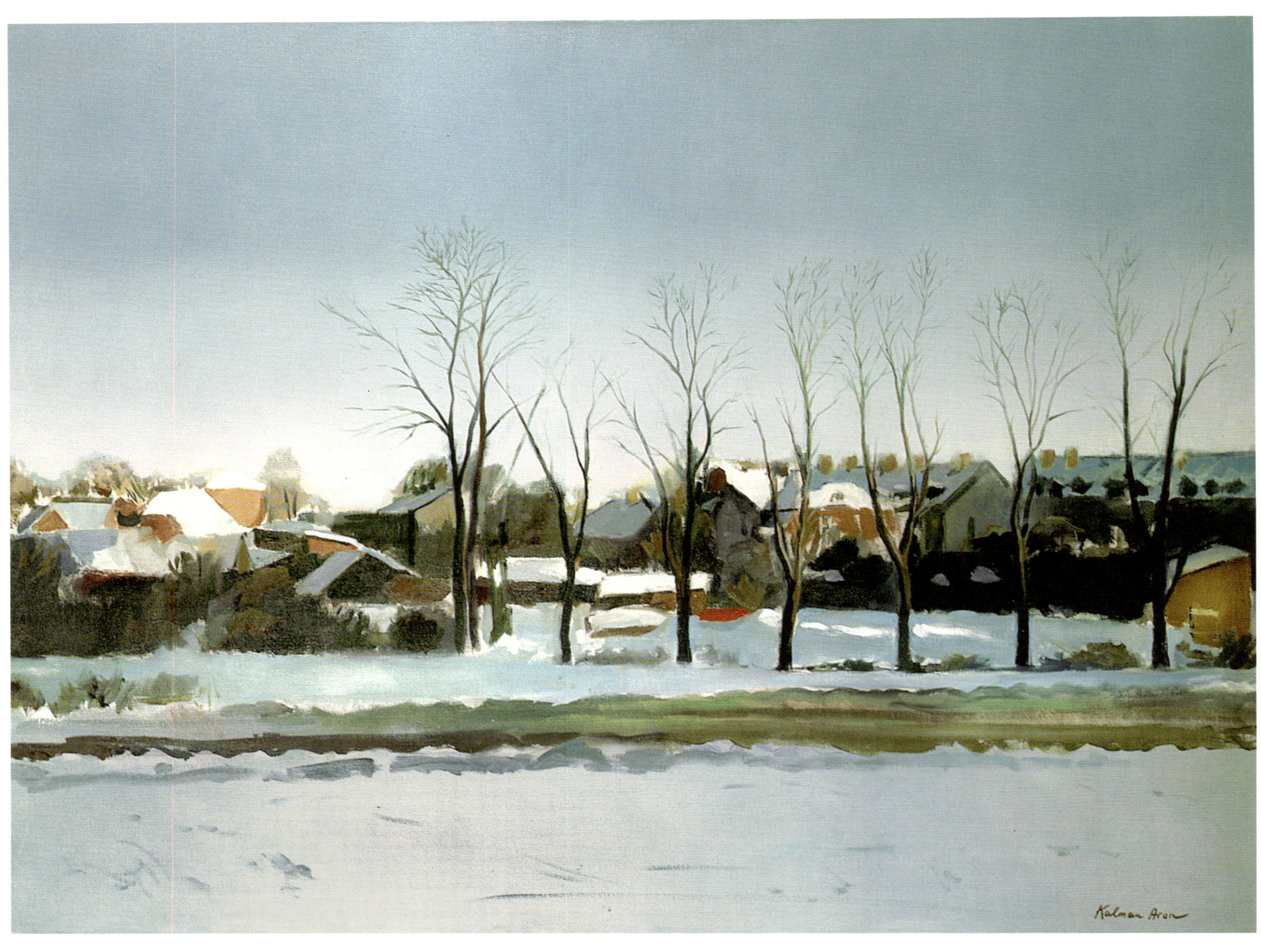
Kalman Aron

Winter in Uppsala (mid 1970s), oil on canvas, 36 × 48 in.

Landscapes and Nature

Los Angeles and its surroundings would prove hospitable to Aron, a home where he could regain his sanity, create art and heal past trauma. It was a far different place from his home in an Old World country that had been invaded by competing cultures and nations since its founding by German crusaders in 1210.

The closest Aron came to his old home in Latvia was in the late 1970s, when a gallery exhibited his paintings in Uppsala, Sweden, and he painted some canvases while there for the opening. He captured the climate he had left behind in his oil *Winter in Uppsala*, a view of the town outside his hotel window. Aron illumines the winter light on the horizon as the sun's rays reflect off the snow, creating a soft glow on the horizon. The blue sky reflects across the white snow, and a stroke of orange-red between the trees and homes completes the composition.

Compared to this world of ice and snow, Aron's new home offered sunshine, warmth and light. No walls confined him mentally or physically in Los Angeles. Living in a creative environment, he was free to paint as he wished and make new friends who didn't share his past. He did not have to relive his Holocaust history on a daily basis. Being large and spread out, Los Angeles also offered Aron a certain level of anonymity. He could have a successful artistic career while staying below the radar. Aron never sought fame. He still carried the instinct, imprinted by the Holocaust, to be invisible. Had he lived in a city like Vienna, Austria's ancient capital of high culture, he could never have maintained such invisibility.

Over the next six decades Aron continued the conversation with nature he began as a boy and cherished during the Holocaust. During those four years he forged a quiet, deep, abiding relationship with nature. The earth's trees, the sky's sunlight and the star-filled night were reliable presences in his life. Nature was a constant the Nazis could not control. Her cycles gave rhythm to his life. The turn of day and night was an anchor. The changing seasons became his calendar. He would recall his movements across Europe from camp to camp by what season it was. Nature sustained and nurtured him.

Throughout his life in Los Angeles, Aron has enjoyed painting landscapes. A favorite subject is the changing views of the Hollywood Hills and the downtown area from his balcony. He has painted these at all times of day and night, in all seasons. This panorama is equivalent to Monet's Rouen Cathedral. The 1985 oil *Balcony View from My Studio* reflects the warmth, color and expanse Aron found in his new home. This landscape is alive with color, movement and texture. A striking apartment building catches the eye with its ochre walls and orange-red roof. Behind it are California trees and bushes in shades of yellow and green with three tall, dark evergreen trees touching the sky. On the horizon the Hollywood Hills roll gently to meet a sky full of colorful clouds in shades of pink, white and purple. Aron captures the vitality of his community that sits easily with its natural surroundings.

In *Night Lights of L.A.* Aron paints the lights and shadows in the night sky in downtown Los Angeles. He uses a variety of colors to create the sky: blues, black, browns and touches of green and yellow. There are shadows in the darkness, but one can still perceive a great deal: rooftops, lampposts, silhouettes of tall trees and buildings, and a variety of colors on the walls of the homes. Aron understands that nighttime is a critical part of the rhythm of life. He understands that there is always light in the darkest night. And he understands that the light of the sun and moon are different. One is warm; one is cool. Both change our perception of the world around us. Van Gogh said, "It often seems to me that the night is much more alive and richly colored than the day."

Aron also enjoyed painting landscapes at the California beaches, in the mountains and in the desert. In *View of Laguna Cove* he captures the dance of light, form and water. All of creation is one: the flowers and glass bottles on the table, the waves lapping onto the sand, the homes dotting the hill of the cove, the wood of the window frame and shutter and the rich turquoise sky. This painting evokes the smell of salt air, the feel of sand under the feet and the warmth of the sun.

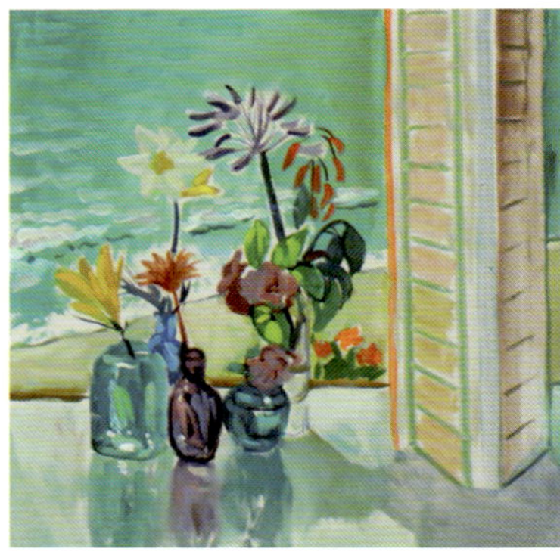

View of Laguna Cove (detail); full image on page 66.

In *Small Boat in San Jacinto Mountains*, Aron paints a lake in Mount San Jacinto, about an hour west of Los Angeles, halfway to Palm Springs. He taught at the prestigious Pasadena Art Center College of Design, and one of his students there introduced him to this land. In 1985 Mt. San Jacinto College hosted a solo show, "Aron, a Retrospective," including a variety of his oils, pastels and charcoals. He had sketched a scene of the boat, water and mountains. Then in 1995 he drew this pastel from the sketch: a peaceful landscape, rich in greens, purple and blue, with the light reflecting the image of the trees and the sky in the water. The clouds clothe the top of the mountain range. Aron captures the warmth, grace and majesty of nature's beauty.

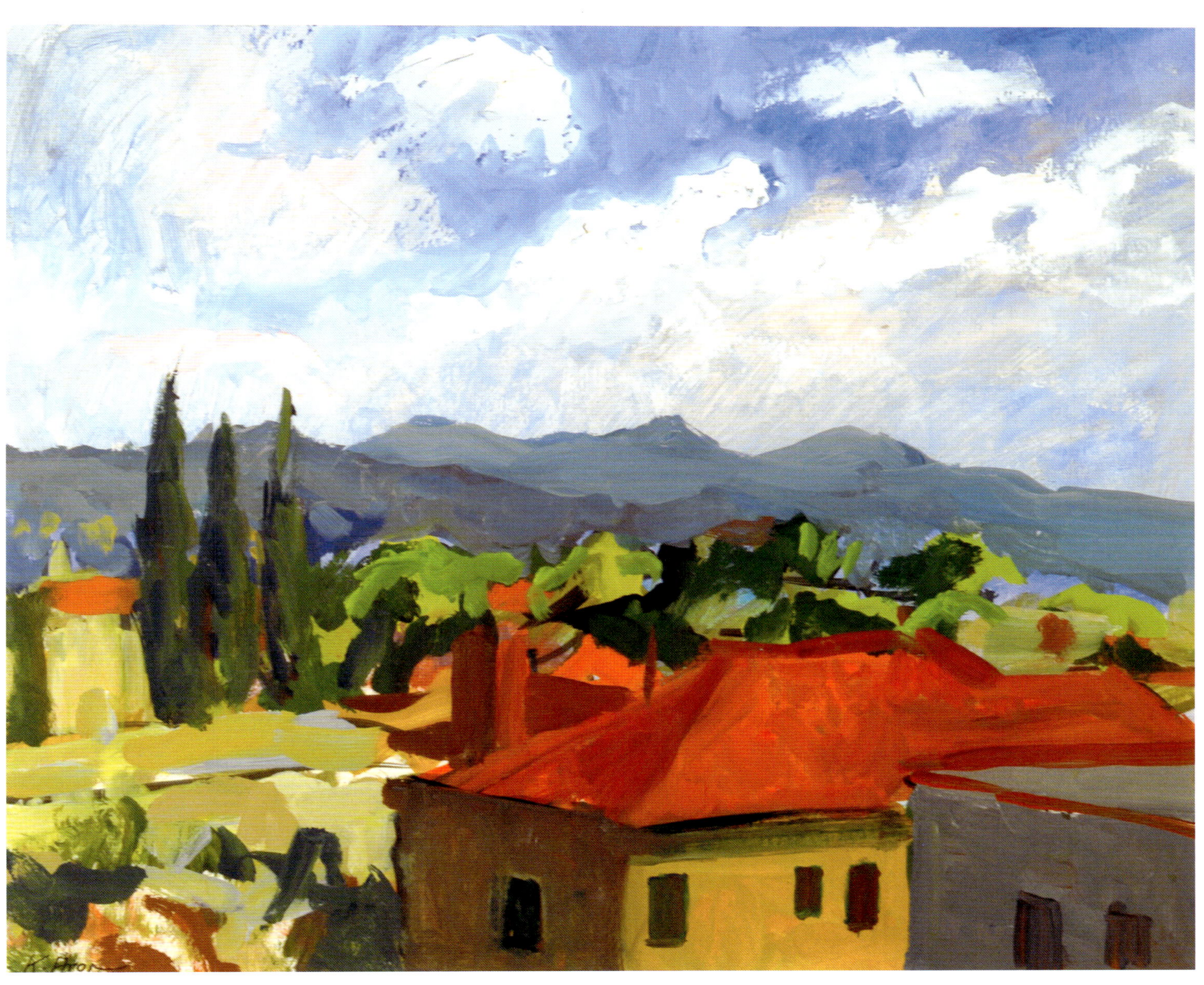

Balcony View from My Studio (1985), oil on paper, 14 × 17 in.

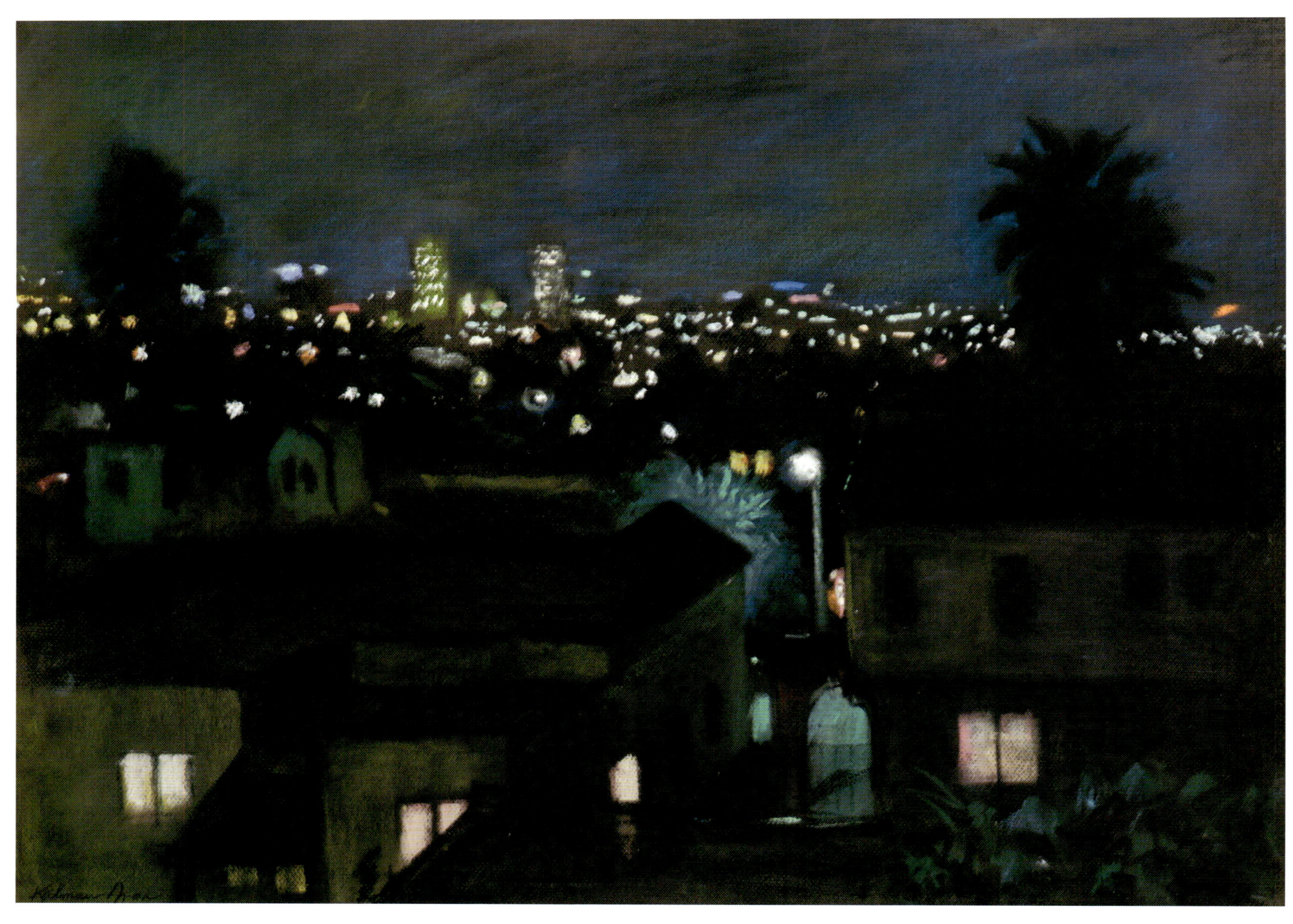

Night Lights of L.A. (1980s), pastel on paper, 21 × 29 in.

Small Boat in the San Jacinto Mountains (1990), pastel on paper, 30 × 21½ in.

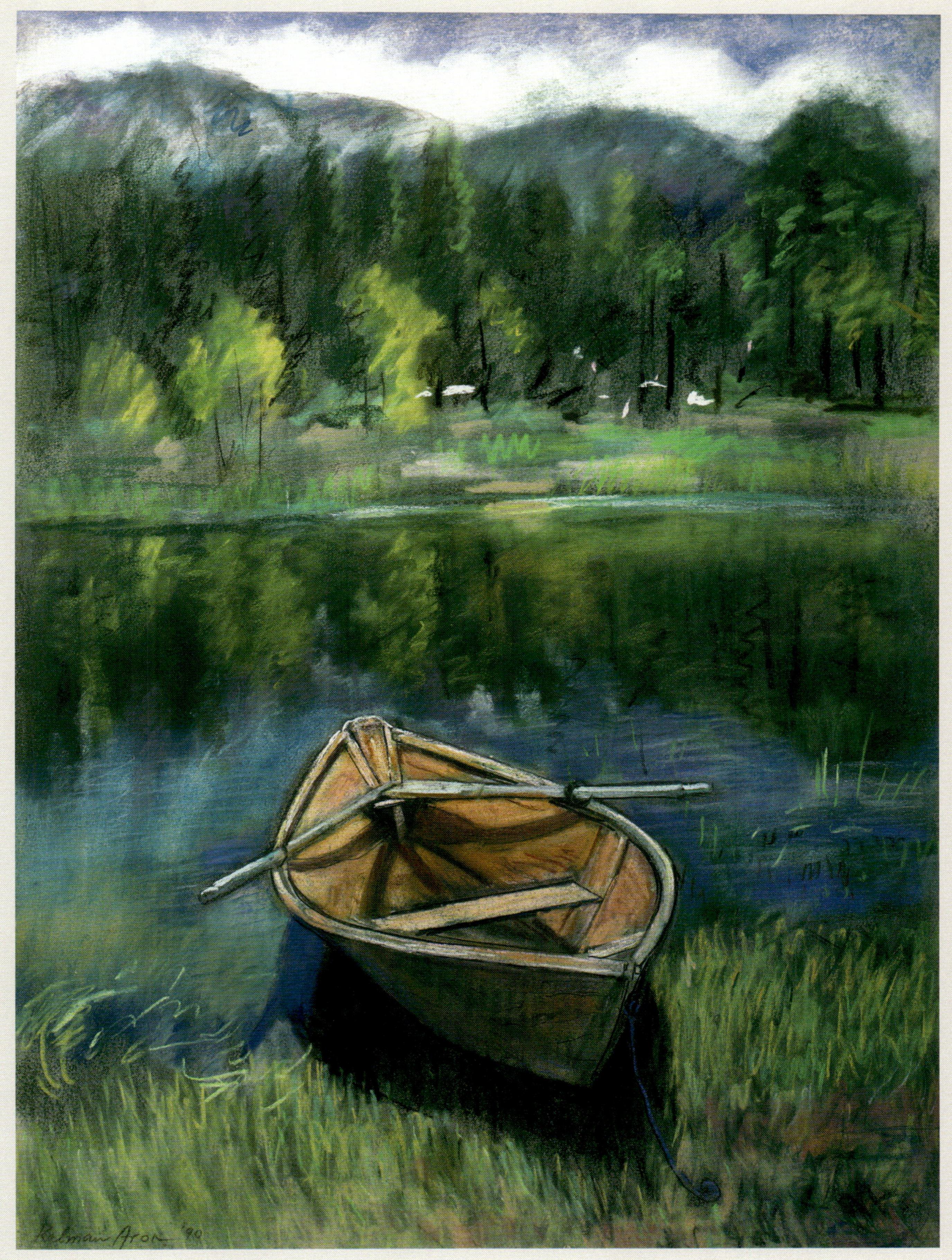

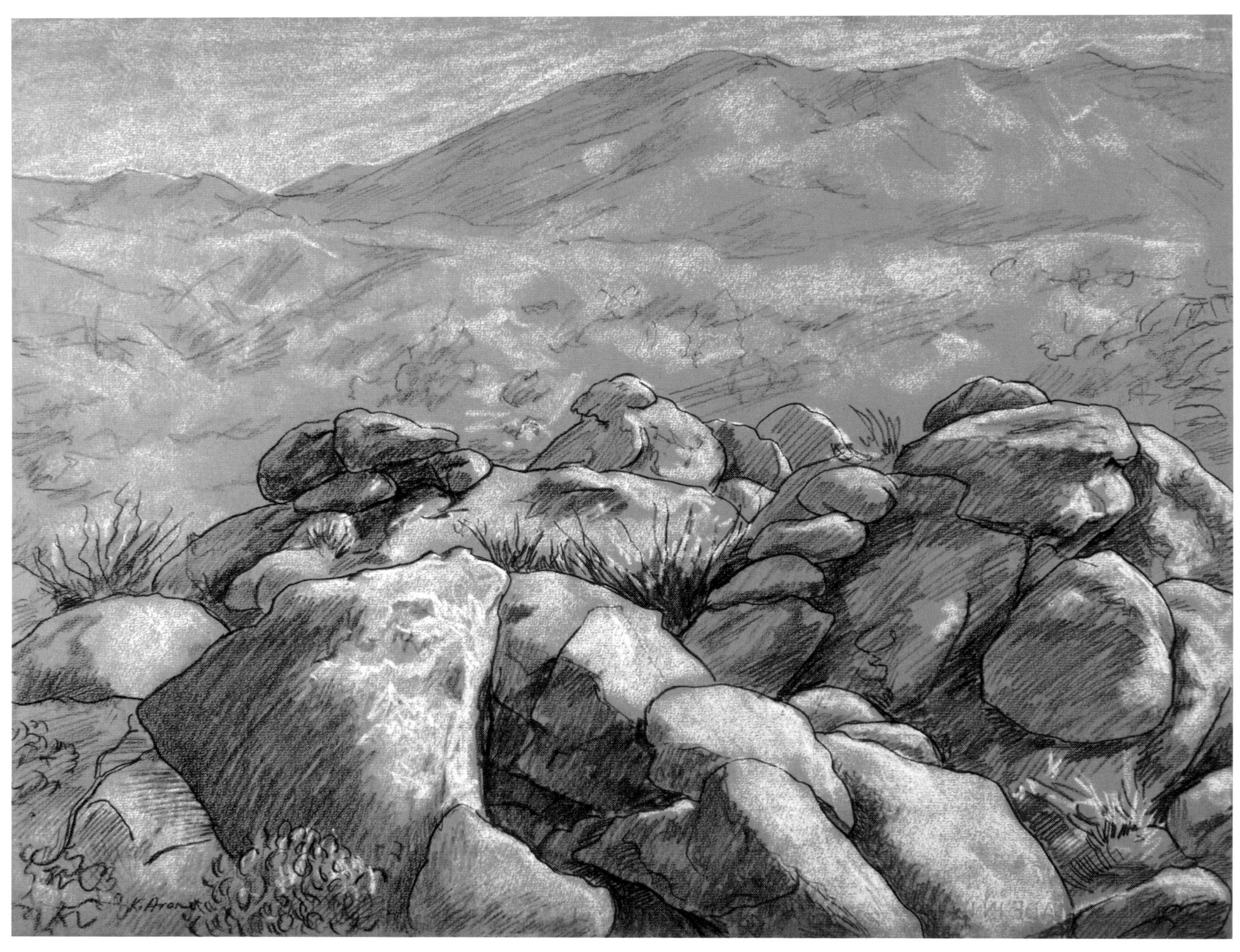

Desert Rocks I (1990s), pastel on paper, 19 × 24 in.

An hour further west is Palm Desert in Coachella Valley, where Aron has also had art shows. In *Desert Rocks I* each rock has its own distinct personality. They dance together, creating a configuration of form, affected by their color and the shadows from the sunlight. There is something pure and clean in this pastel of rocks.

Around Los Angeles Aron painted garden landscapes in different styles, as seen in *Bel Air Garden*, as well as *Beverly Hills Garden* and *Backyard Garden and Pool*, all from the 1980s. He painted portraits of a family's children in Bel Air. When he completed them, he asked if he could paint an interior scene in their home that looked out on their garden. *Bel Air Garden* was the result. He paints the beauty, light and harmony in the outdoor garden. A white statue of a beautiful woman stands among the plants. The pattern of the doors casts shadows on the floor inside the room. Inside is a bronze sculpture of a person's head. It is dark, in the shadow. No details of its face can be seen. This could be Aron still inside in the shadows, even though he knows this vibrant world lies just outside. Being seen in the camps meant death, as he told me: "To survive, I must be invisible." The Holocaust experience still lies within.

The mayor of Beverly Hills, Max Saltzer, and his wife commissioned Aron to paint family portraits, including a large one of Saltzer playing chess with his son. When he finished, Aron asked permission to sketch their backyard garden. He returned to his studio to paint this large canvas, *Beverly Hills Garden*. An old tree stands firmly in the ground as it spreads its canopy to shade the garden. Around it are neatly pruned green hedges, with a group of tall rosebushes blooming next to the tree. The red-tiled roof of the white stucco home balances the red brick pathway, and sunlight shines through the leaves to dapple its light on the lawn, path, bushes and flowers. Aron's brush strokes create the reflection of sunlight on the plants, ground and roof. There is order in the composition of the garden, power and movement in the trunk of the tree, and safety in the home nestled among the plants. The sunlight brings everything to life.

In *Backyard Garden and Pool*, Aron painted a friend's house that had been a part of the Will Rogers estate in Pacific Palisades. He paints a quintessential California scene with a red brick patio, deep blue water in the swimming pool, green trees and red, white and yellow flowers. Sunlight filters through the trees to highlight what might be a potted lemon tree and a bunch of begonias.

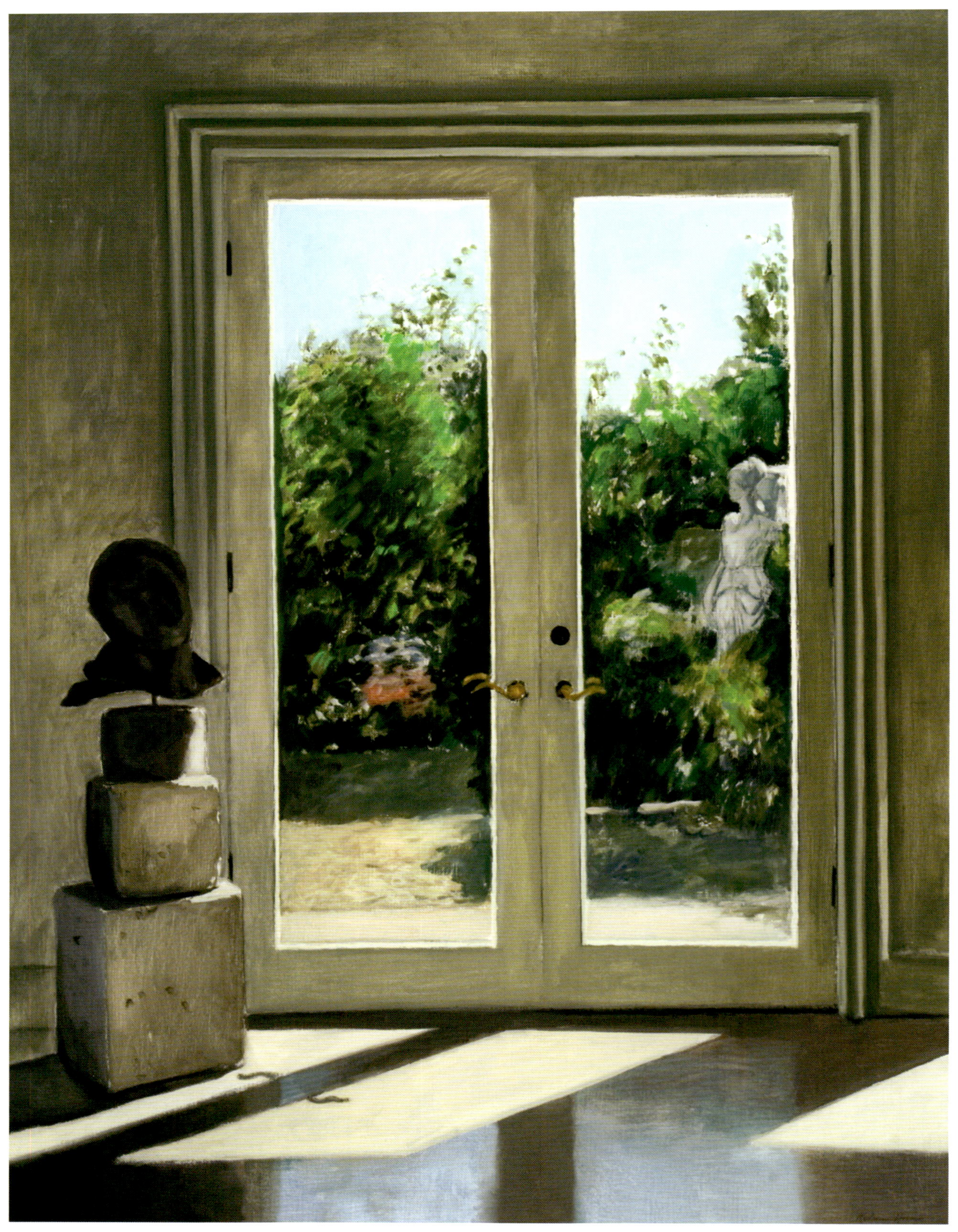

Bel Air Garden (1980s), oil on canvas, 48 × 36 in.

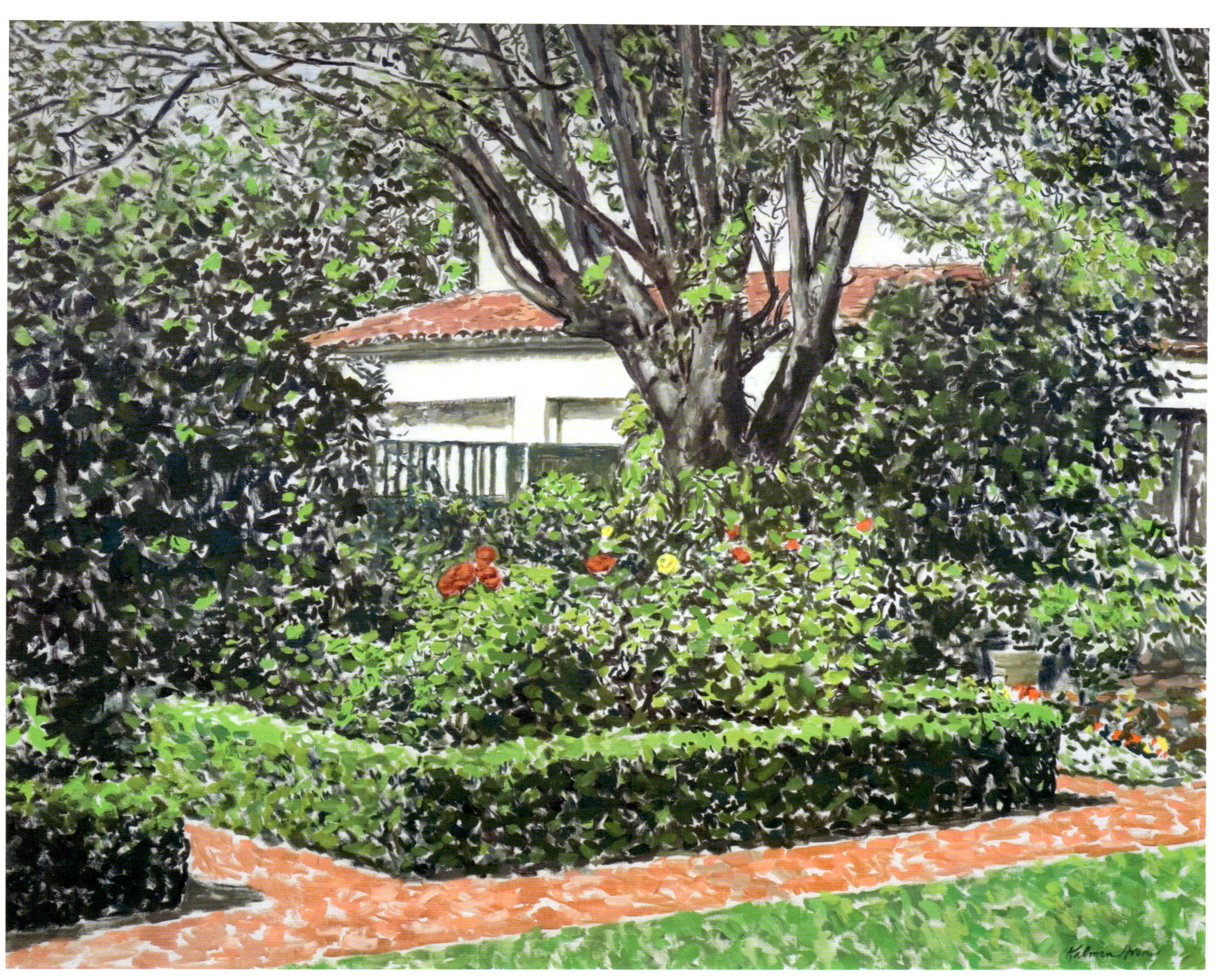

Beverly Hills Garden (1980s), oil on canvas, 43¼ × 53½ in.

Musings of the Mind

Although best known for his portraiture and representational art, Aron painted semiabstracts and abstracts of nature. *Abstract Freeways* offers a different vision of Aron's land of sun, with living patches of color bordered by a crisscross of "freeway" lines. In *City-Sky Abstract*, Aron paints the Los Angeles sky with roads crossing the land, leading to the far horizon. Within the clouds is a face. Aron's friends call this painting "God in the Sky," a title Aron refuses to use. He gave up any belief in the God of his childhood when Germans locked Jews inside his local synagogue and set it on fire. "How could I believe in a God that would permit this to happen?" he would ask.

Aron began painting with acrylics in the 1990s. He explains:

A painter I met got me experimenting with the acrylics. He had been using them for thirty-five years. One day he said: 'Why don't you try acrylics? Maybe you will like them.' I told him that I had used them once on a portrait. It was okay, but they dry too fast . . . not the same as oil. So one day in 1993 I started experimenting, and out came a series of trees. I always like drawing trees, and I have a lot of black and white pencil drawings of trees. To me they are almost like people. Each one has a different character. When I picked up acrylics, I started fooling around. I don't look at anything; I just do these spontaneously and quickly. If I don't like the result, I tear it up and throw it away. *Trees I* is an example. My friend, the painter, came back and said: 'I can't figure out how you did that with the texture, colors, and form.' I told him I just did it, and I liked the way it came out. I kept doing it.

Aron has also painted a collection of "musings" on softer paper, no two exactly alike. Most done in acrylics, they are abstract dances of movement and color and form, which spring forth from his mind.

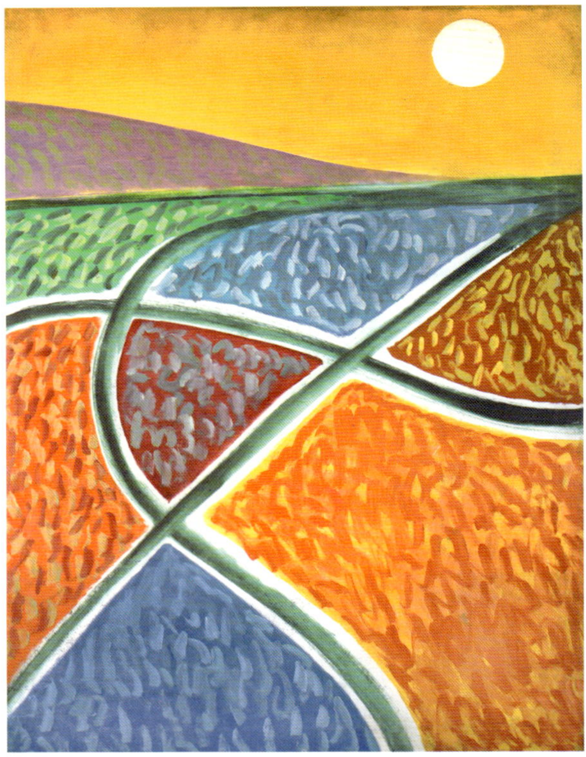

Abstract Freeways (1990s), oil on canvas, 40 × 30 in.

City-Sky Abstract (1996), oil on projection screen, 40 × 30 in.

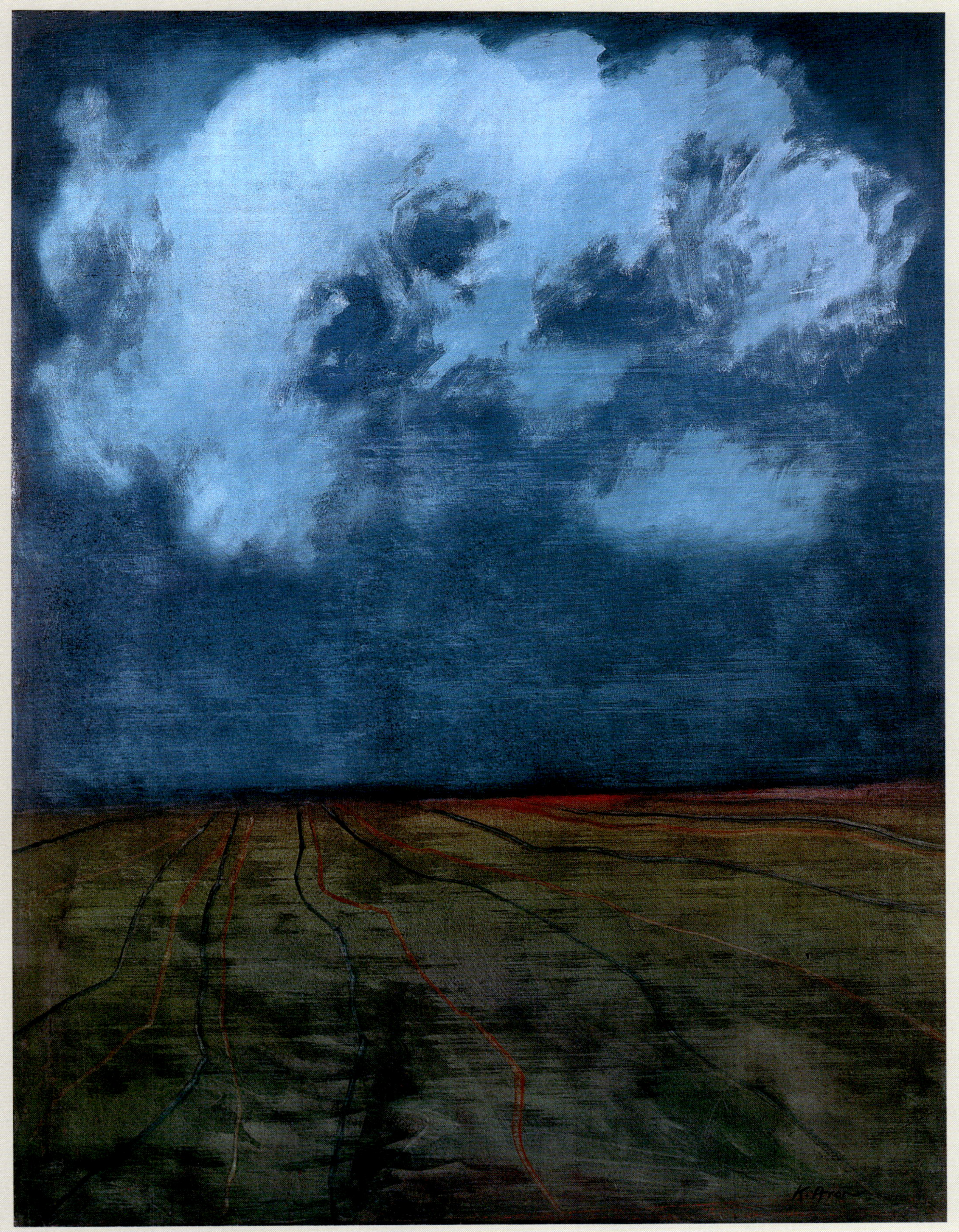

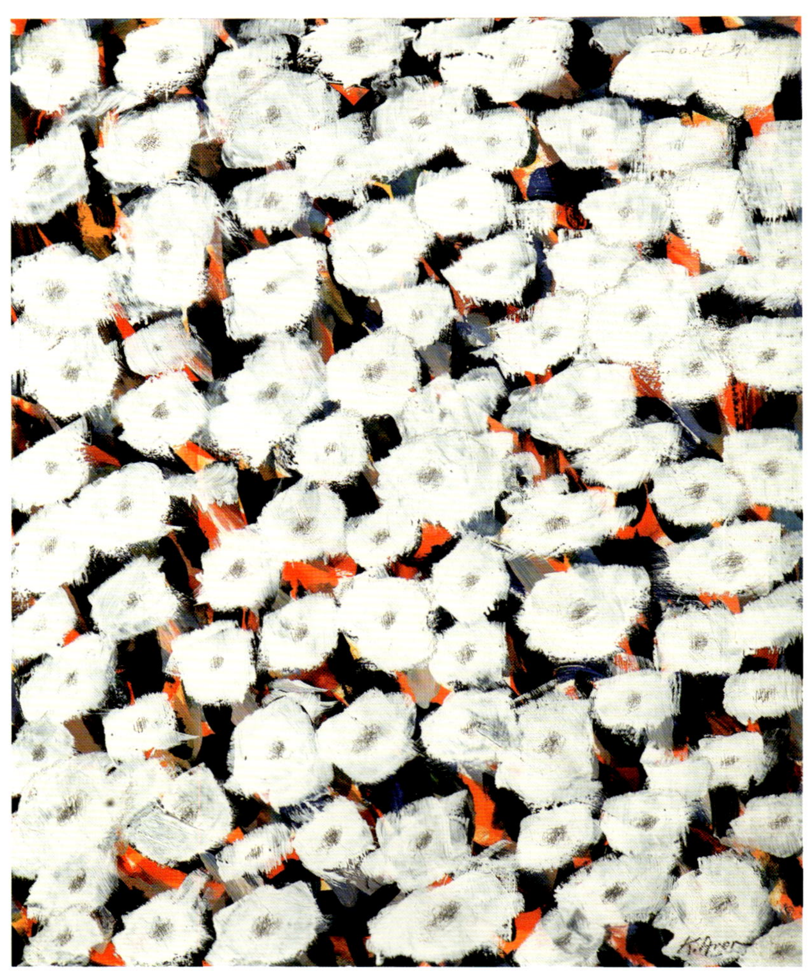

White Flowers (2000s), acrylic on paper, 14 × 11 in.

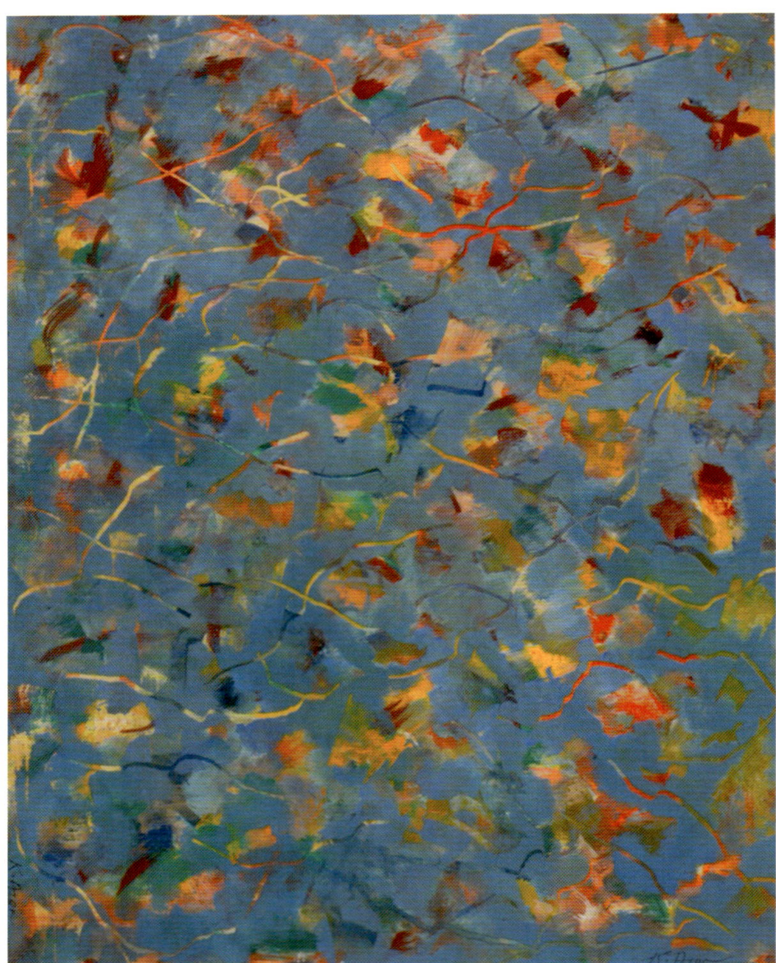

Abstract Flowers (2000s), acrylic on paper, 13½ × 10½ in.

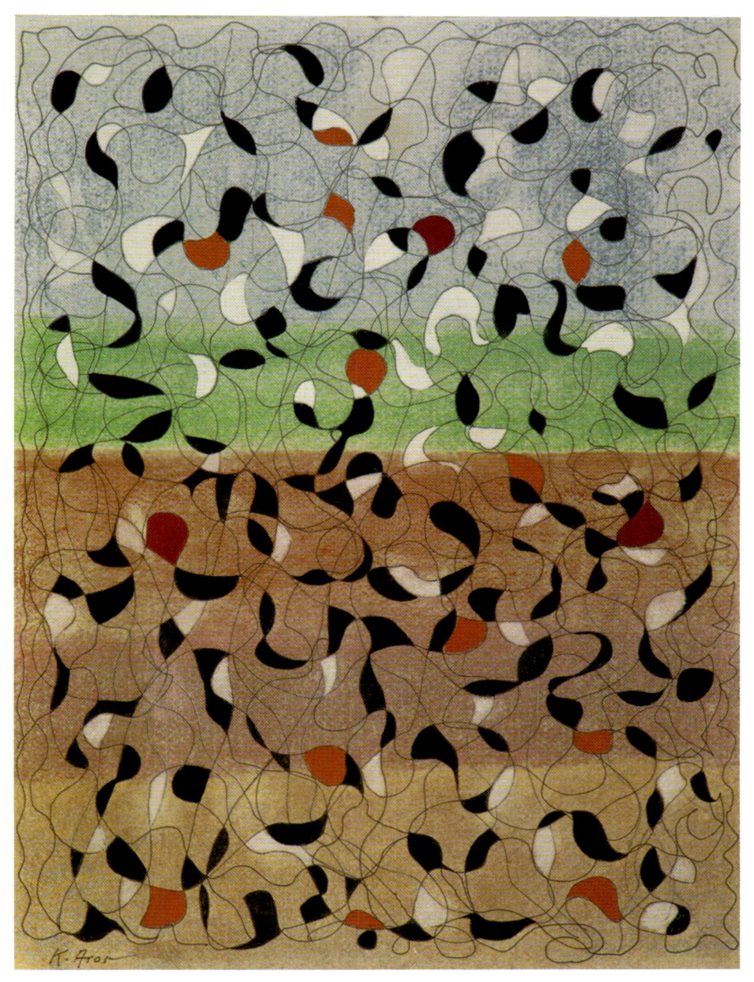

Non-Objective I (2007), acrylic on paper, 14 × 10½ in.

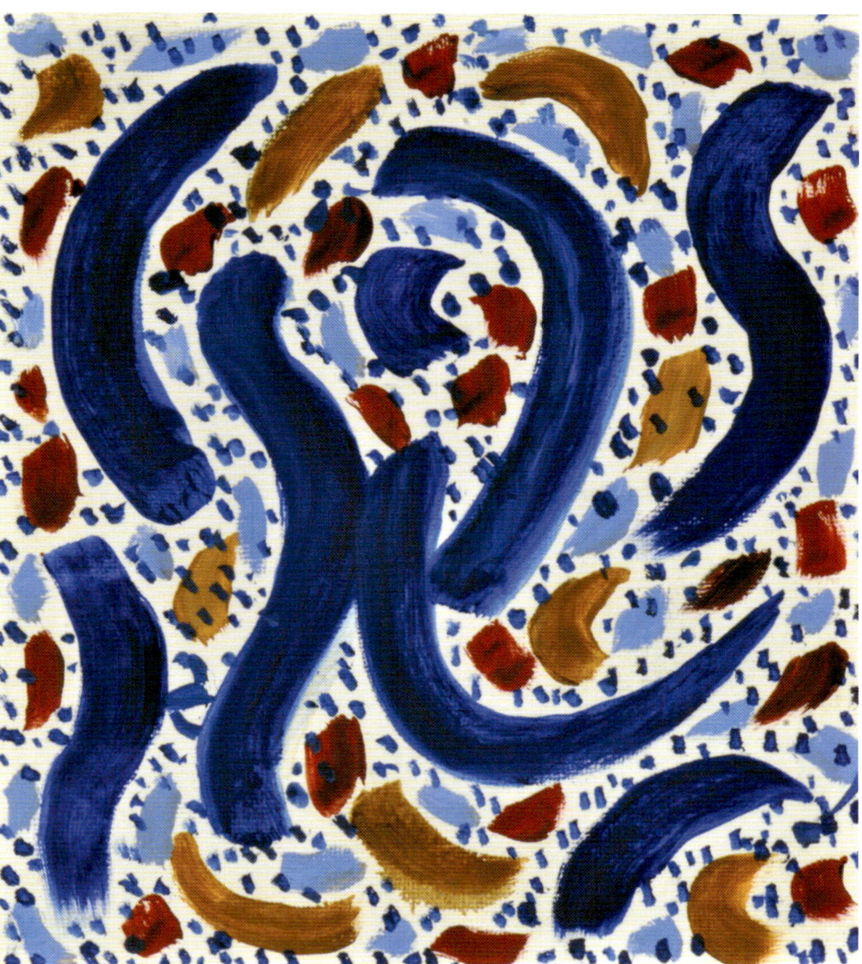

Non-Objective II (2009), oil on board, 15 × 13 in.

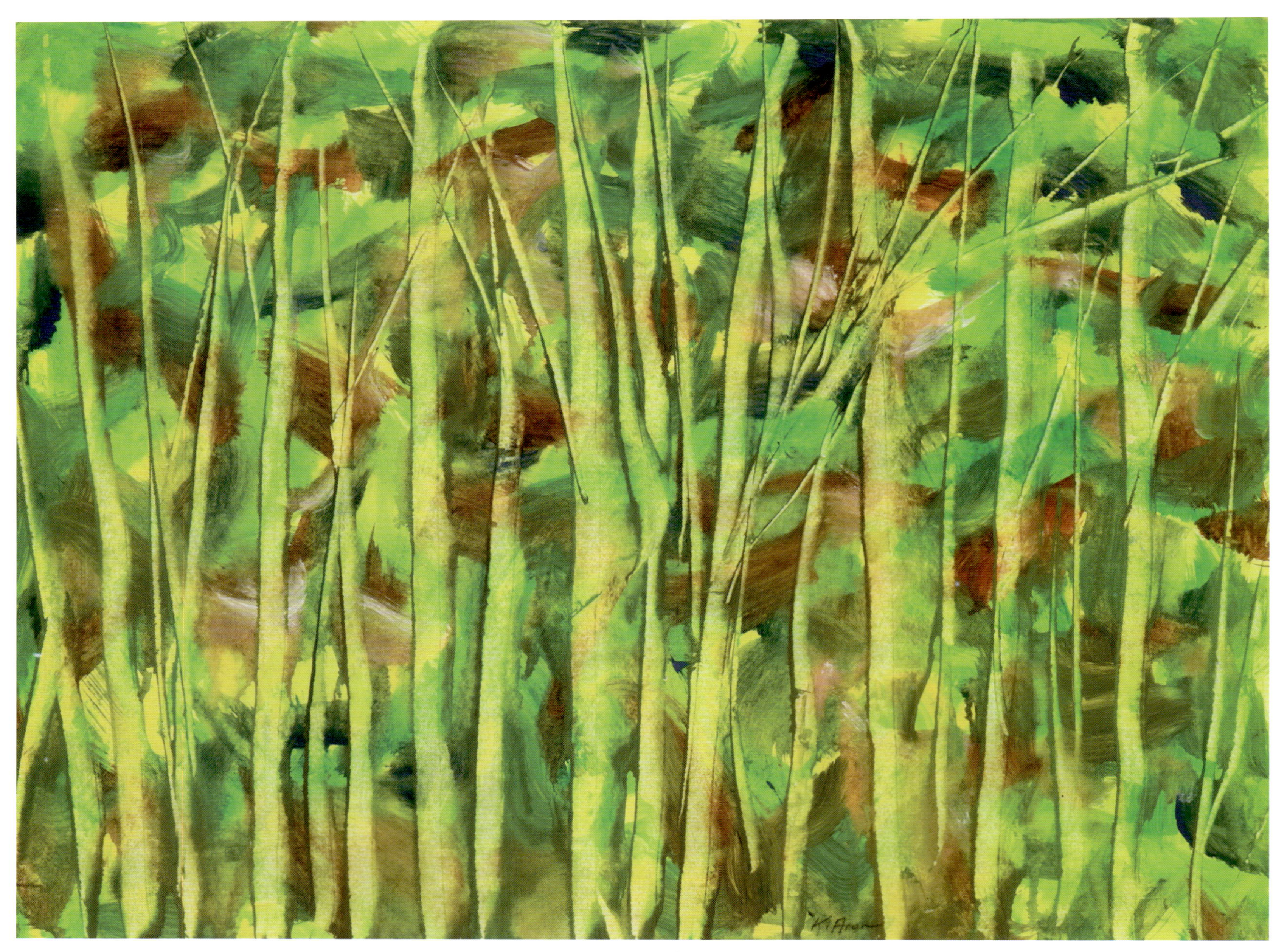

Trees I (2003), acrylic on paper, 18 × 23½ in.

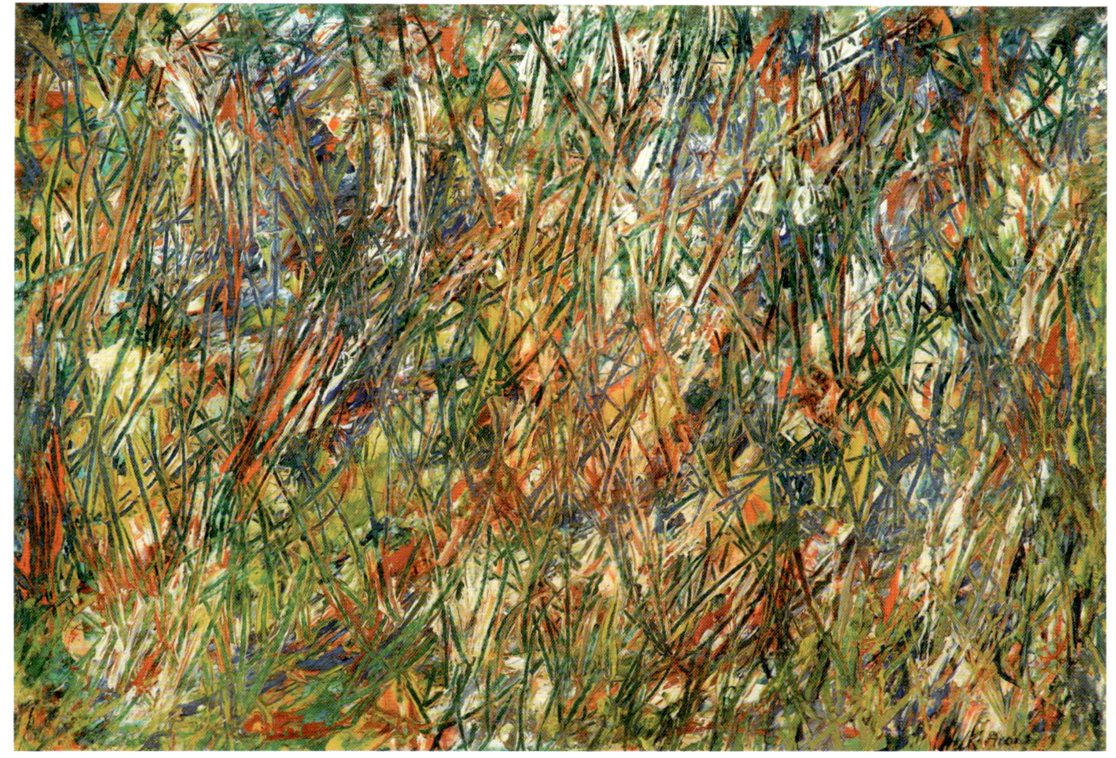

Gardener Didn't Show Up (2000s), acrylic on paper, 8½ × 12 in.

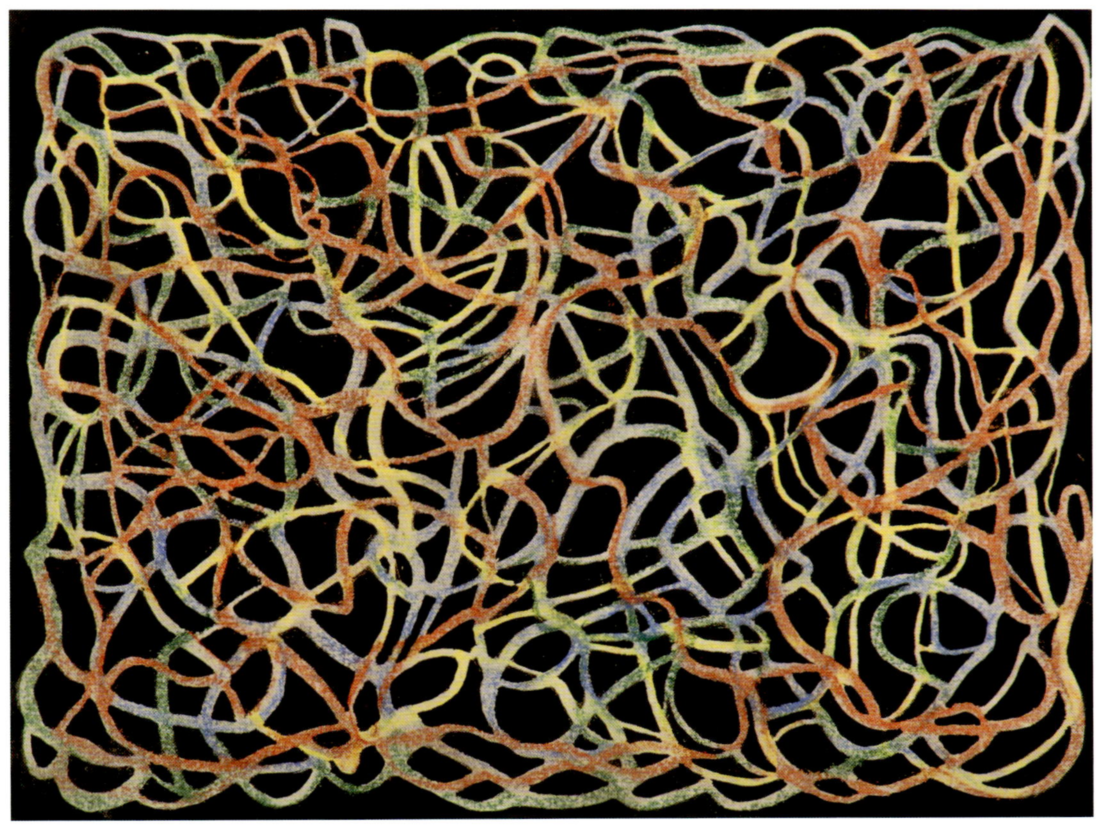

Non-Objective III (2010), pastel and black ink, 10½ × 14 in.

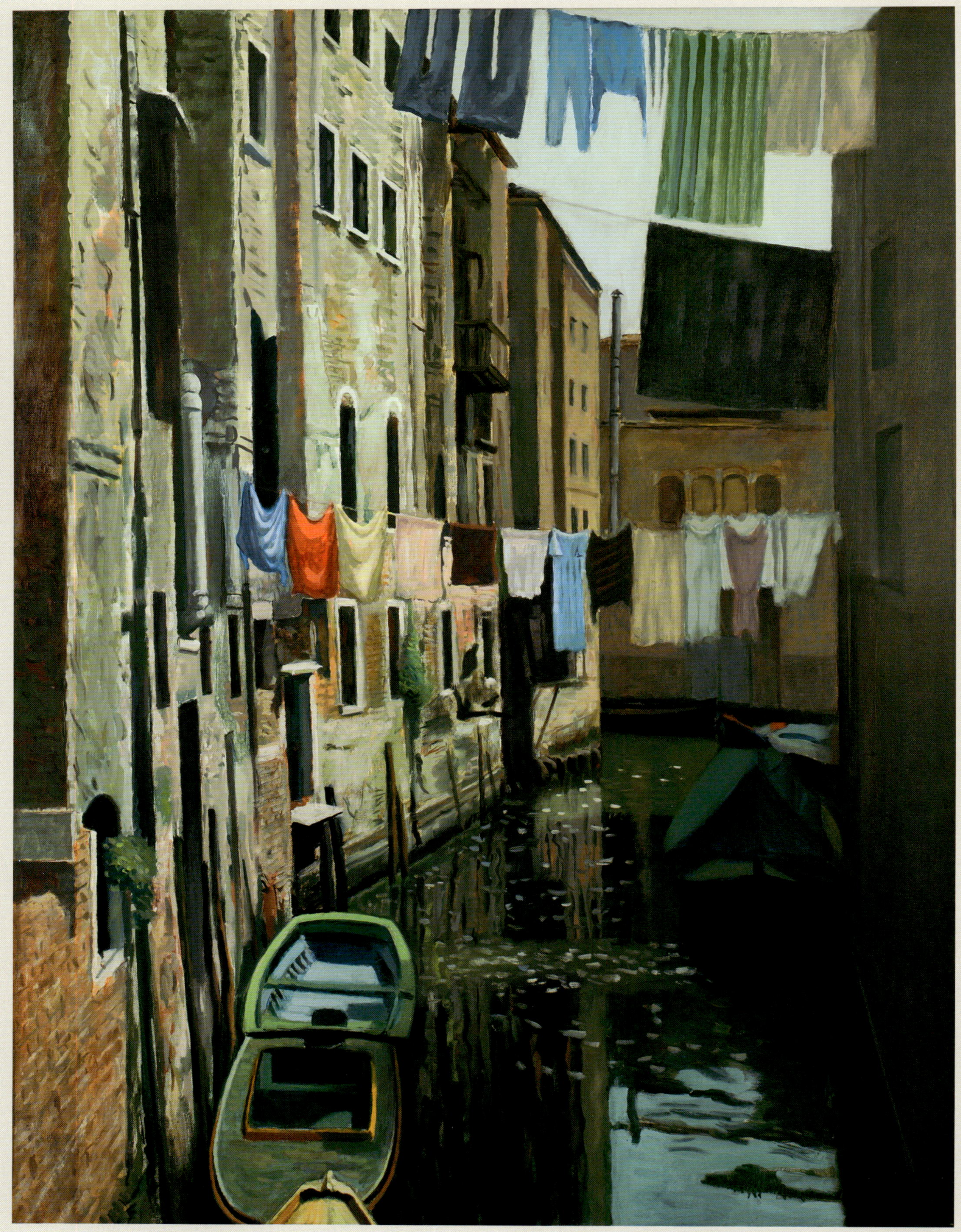

5

DISCOVERING COLORS

Return to the Old World

Ghetto (1960s), oil on canvas, 48 × 36 in.

In 1960 I decided I wanted to get out of Los Angeles and all of the stuff that was going on, the smoking and partying. I decided to go to Europe because I had never seen the original paintings by the masters, only black-and-white photographs in my six years in two art schools. I wanted to see the originals, and I wanted to see Europe.

First I went to Paris and saw paintings by Monet, Cézanne, Manet, and Pissarro. Then I went to Venice to study the Tintorettos and Titians, hung in dark rooms. Later in the 1960s I returned on a commission to paint its buildings and canals. One of these I called *The Ghetto*, an oil of the neighborhood where that word originated. Another is *Gondolas in Venice*.

During my travels I met interesting people. In Venice I started talking with a Parisian who was staying at the same hotel. He was a painter who had inherited a lot of money. He said, "I don't have to work. Three times a year I go and paint. My wife stays home." I asked, "What does your wife do when you are away?" "Well, she stays with my mistress." What kind of nonsense was this? He said that his mistress visited his wife and kept her company.

In Florence I met a tall American from Cambridge, Massachusetts, who was a sculptor and art historian on sabbatical. He spoke perfect Italian. We went to museums together, and one day we went to a private home that was never open to the public. The houseman opened the door and told him that it was a private home. My friend responded in elegant Italian that he was the nephew of the prime minister, and the houseman let us in. My friend made up the story, and we saw Rembrandts never shown in public.

I love Rembrandt's etchings and the paintings he did for himself after his wife died, when he moved to the Jewish ghetto. His strokes were looser and his paintings more fluid and expressionistic. The painting of his son, Titus, was done quickly; it looks unfinished. I believe this was the beginning of expressionism. Artists who followed drew on these later paintings by Rembrandt.

We went together to Spain and spent time in the Prado in Madrid. He knew that there was a collection of Goya drawings and etchings upstairs, and he asked to see them. Up we went into an air-conditioned room to see Goya's drawings. I didn't even know the collection existed. I was lucky to be with him.

Then we walked through the regular galleries. My favorite painting was hanging in a dark small room, *Las Meninas* (The maids of honor) by Velázquez. It is beautifully painted. I liked the composition. When this friend and I went through museums together, we didn't talk until we got out.

Gondolas in Venice (1960s), pastel on paper, 21½ × 29½ in.

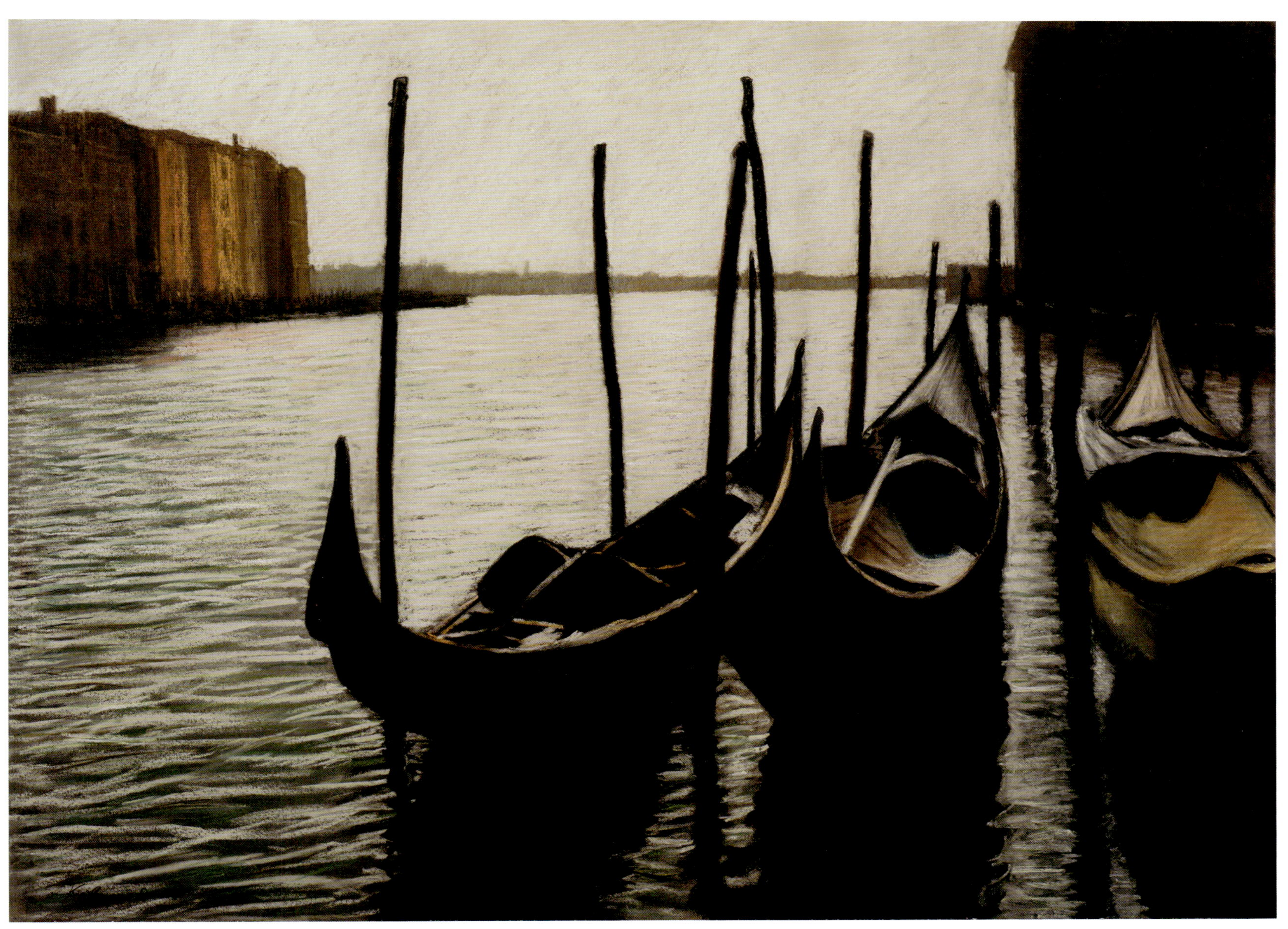

After six months I ended up in Athens. I got into an American hotel. Next I took a crowded bus to see the Acropolis. Suddenly I heard this beautiful British accent from a woman sitting next to me. I hadn't spoken English in a long time. We started talking. She liked my drawings. She asked about the war and the camps. We saw each other on a tour of the Greek islands, and at the end she said, "I want you to meet my daughter and husband if you ever get near London." She told me that her daughter was brilliant, plays the piano and sings . . . but was a little neurotic. I should have listened to her. After Greece I spent another six months traveling around Europe before going to London, my last stop on my way home.

On the continent I was free, free to see Europe with fresh eyes. Looking at paintings, I could smell the paints as the artist mixed them. I wondered: What did this artist choose to paint—people, surroundings, intimate rooms or vast landscapes? How did he paint, loosely or firmly? Did he draw on paper or paint on canvas? What mediums did he use: oils, charcoal, pencil, pen and ink? What colors did he choose? Did he experiment or did he get stuck in a commercially successful style? For an artist the only thing better than seeing the great works of others is painting your own.

Within a few months I would return to Paris and the French countryside to sketch and paint all day long, with only a break for lunch. But now it was time to go to London. On the second day there I found the British woman's phone number and called her. She picked me up and took me to the Tate Gallery. She invited me to lunch at her home. She and her husband lived in a plush apartment with paintings on the wall, a chauffeur with a Bentley, lots of money. Her husband was a small, short man with a bit of a Napoleon complex. He looked me over: Who is this guy? Does he have any money?

His father came from Poland and had opened department stores. Having inherited these, the son sold them and built houses and apartments. While we had lunch, their daughter, Suzanne, never said a word. She just watched me. He gave me a hand-rolled Havana cigar. I had never smoked a cigar before. His wife had already told him that I was an artist and that she liked my drawings. She had seen me sketching all the time in Greece. He started to ask me about his paintings on the wall. Some of the impressionist paintings were okay, though not the best. But there was a small painting by Oskar Kokoschka, a famous Viennese expressionist, who lived in England during the war. As a student I had liked his work.

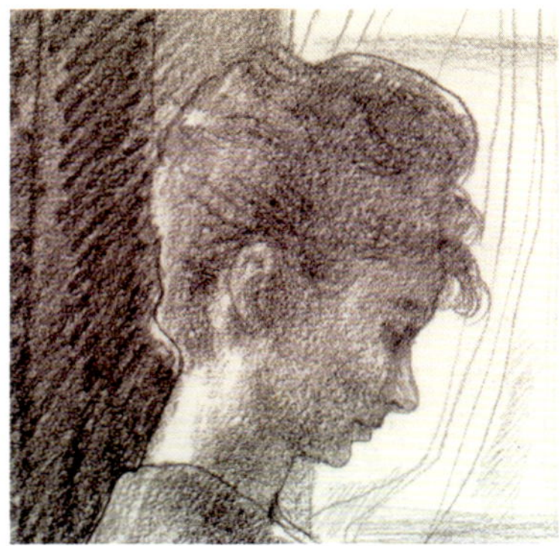

Suzanne Reading (detail);
full image on page 150.

He showed me two paintings by a local English painter that I didn't like, and he asked me about them. I didn't want to be rude, so I told him that they didn't have the quality of the others. The two women looked at me with an expression: what is this guy doing, talking to *him* like this, saying he has lousy taste. I couldn't care less. I was going home to Los Angeles the next day. I was not going to lie to him.

To my surprise, after not saying a word, the daughter got up and said, "Mr. Aron, you haven't seen London yet, have you? I want to show you London." I think she wanted to get me out of there because she knew I was going to get into an argument. Later she told me that nobody had ever dared tell her father he had lousy taste. That was the beginning of a big love affair.

I stayed in London for ten days with her. She was educated, sophisticated and interesting. I found out later that there was a problem between her and her father. She had played the piano since she was a little child. But she really wanted to sing onstage. She had a beautiful voice, and a male soprano was teaching her to sing. But a ninety-eight-pound woman cannot be an opera singer. In addition, her father didn't want her to sing onstage. When she went to sing at a concert in Switzerland, he wouldn't go with her. While she was gone, he removed her Steinway grand piano.

I finally decided that this was getting too hot. I had been traveling for over a year. I had obligations for commissions in America and a possible show. I had to get out. I left. At home I got a telegram from Suzanne every night, and for a few months every day I got a seven- or eight-page letter in beautiful calligraphy.

Four months later, I called her on the phone and said, "Suzanne, I am coming to London. We are getting married." I was a little apprehensive because I didn't know her well enough; we had spent only ten days together. I knew there were some problems. She worked for the BBC, writing. She was smart, and she had a good sense of humor. There were a lot of good things about her. But the father thing was bad. And that difficulty showed up in the marriage.

We got married in London in a civil ceremony with her sister and parents present. I don't think her father liked it, but her mother loved it. Her sister gave us a big wedding reception. Her sister's husband was an executive in the film industry. Occasionally we would join them for lunch with Charlie Chaplin or Gina Lollobrigida.

We lived in Chelsea, which is now very expensive. At that time it was not. What I liked about her was that she didn't take her parents' money, nor did she use her father's name. She made up a last name and called herself Suzanne Creyson when performing. She lived in a modest two-bedroom apartment. Occasionally her father would send his chauffeur to pick us up and take us out. So we were living high on the hog, but I liked that she didn't depend on his money. I paid for everything when we went out, because she had no money. She drove a very old, small car.

Suzanne and I went to France to sketch and paint. Before I left, I met a gallery owner, Jack O'Hana, through my father-in-law. A collector of Matisse and Chagall, he had an excellent gallery in Grosvenor Square. He offered to do a show of my paintings when we returned from France.

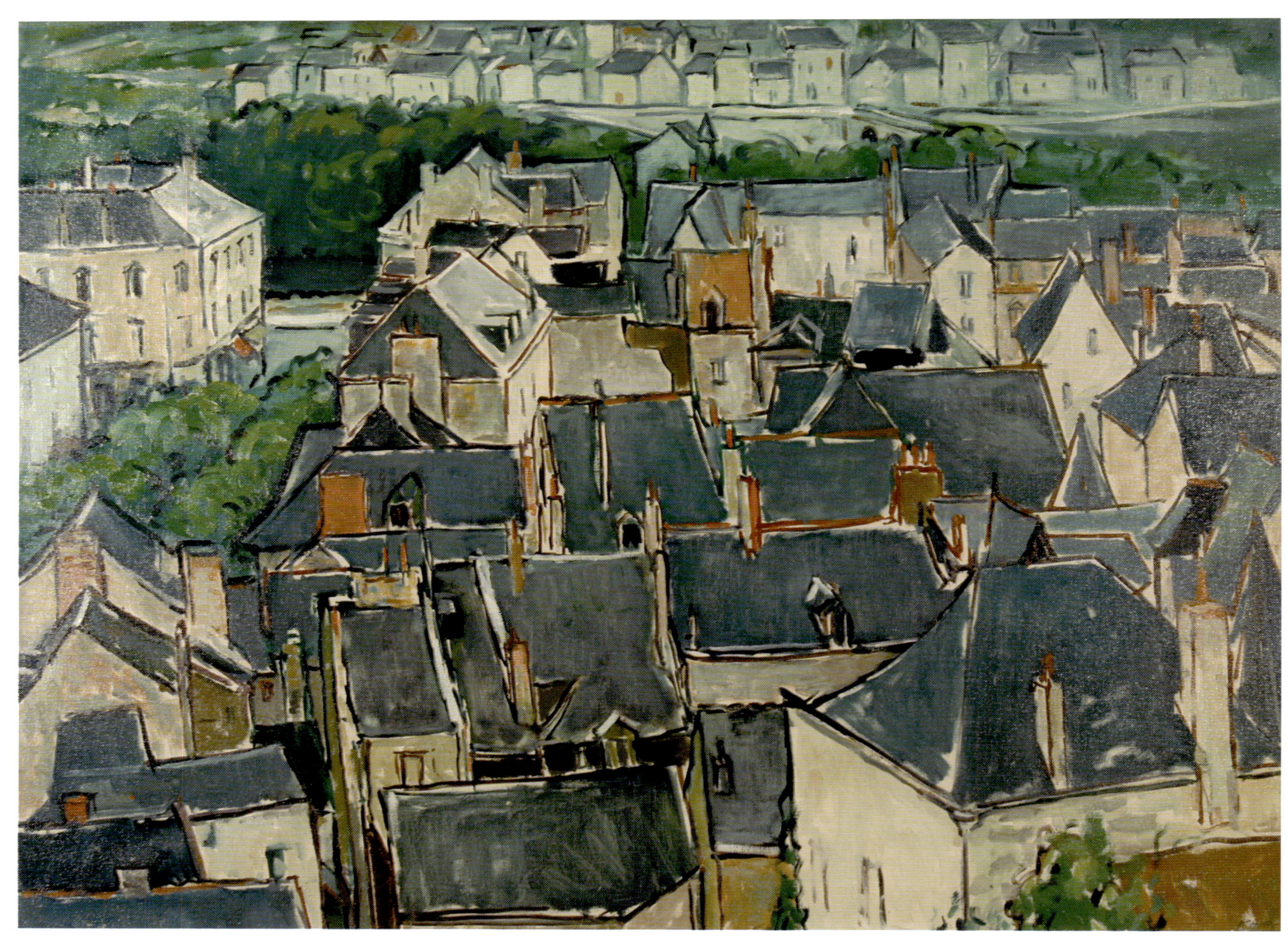

Chinon (1962), oil on canvas, 30 × 40 in.

We were in France ten months, painting in places like Chinon, an old village in the Val de Loire, where Henry II, the English king, had his castle. I couldn't stop. Some were studies; I came back to Los Angeles to finish them. Others were paintings. They are practically all gone. I still have a good oil of the village and one of a French woman looking out her window.

I painted mostly small landscapes and peasants. Ten months later I came back with thirty-five paintings. I was painting every day. I got up at six in the morning and went all day long. To be a good husband, I made sure that Suzanne and I had lunch together.

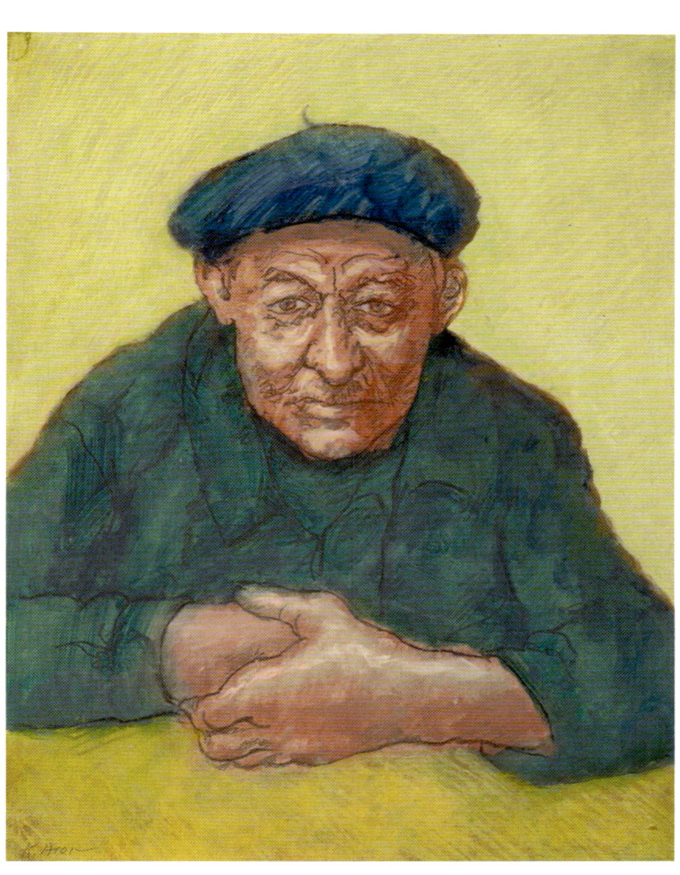

French Peasant with Blue Hat (1962), oil on paper, 14 × 11 in.

The sketches I drew in France gave me good material for years afterward. Thirty years later I painted the oil on paper, *French Peasant with Blue Hat*, from a sketch I made in a small village.

I really liked what I saw in France: the light, colors, characters, buildings, houses. You have to be very strong to go to the places I went. I walked up with a big canvas, easel and paints, and I was there half a day in the sun. Without help I couldn't do it now.

Suzanne spoke French well enough to interpret for me. We went everywhere: small villages, big cities. Wherever I saw something I liked, I found a place to stay, an inn. There weren't many hotels then, just little inns. That was the best time of my life.

Suzanne described it in a letter she wrote from the Hotel Terminus in Nantes to the art journalist Janice Lovoos:

I'm sure you would be amused to know how Kalman is working. We spent last week in a tiny village . . . on the bank of the River Vienne. The first thing Kalman saw were the rooftops. How many times have we arrived exhausted at the end of the day to find a hotel where we can rent a room . . . Kalman insists, however, that the room must be right at the top of the house. He rushes to the window to see if there is any roof to draw, while I collapse in the bed.

At Michel we climbed three hundred stairs straight up, but the view wasn't good enough so down we went again.

Last week he found a house he particularly liked, so he set up an easel and began painting. Various people came up, watched and commented, and we were invited to have a drink later. We then found a real gold mine. The old peasants and farmers were so friendly and were easily persuaded to sit still for five minutes—and he would do the loveliest charcoal drawings. They would look at the drawings and burst out laughing with sheer delight. Then they produced their friends who would "sit" with great savoir-faire. They really were marvelous people, and he must have done about fifteen or sixteen drawings.

Kalman's only lament was that he wasn't able to get the peasants to sit for any portraits in oil, but he hopes to work from the many sketches he has made.

He has done a lot of landscapes, seascapes, old houses, chateaux, in oil. There is so much to paint and draw in this country. If Kalman had his way, we would still be at Le Touquet where we landed with the car. We were just five feet into France, and he had already found a subject.

He designed a marvelous box to go on top of the car. It has six shelves that pull out and hold wet canvases. In this way he is able to have six canvases at one time. As they dry, he takes them off the stretchers, then stretches a new canvas.

When I returned to London in the fall of 1963 with Suzanne, I had a solo exhibit at the O'Hana Gallery. It included many oils, also some drawings and pastels, all of my favorite subjects: children, seascapes and landscapes, chess players and studies of old people. There were reviews in the newspapers, and Jack O'Hana gave me another show later. I liked painting the buildings there, like in *London Rooftops*. I also got some important commissions; for example, the French car maker Peugeot sent his grandson to sit for his portrait.

London Rooftops (early 1960s), oil on canvas, 30 × 24 in.

In London a woman art critic took Suzanne and me to meet the painter Francis Bacon. As Suzanne and the art critic walked into his studio, Bacon held me back in the hallway. He turned to me to complain that he could not change his style of painting; his gallery owners said he must continue to paint in the style that was successful.

When I faced the same problem, I chose differently. I always wanted to be free to paint what and how I wanted at any time. I never knew what I would be painting six months or two years from now. As a result, I have bodies of work that are completely different from each other. You wouldn't know they were painted by the same man.

I liked London. I was painting. I had this wonderful gallery. It was cold and windy, with fog and all, but I didn't care. Suzanne and I returned to Los Angeles to close my studio so we could live permanently in London. It would take a long time to pack everything up. I had a lot of things to box and send. She sat in the sun every day. Then one day she said, "I am not going back to London. I like it here. Why would I want to go back to London?"

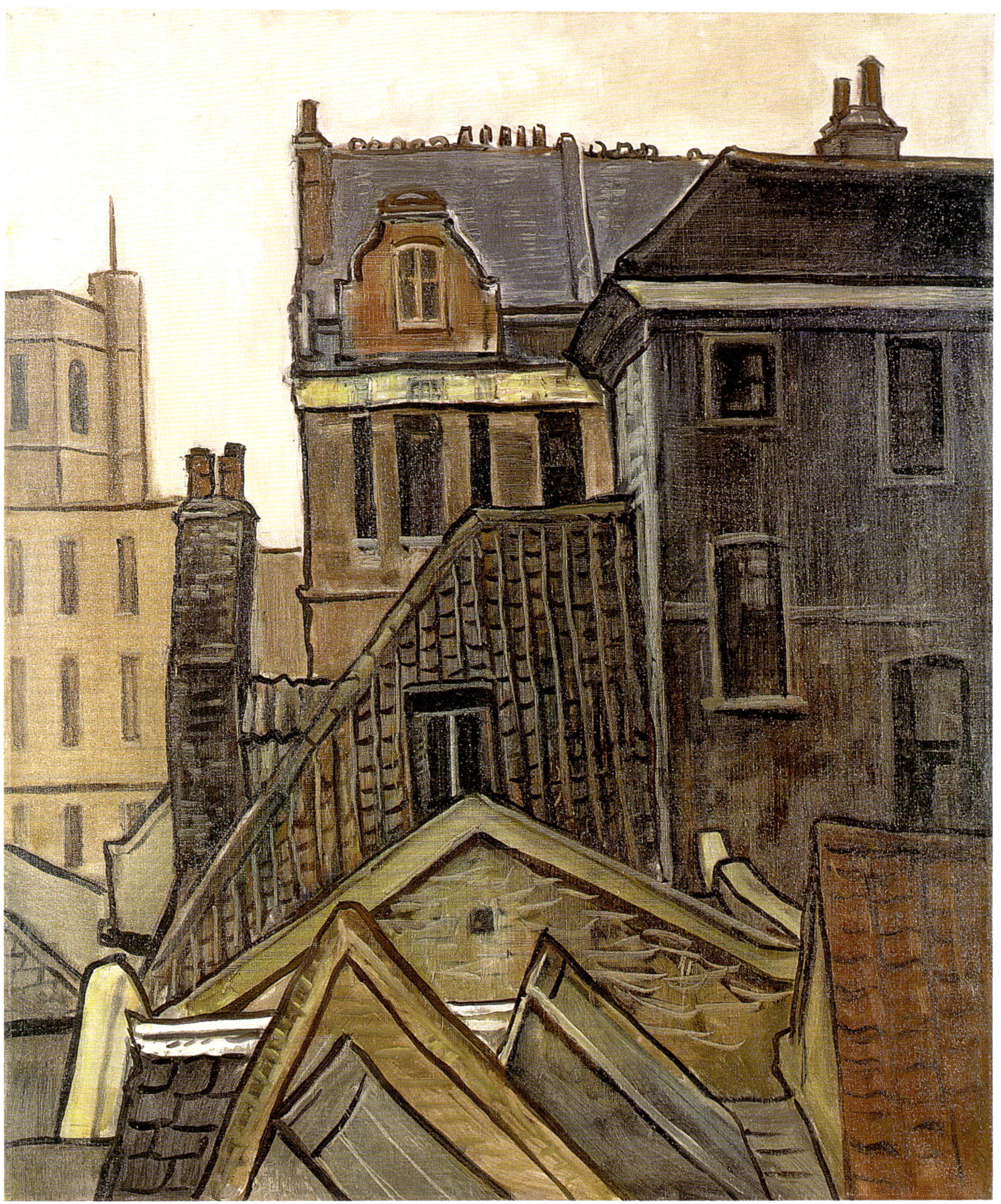

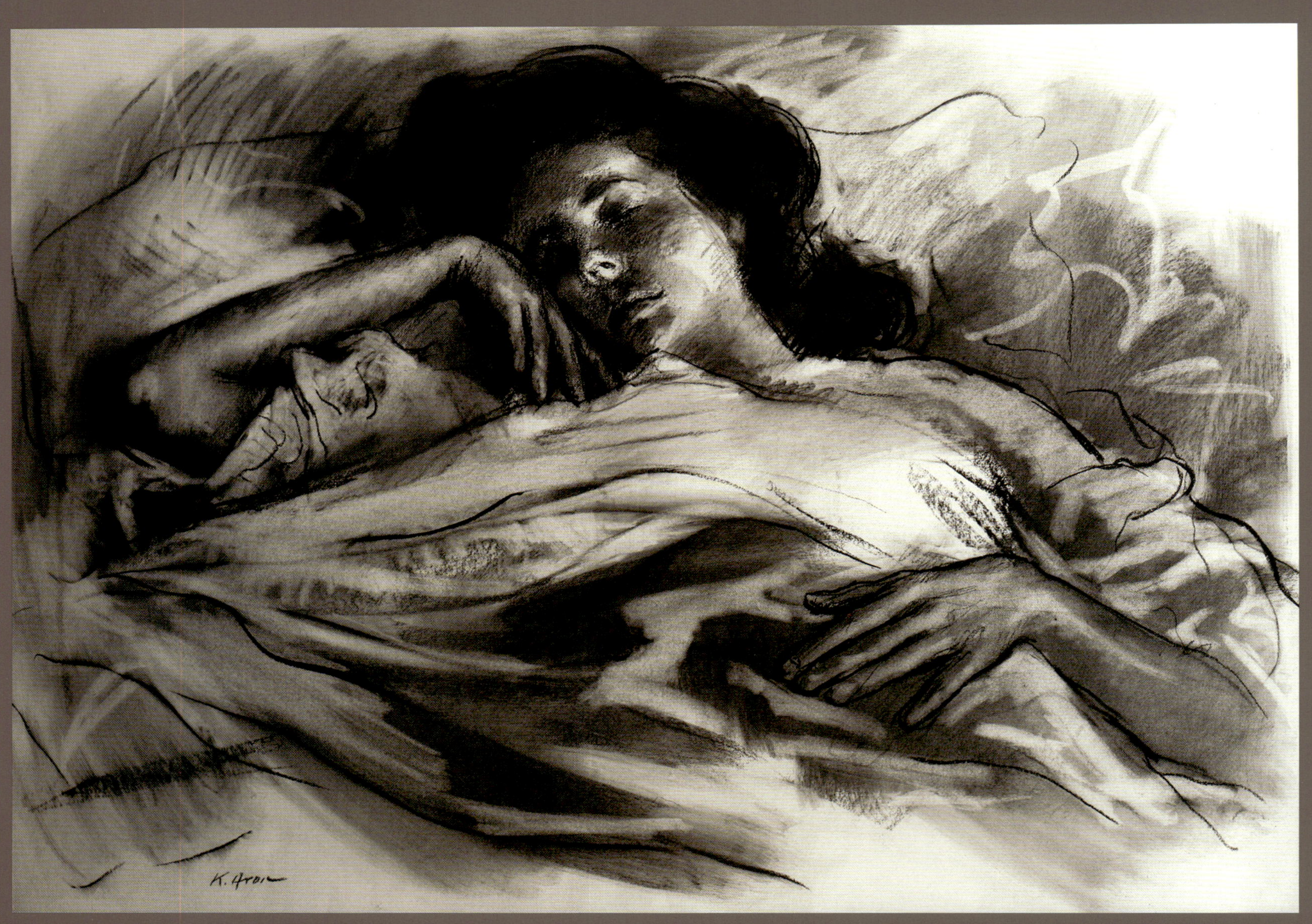

Suzanne (1962), charcoal on paper, 21 × 29½ in.

So we stayed in Los Angeles, and everything changed. I was painting all the time. A coloratura soprano, Suzanne sang and played the piano. Sometimes I would pick up the mandolin and accompany her. I invited three musicians from the Los Angeles Philharmonic to accompany her in concerts for friends in my studio. With the high ceiling it had perfect acoustics. We had a good time.

She was happy for a while. People came and praised my paintings, and I made sure they heard her sing and play. People liked her a lot. She was charming and intelligent. But she was frustrated that she couldn't go onstage and be a big opera singer. She also had bad rheumatoid arthritis. I tried to get her to different doctors, but they couldn't cure it. She had a lot of things she wouldn't tell me; she would hide. She was trying to pretend she was okay, but I knew she wasn't doing well. I could see that she was getting depressed, because she didn't sing anymore. But then she started doing other things I didn't like.

We used to go to the Santa Monica beach every Sunday, where there was a group of people we saw, including a French woman and a man who was a computer genius. Suzanne liked to talk to him. People drank and talked to each other. Then she said to me, "I was invited to make breakfast for this man. Why don't you come along?" I said, "He didn't invite me." "Well, I am going," she said. Then I realized what was going on. I warned her, "If you go there, it will be over." She came home the next afternoon; the next morning I went to see a lawyer, and that was it. She moved out.

She didn't want the divorce. Her father sent money to buy a house. I didn't want it. We had been looking for a house, but I would not take his money. We were married for three years. She told me after we were married that she couldn't have children. I wanted to have children. I also learned from this marriage. If a woman doesn't like her father, stay away.

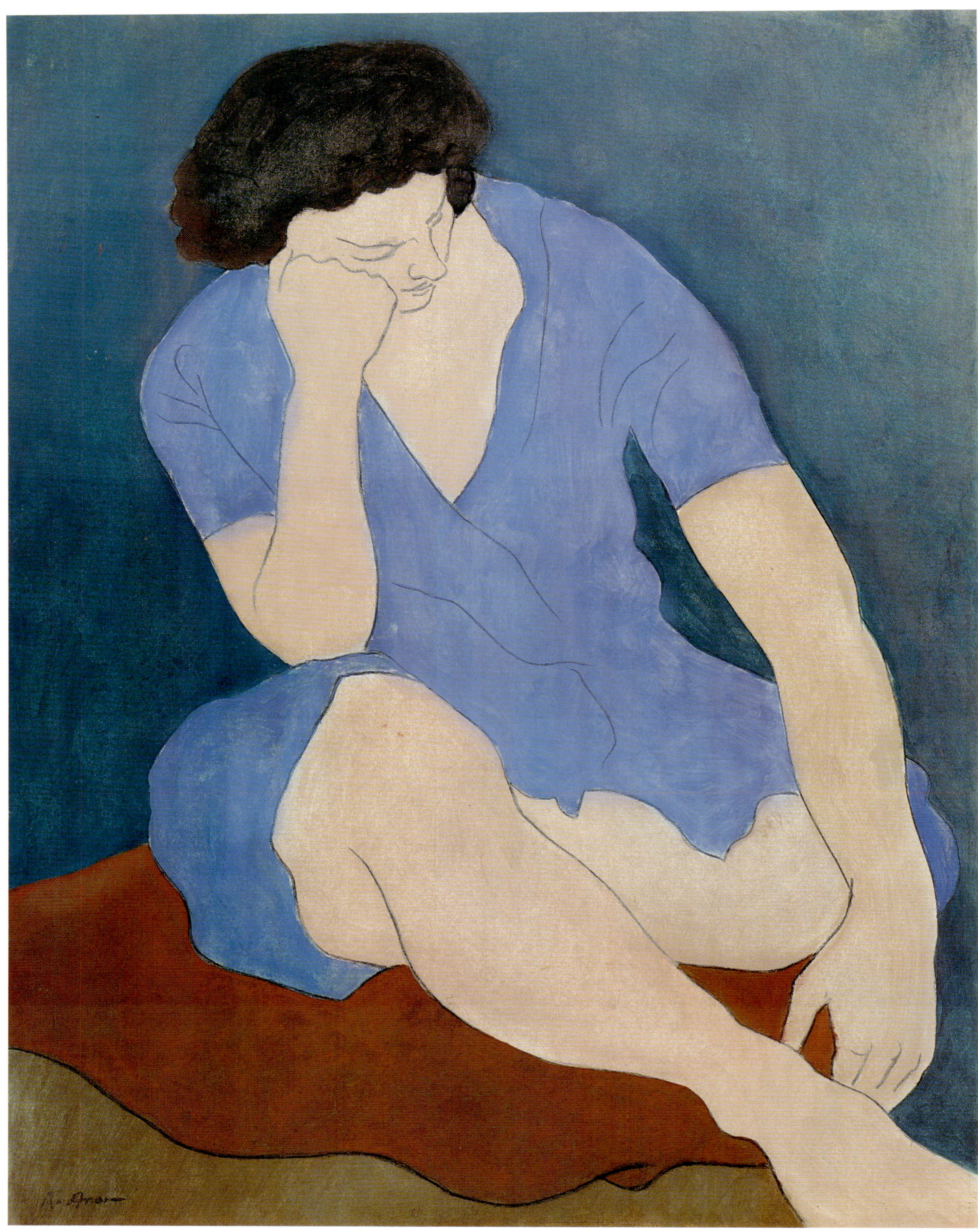

6

IMAGES

Portraits, People, and Psychological Realism

Woman in Blue (1970s or 80s), oil on paper, 14 × 11 in.

Aron quickly became a successful portrait artist. In the 1950s he began doing commissions for my mother's clients. As he became more widely known, he was hired to paint a wide variety of people: luminaries such as Ronald Reagan, Henry Miller and André Previn, as well as businessmen, art collectors, artists, musicians and children. In his own words:

I like to draw people. I have been doing it since I was a little kid. I remember drawing in my parents' bedroom. I would watch friends who came over and try to draw them. I must have been about three. I still like to do it because to me each is a different character.

Then in the camps I looked at and studied people. When I paint, I'm trying to capture their character, their spirit, the certain look they have. Each one has a different kind of look. There are no two people alike even if they look alike. The Holocaust gave me an understanding of people that most people won't understand.

Everybody is worried a little bit how I'm going to paint them. I make them feel comfortable by talking to them and distracting them from their worries. I tell them to relax a moment and look around the studio while I prepare, and during this time I observe the person. I see what they look like in profile, from the left or right side. Do they keep their head straight or turn it sideways? They don't even know I am doing it. Then I choose how to have them pose to show more of their personality. I look into their eyes.

There is a story with every portrait. I am part psychiatrist, part psychologist. Like psychiatrists, I don't talk about it. People want to be painted this way or that way. "Take my wrinkles out," they say. I say to them, "Why would I want to take your wrinkles out? When you hang it on the wall, and you are standing next to it, you will look much younger in the painting than you are." It doesn't make any sense, does it? "You look terrific," I tell them. This is people. They don't think. They want something that they are not.

What is nice about portraiture is that you meet people you may not meet otherwise. Here they are sitting for a couple of hours. They come back for another two hours. You get to talk to them on different subjects. That is an education; it is interesting.

I never intended to do portraits. But there are very few artists that make a living from painting. I came to the conclusion that if I did portraits, I would be free to do my own paintings. After a while I enjoyed doing them, not just to make money but also for my own pleasure. . . . I liked capturing personalities and poses, sitting or standing. I particularly enjoy doing portraits for myself without being influenced by the sitter's expectations of how they like to look.

Aron sees, senses and paints the humanity that sits in front of him. He removes the veil and reveals what lies within. His time in the camps honed his concentration skills, resulting in an ability to read a person's emotions. If you are sad when you sit for his portrait, it will show in your eyes. If you have a cold, as my sister did when Aron painted her in 1951, it will show on your face. If you are grounded and strong, your strength emerges. Aron paints what he sees, and he sees deeply.

Aron deftly uses the artist's tools. He learned human anatomy in art school, which allows him to create a likeness with a few lines. He mixes his own colors, so he understands how they relate and influence each other. He is equally at home with pastels, oils, acrylics, pencil, ink and compressed charcoal, using what is appropriate for the subject. For example, for children he likes pastels because they are softer and allow him to work quickly.

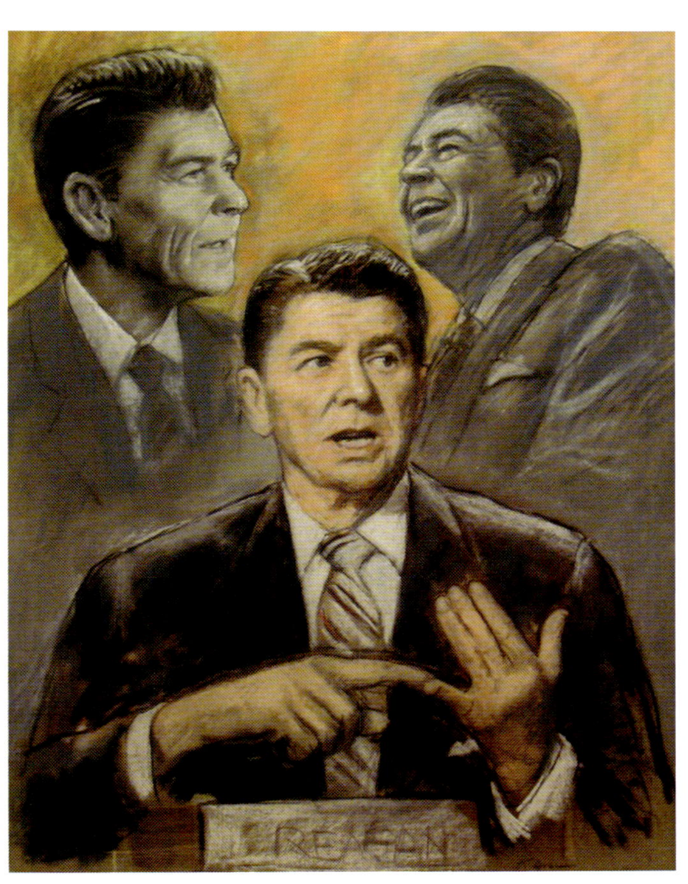

Reagan Sketch (1980), pastel on paper, 14 × 12 in.

Most of his commissions have come through client referrals. In 1980 he received a phone call to paint the former governor of California, then a candidate for the presidency: Ronald Reagan. In Aron's words:

His bodyguards and driver came to check my studio. They didn't want him to come and sit there because my studio was at the back of the property, and they didn't feel it was safe. The driver with the broken nose and the hand in his pocket said to me: "I think we should have it done in the Valley." There was a building where he used to give Saturday afternoon commentary on the radio.

So I followed them, got out of the car with my easel and paper, and I met Governor Reagan at the elevator inside the building. He is very friendly, shakes my hand and looks at me like he knows me. It was nice. I didn't know much about him. Then suddenly the guy grabs both of us and pushes us into the elevator. I was talking to him, and suddenly this man pushes us in. Well, he must have seen something or somebody coming, so he was making sure he was safe. This was during the campaign.

Reagan was doing a recording session. I watched. I learned that he was a stickler for detail. When he didn't like the way he said something, he would stop and redo it. I had two sittings with him, and I drew the middle figure from these two sittings. I drew the other two from photographs.

I first did a sketch. I was told that Nancy Reagan looked at it and insisted that I paint one of the figures wearing his cowboy hat. I did.

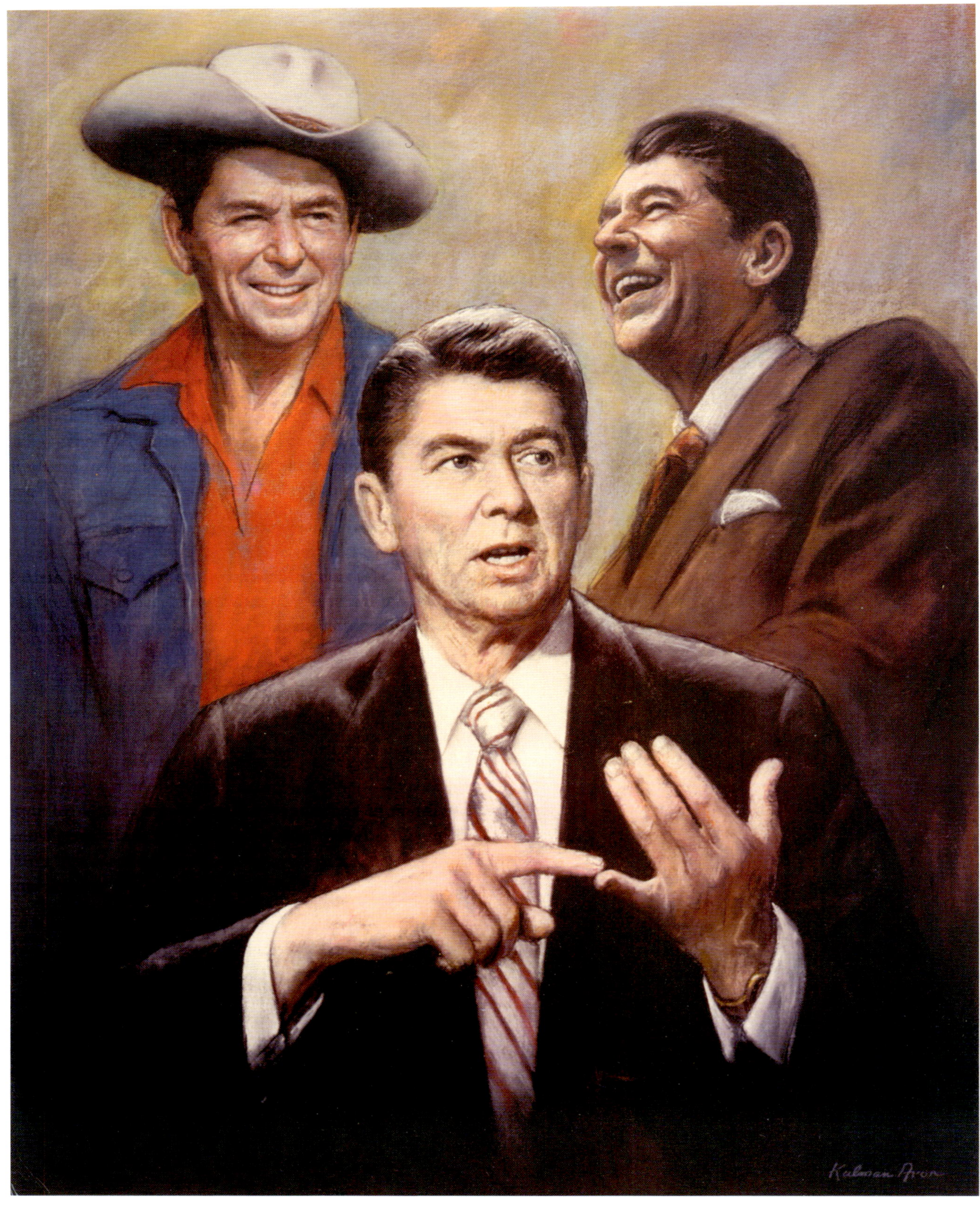

Portrait of President Ronald Reagan (1980), pastel on paper.

Aron captures the character of Reagan in the center figure: the great communicator. He is speaking, making his points. The other two figures reveal an engaging man at ease with himself and others. Aron relates, "His people intended to print a poster from the portrait to use in the campaign. When they showed it to me, I didn't like it. Because of the printing process it was missing a color. It was bland. To do it right, they said, was too much money. I told them, 'I won't let you use it.' So they used a photograph of him for the poster. That is the story with Ronald Reagan. He was very charming, very nice. But I didn't know him." Aron was told that this portrait later hung in the White House.

He often became friends with those he painted. In 1966 he was invited to paint author Henry Miller. He recalls:

Henry Miller was a character. A gallery in Westwood had a show of his watercolors. The owner asked me to meet him and do a portrait to hang in the show. I went to his house and did his portrait. I did three drawings of him and one portrait in oil. He wasn't writing anything at the time. He told me about his good friend, Anaïs Nin, who saved his life in Paris in the 1930s. Starving, he was going through garbage cans to find a piece of bread. They met, and she got him jobs for the magazines . . . and later arranged the publication of his first book, *Tropic of Cancer*.

What was interesting was that he watched me drawing. He said, "I really like what you are doing. I don't know how to draw. But people like my work, and I enjoy doing it." He was apologizing, so I went out and bought a box of compressed charcoal for him. He was like a little kid: "Oh, I like it. Thank you."

The portrait hung in the show with his watercolors. Some people wanted to buy it. He said to me, "Kalman, keep it. Don't sell it now. Wait till I die. It will be much more valuable then."

When they met in 1966, Miller was seventy-five, Aron forty-two. They had several things in common. Like Aron, Miller had experienced starvation, humiliation, despair and frustration. Born in Manhattan and raised in Brooklyn, Miller was a hungry boy. He begged for money and food. In a recorded interview he recalled, "Every bloody street I look down, I see nothing but monsters. No wonder I had recurring nightmares. I don't know how I ever survived, why I'm still sane. . . . My whole past seems like one long dream punctured by nightmares."

Although quite different in character, Aron and Miller were both creative artists. Their eyes were wide open, they shared a knowing. In painting this living witness to humanity and human appetites, Aron places him comfortably in a chair. He paints his body with broad strokes in a range of cool blues and outlines it in black. This rendering suggests that Aron sees a man in his midseventies who is comfortable with himself and the world around him, at ease with his notoriety and success. This portrait illustrated a *New York Times Book Review* article about the author's work in 1976.

A more idiosyncratic work is the portrait *Mr. Bachrach*. A Russian-Israeli immigrant, Bachrach became a successful chicken farmer in California and tried to sell Aron eggs when he came for sittings. He was well read, and Aron enjoyed his company. He painted his family as well.

Portrait of Henry Miller (late 1960s), oil on canvas, 40 × 36 in.

Aron painted other notable figures such as the mayor of Beverly Hills, Max Salter; California Supreme Court Chief Justice Rose Elizabeth Bird; the chancellor of the University of California, Riverside, Herman Spieth; contemporary art collector Frederick Weisman; and multitudes of musicians: classical guitarist Andrés Segovia, composer Mario Castelnuovo-Tedesco, cellist Nathaniel Rosen, composer Henri Lazarof, flutist Burnett Atkinson, jazzman Robert Mercer, and Juilliard Music School professor Rosina Lhévinne. In 1988 he received a commission to paint André Previn, music director of the Los Angeles Philharmonic and a renowned composer and pianist.

In *Art in America*, Janice Lovoos praised "Kalman's ability to sketch rapidly, obtain a likeness and the true personality of the sitter." In the 1960s Aron did a charcoal drawing of Italian flutist Severino Gazzelloni, *Playing Debussy*. Lovoos described their encounter, quoting Aron: "A few years ago a famous Italian flute player came to my studio to sit for a portrait. I don't speak any Italian, and he spoke no English." So Kalman suggested that the musician pay no attention to him, but just play his flute. "He played Mozart and Debussy, and I drew two large charcoal drawings. When I finished, he stopped playing his flute and looked at the two drawings. He pointed to one and exclaimed 'Mozart!' and to the other, 'Debussy!'"

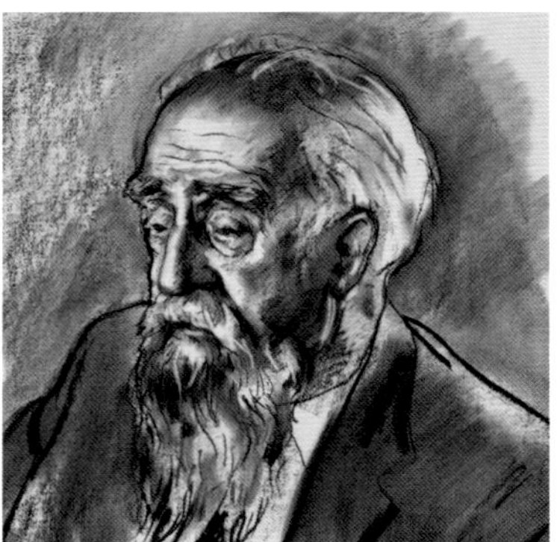

Rabbi Jacob Sonderling (detail); full image on page 93.

Aron knew local artists such as Leonard Kester, Ted Gilien, Gerd Koch and Michio Takayama. In the 1960s he used compressed charcoal to draw many of them, including artist Bettina Brendel, artist Arnold Schifrin, and photographer and painter Mark Cheka. He also drew a charcoal of Rabbi Jacob Sonderling, whom he met at an art gallery. They talked together over coffee about art and religion. Later Aron received a letter from him, saying, "you are not a religious man, but you are a man of great spirit."

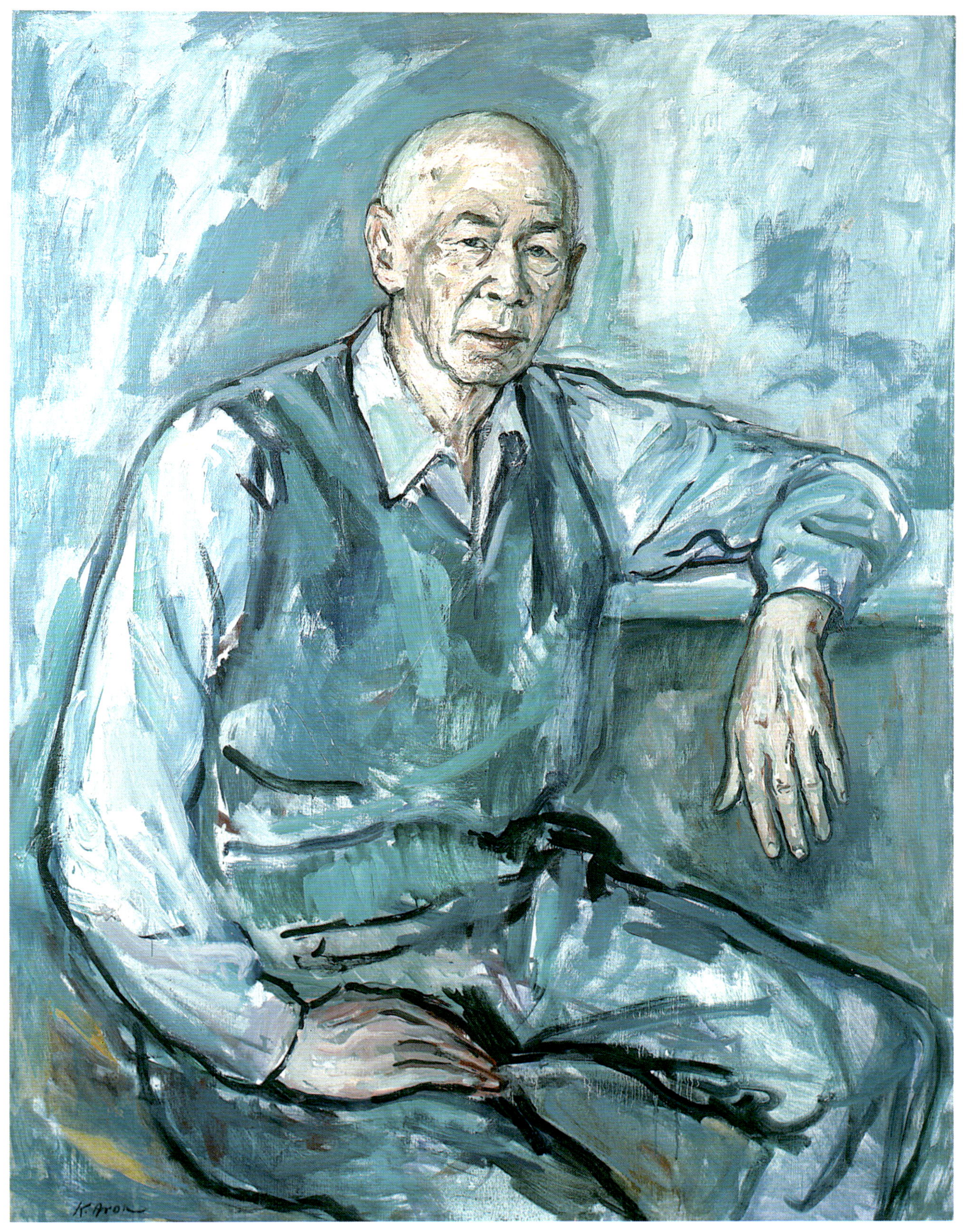
K. Aron

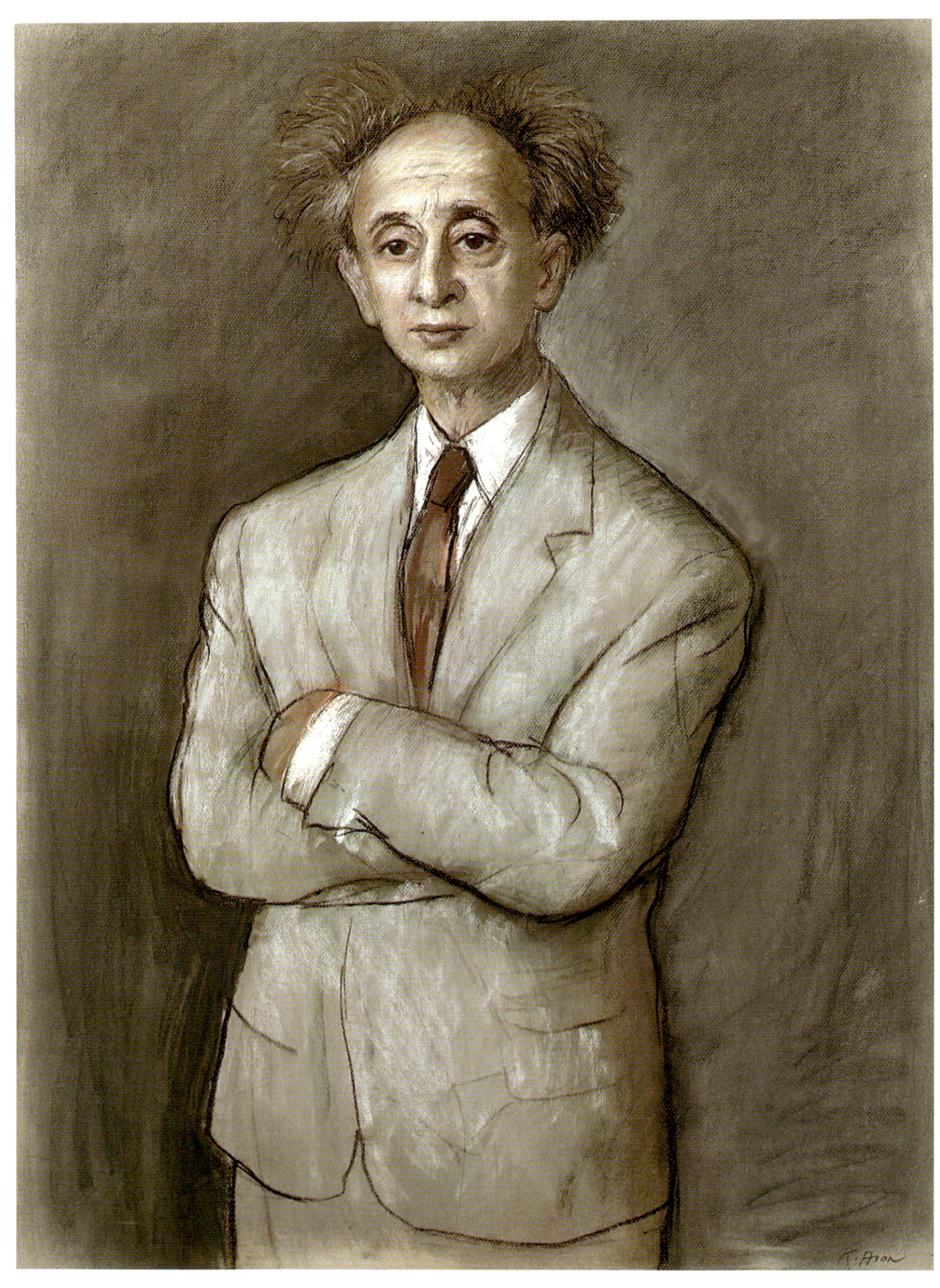

Portrait of Mr. Bachrach (1965), pastel on paper, 38 × 28 in.

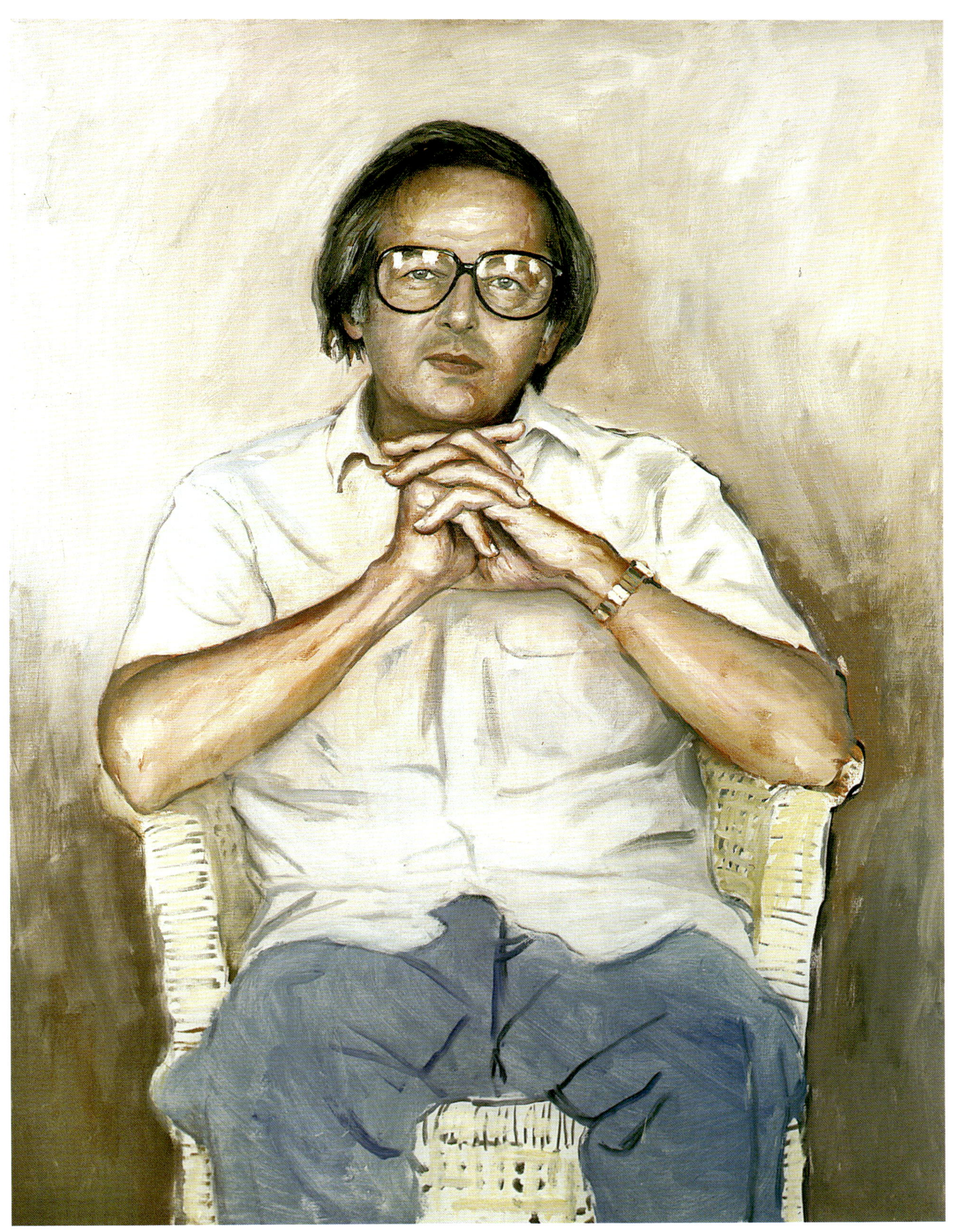

Portrait of Maestro André Previn (1988), pastel on paper, 48 × 36 in.

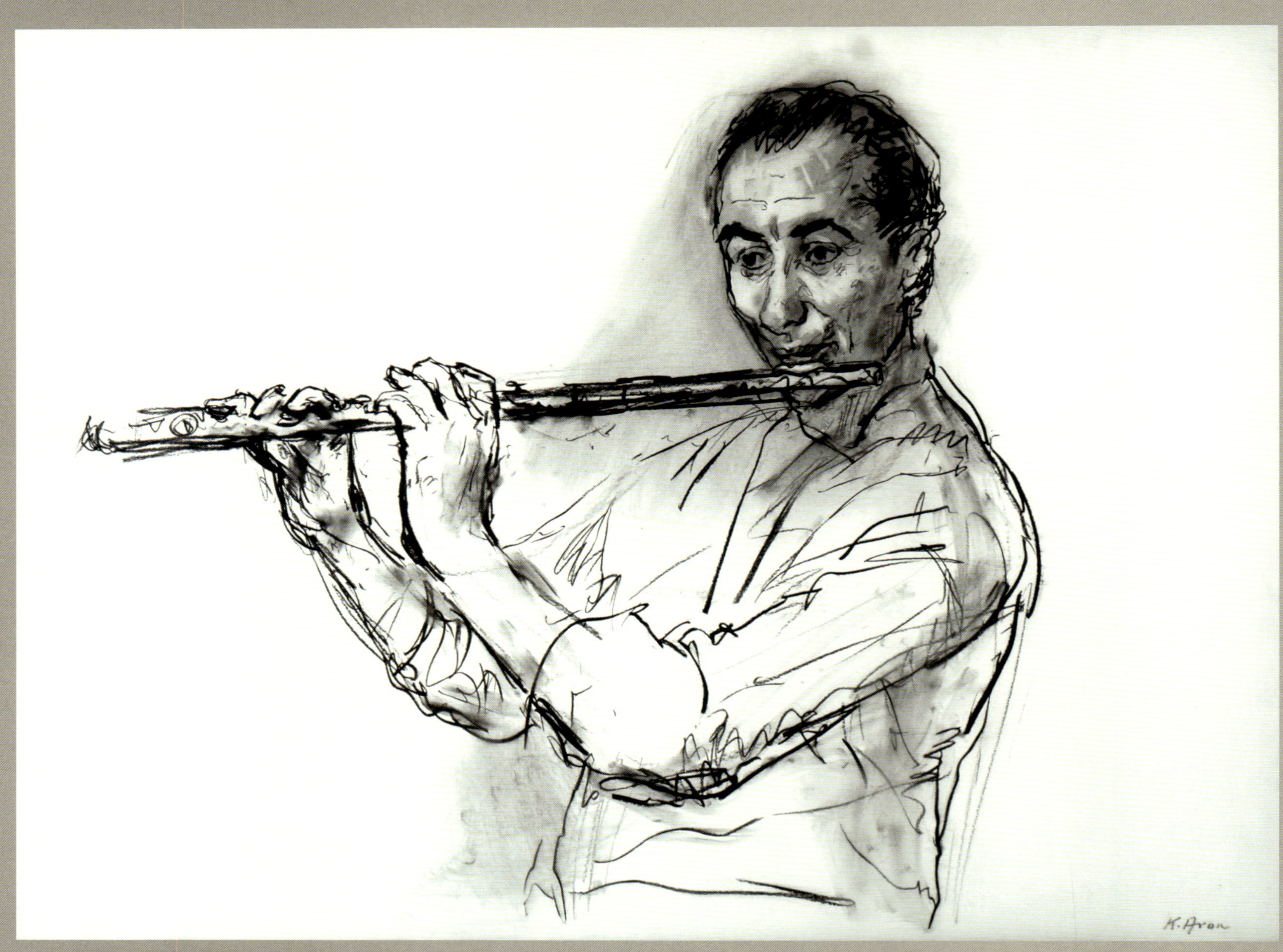

Italian Flautist Severino Gazzelloni (early 1960s), charcoal on paper, 30 × 40 in.

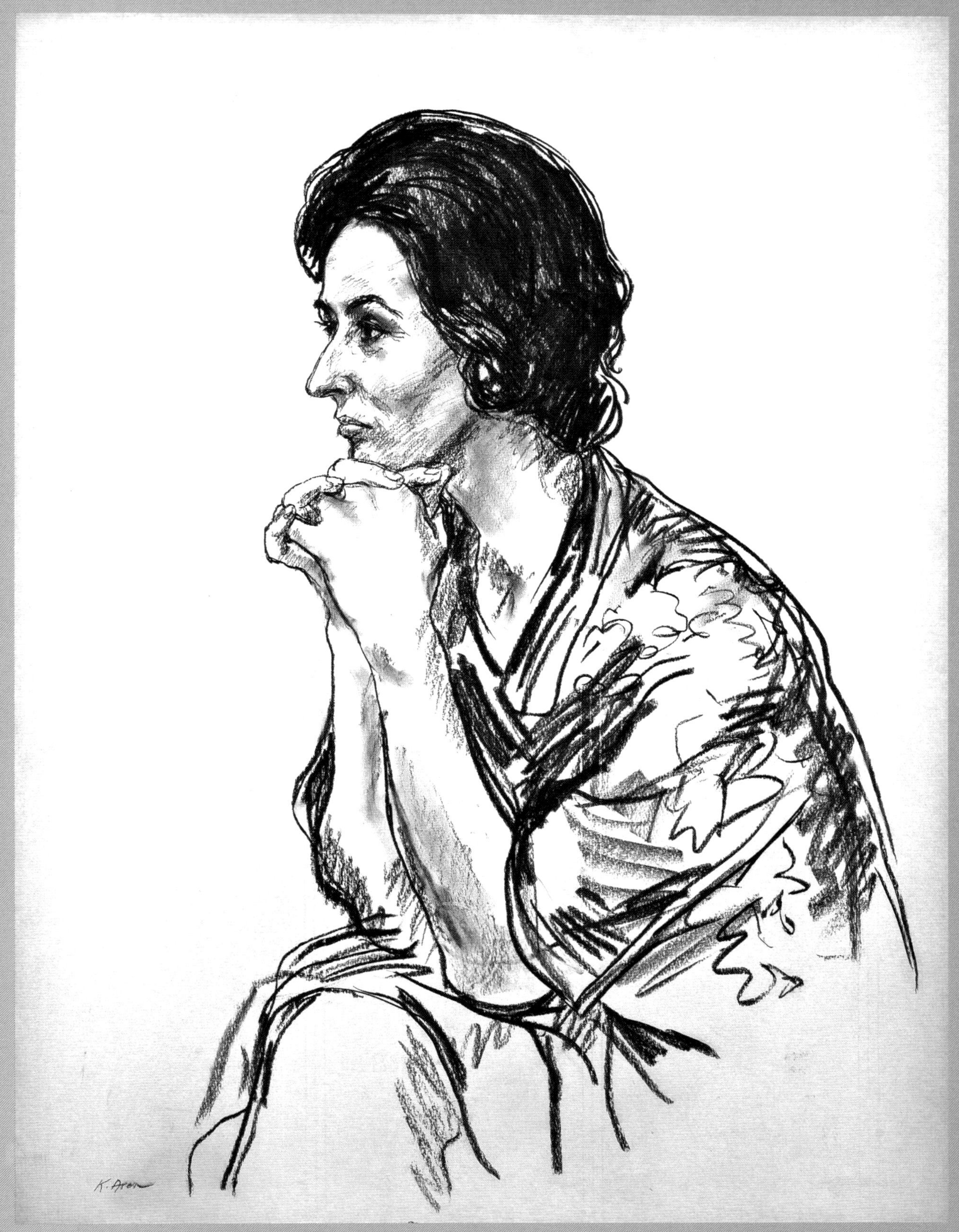

Artist Bettina Brendel (1970s), charcoal on paper, 40 × 30 in.

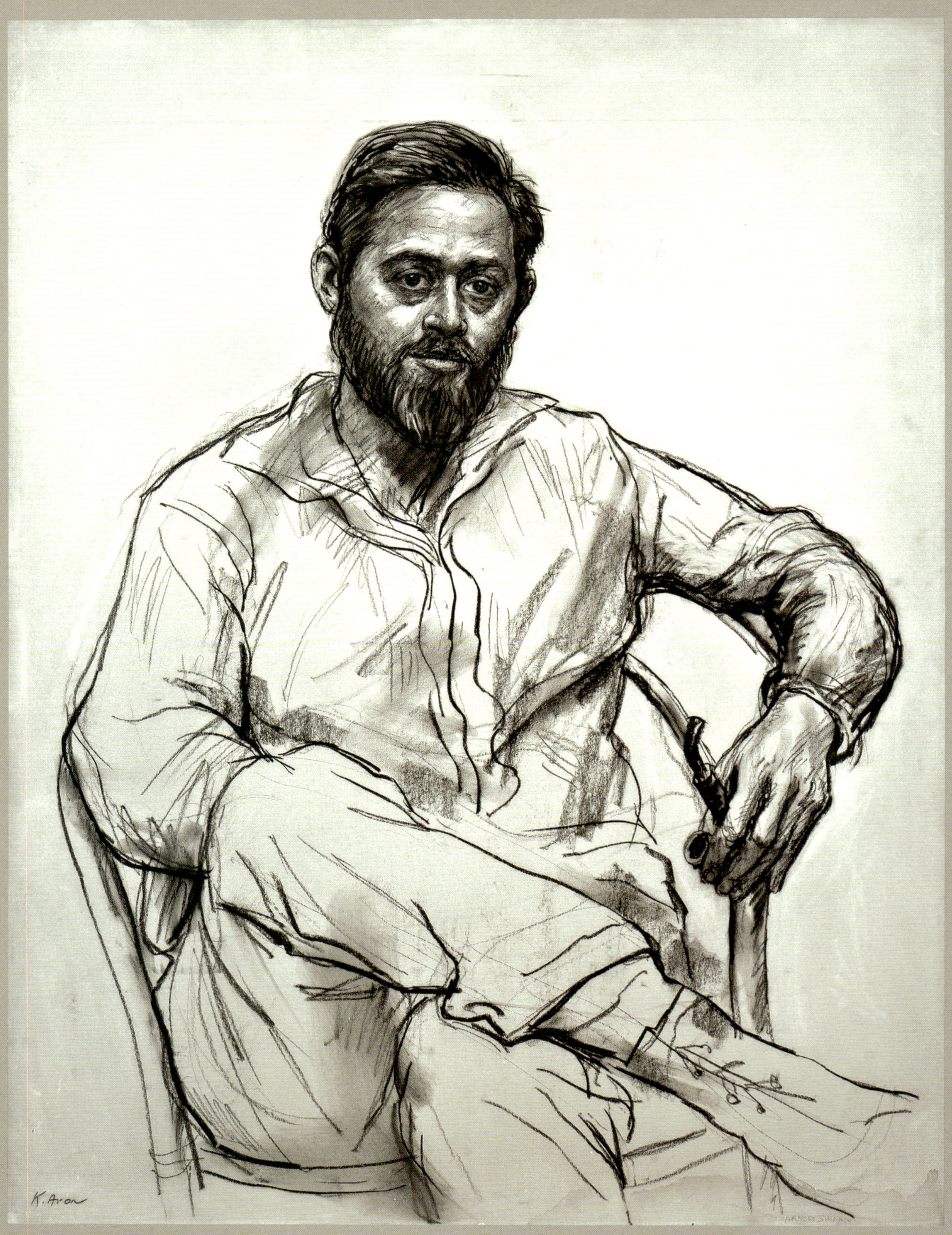

Artist Arnold Schifrin (1970s), charcoal on paper, 40 × 30 in.

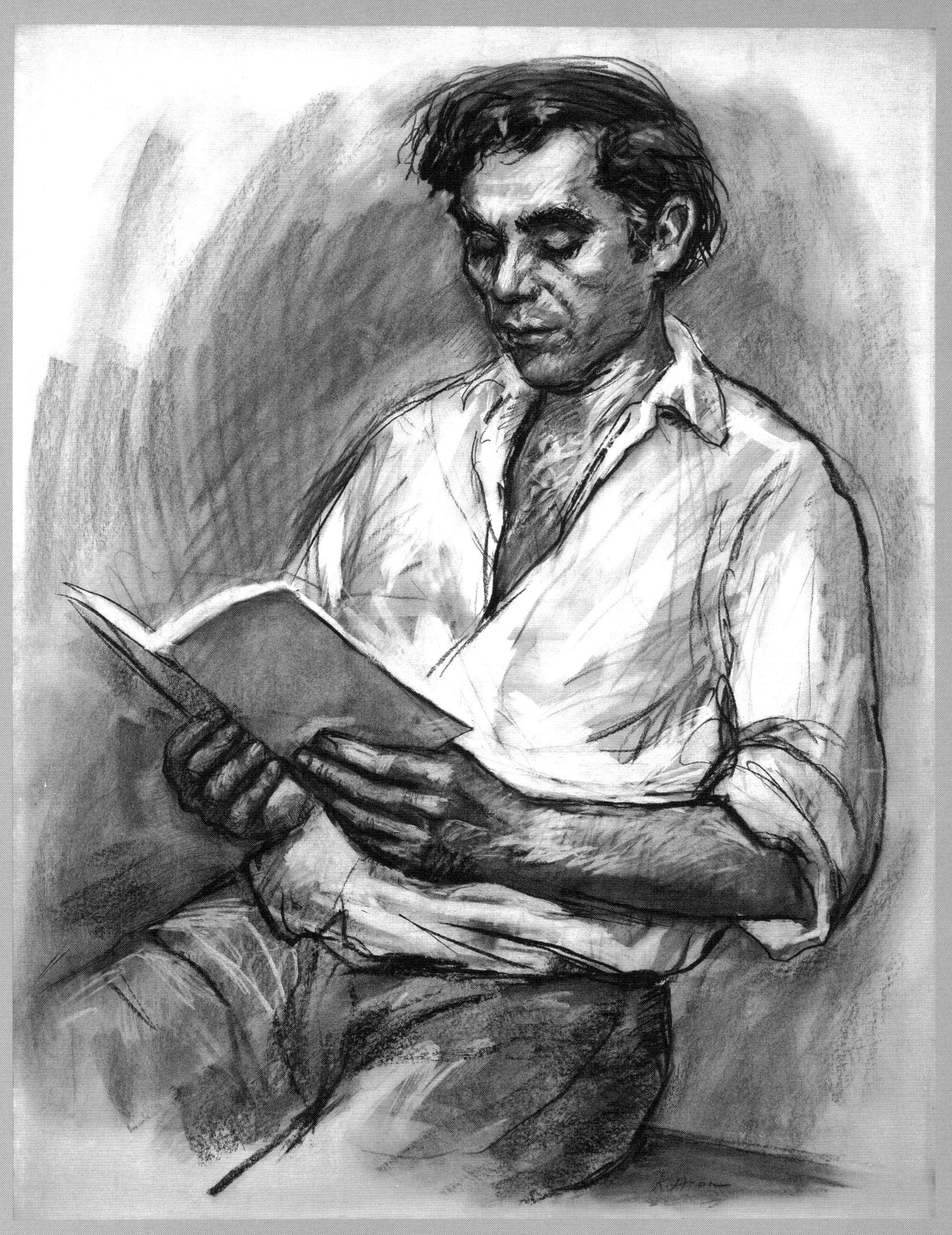

Artist-Photographer Mark Cheka (1970s), charcoal on paper, 40 × 30 in.

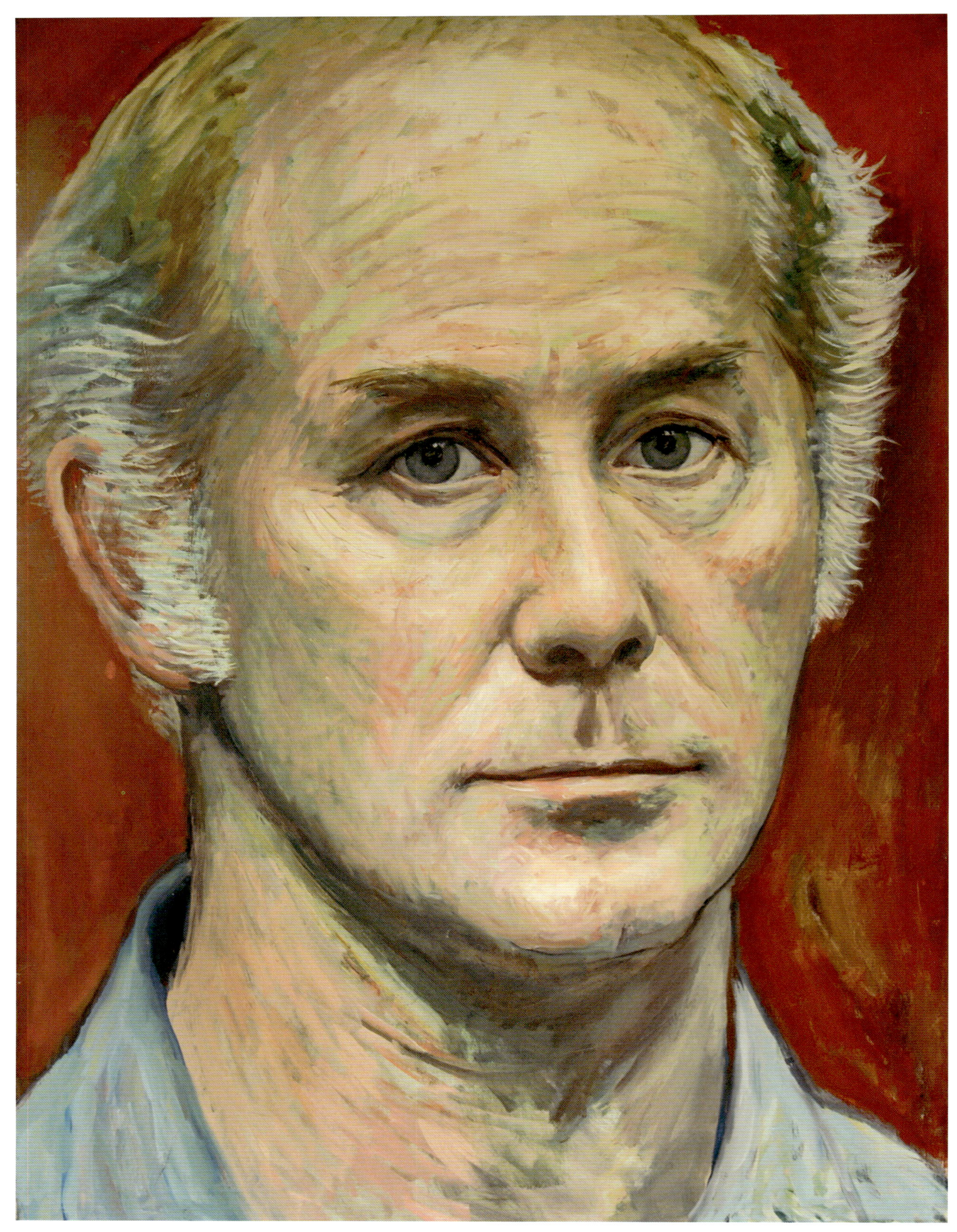

Self-Portrait (1967), oil on canvas, 48 × 36 in.

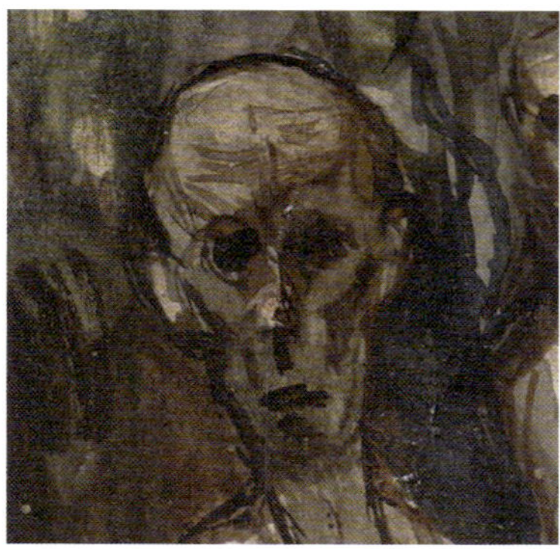

Kalman Marching in the Camp (detail);
full image on page 50.

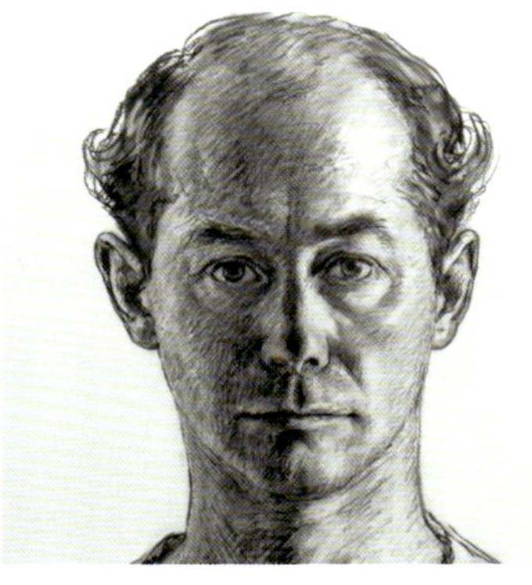

Self-Portrait (detail);
full image on page 89.

Aron's art is equally revealing of himself. In 1967 at age forty-three he painted a self-portrait in oils. He had changed since his self-portrayal in *Marching in the Camps* in 1951 and his *Self-Portrait* at age 30. Here he uses a rich palette and strong brush strokes. Color has returned to his skin. It is not the smooth skin of an innocent baby; it has the robust markings of a man who has lived. There is power in his face, an awareness of all he has seen, an intelligence. The firm set of his chin and lips underscore a determination, much like that seen in the portrait of the *Child with Black Eyes*. His eyes reveal an intense watchfulness as well as some sadness, confusion, a slight wariness or holding back. Most striking of all, there is no hatred in his eyes.

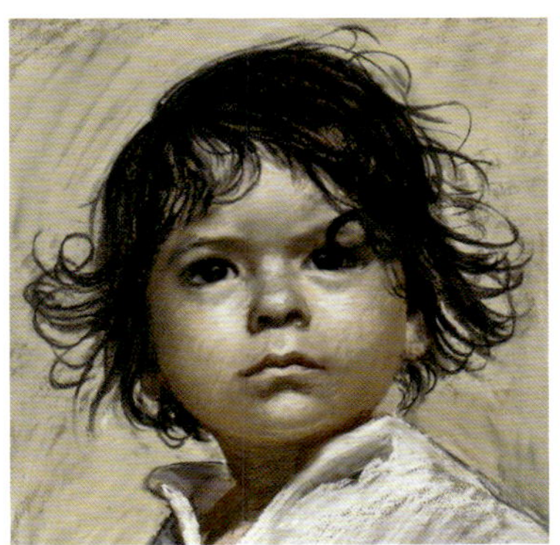

Child with Black Eyes (detail);
full image on page 8.

Some patrons who knew his talent returned with further commissions. I asked Aron to draw my daughter Elizabeth in 1987. My sister Elena commissioned pastels of her children, Eric and Laura, in the 1970s.

In studying people as he paints, I believe that Aron is looking for the light in them, while also seeing the dark and the shadows. A human being is an ever-changing kaleidoscope, a configuration of crystals and colors that reflect our joys and sorrows, unconscious fears, traumas, vows and beliefs. In Aron's portraits—especially in this self-portrait—he captures the unique configuration of humanity that sits before him in that moment of time.

He could not do this with the same power or perception had he not lived through the Holocaust. Having witnessed the killing, he knows man's capacity for evil and courage. With the eye of a witness, he penetrates the mystery of his subjects and portrays it on canvas. Just as the Dalai Lama transcends the polarity of good and evil without judging Mao Tse-tung, so Aron paints what he sees in a person without judgment. He does this with grace and reverence. In the process he makes sacred the complex human being that sits before him.

His portraits are alive. Try an experiment. Sit quietly with one of them. Look into the person's eyes, and ask: How does the person feel? What is important to him or her? If you are still, you will sense volumes. You will connect with some aspect of the person's personality Aron has captured.

Portrait of Elizabeth (1987), pastel on paper, 23 × 19¼ in.

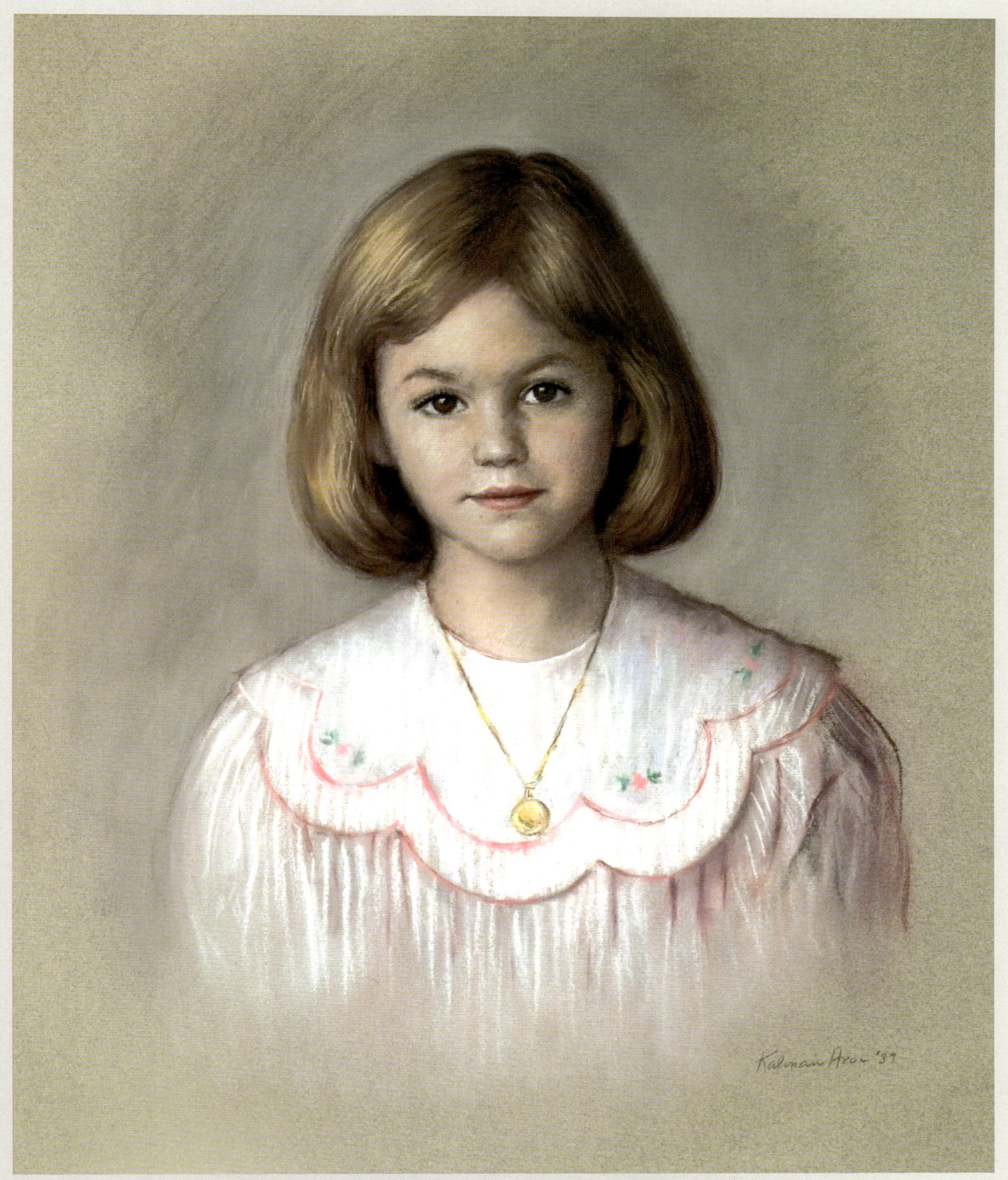
Kalman Aron

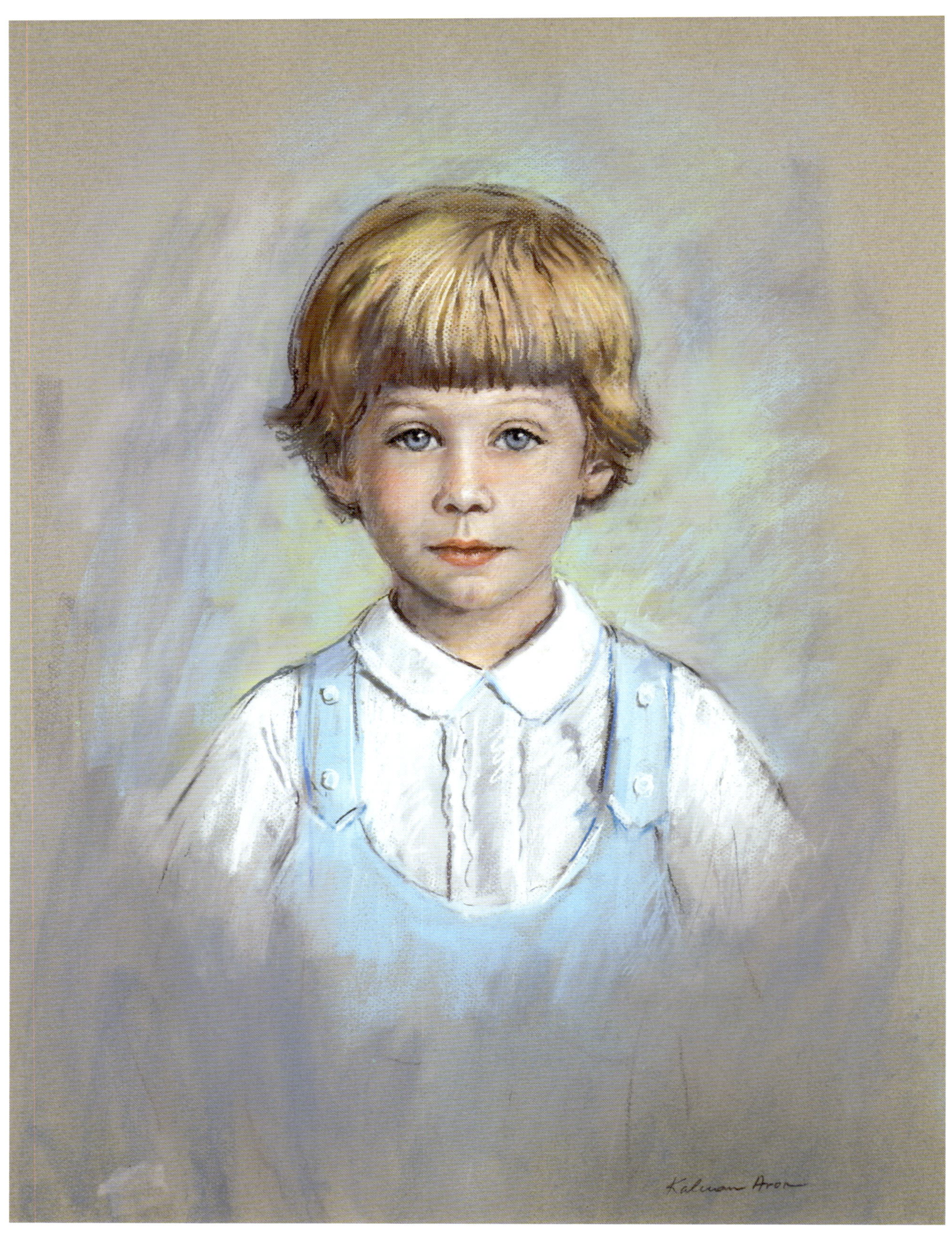

Portrait of Eric (1977), pastel on paper, 25¾ × 20 in.

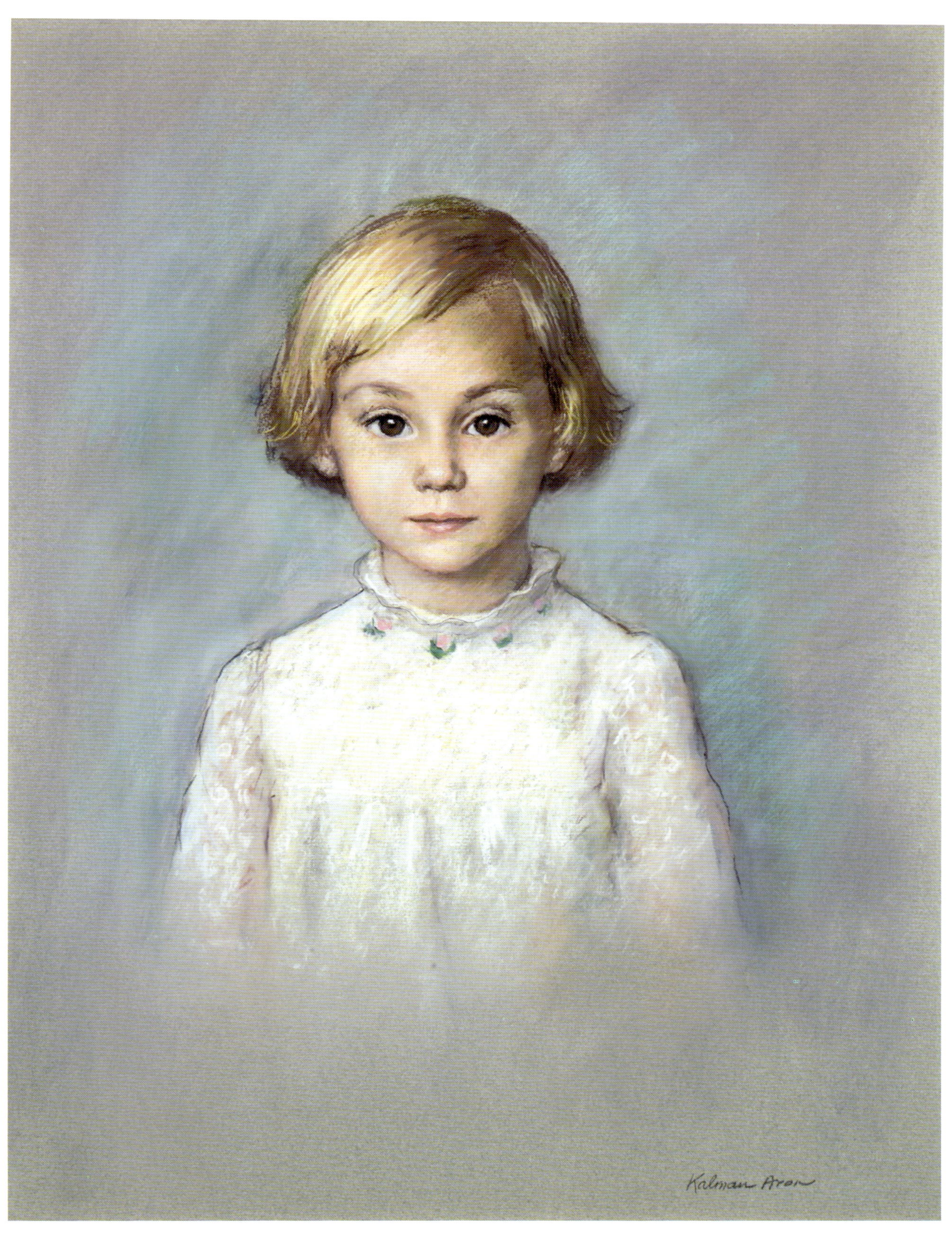

Portrait of Laura (1977), pastel on paper, 25¾ × 20 in.

An Affinity for Women

Throughout his career Aron has painted individual women in all stages of life. Exploring facets of the feminine connects him to his own sensuality, expands his emotional realm and invites an opening of the heart.

A recurring theme has been the mother and child. In his eight-foot masterpiece, *Mother and Child,* Aron drew a mother in the ghetto desperately holding on to her child. In the large oil, *Mother Nursing Her Child,* he painted the bond in a different way. Here he renders a tender image of the mother caressing her baby at her breast. On the left side he uses a rich turquoise-green background, creating negative space that moves and changes in intensity. It joins with the light shed on the mother and child, illuminating the love between them. Aron captures the intimacy experienced by a mother nursing her baby; her contentment is evident in her face as the baby rests gently in this nurturing cocoon. What wonder, a new life, the mother thinking: *You are a miracle, and you are mine.* It is a testament to the human spirit that Aron can still feel such tenderness after the horror he experienced.

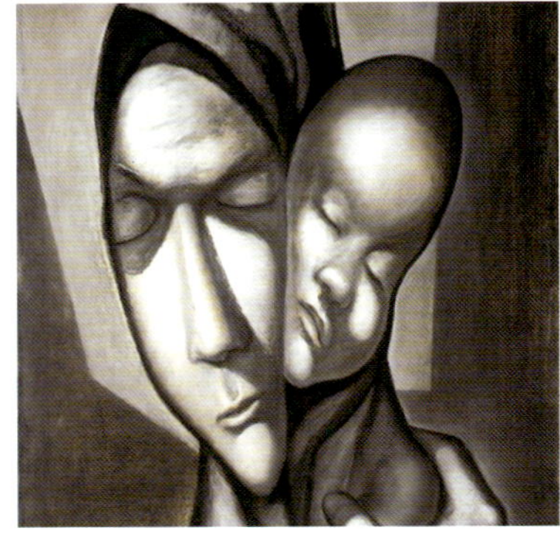

Mother and Child (detail): full image on page 85.

In *Woman Seated* Aron captures the beauty and sensuality of the female body. He used a small drawing of a girlfriend who modeled for him as the inspiration for this larger drawing. Aron depicts her sitting comfortably on a chair, with a cloth draped loosely around her naked body. Behind her are suggestions of his paintings against the wall in his studio. With just a few lines he captures the grace and curves of this woman's body. The paintings behind her form a plane that frames her face, and the detail on the chair completes the composition.

Aron also portrays young women in their formative years, as in the pastel *The Ballerina,* one of his favorites, drawn in the 1950s. This lithesome young girl has a faraway look that is mysterious to men at any age. The form of her body is light and delightful. There is a touch of sadness in her face. One cannot guess her thoughts. She is unreachable as she looks into the distance.

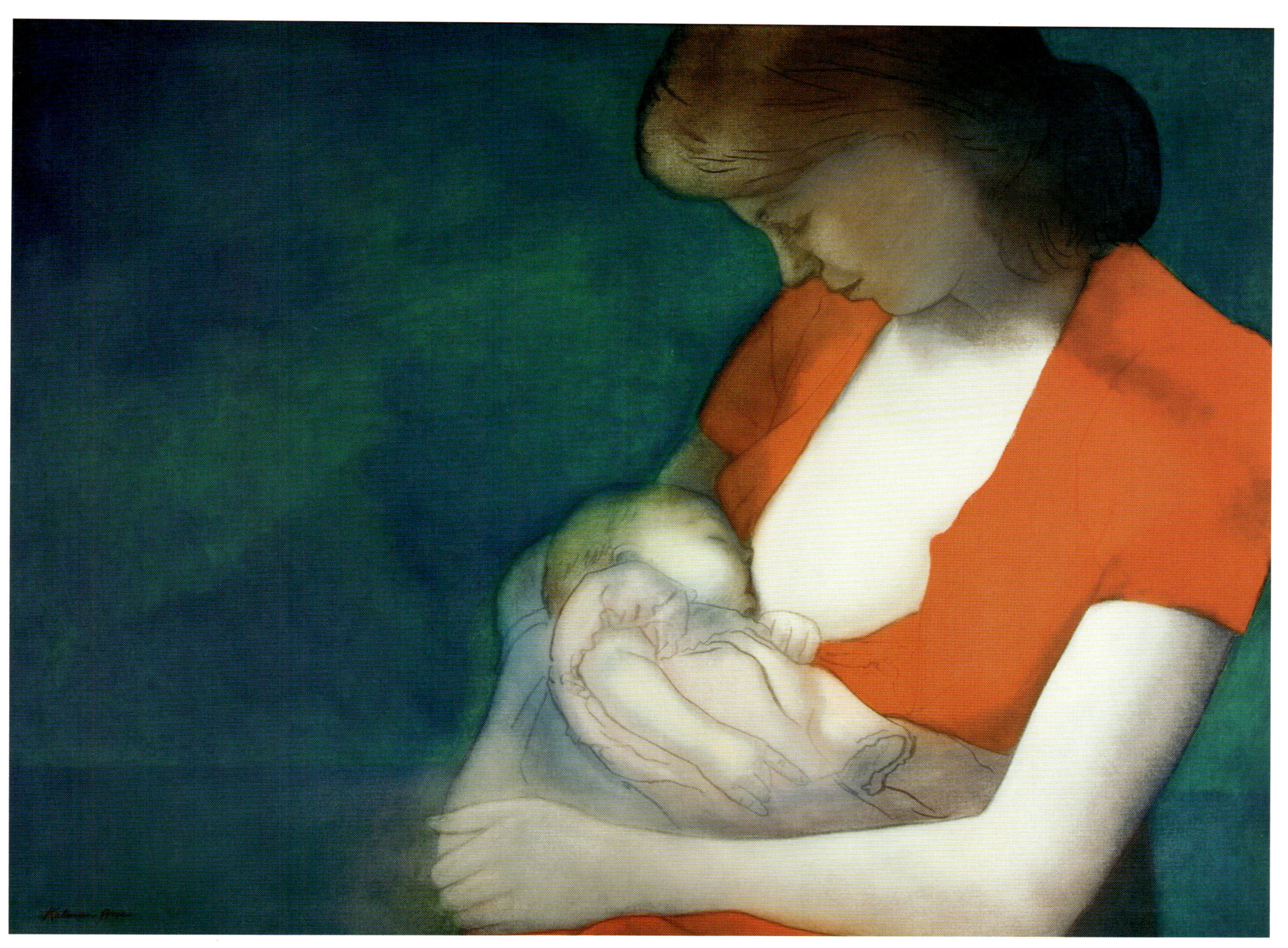

Mother Nursing Her Child (1980s), oil on canvas, 36 × 48 in.

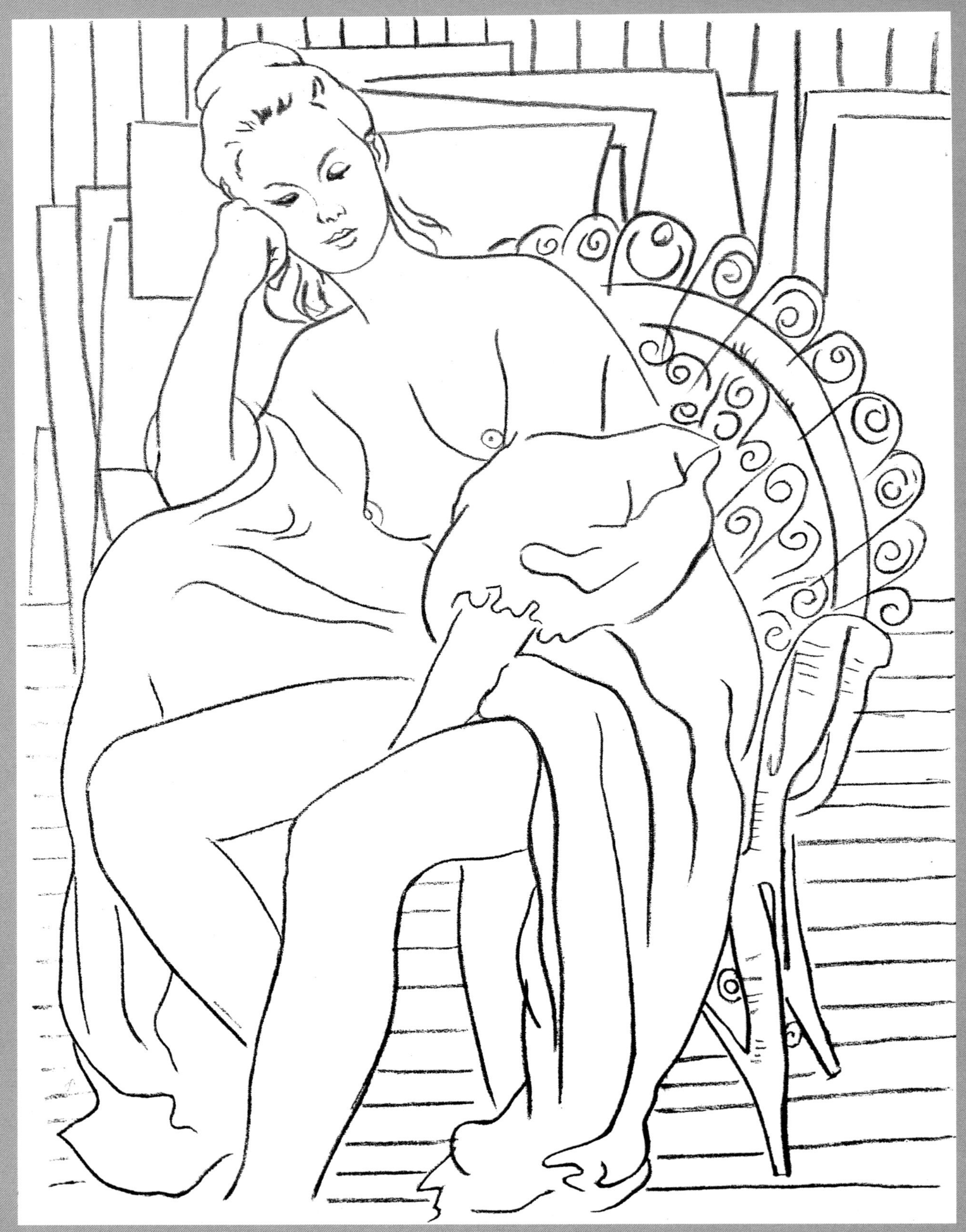

Woman Seated (1959), charcoal pencil, 40 × 30 in.

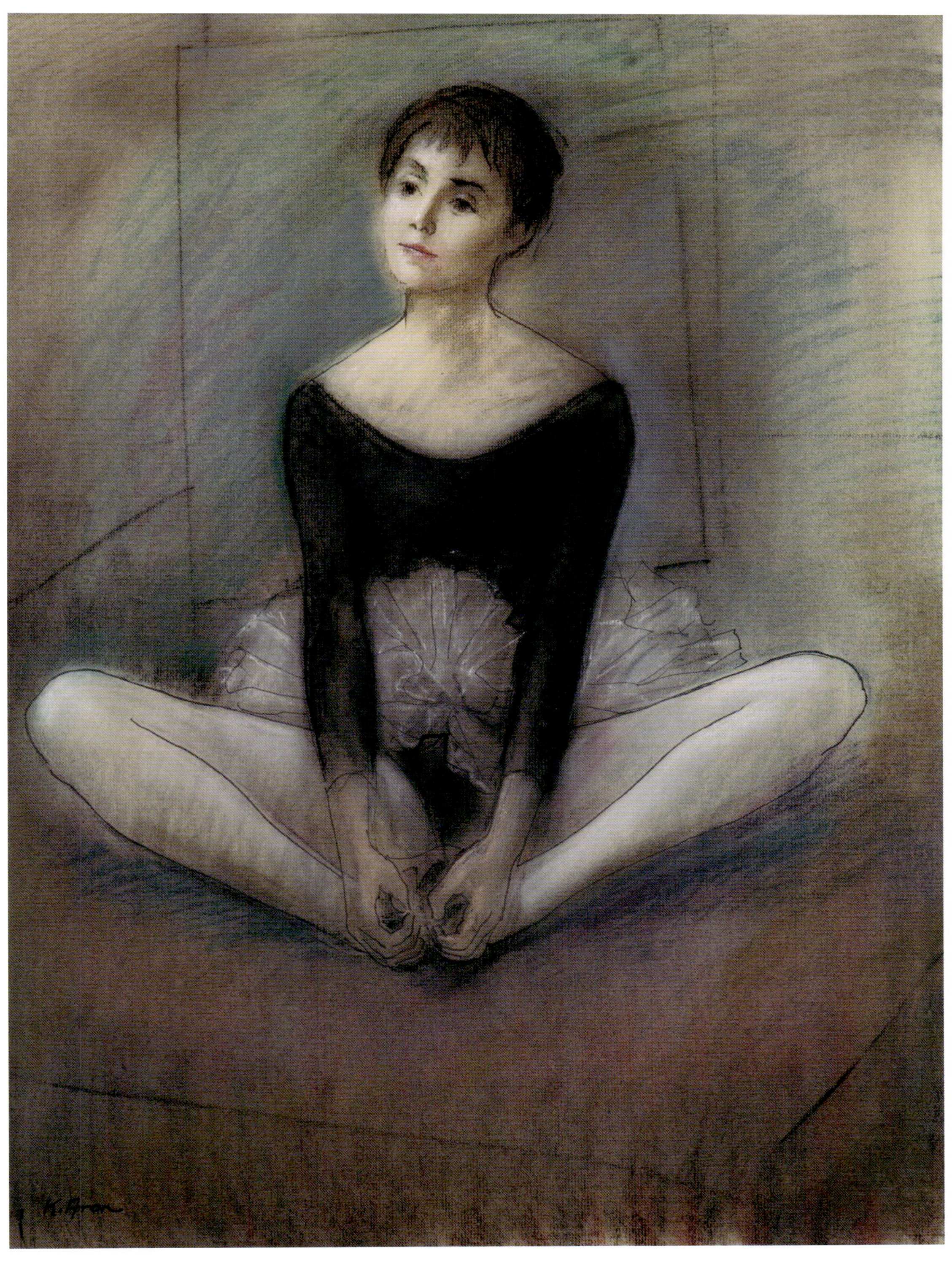

Ballerina (1957), pastel on paper, 23 × 17½ in.

Aron explores the femme fatale mystique in the line drawing and the stunning oil of *The Lady in Waiting*. He explains:

I did a simple drawing, maybe a five-minute drawing. I remember the girl. I used to draw her a lot. She was interesting. Some time in the eighties I went through old drawings and chose this one. I wanted to do something with it, make a painting out of it. I tried to capture some mood. I changed maybe a little bit of the face, the mouth, just to get a certain mood in it.

See, there is no white paint in this painting. That is why it is so translucent, transparent. This is all rubbed out with rags. In the skin I use very thin layers of paint, but no white because white makes it opaque. I don't want it opaque. I want it transparent.

Here he paints a striking, bare-chested woman, gazing into her own world. He uses three moving masses of color—blue, black and chartreuse—to frame her head and torso. He captures the alluring and surprising nature of women in this temptress. She is beautiful; she is seductive.

In the oil *Study of a Woman,* Aron paints a woman standing alone. Drawn with strong colors and full brush strokes, this woman is physically fit and mentally strong. Her stance suggests: I'm ready for whatever life throws my way. While she appears tough and strong, she also looks like she wants to protect herself. This ready stance belies a pool of sadness in her eyes.

Aron has always appreciated a woman's intellect. This is reflected in oils he painted in the 1960s of women reading, such as *Girl Reading a Small Book* and *Suzanne Reading*. Aron also portrays older women with great respect and sensitivity. In *Woman Looking Out the Window*, his subject is standing inside her country house gazing out. Aron painted this large oil sometime in the 1980s from a sketch he had done decades earlier in a French village. Given her age, this woman probably lived through two world wars. A child during World War I, she surely lost men in her family. Then, twenty years later, she lived through another war, perhaps losing a son this time. She holds on to the window ledge with her long fingers. Her background—the wars—is black. But life abounds in her rosy cheeks and the new growth in plants resting before her. The whitewash of the exterior walls and touch of yellow trim balance the black panel that frames her head.

Such is life. We always live with a balance of light and dark. We are the integrators. No matter what we see and experience, we carry our own flame, our spark of life, and we choose to endure. We live alongside our flowers and plants. We grow, no matter the challenges, droughts and rains that come. She is still watching. Her home provides her safety, and the living plants are her companions.

In Aron's paintings women are living, breathing human beings with a full range of feelings. His art portrays their beauty, power, tenderness, allure and mystery. He captures on canvas the mysterious dance called "the feminine."

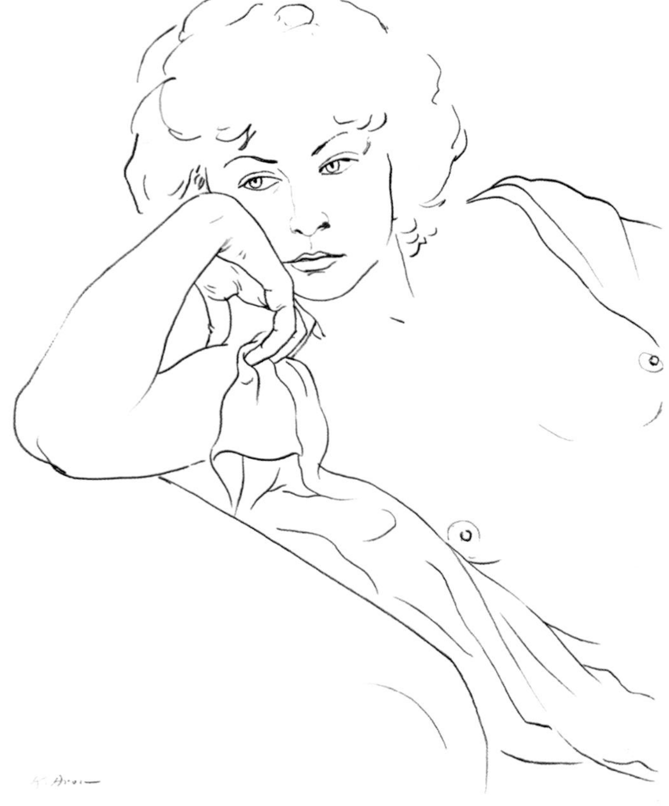

Line Drawing of the Lady (1970s), line drawing on paper, 24 × 18 in.

The Lady in Waiting (1980s), oil on canvas, 48 × 36 in.

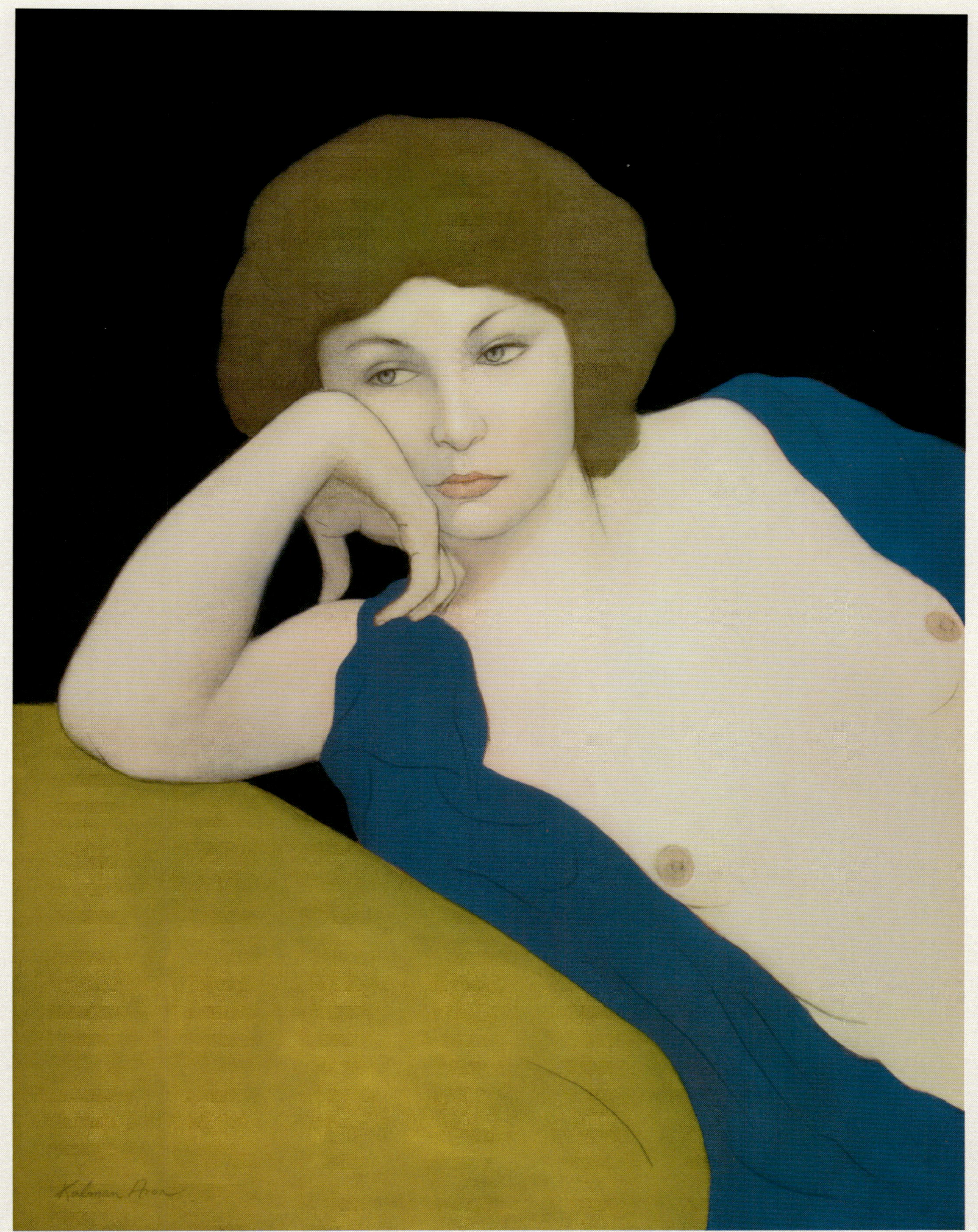
Kalman Aron

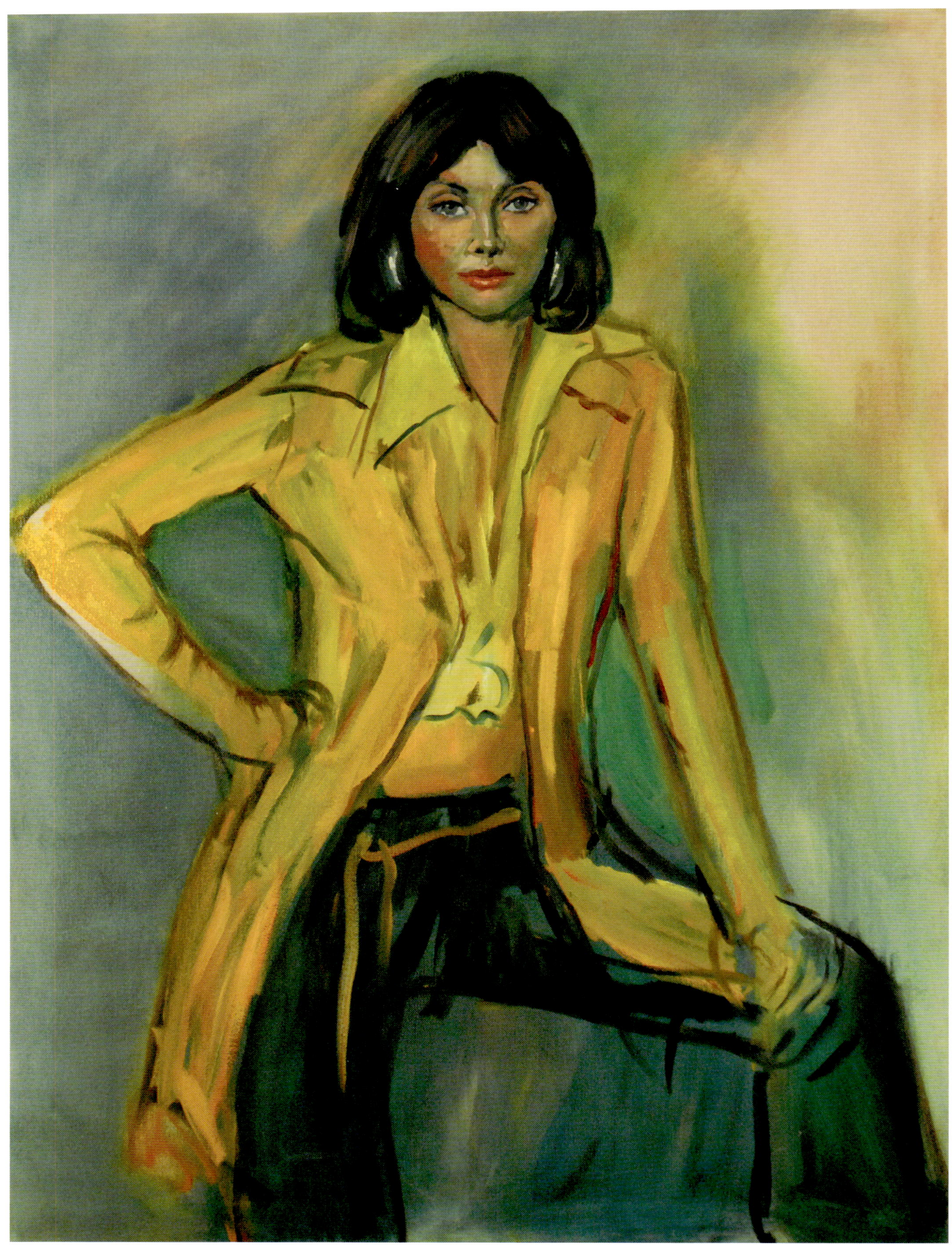

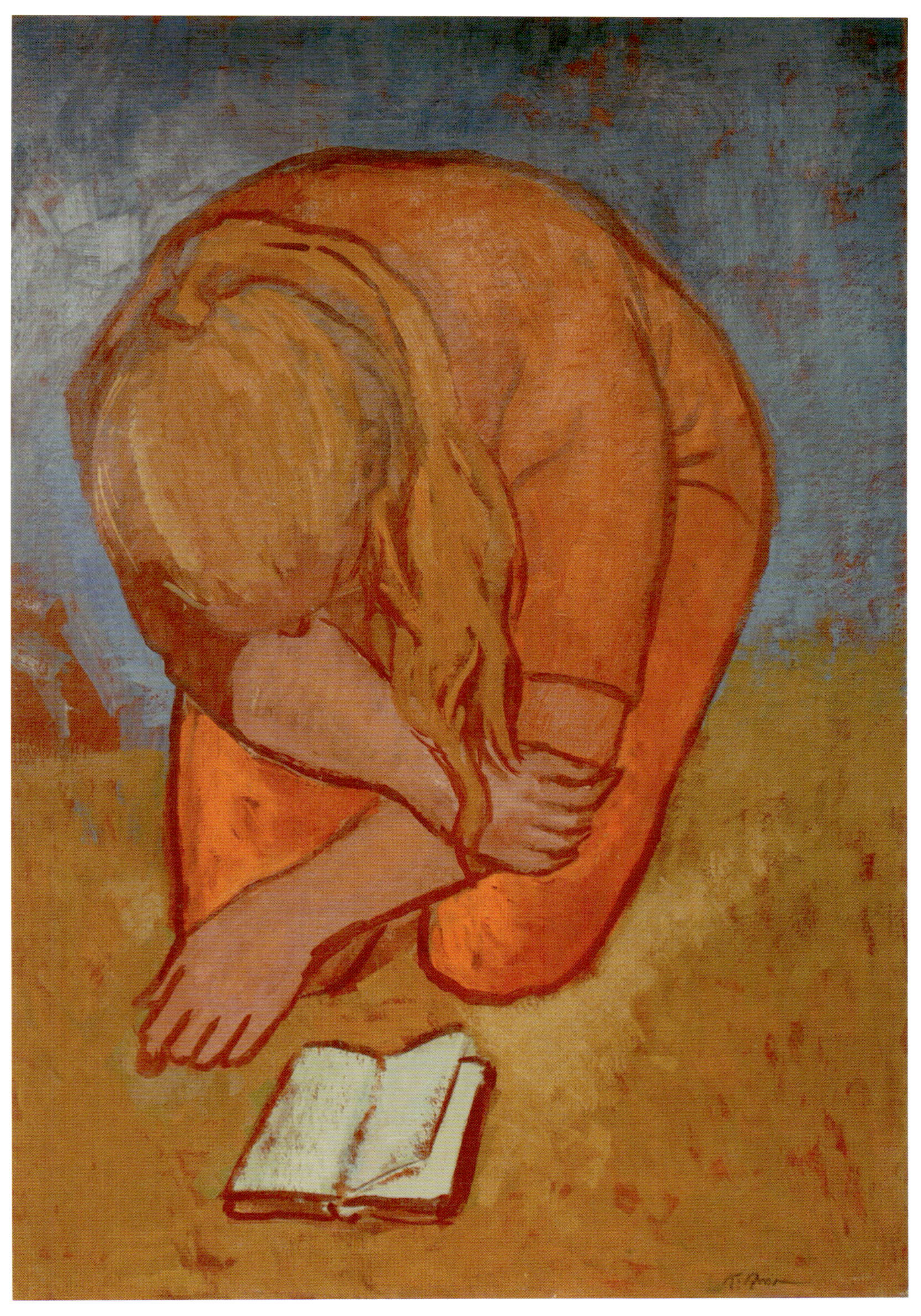

Girl Reading a Small Book (1960s), oil on board, 40 × 26 in.

Study of a Woman (1975), oil on canvas, 48 × 36 in.

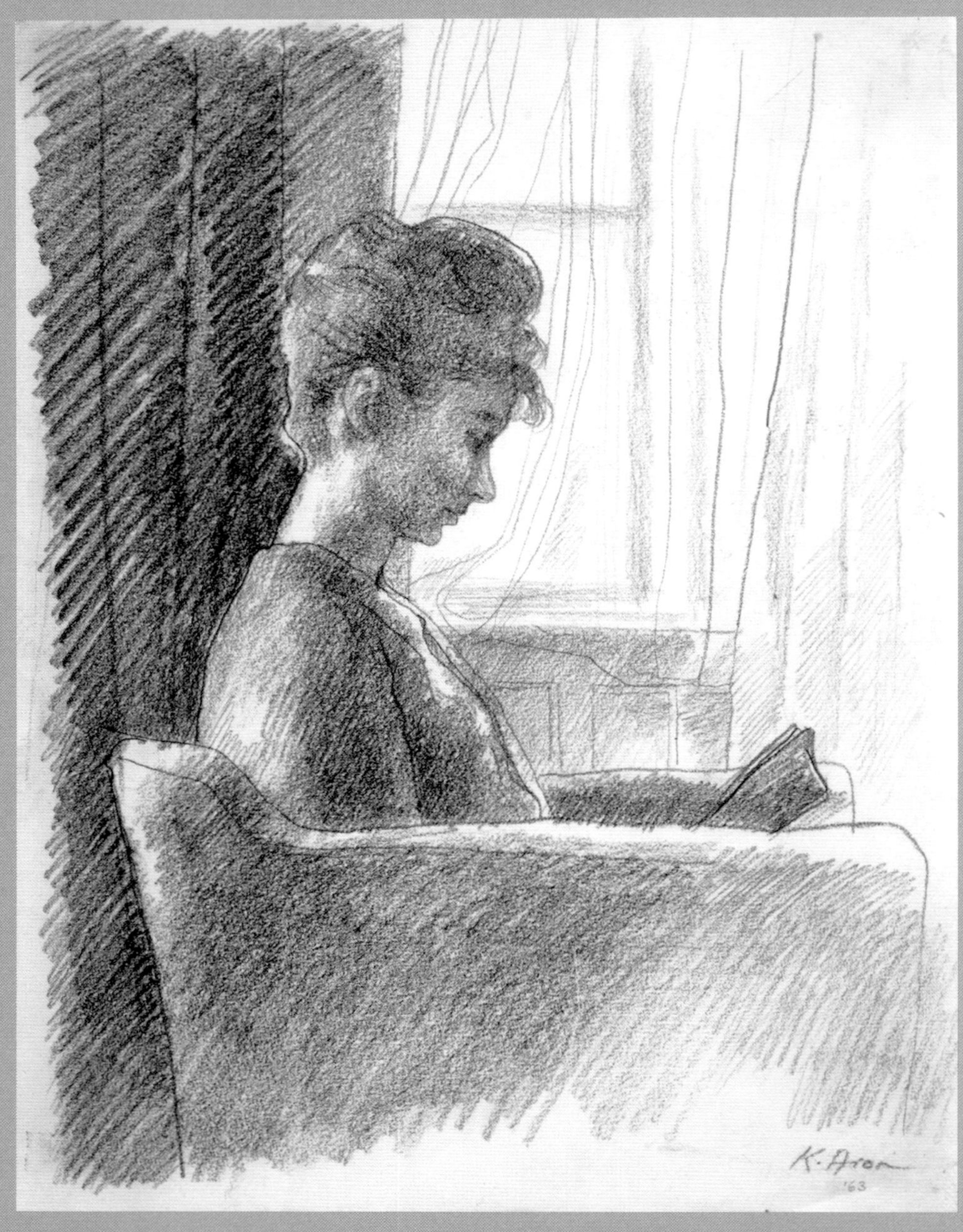

Suzanne Reading (1963), charcoal pencil, 14 × 10½ in.

Woman Looking Out the Window (1970s),
oil on projection screen, 54 × 34 in.

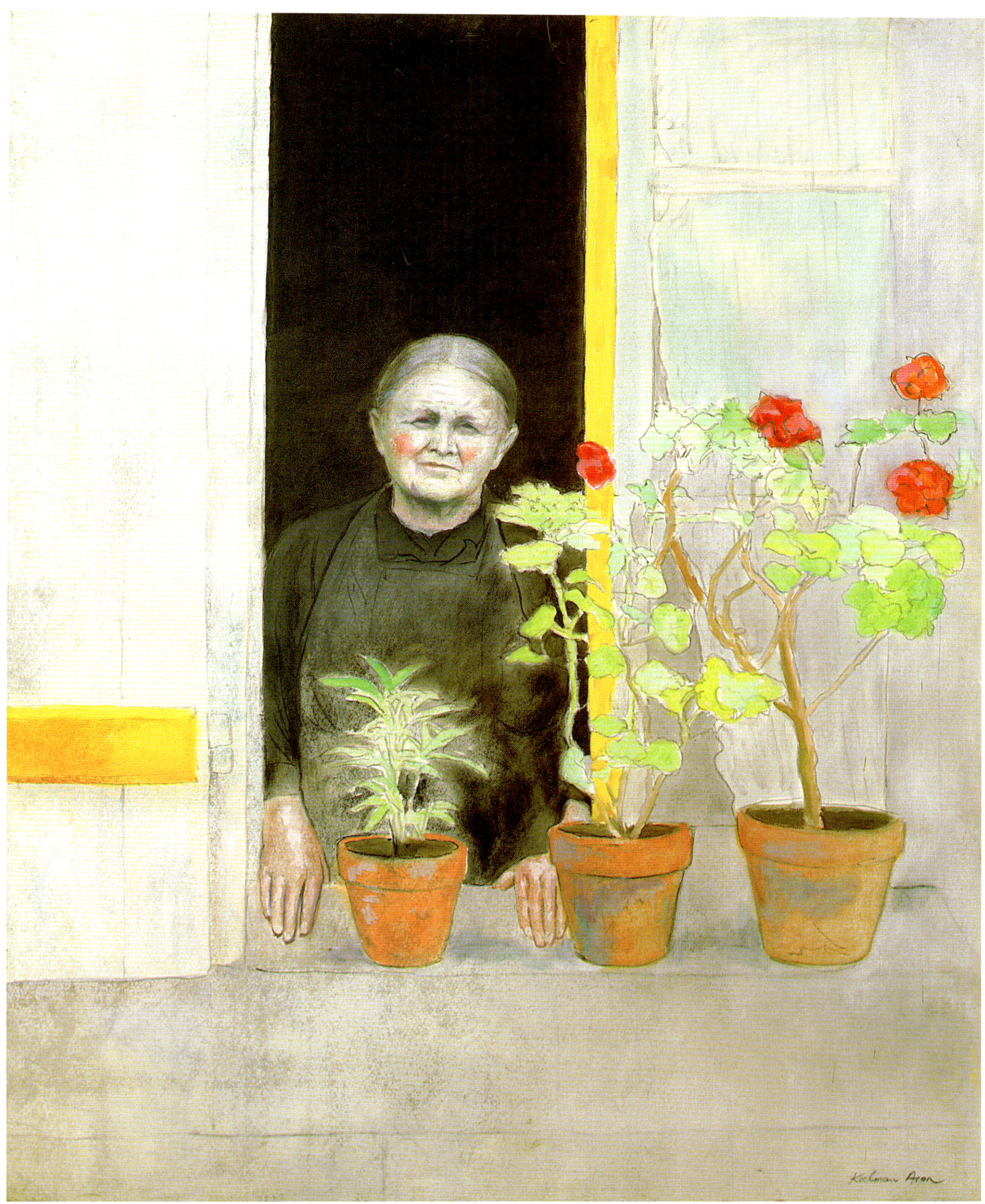
Kalman Aron

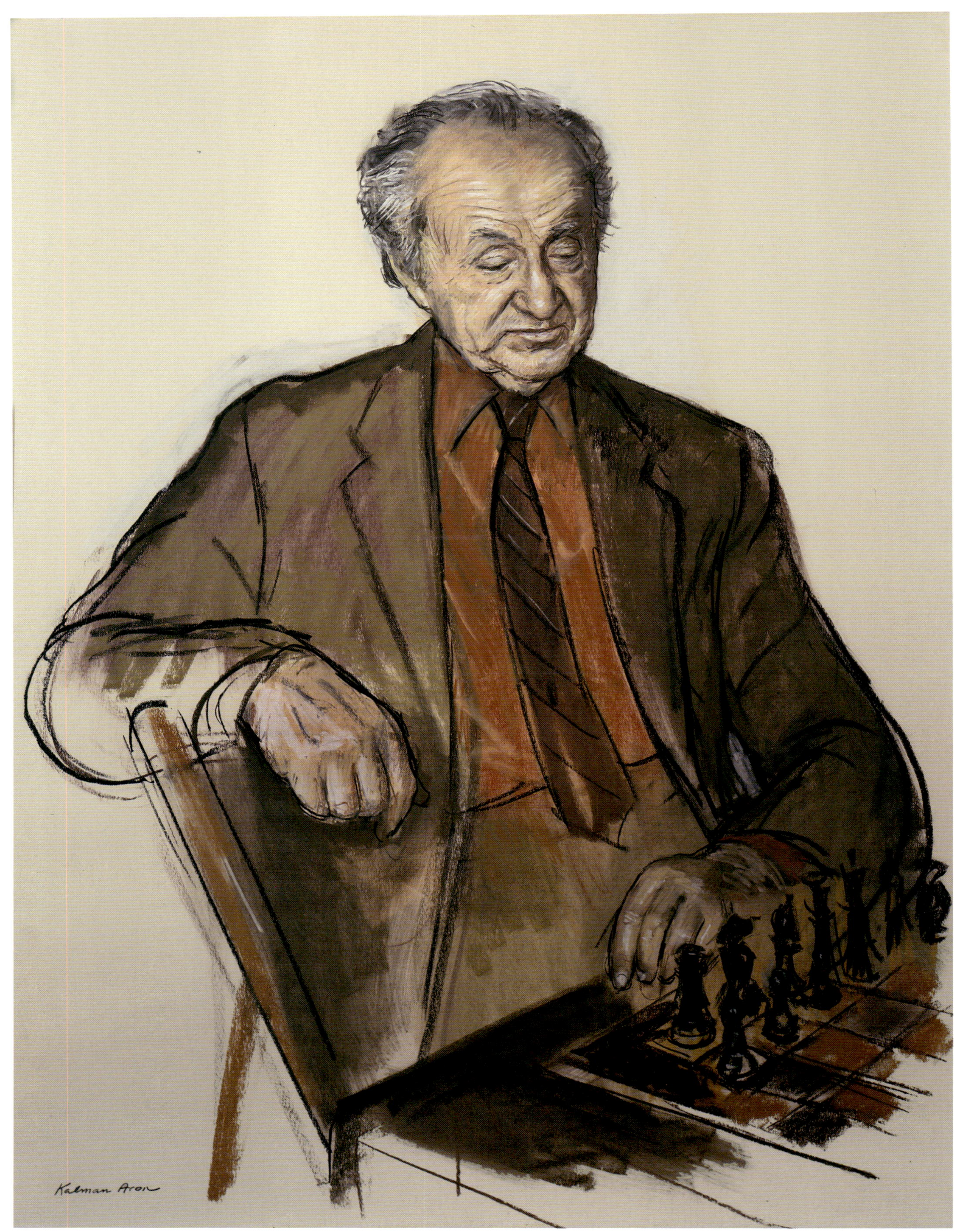
Kalman Aron

The Chess Player (1970s), pastel on paper, 46 × 34½ in.

Players of Games

A second recurring theme in Aron's art involves men gathered around tables outdoors, playing checkers, chess and cards. He began painting these in the 1950s and continued throughout the years.

Like painting, chess has been a constant in Aron's life. His father and uncle played. He started sketching men playing chess at a Santa Monica beach when he came to America. A lawyer began coaching him and brought him into a private chess club. He played the California state chess champion four times.

In some ways chess is a metaphor for his life. Players move objects on a board: kings, pawns. Why? To win. The objective is clear. One may sacrifice a piece, but in the end the winner stands alone. His purpose is to survive.

In 1967 he met a professor at UCLA, Marvin Chester, with whom he played. Chester remembers the importance of play and art in Aron's life: "We were friends in 1967 for about a year. We did play chess a lot. What does a game mean? We casually while away our precious life's moments in one inconsequential activity or another. Playing is the most blessed of all ways to spend one's time, is it not? Aron's art has rescued and sustained his life. He is devoted to his talent. It even allowed him to 'play.' Not too many men's working lives allow them to casually take off a weekday afternoon to play chess. My working life permitted me that luxury, as did his."

Chess also connects Aron to his history in Europe. Life keeps reminding us of our past so we may integrate and remember it without bitterness, so we may complete the lesson for our soul. Through chess Aron met interesting people who had ties to his old world. In the 1970s at the local chess club, he met a Goethe scholar, educated in Vienna. They spent time together talking and playing. Aron drew him in *The Chess Player*. Playing with him reminded Aron of reading Goethe after the war when he was at art school in Vienna. In *Theory of Colors*, written in 1810, Goethe argued that light, shade and color are associated with emotions: "Every color produces a distinct impression on the mind and thus addresses at once the eye and feelings." He could have been describing Aron's art.

Goethe was a leading figure in the city of Weimar from 1775 to 1832. Germans look back on this period as their golden age of philosophy and art. Over a century later, up the hill from Weimar, the Nazis built the notorious Buchenwald concentration camp, where some 57,000 people died. What a juxtaposition of light and dark.

Playing chess with this Goethe scholar from Vienna permitted Aron to remember Buchenwald and the Fine Arts Academy in Vienna; it enabled him to play, to turn again. Like moving up a spiral, life turns, ever returning to "where it all began."

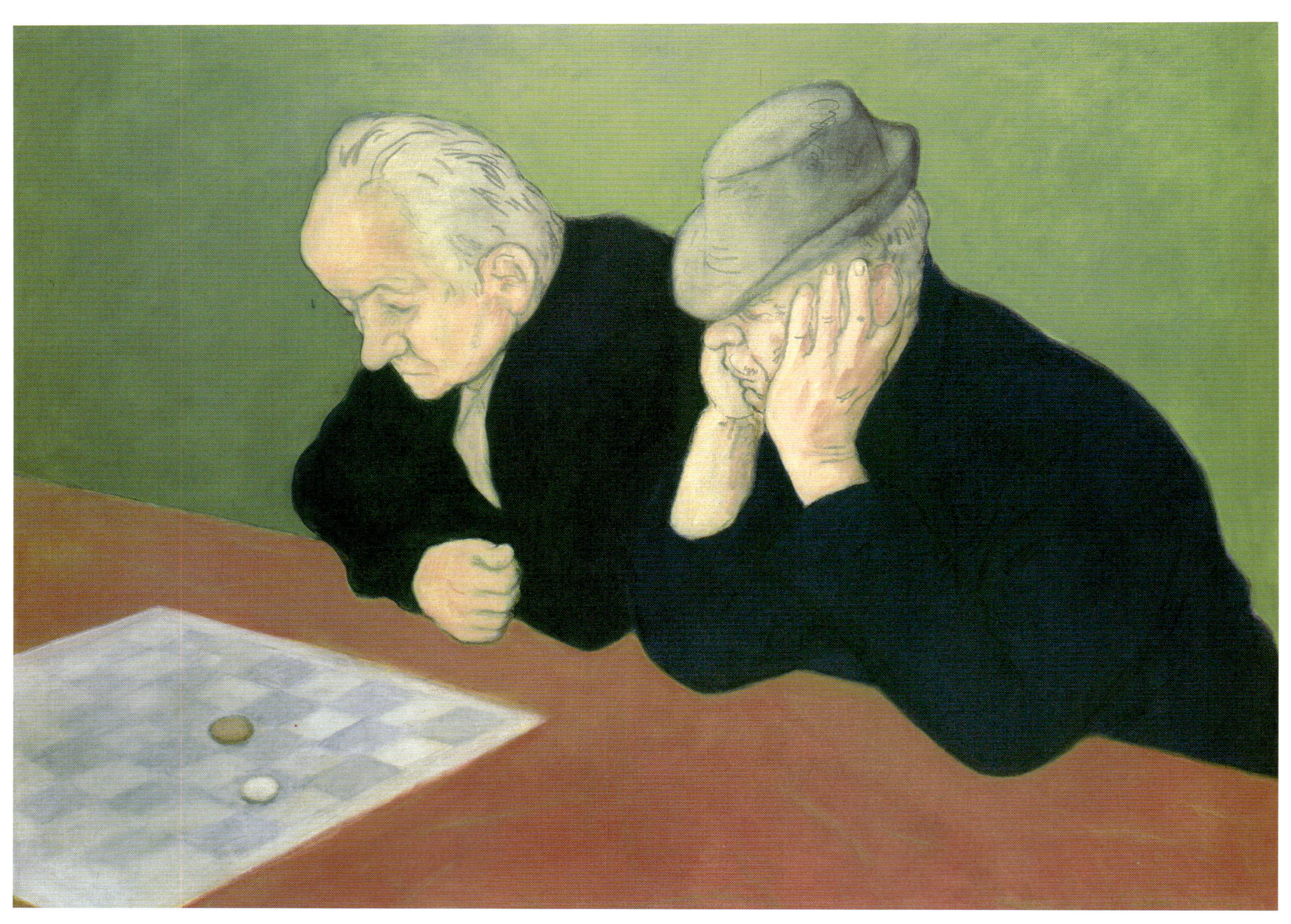

Checker Players I (late 1960s), oil on canvas, 36 × 48 in.

In *The Chess Player* Aron captures the thoughtful demeanor of his friend with salt-and-pepper hair. His character is reflected in the lines and shadows around his forehead, eyes, nose, chin and mouth. The use of browns and oranges suggests a substantial level of experience in living. He looks like a man who has thought about the game of life. What he has seen has neither lifted him to a state of joy nor thrust him into the depths of despair. The game is just beginning. Will he passionately jump in or hold back to protect himself?

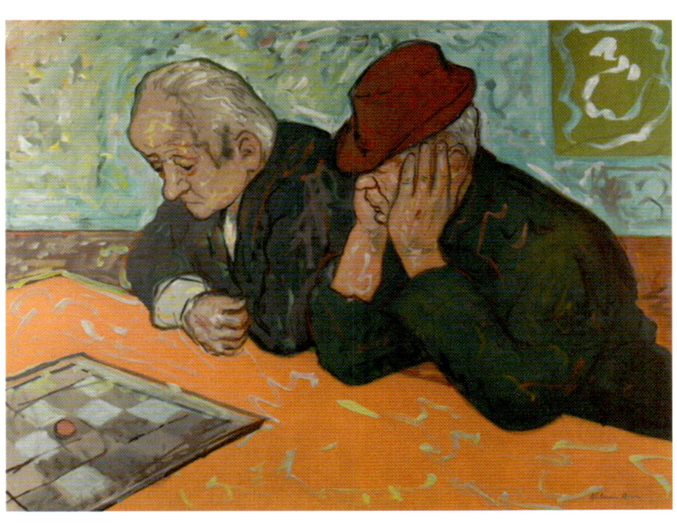

Checker Players II (late 1960s), oil on canvas, 48 × 60 in.

Aron also painted men playing checkers. In one pair of paintings from the late 1960s, two men rest their elbows on a table, concentrating on the board. *Checker Players I* distills the men's world to its essentials. The game lies simply before them. Thinning his paint and using three major bodies of color—the orange-red, lime green and dark jackets, Aron creates a timeless quality on this three- by four-foot canvas. *Checker Players II* covers a larger, four- by five-foot canvas. Aron improvises, changing his palette, applying rich, thick strokes on the jackets, table and background. This painting conveys an Old World feeling.

Also in the late 1960s Aron painted the oil *The Chess Players*, depicting a group of men absorbed in a game, some sitting across from each other in pairs, some standing. A decade later he painted *Observation in Echo Park*, a more ephemeral painting, which uses a softer palette to capture the backs of men with heads bowed, watching others play chess on a park bench. These two paintings recall a time in America when immigrants gathered as their forefathers had in Europe.

In the 1980s Aron painted *A Gathering of Chess Players* in an entirely different style. Compared with the two earlier oils, this has a mystical feel. Aron has moved from the concrete to the ethereal. In what dimension are these men and one woman gathered? Are they ghosts, at a universal gathering that could occur anyplace on this earth? Aron's art is multidimensional, suggesting that there are many planes on which we live.

As these paintings suggest, Aron is both an observer and player in the game of life. He enjoys the camaraderie of men, and he likes playing chess because it is mentally and strategically challenging. He must plan multiple moves while intuiting those of his opponent. He concentrates, observes and anticipates, much as he did to survive in the camps. Only in this game the stakes are not life or death. He returns to play once again in the game of life, integrating his past experiences and strengthening the foundation of his life.

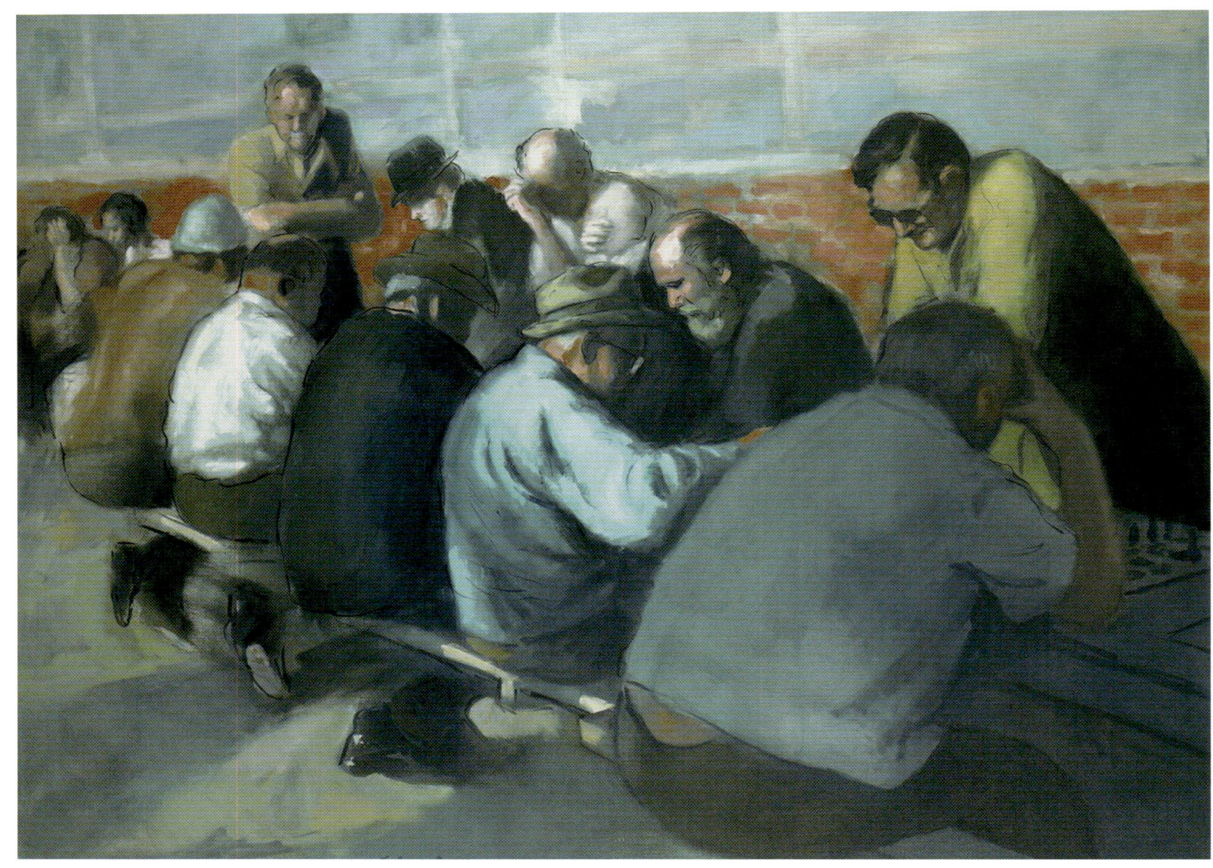

The Chess Players (late 1960s), oil on canvas, 36 × 48 in.

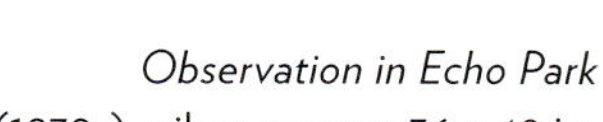

Observation in Echo Park (1970s), oil on canvas, 36 × 48 in.

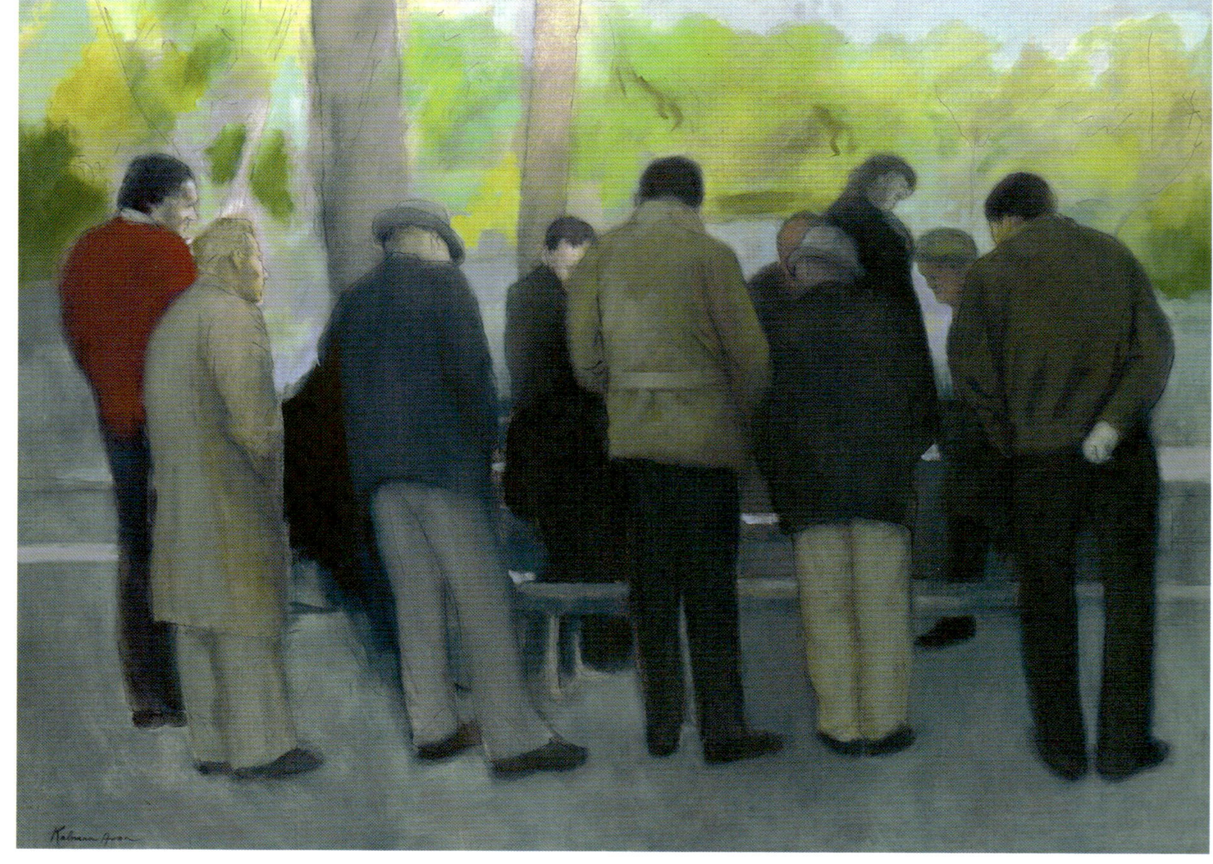

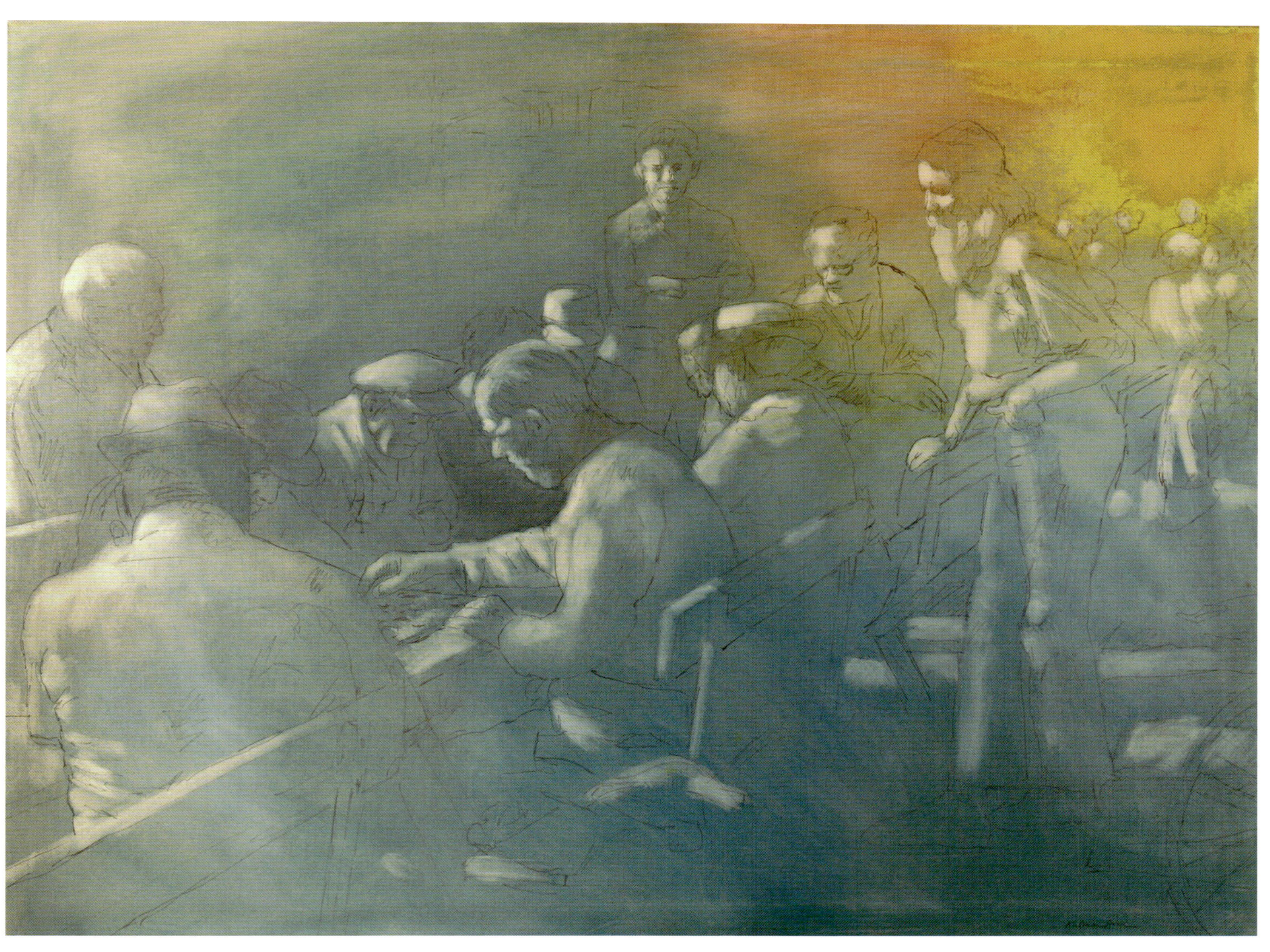

A Gathering of Chess Players (1980s), oil on canvas, 36 × 48 in.

Psychological Realism

Throughout his career Aron has painted in a wide variety of styles. In the late 1960s and early 1970s he developed a particularly distinctive approach, which a European admirer called "psychological realism." This term describes both the technique he uses in painting and the way he portrays character and creates moods. It combines his artistic talent with his intuitive understanding of human nature. The result is a body of art that is powerful, interesting and at times mystical.

Aron first showed work in this style in Sweden in the 1970s. The gallery exhibit of twenty-nine paintings was in Uppsala, outside of Stockholm. It is the home of Sweden's oldest university, and the president of Uppsala University attended the exhibit. Struck by the power of the drawings, he called the style "psychological realism" and promptly bought three or four large canvases. The Swedish press picked up this name in reviews.

Aron explains: "I started doing these in the sixties. In Sweden they were very interested in this kind of thing. I didn't show them in Los Angeles." He continued to paint in this style through the nineties.

Visiting Stockholm in 2004 on my way to Riga, I met Johan Wallin, who worked in the gallery during the show in the 1970s. Currently an art gallery owner, he remembered Aron well. He showed me a painting he purchased from the exhibit and a portrait Aron did of him. Like others who have met Aron and spend time with his work, he still finds pleasure in their company.

Wallin did not know that Aron was a Holocaust survivor. When I told him, he said that it explains the intensity and power of his art: artists talk with their brushes, not words. Their life experience, struggles and victories are reflected in their art. I asked him how Aron's work related to art in the principal European traditions. He responded, "I don't think he is part of a European tradition. I don't think he is part of any tradition. He's very much an original personality. . . . What I liked most of all was his fantastic capacity of painting human beings . . . a fantastic drawer." Wallin called him a master.

In a small oil on paper, *Two Men Seated*, Aron explores the relationship of two men, sitting across from each other. They do not appear to be talking. The man on the left is gazing away, perhaps remembering a time past as his friend listens in silence. With few lines and a touch of rusty shadowing, Aron creates the features of his face. This is the painting that suggested the term "psychological realism."

In 1980 Aron painted *Woman in Blue* from a sketch he did in the 1950s. Using a few large concentrations of strong colors, he captures a women thinking as she sits comfortably on a pillow on the floor. Her dress flows gently around her body, and a few black lines define her face and outline her body and dress.

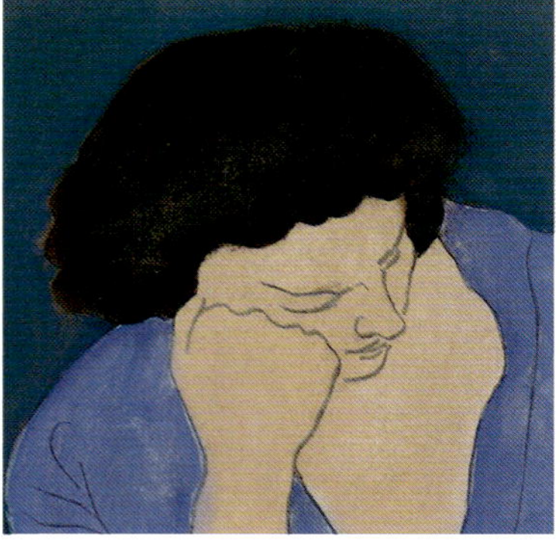

Woman in Blue (detail); full image on page 122.

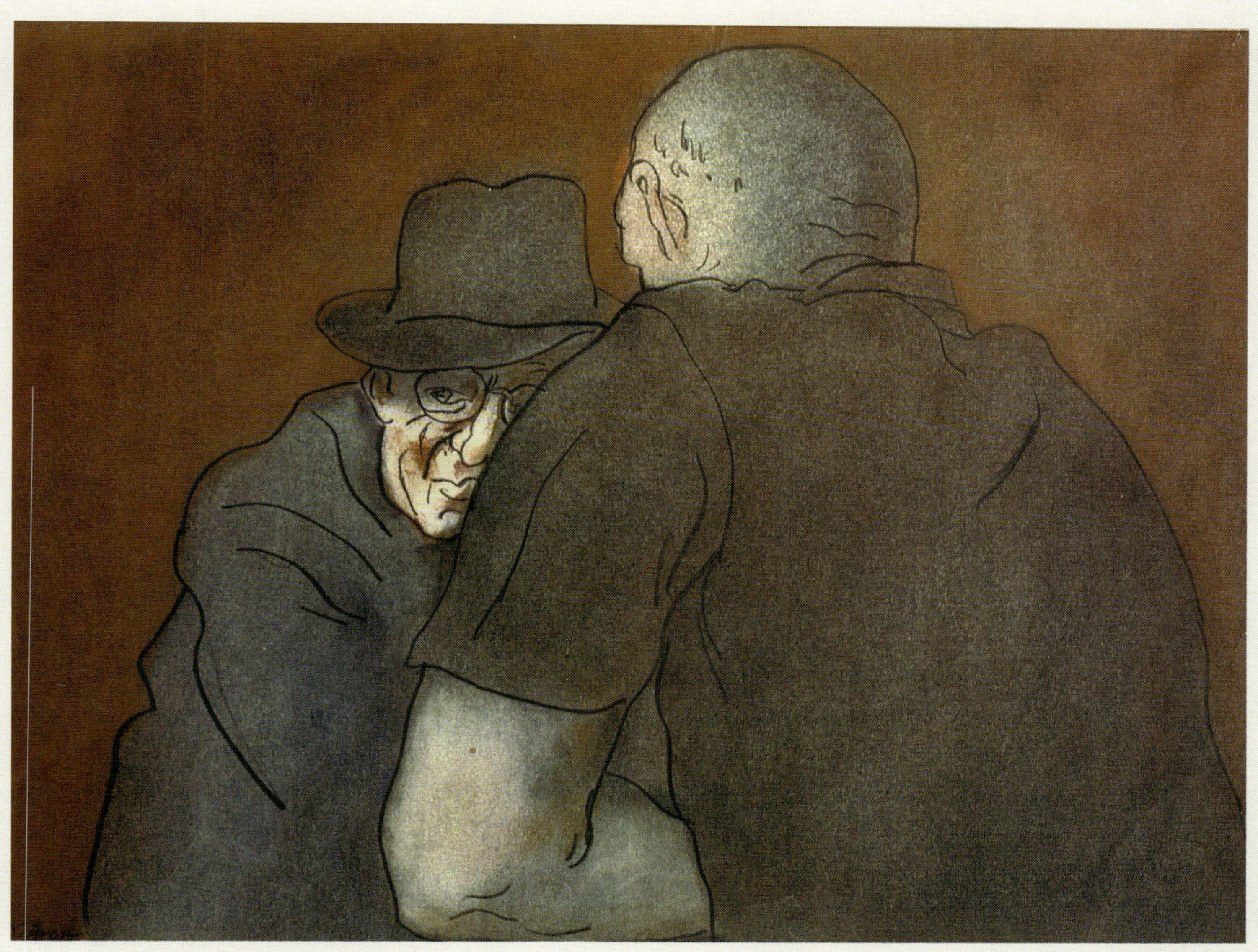

Two Men Seated (early 1970s), oil on paper, 10½ × 13½ in.

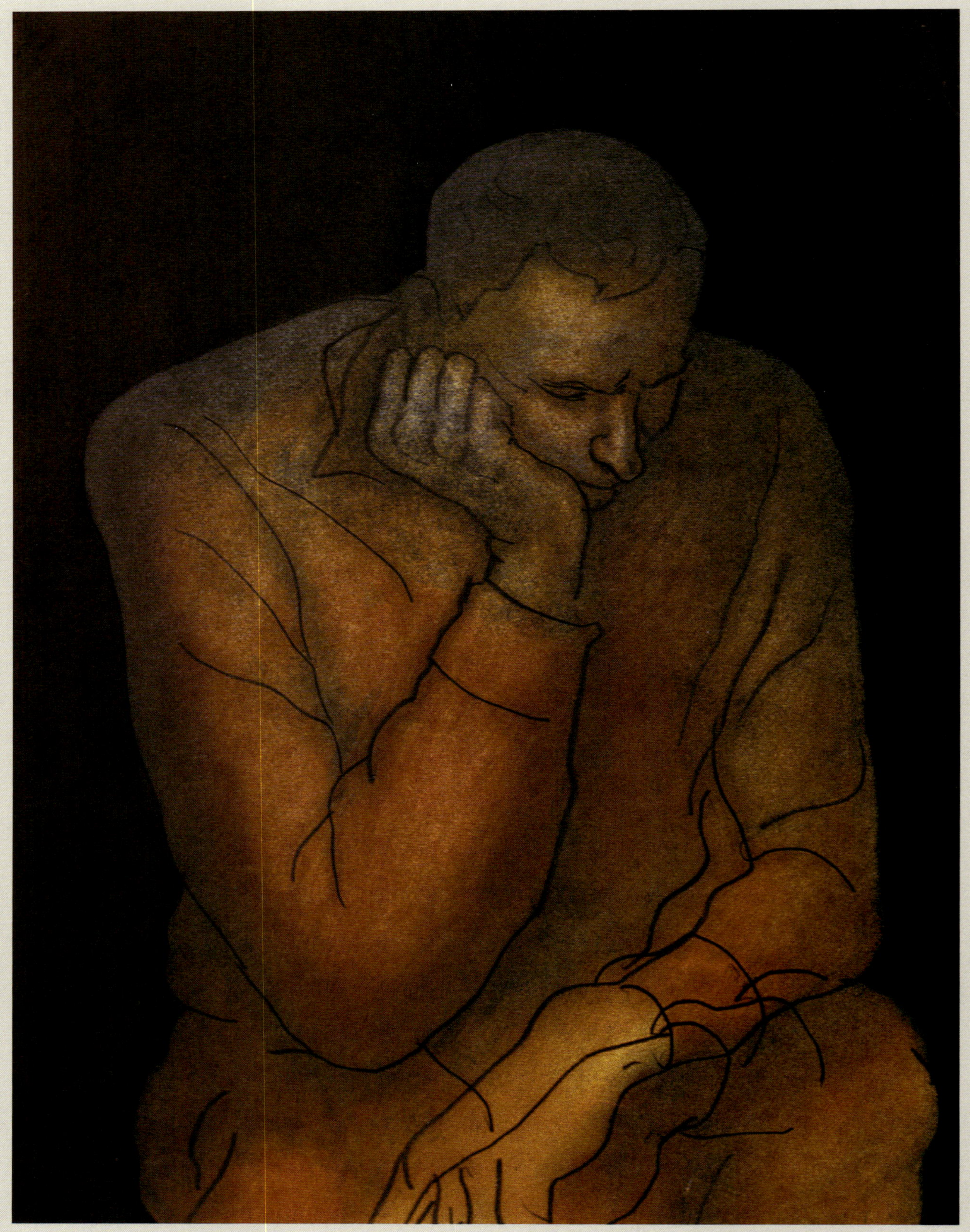

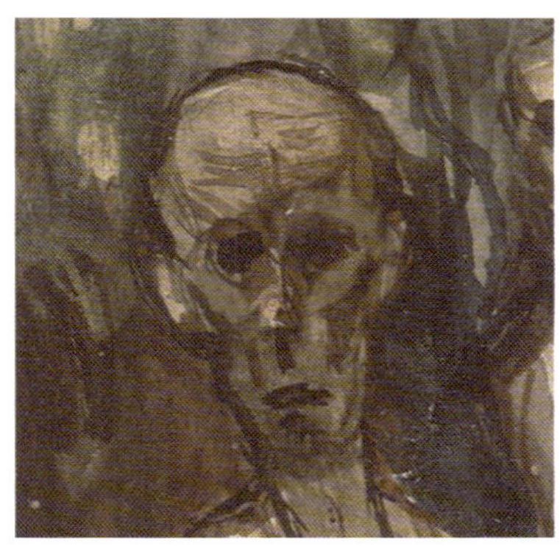

Kalman Marching in the Camp (detail); full image on page 50.

A fourth small oil on paper, *The Thinker*, recalls Rodin's sculpture, portraying a man deep in thought. Once again Aron's black lines and bodies of color define the mood and the man. He highlights parts of the man's body and places him against an ink-blue and black background. The colors and the repeat of the man's left hand and wrist suggest that he is in another dimension, perplexed with his thoughts. There is an ethereal, mystical feel to this drawing, amplified by the texture, thin layers of paint and rubbing of oils on paper. The dark background and black lines contain the energy of this figure, just as they contained Aron's own life force in his painting of himself in *Marching in the Camps*, drawn twenty years earlier. Life feels tenuous, his hold on "reality" somewhat loose.

Aron describes the process of painting on paper:

Once you put a color on, it stains the paper. You can't get it back. On those I don't use white. I want it transparent. I want the glow. The interesting part is that the paper gets a little bit more yellowish over time. It depends on what kind of paper I am using. It is like the old master paintings that were painted five hundred years ago. The color is different as a result of the varnishing. It gets a yellow-brownish glow, which makes it more interesting, actually.

The university president said that I should start a new 'ism' if I meet other people who are doing a similar kind of painting, like impressionism or expressionism. I haven't found anybody who does it. You have to know how to draw, where to display the color, and once you stain the paper, it is gone. If it is not right, you might as well tear it up and throw it away.

The Thinker (early 1970s), oil on paper, 13½ × 10½ in., p. 164

Aron has also painted large oils on canvas in this style. These illustrate his mastery of form, movement, color, technique and drawing. While in Sweden, he sketched a man on a train going from Uppsala to Stockholm. Another day he sketched a woman as he was traveling back to Uppsala. When he returned home, he put them together in the painting, *A Couple*. There is an elegance in the man's face and the way he holds his head, a gentleness in the movement of his coat and shape of his hat. Aron captures his quiet humanity and pride; he presents him with humility and respect. The woman is looking down, her back rounded with time. Not as erect as the man, she carries her burdens somewhat differently. Aron achieves a balance with the colors he uses. The woman's black hat plays off the man's dark gray coat, while his green hat dances with her orange-red coat. He draws their faces using a few lines, and he colors their skin with a tone of the blue-gray background. Having appeared in various newspapers and magazines, including the *Los Angeles Times*, this oil keeps Aron company in his studio.

A Couple (1980s), oil on canvas, 48 × 36 in.

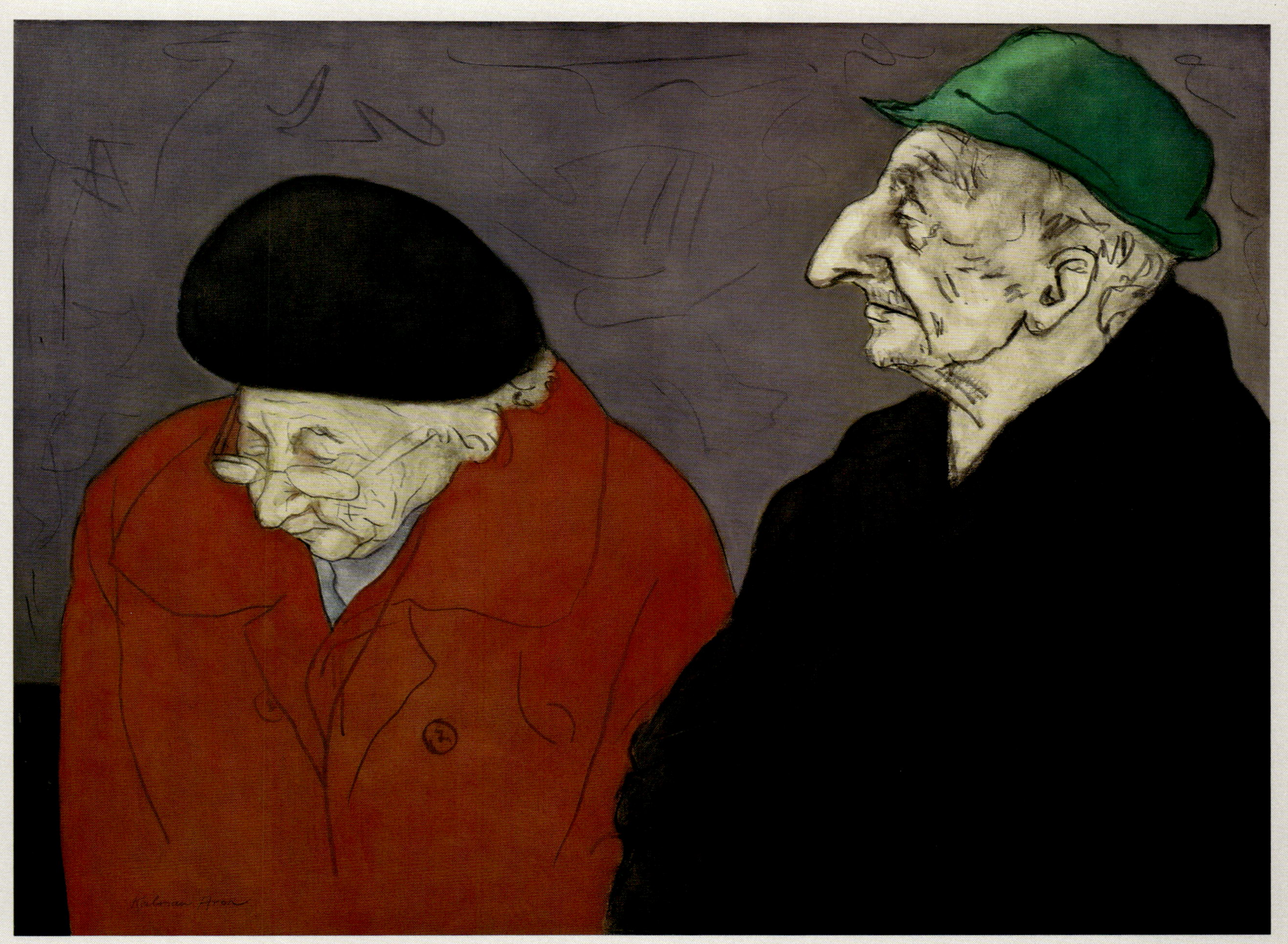

In a large oil, *The Dreamer*, Aron creates a woman resting, perhaps dreaming, occupying an ethereal space removed from everyday life. He uses gentle curves only, no straight lines, and he varies the intensity of the rich coral background around her. He transports the viewer to a timeless place of peace and respite, perhaps similar to the one he inhabits when he paints. It is a vision of tenderness, simplicity and beauty.

In *Woman in Repose* a woman is resting with her legs up. Aron uses three large bodies of color and a few lines to define her. She is floating in space, inhabiting a realm of silence. In another oil, *Woman in Black*, Aron captures the face of a woman with her hands touching her chin. The rest of her body is wrapped in black clothing. As though inside a cocoon, she gazes into the distance perhaps dreaming a new reality and transforming herself to soar into a new life.

In all three of these paintings, Aron creates a timeless space in another realm, a realm he has clearly experienced. As a child artist, he delighted in a world of love, beauty and community. At age seventeen the lights went out; his world disappeared; and he found himself in a black hole of evil. Since that time Aron has moved in and out of worlds of horror, dreams and visions. In America he projected his experience in these worlds and dimensions onto canvas. In this body of work he explores our ability to remove ourselves from the everyday business of living and move into the realms of dreaming, resting, floating and wandering. There are no walls confining Aron's people here. These paintings rank among his masterpieces.

The Dreamer (late 1970s), oil on canvas, 48 × 36 in.

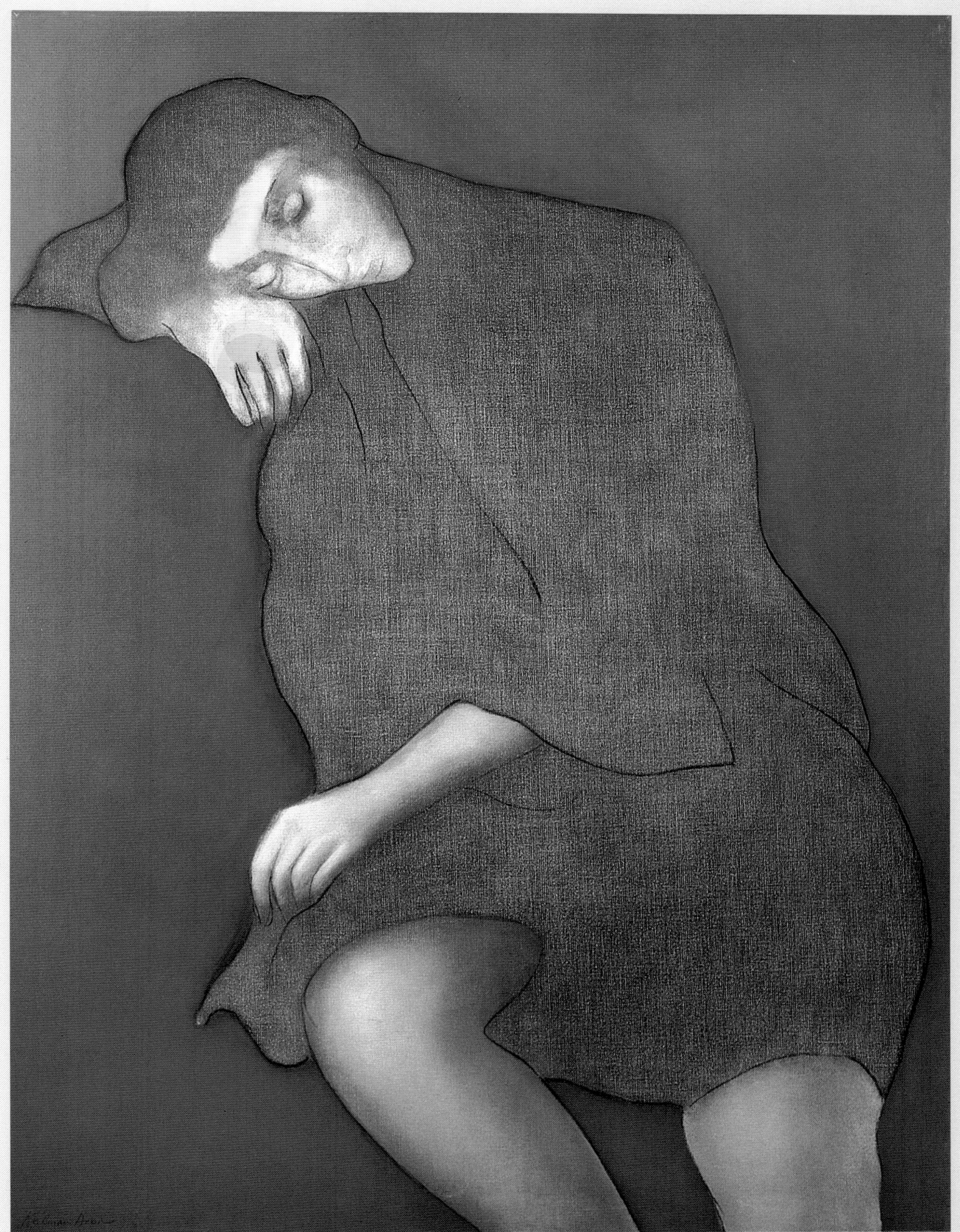

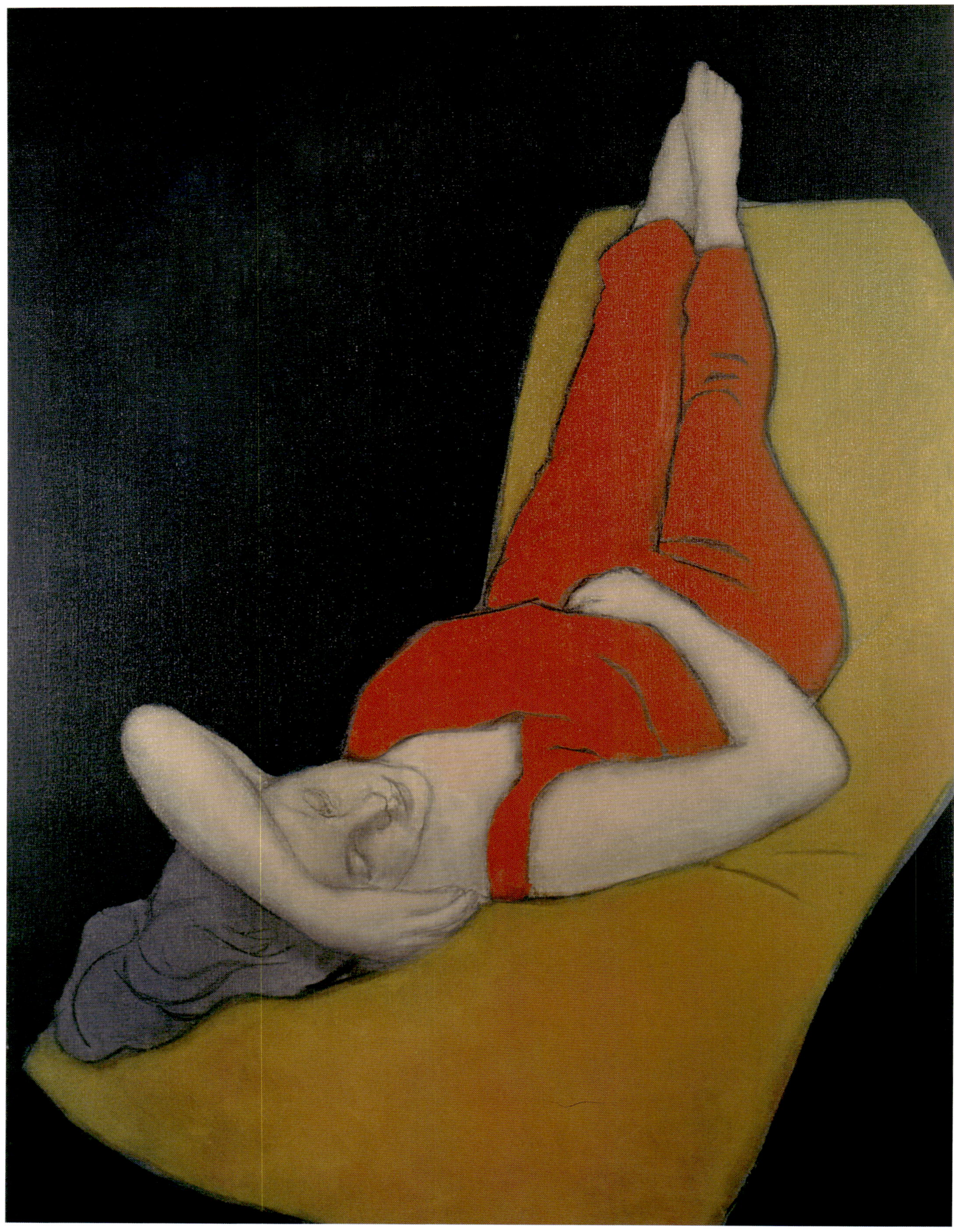

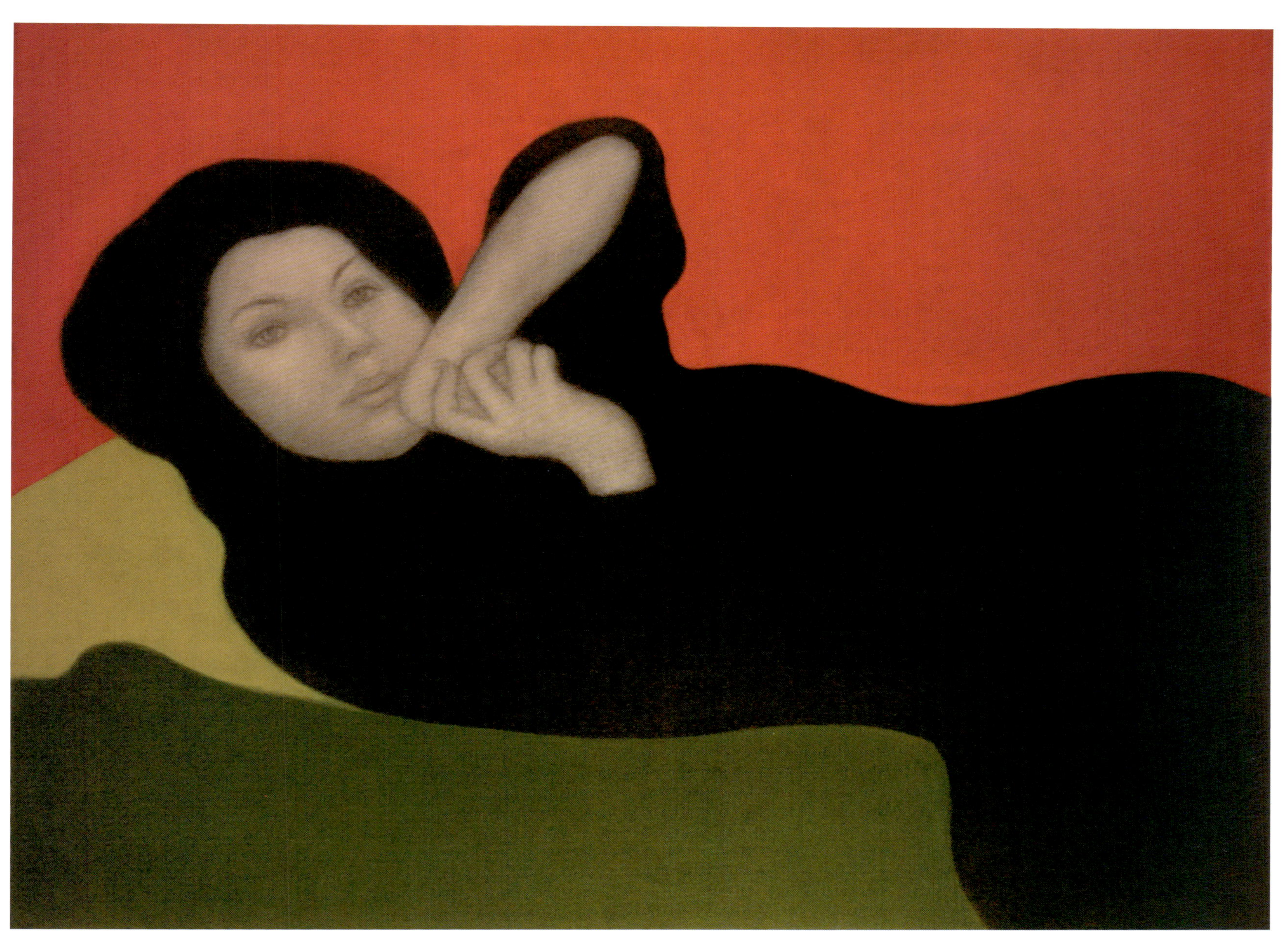

Woman in Black (early 1980s), oil on canvas, 30× 40 in.

Woman in Repose (early 1980s), oil on canvas, 40 × 36 in.

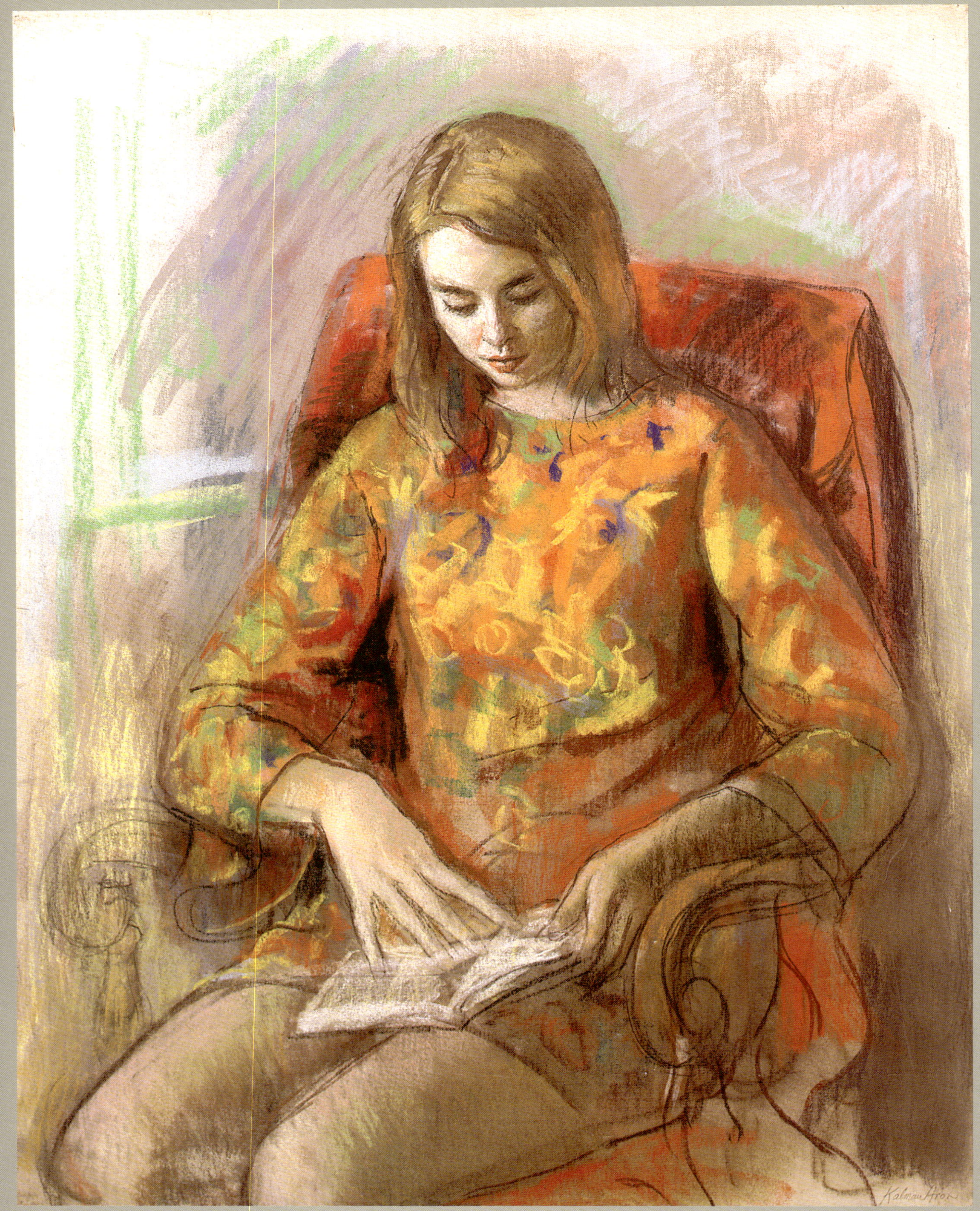

7

PORTRAIT OF A MARRIAGE

Kalman and Tanis

Tanis Reading (1968), pastel on paper, 40 × 30 in.

He met her at a party. As Aron remembers:

I was socializing. I was divorced at that time. An art collector invited me to a big luncheon. I didn't know if he was trying to fix me up. Tanis Furst came with her boyfriend. She walked in. I thought, "Whoa, look at this." She was young. The host sat her next to me, and her boyfriend was across. Someone must have told her that I had done a portrait of Henry Miller. She had a degree in English literature, and she read everything. She had read Henry Miller. She was kind of demure; she wouldn't say a bad word. Looking at her, you wouldn't think that she would read Henry Miller. She kept asking me these questions about my background and the people whose portraits I did. She told me that her father was a painter, and when he couldn't make a living at it he became a very fine architectural designer. She wanted me to meet her father because we had something in common; he was only three or four years older than I was. She was twenty-five when I met her. I was eighteen years older.

Tanis describes her first encounter with Aron:

I'd been dating a screen editor to whom I was introduced by my father and my stepmother. They thought he'd be a good catch. Things were going from bad to worse. Anyway, on one of our final dates we went to a very elegant party in Beverly Hills, a sort of Pickfair kind of place. I was seated next to this very interesting man, Kalman, and had a wonderful conversation with him. I was impressed that at the end of the party, when we were all going in different directions, Kalman asked my beau if he could borrow a pen so he could take my phone number. I thought that was a lot of chutzpah, you know. He wanted to show me his paintings. This was in the spring of 1967.

He called me at some point and invited me to come over and see his paintings. I thought, "Oh, great. If I don't like his paintings, this is going to be a disaster." It's pretty hard for me to say, "Oh, isn't that nice," when I'm thinking "Oy!" Needless to say, when we walked into the studio and he flipped the light on, I was just bowled over. I thought, "This guy can draw." That was my first criterion. I was just very, very, very impressed with it. I love portraits. I love Holbein. I'm critical. I've seen a lot of art in my day. If this guy's some schmearer, I'd just forget it, no matter how nice a guy he is. When I saw how good he was, I was relieved, because I was very attracted to him.

What I saw in the portraits was something more than you'd get from a photograph or a painting from a photograph. There was a real connection with these people, like you get when you look at the great portraits. They just look right out at you. I love the one of a woman, *Jaffa Flitterman*, wearing a hat and a kind of pink sort of flowery dress. There was a sort of sadness about the eyes, in a way. Kalman said later that she'd had him do the portrait just as she was getting a divorce. She let him keep the portrait. They became very good friends.

Portrait of Jaffa (1966), pastel on paper, 46½ × 34½ in.

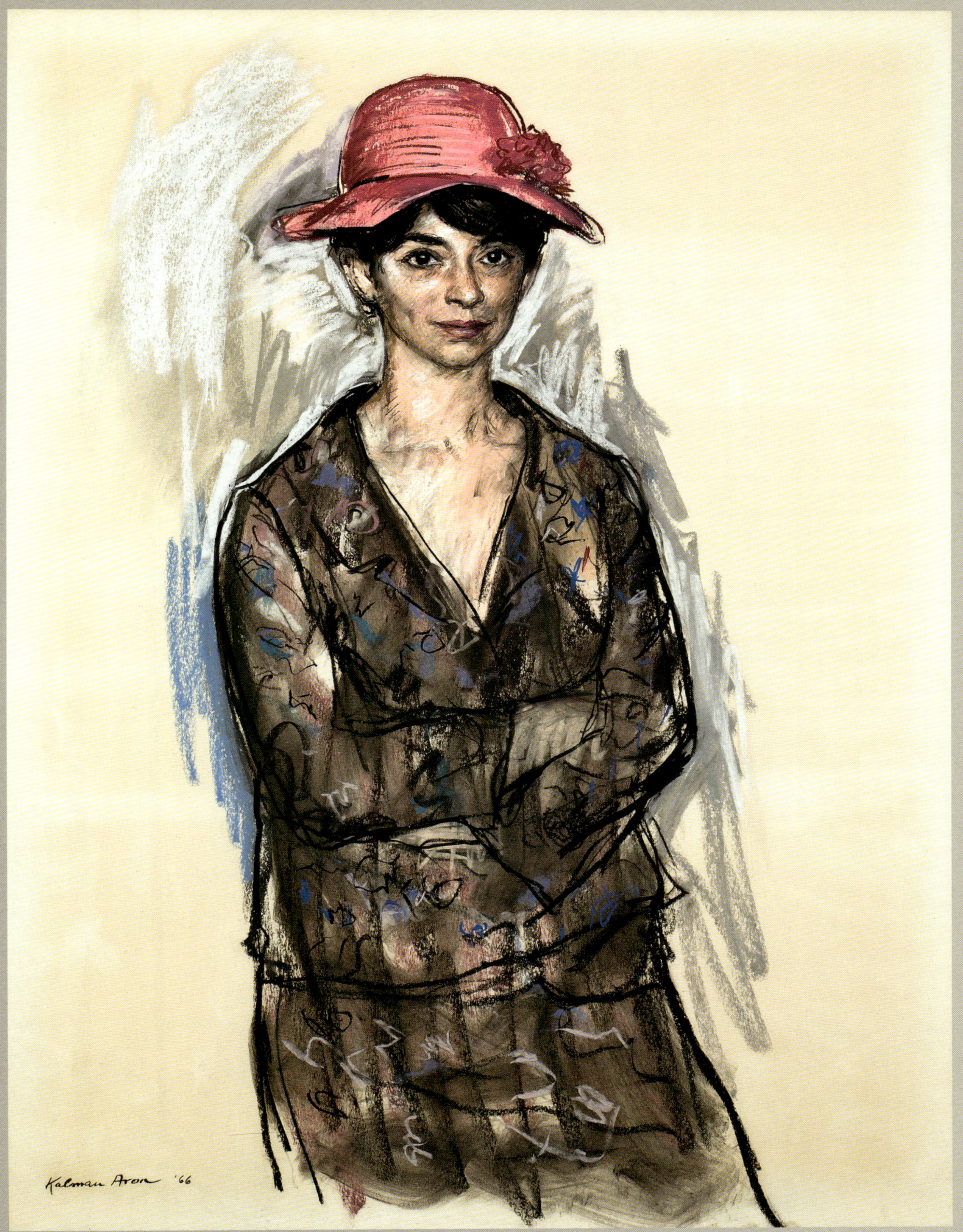
Kalman Aron '66

The first time I met him at his apartment, Kalman was very charming. I thought he looked like a cross between Rex Harrison and somebody else who was attractive. He was bald, of course; big deal, who cares? He was attractive. We got together. At some point we actually moved in together, which wasn't really done in those days that much, but we did.

Aron remembers:

She came over to my studio, and I said, "I have nothing in common with you." She was a young girl, you know. I met her father, and we were talking all the time about painters. I painted a portrait of him. He was knowledgeable, a very bright guy. She was a reader, very bright; she used to read all the time. So she came over to my studio a few times. Little by little, you know, things happened at the studio, and we started seeing each other more often. She was very nice, and she was different from any girl her age. She was very well educated. She was calm. She was very attractive, by the way.

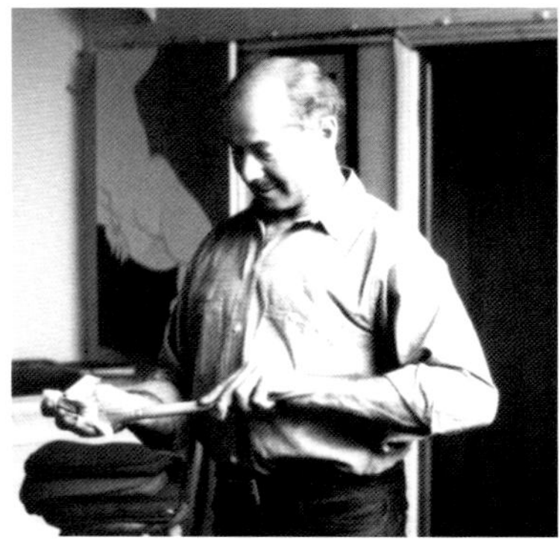

Kalman in his studio (1969).

I could see that it was getting hot and heavy. I just had a studio with one bedroom. We rented an apartment so she would have a place to read, and we moved in together. After one year, she gave me an ultimatum: if you don't marry me, I will move out. She knew exactly what she wanted. She made up her mind, packed her bag, and moved to New York.

We talked by phone a lot, so I gave it another chance. I will go to New York, and maybe we will stay in New York for a little while. I stayed for three months. She wanted to get married and have a child. I had two wives and no children. So I decided to marry. We came back to Los Angeles. We got married. Then we went for a whole year on a honeymoon.

Tanis remembers it differently:

In the spring of '68, I said to myself, "I'm going back to New York. The heck with this." And off I went. I subleased an apartment, and I got myself a temp job at Revlon. Kalman and I talked by phone. Eventually, one day he called and said, "Let's get married." And I said, "Okay," thinking, "Yes!!"

We got married at City Hall. Lou Lenart, his dear friend, stood with us. It was bizarre because it was not at all what I had in mind, a nice Catholic girl, standing in a long line of people—people in Bermuda shorts, in wedding gowns—all at City Hall. We went in front of this judge, and it was *Brrrrrrr*—really fast. Then we went to Cantor's Deli afterwards to have corned beef sandwiches, and I'm thinking, "What the hell did I just do?" But I was glad. I was happy. Then in 1969 we went on this long honeymoon trip to El Paso, Texas, for about four months, and then back east and on to Canada.

Aron had a commission for a portrait of the two children and wife of Amen Wardy in El Paso, Texas. Wardy owned a dress shop in El Paso and one on Rodeo Drive in Beverly Hills. He sold high-fashion clothes to movie stars and wealthy people. Aron and Tanis stayed for three months, while Aron completed nine portrait commissions.

Tanis remembers:

We were just traveling. We went to Montreal. We were just going to go through it, but it was nice, so we found a place and stayed for about a month. One reason we stuck around was because he loved the buildings there and painted them. I remember he stopped in front of one place and said, "I've got to paint that." He got out and set up his easel in front of this person's house. It was in some dicey part of town. It turned out to be a house where a woman had thirty cats. These cats were all over the place. There were all these kids that were hanging around Kalman, watching what he was doing. Kalman doesn't speak French, but he was saying, "Allez, allez, allez! Go away." He kept persisting and painting. I'm sitting in this station wagon, and thinking—wow. This happened all the time on this trip. He would drive along and stop: "Gotta paint that." We had a lot of fun. Being on the road was great. I thought, "He's really got to do this more."

We went to Quebec City and then traveled back into the States. We spent some time in the Boston area, where we subleased an apartment for the summer of 1969. Kalman had a friend there he'd met in Europe, a young guy, a sculptor, who was hysterical. Tall, skinny and dark-haired, he was an American with a Sicilian background. He was so fun. We had a good time with him and his wife. Kalman and I had a lot of good times.

We went to art museums all over the place. The most memorable was the Barnes Foundation [in suburban Philadelphia]. I think Kalman was drawn to Cézanne and Degas, the great draftsmen.

Getting out on the road together was the best, even though Kalman felt secure in what he had created for himself in Los Angeles. I was pregnant when we returned. At five and a half months, I almost lost David. I started to have contractions. I was bedridden for a while and actually spent a little time in the hospital. David was born about ten days early on February 2, 1970.

Aron remembers:

I was a very happy guy when my son was born. In fact, it was the happiest day of my life. I named him David after my uncle, David Aron.

Tanis had an interesting background. Her grandmother, born in Transylvania, fled the chaos in Europe after World War I and brought her six-year-old daughter, Mitzi, to America. Eventually they moved to Hollywood, where Mitzi got some bit movie parts. Her father was born in Los Angeles and met Mitzi in Palm Springs. They married, had Tanis, and divorced when Tanis was seven.

She recalls:

I had met a lot of interesting people through my father: Herbert von Karajan, Europe's greatest maestro from the 1950s to the 1970s; Zubin Mehta, the conductor of the Los Angeles Philharmonic; and actors like Henry Wilcoxon, who had played Mark Antony to Claudette Colbert's Cleopatra. Having grown up in this milieu, I enjoyed meeting Kalman's friends.

The most interesting person who stood out was Henry Miller. We went over once to his place. He was living with a young woman, which amused Kalman. Miller was painting. He wouldn't let just anybody in. But he liked Kalman. They got along very well. I thought he was just cool. I can't stand his writing. And I told him so: "I think it's too masculine for me to relate." And he said, "You're probably right." He could hear that. He was very secure.

Another time we went to a party hosted by Kalman's friend Jaffa Flitterman. It may have been one of the last parties Aron and I went to together. Henry Miller was there, along with a famous Polish pianist, Jakob Gimpel. Kalman did the most amazing thing. He's very good with stringed instruments. This famous concert pianist, Gimpel, sat down at the piano, and he'd go *mm-pa, mm-pa*, mimicking a sort of Russian rhythm on the piano. Kalman picked up a mandolin and would go *chinga, chinga, aching* . . . mimicking Russian folk music.

I spent the whole evening with Miller. He was really nice. He said to me at some point, "Is your marriage in trouble? You don't seem very happy." He was very astute. He wasn't being nosy. But things were definitely not good, at least from my point of view.

Things started to deteriorate back in the real world. After David came along, I found myself feeling very protective of him, my part of David. These yentas would come over and say, "Oh, another boy to die for Israel." That frightened me. I was saying, "These people are crazy." And Kalman's like, "You don't get it." I was young emotionally. I just didn't get why people weren't more reasonable.

I had grown up in Beverly Hills in the Jewish community. My high school was 85 to 90 percent Jewish. Kalman was a tribal Jew more than a religious one. Most of his friends and mine were Jewish. It was where we were living. I was born a Catholic, and had I not been a Catholic I would be a Jew. Kalman never asked me to convert. His Jewish women friends did.

I think it was important for him to have Jewish friends. He trusted them. I was an anomaly. Somehow I felt Kalman's friends were saying: "We're a unit of some sort, even though we don't all do things the same way."

In addition, Kalman was disillusioned during the Holocaust about religion. "If there's a God, why would he let these horrible things happen?" How do you argue with that? And the life of the spirit has always been important to me. But there was no way you could talk about anything spiritual. It's like, "If God exists, I don't want to know Him. He caused this. He let this happen. I'm an atheist. When you die, you die. And that's it." I think he feels betrayed by the guy upstairs. In this way we were not compatible, because I'm all about the soul. What's interesting is that the spirit is so powerfully alive in Kalman. I wish he would acknowledge it before he dies.

When we lived together, Kalman could paint for hours and hours. He often painted all night long. Then people would come for a sitting. And he'd have these models . . . nice naked girls who would come and sprawl around, and he would draw them and paint them. His painting was never a problem with me. I loved my reading just like he loved his painting. But when we had David, I had to get up in the morning. I couldn't stay up all night like I had.

Kalman shared some things about his family and the Holocaust, but not in a great deal of detail. He alluded to his family being gunned down. He talked about how his brother would come home and say, "Look, we've got to get out of here," and people would say, "Oh no, we can't leave," "This isn't going to happen" and "We'll be fine." As Kalman put it, "They were afraid to leave their grandmother's teacups; they couldn't leave their stuff. They'd have to leave the home, and this and that." So they delayed. Kalman and his family were at the train station when they were gunned down. He said it might have been different had they gone a week earlier. But by then the Germans had just swept across. They were there. It was too late. He talked about that.

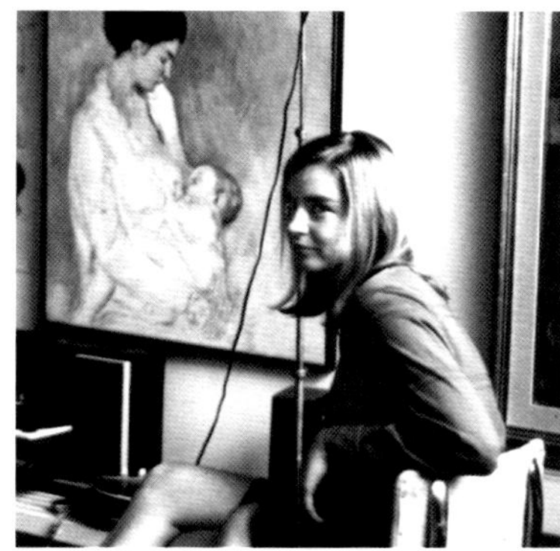

Kalman's wife Tanis in his studio (1969).

He also talked about not going back to Latvia after being liberated. He said: "I didn't want to meet anyone who may have killed my mother and my father, and I didn't think anyone was alive."

I had the feeling that he had a very good relationship with his older brother. I think the brother more or less followed in the father's footsteps as a shoe designer. They finally reconnected through the Red Cross and wrote back and forth in Yiddish. His brother was saying, "Why don't you come back? The state will take care of you. You can paint." Kalman was just, "No, no, no. I can't do that. I wouldn't go back there." Kalman was the young prodigy and probably danced to a slightly different drummer.

Kalman continued to stay in touch with his brother, and eventually they actually talked on the phone once in a while. Kalman talked about going over for his brother's seventieth birthday in 1989, when the Soviet system collapsed. At the last minute he pulled back. He couldn't go. He was afraid he wouldn't be able to get back to America. Kalman worked hard to disconnect from all that awful stuff in his life and just live in the present moment.

The last time Kalman saw his brother was at the Stutthof camp near Gdańsk in the summer of 1944, when the Germans separated them and sent Kalman to Buchenwald. He started looking for Henech as soon as the war ended. He asked at the relief agencies; he asked people who came from Latvia, from Russia, "Do you know Henech Aron?" "No, we don't know him." Around 1960 he finally learned from the Red Cross that Henech was alive and living in Latvia.

Aron relates the rest:

First we only wrote letters, in Yiddish. Somebody, a censor, perhaps a Jewish Communist, read the Yiddish letters and crossed parts out. His letters came with sections crossed out. Later on we would talk on the phone in Yiddish. He couldn't leave Latvia because the Russians wouldn't let him out.

At the end of the war when he went back to Latvia, he met a woman, a Russian Jew, and married her. I understand that she was very sick and had lost a leg to diabetes. He was very poor, doing the same thing my father had done, designing shoes. They had three boys and one girl. The daughter came to New York with her husband. Later she divorced and married an Israeli. I met her twice, but I don't know her married name.

My brother and I talked on the phone in the 1960s and 1970s. Then one day when I called, his wife said that Henech is very sick. He cannot speak. He had a stroke. So I spoke to her, but it was very difficult. I couldn't ask any questions because the Communists were listening, I am sure.

When I was in London in 1961, I wanted to go to Riga to see him. I went to a Jewish organization to help with the paperwork. But the people there told me not to go, as the Russians would keep me as one of their own. My passport showed I was born in Riga. Later on I could have gone. But they told me, "If you go there, you can't go to his house. You have to stay in a hotel, and he has to meet you there."

In the 1960s the Russians jailed him for four years. I could never find out why. He couldn't tell me on the phone. They let him out because he had bleeding ulcers. After that he was very sick. He started playing the piano and the violin. Apparently he was very good. His wife told me he played for five or six years. He was a very talented musician. Being home and not doing anything else, he had time to learn to play the piano, the violin and the mandolin. I never heard him play. At one point I was going to take a chance to visit him, but his wife told me he can't speak. So I never saw him again.

Over time friends have said to me, "Riga is beautiful. Why don't you go back?" I don't want to go back. I don't want anything to do with Latvia. I would never go to Germany either. They wanted to give me a show in a gallery in Munich. I said no, I am not going to Germany, period. These two places I wouldn't go.

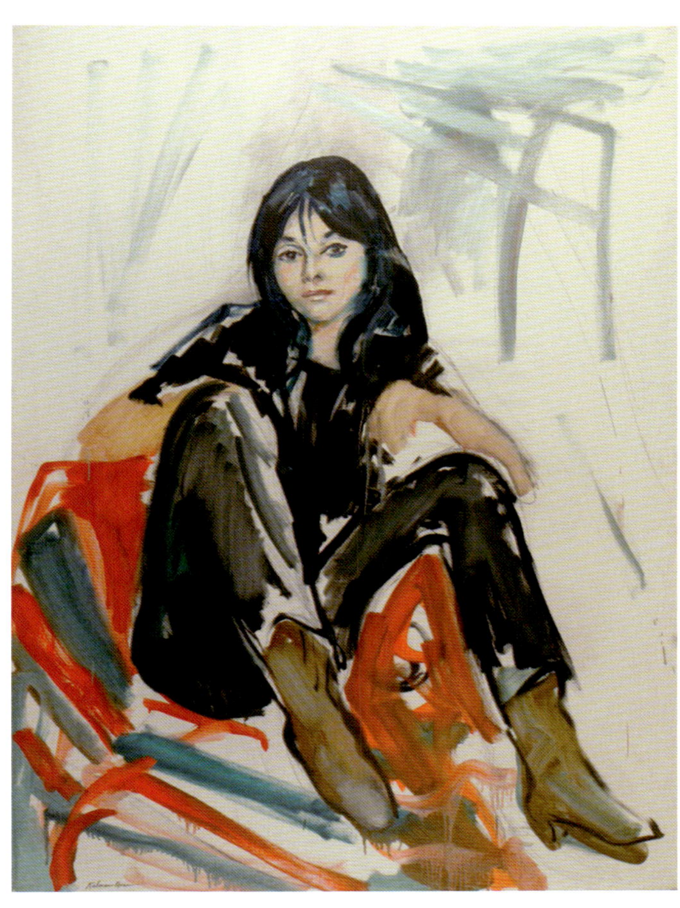

Young Woman (1980s), oil on canvas, 48 × 24 in.

Tanis asked Kalman how he survived in the camps. He told her, "First, by not being conspicuous. Second, I was young, and I could work."

She continues:

He didn't tell me any details about the camps, but he did talk about being inconspicuous and not standing out in a crowd. He also told me what happened after they were liberated. Suddenly there was food, and people died because they ate too much too fast. They got sick. He said he just sat on his hands. He wouldn't eat until he could handle some food because he saw people getting violently ill. He was just very careful, and maybe by nature he's that way. Of course, it translated into being very careful about not spilling the beans too much.

It's always safest for Kalman to skate along the surface of emotions, because getting to the heart of something was just too hard. Sometimes he would just back off and become unreachable. I understand this distrust after what happened in the Holocaust.

His experience kept David from being a smug, self-satisfied, shallow American kid who feels entitled. David recognizes that things happen. The Russians happened. The Germans happened. The world came apart. Life goes on.

I love his paintings and drawings of David, because it's David. I love many of the portraits, especially the ones that have sort of unfinished parts to them. That gives them life, somehow. Like they are emerging off the canvas. The oil *Young Woman* illustrates that. Aron painted quickly, using broad, strong, colorful strokes. He captured a moment in time as this woman rests easily on canvas, engaged in her own thoughts.

I love a lot of his charcoal work and the portraits not developed yet in paint. Kalman is very bold with his colors. He's assured in the way someone is who has ground his own pigments. At the Academy in Vienna, he had to make his own paints—measure out a bit of blue with a bit of green. Kalman had that training. So when he selects paint or a brand of paints, he understands how they're going to work. He understands the chemistry of it.

His colors have changed over time. In oils his attack on the canvas got brasher, bolder and quicker. With pastels he is able to do weird things that most people don't do. He has a whole series of pastel night scenes of L.A. I also love his use of negative space. It's essential in his compositions. His figures emerge from the negative space on the canvas. Some of his landscapes are really quite sunny and light. Kalman needs to be in the sun. I think he said that during the war his circulation suffered, and in fact his hands would just go white in Vienna in the winter. It's very hard for him to stay warm. So he needs to be in the sun. I also think it's psychological. Los Angeles is the antithesis of Riga and the camps.

He has one magnificent pastel done in the 1950s which is unlike anything he's ever done. It is the eight-foot-tall *Mother and Child*. I think it comes from a vision. It's something he envisioned, and it came out of him like he was channeling it from somewhere. And I think he knows that. I was struck by the universality of it. This painting means everything to him. He won't let it go. He says if he ever does, it has to be in the right setting. He says, "It's too personal."

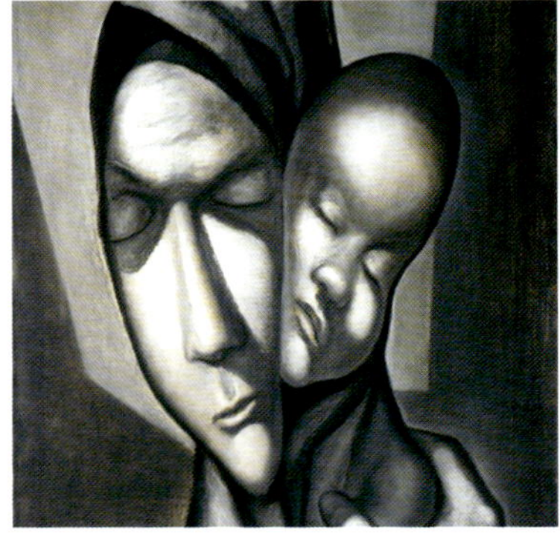

Mother and Child (detail); full image on page 85.

Why is he not more famous? He's been a successful artist all his life. Anyone who sees his art asks this same question. The answer: he holds himself back. He doesn't put himself out there. When we were married, people in New York wanted to represent him in the galleries. I'd say, "Come on, let's do the show in New York." He'd respond, "Ah, it doesn't pay. They take too large a percentage. You have to ship things. You have to do this; you have to do that." And I'm saying, "Who cares? Just do it. Get an agent." It was so frustrating. Oh, he's been written up in magazines and all this kind of thing. But it's very minimal, considering his talent.

Regardless of whatever problems we had, Kalman is a very decent, good human being. He's honest. He is a man of integrity. He may be unfathomable at times, but he is a very honest, decent person, and he has a sense of responsibility.

I became desperately unhappy. I was too young to comprehend that I couldn't understand fully Kalman's experience in the Holocaust. I began to feel like a "toy wife." At one point that was okay; I loved that. But then I stopped loving it.

Kalman will tell you that I was young. I was touchy. I was nervous, and I was emotional. I am not the easiest person to be around sometimes. I have no political skills whatsoever. And half of my family background is German, Transylvanian Saxons, but German nonetheless. Maybe without even realizing it, he may not have trusted me after his life experience in the Holocaust.

It was a horrible day, the day I said I wanted a divorce. I just felt terrible about it. I couldn't explain to him why.

Aron recalls:

It didn't work out. Why? I used to change David's diapers and feed him. Tanis was reading all the time. She suggested I take a little vacation and go to San Francisco to a gallery and do some painting. I went reluctantly with my canvases. I was supposed to stay two weeks. I couldn't take it any longer. A new daddy, you know. I came back a week early. She wanted a divorce. I moved out. I lived in my studio. I was very upset about it. Here was a young child. She left with him, getting a job somewhere in the Midwest. She went and left with him. I didn't see the baby for a long time.

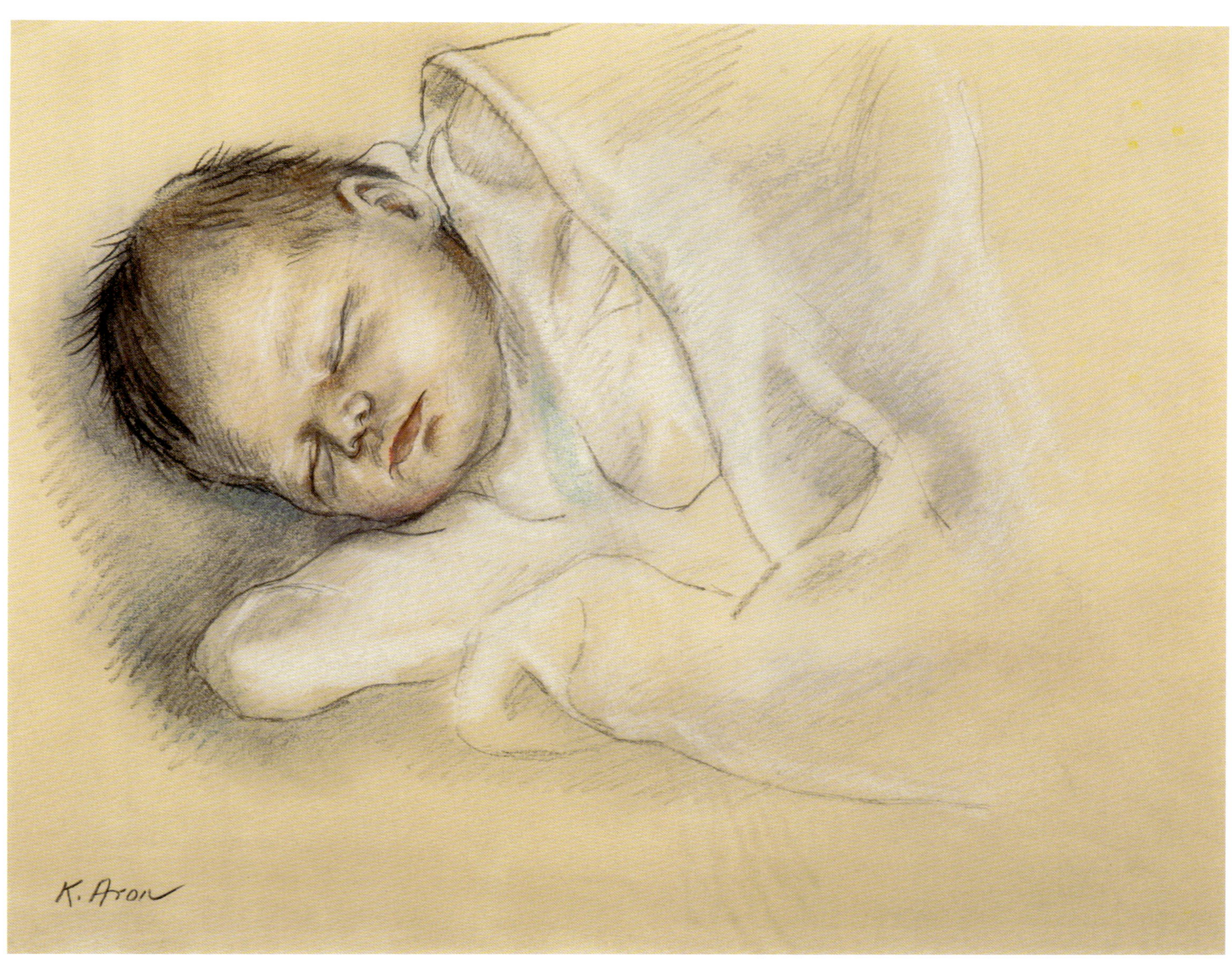

Baby David (1970), pastel on paper, 10½ × 14 in.

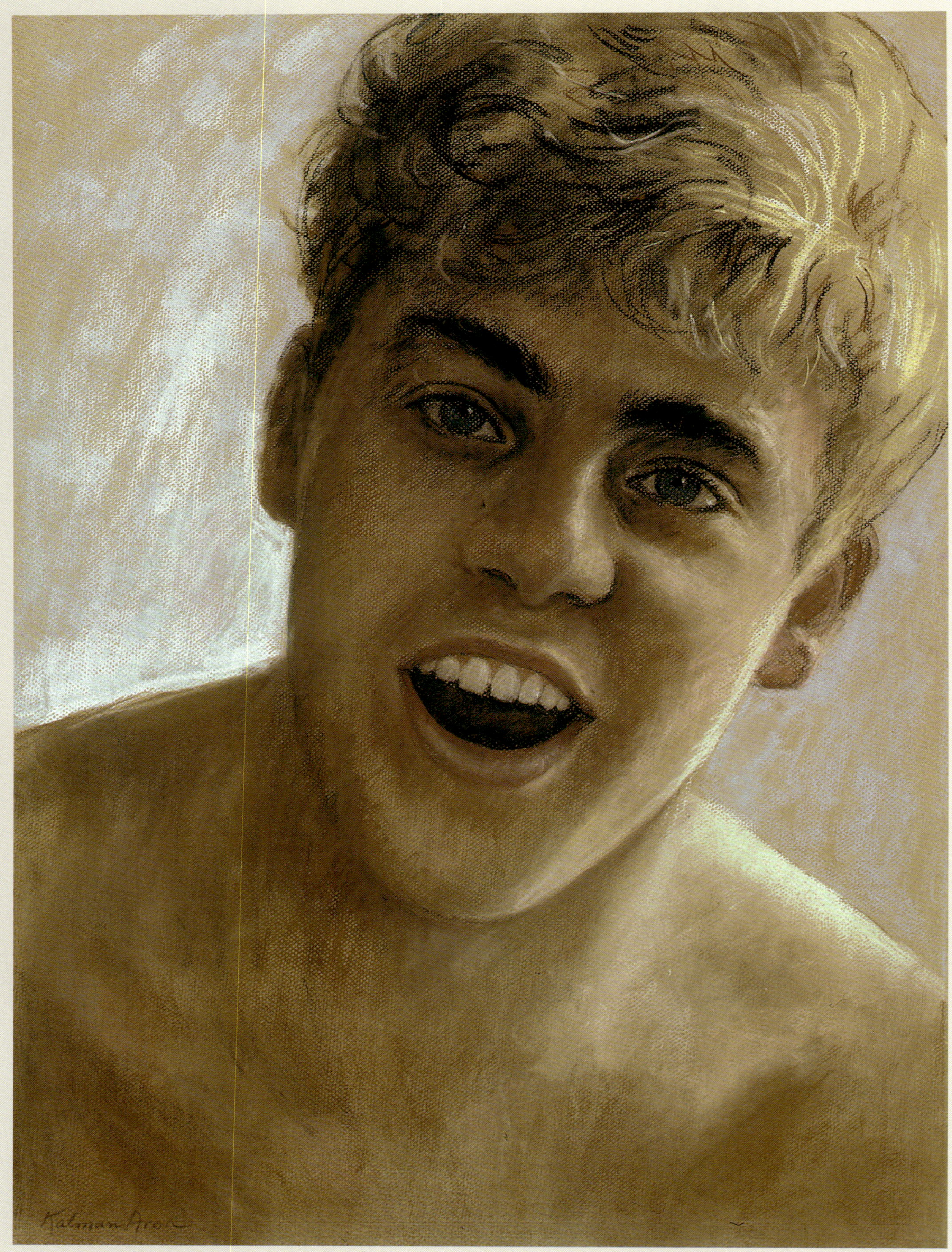

8

THROUGH DAVID'S EYES

A Son Looks at His Father

David as a Teenager (1985), pastel on paper, 30 × 21 in.

Born in 1970, David lives today in the Hudson Valley outside of New York City, an artist too. Offering insights into his father's character and experience, he remembers the signature scent of oil paints and turpentine in Kalman's West Hollywood studio, and more.

It had high ceilings, a whole wall of windows with north light, which is good for an artist. I always really liked the fireplace and the little nooks. I remember art objects and sculptures. There's a certain kind of atmosphere that I still feel with my dad. It's always a gentle atmosphere. I equate anything artistic with that atmosphere.

Dad never took photos of me; he just drew pictures. That was his way of capturing those times. He still has those drawings hanging on his wall in his bedroom. He cherishes them, and to this day he still calls me names he called me when I was a baby. He called me "Deidel Dreidel," Deidel for David and dreidel after a Jewish toy.

When you watch him work and handle his work, there is a gentleness, just the way he is in his body. Of course, he can get upset. But my father does not have what you would call a dark side. There is a lot of discomfort, ups and downs, but he does not have a hardness to him. He is a loving person, and he is kind of an upbeat person. He's not a heavy-handed person. It's amazing because of what he's endured. So in this way I always felt safe. I always felt at home. I always felt loved and nurtured.

My mom moved away from Los Angeles after I was born and then moved back for two years when I was three. I saw a lot of my dad then. Then she decided to move to London, where we stayed for five years. I missed my dad a lot.

When I was ten, we returned to Los Angeles for three years. My dad left his West Hollywood studio and moved into his current apartment, so he was near my school and where we lived. He'd always take me to the beach in Santa Monica or Venice. I would play in the sand, go looking for things and feel the water. I remember swinging on a swing and walking on the boardwalk. Dad would play chess. He's a really good chess player. He beat some serious chess players and was called an "unofficial chess master." He is bright.

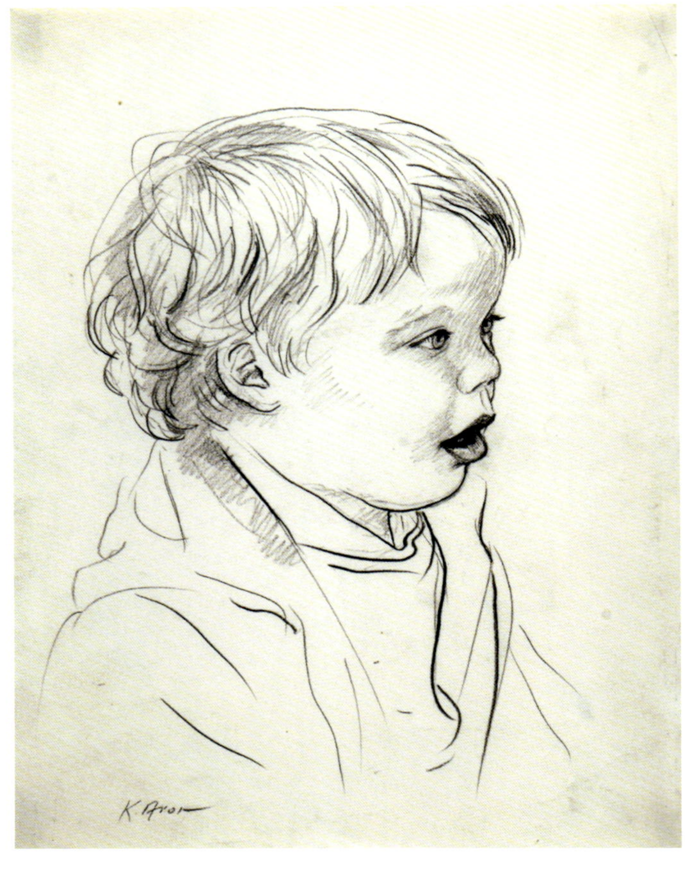

Profile of David (1971), charcoal on paper, 14 × 10¾ in.

David Sleeping (1971), charcoal on paper, 12 × 17 in.

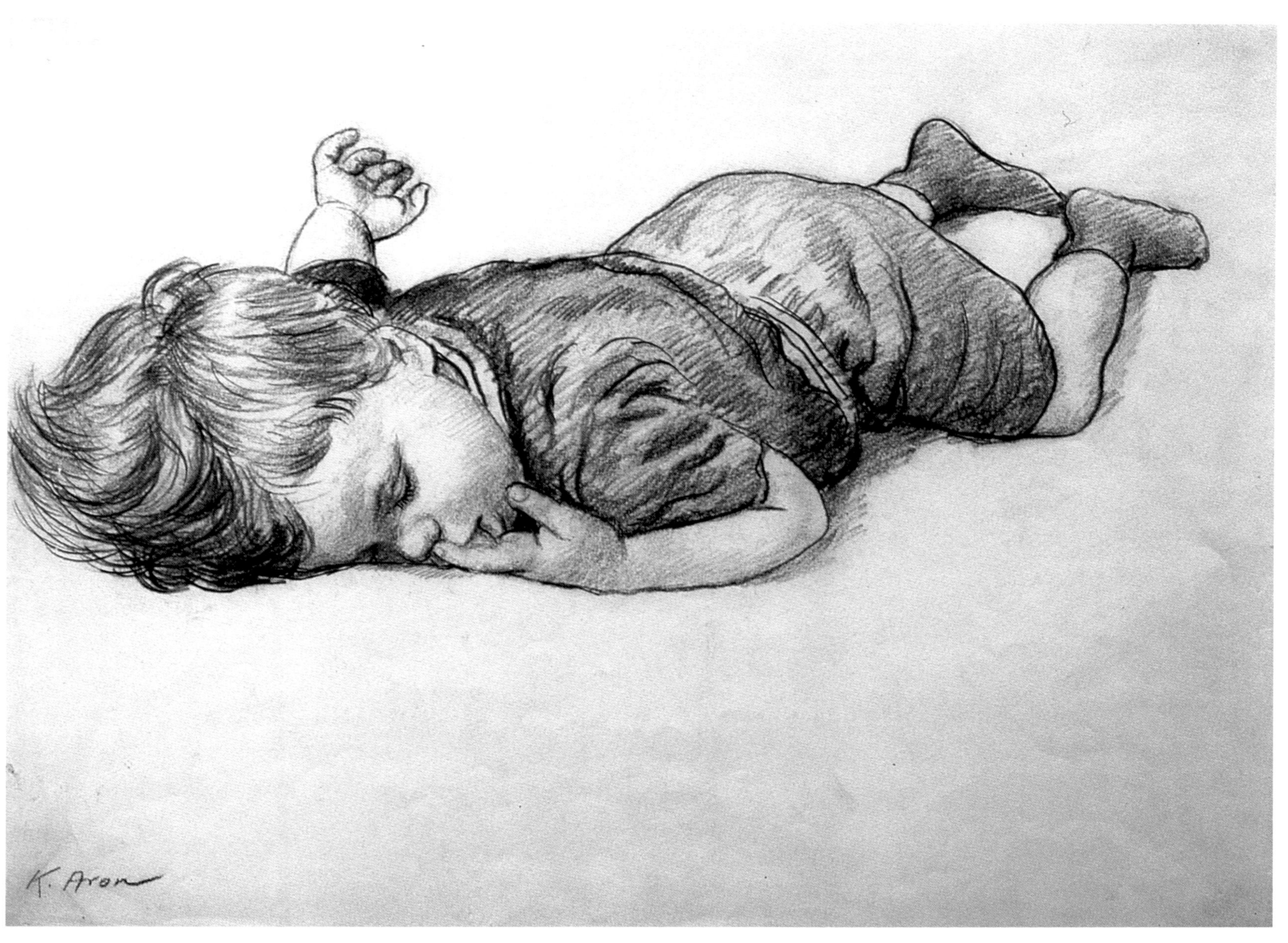
K. Aron

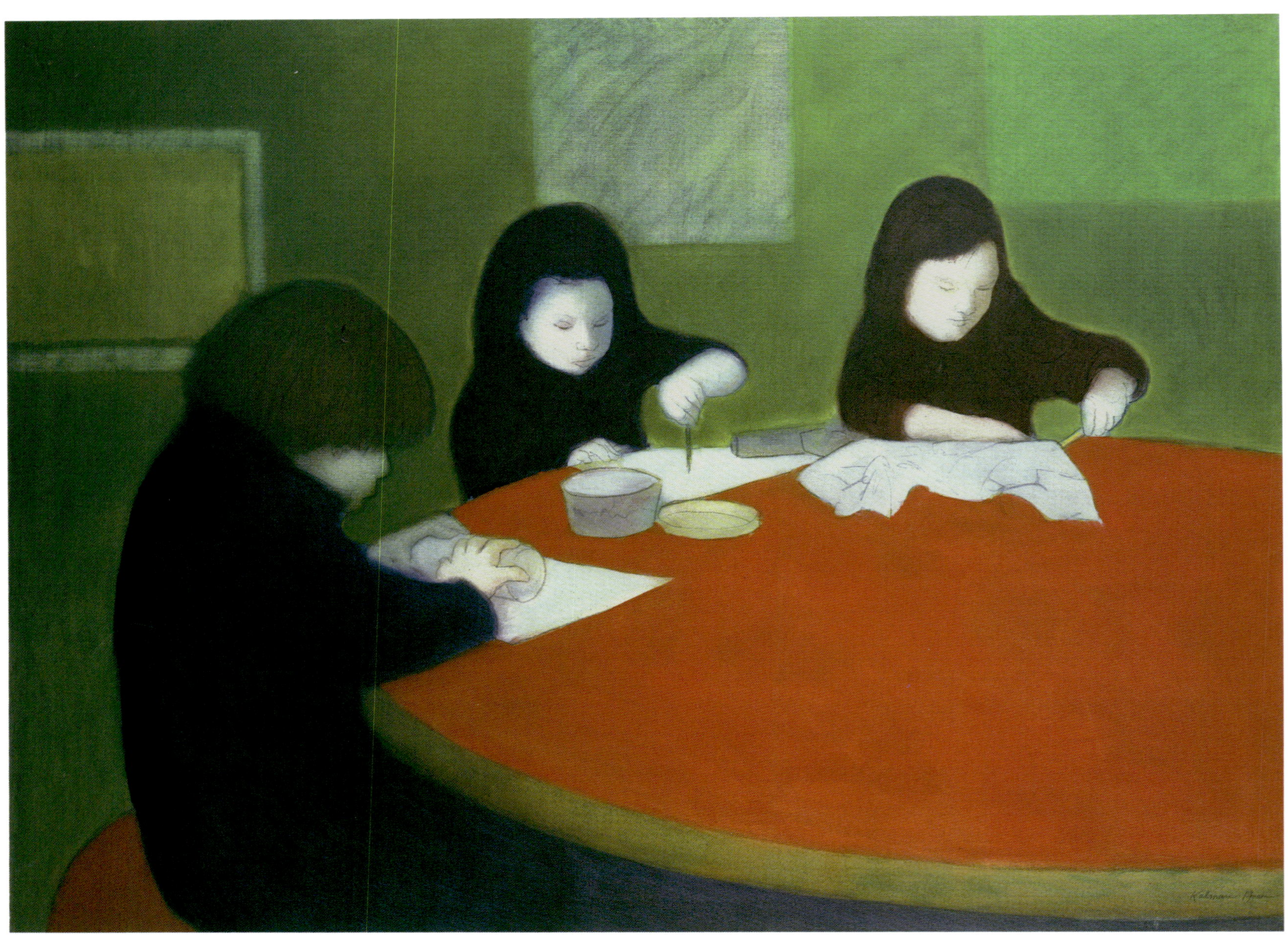

Children with Green Wall and Red Table (1976), oil on canvas, 36 × 48 in.

When I was thirteen, Mom wanted to move again, so we chose Ithaca, New York. Dad visited once, I believe, and I probably went to see him quite often. After two years I wanted to live with him, so I moved back to Los Angeles.

Living together was pretty hard for him. I was fifteen. I was getting into trouble. We would argue about stupid stuff—just things that a teenager would argue about with his parents because I thought I was right about something. Once when my father and I had an argument, he had a panic attack with a racing pulse. It was scary. I thought I was going to lose him. I blamed myself for igniting this thing in him. His experience in the past is far away, but in actuality it is physically inside his body, very close, and dictates his life more than he might realize—this fear, pain and loss. When the panic attack was happening, it was almost like a screaming. It was his fear that was frightening me. It was a real shock. My fear of losing him created a kind of clinging in me after that. Today I can still feel that fear of losing him. When this happened, I also decided that if he gets upset, it's bad.

From that incident I learned that he was fragile. He has a fragile heart and system. These panic attacks reoccurred over time. In more recent years, he's learned that he had a heart attack when he was in his forties. I think that he just forgot about it. He has a way of just getting back on his horse. He doesn't want to dwell on his ailment. If he does, he's losing what life he has to do things. He is upset if he can't get up and paint, arrange things or work on archiving his work.

After a rough year at Beverly Hills High School, I went back to Ithaca to go to a different school where there were more kids like me, and I would visit Dad all summer. Following high school I attended art school in Denver, went abroad and found my way to New York City to attend the School of Visual Arts for two years.

Around 2001 I went through two years of hell—what some people call a "dark night of the soul" or a "Saturn return." I was drawing waves, and I experienced a tremendous amount of fear, like a tidal wave was going to hit me. I was digging for answers as an artist. I dug a hole, went into the dark places and didn't have a rope to get back out. I was kind of lost there for a while. While I was going through this crisis, I just didn't want to live. As a child I had experienced a paralyzing fear—I would freeze. I noticed that others were less afraid in so many ways.

All of this is my own stuff, but I feel that I also inherited some from both sides of my family. I realize that my father's experience must have shaped a kind of horrific fear at what he'd been through. I felt that I was living his fear and terror. But not only that, I felt the oppressor in me as well. My grandmother on my mother's side of the family came from Hungary. They were called Saxons, like the Germans that came to Hungary, and had been there for a long time. These people were the oppressors.

During this time, on one of the trips to see my father, I was try ng hard to be good with him, even though I was still struggling deeply inside me. I made an effort to explain to him what was happening and how we might deal with it. I suggested to him that every time we get in an argument, I'm going to walk out the door. That would upset him, and I'd come back to say, "Dad, if I don't leave, you will have another episode. This whole thing could blow up and turn into an explosion between us." I started doing this actively, and he appreciated it. He said, "You're right. If we get into a little scrabble, your leaving is helpful because I don't go past the red line."

We started working together. One time in L.A. when I was crying, he brought out his guitar. He said, "Remember when I used to play this to you?" The moment he started playing his guitar, I recalled that this was what he was giving me when I was a child. When I was a little baby, he would play his guitar and sing to me. At that moment, everything changed. I could hear the music again. I was being pulled out of this murk. He gave me a guitar. I went back to New York, and I was playing it every day, and my life was getting better and better. So music is very important.

My mom will tell you that she chose my father in part because he was musical. She wanted to have a child with him, and she wanted that part to be in me. So it is.

The music is in my father. It is in his artwork. Visual art and music are companions. Whether he thinks about it or not, he's a musician in a sense. He's composing. He's making decisions. He's creating something that's going to be heard with the eyes. So ultimately he's a musician.

Dad shared stories with me about the Holocaust. I think he survived because some kind of grace has been with him. Based on his own goodness, he has some kind of guardian. He was able to keep his wits about him and keep his integrity—keep himself straight. He was able to see what it was doing to other people around him and not let that happen to him. He was also able to isolate himself in a kind of inward way to protect himself in a mental way. He made himself invisible, as he often says. He would say that if people were standing out in the middle of the yard, he would be one with the building. It was a real hiding game, but maybe more about keeping his persona quiet somehow. Dad had a constant awareness. Something inside him kept saying, "Don't let them get you."

But there was something else. I remember some of the escape stories, like when he got away from the Russian soldiers on his way to Vienna. That takes some kind of fearlessness. Maybe he thought, "I've got nothing to lose. . . . I don't see any future. I'm gonna make a run for it." That's probably a really human place to be. I think something inside him told him that he had to live because he had a life to live.

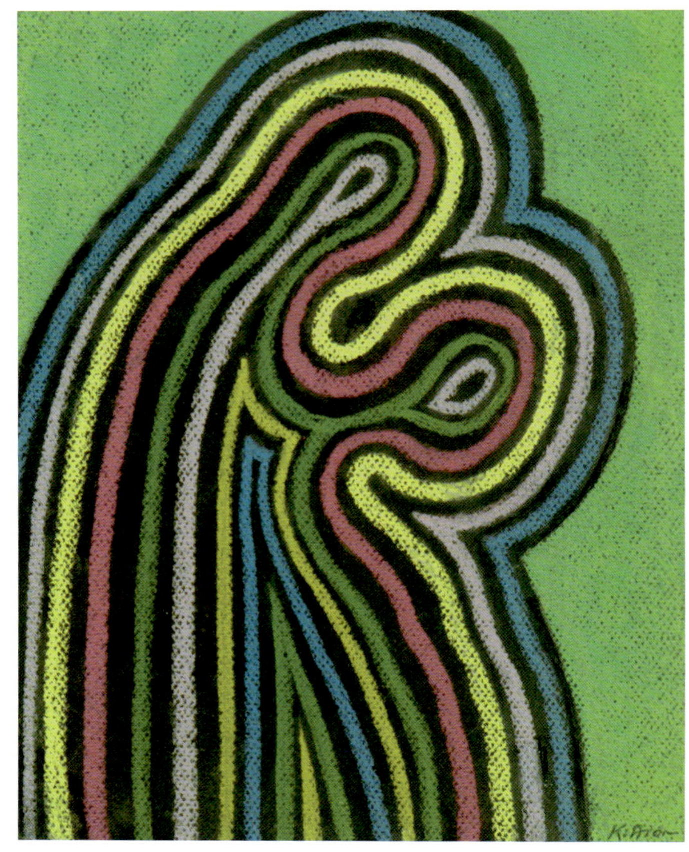

The Embrace (2003), pastel on paper, 12 × 9 in.

When he first got to Los Angeles, he protected himself from being hurt by not spending time with those who were dwelling on the war and just commiserating continually. Some people chose to remember and embrace what happened in a way that was not making them happy. He didn't want any of that. He's like, 'I lived through this. As far as I'm concerned, I've got a second life here.' So he avoided diving back into that history. He just made sure that he wasn't absorbing too much of the other people's misery. He also would go hang out with Americans and learn. They were having fun; they didn't have this history. Life in L.A. was new, and he's kind of adventurous.

The biggest protection he has is his art. He's such a real, genuine artist. He could be anywhere in any part of a city with his easel, painting. People get drawn into what he's doing, and they say, "Wow." Dad becomes this luminous figure, untouchable, because he has this magical skill.

The Holocaust affected his art in a number of ways. He has a compassionate view of his subjects, especially when he's painting the elderly and children. He has a concern for portraying somebody well. Deep down he has a lot of humility. He doesn't think that any one kind of person's life is more important than another's. That's important to know. He has had to take care of himself and raise himself to a comfortable quality of life. He understands the hardships of other people. He's sensitive to that. He draws older figures, the chess players and the young people with great warmth. You feel and see their emotions. He is a master at capturing the spirit of human beings.

In addition, the color palette he uses actually changes. Some of his early work was really dark and heavy. Sometimes in his work you can see a heaviness, like the color of his mind. Look at his chess players. They're very delicate, they're soft, but there's always a kind of dark coloring. He has also done bright works. Even these are lean; they're not whimsical. I think he draws and paints what he feels. There are times when he has expressed love, loss, loneliness and passion in a very personal way. He has told me about a few drawings like that. You can see it. For example, he has done some brightly colored pastels on black paper with figurative images built up in different colors. He referred to them as a kind of embrace. They might represent someone he met, had feelings for, and felt her come and go. The pastel *The Embrace* captures the timeless human experience of longing and loss. When I saw it, I thought: I have felt this loss, and I realize that he's the same as me. We are different ages, but we share the same longings.

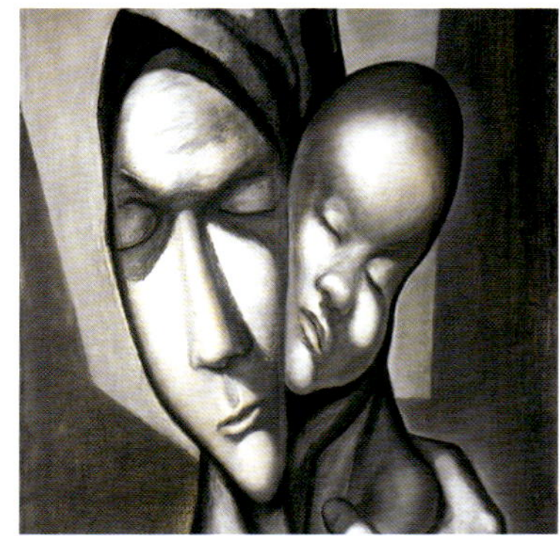

Mother and Child (detail); full image on page 85.

In some early works he processed the war experience—the large pastel of the *Mother and Child* and some small paintings are examples. *The Mother and Child* is important to him. The color is murky, muddy for a reason. In addition, artwork around Los Angeles at that time had a certain vibe, and weight in your work was a good thing.

Dad also processes the horror in his dreams. He says he doesn't remember any dreams. But when I'm with him at his house, I see him sleeping. I can see that he's dreaming about what happened. He'll make a noise or something. I can feel and hear the horror in his voice.

The night after learning about the killing fields outside of Riga where my grandmother was executed, I had a dream, witnessing people killing each other in a really horrible way. When you're dreaming, you're unaware that you are dreaming. You are experiencing all that horrible imagery. When I woke up, it felt like, "Whoa, that was horrible." My father must have experienced that all the time, over and over again. That's really got to kill a part of you.

He doesn't cry. During my own dark night of the soul, I was so hardened because I had anger, hatred and all these things, and I couldn't cry for about a year and a half. The feelings wouldn't come up. I knew that if I could cry, it would be a release. It's so painful not to be able to cry. I would think that in my dad and all those who lived through the Holocaust, there's still a lot of anger, hatred and resentment. How could there not be? It gets stuck down real deep.

My father has a Renaissance quality about him. He is secure in himself. He's good with people. He's really open and passionate about things. He has a strong constitution, but he also has this gentle heart. My dad's got a really young mind. He's a kid. As with us all, there is more for him to know about himself and his behavioral patterns.

He is real magnetic, and he was kind of a ladies' man. But he's never been greedy. He's always been self-made. He has integrity. He sees beforehand if something is going to turn him into something he doesn't want, and he avoids that.

Through past relationships and marriages, it's been hard for him to open himself up to somebody. There's a wall. He has trust issues and for good reason. His experiences have molded him. With his decision to remember and share his story in this book, he has a new opportunity to break through this wall.

French Village (1978–79), oil on canvas, 36 × 48 in.

I didn't hear much about his parents. The way he talks about his father and mother is a bit detached. He didn't know them for long, and he was raised in the religious atmosphere of a Jewish family. He once told me that his father, Chaim, and his father's brother, David, were anarchists. He remembers them in their workshop, talking about being anarchists. He tells me how his father was the best shoemaker. I never really hear anything about his mother. It must be so hard for him to even think about her.

My favorite paintings are the landscapes. They're imaginative, and some have a sense that he's found himself. He'll do them from life, but then he switches the colors around or just shifts everything, and it looks like some kind of inner world. An example is *French Village* with a view down the street. It is an oil done in the psychological realism style. The light source is strange. It's like a white light, a kind of nonexistent light, appearing in the darkness and hitting these buildings. This painting has always suggested to me this grace—something that will carry him through hard times. It is not realistic. It has something that goes beyond. It's personal. It has a lot to do with me. It has a lot to do with my mother and some of the things she's expressed to me about the light and how it comes into play in our lives. You get the sense of just light, maybe suggesting transformation and hope. And there's something distinctly Jewish about it. I feel it, that half of me. I feel a strong cultural resemblance.

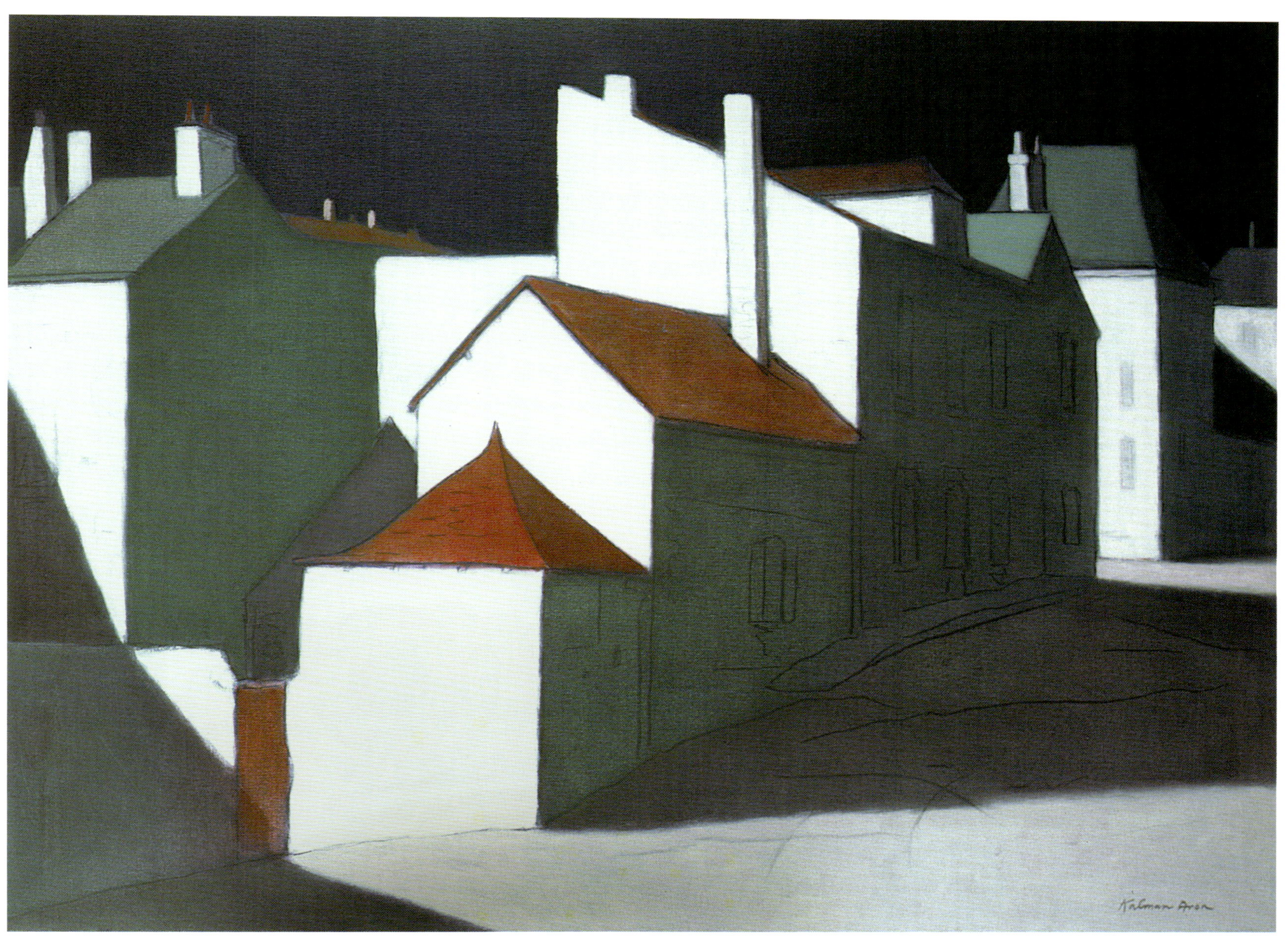
Kálman Aron

I also love the night scene from his balcony of Los Angeles: *Night Lights of L.A.* What an incredible feat to capture the city at night.

The most playful are the ones he did a number of years ago when he started working with acrylics. He never used them before. The color palette is different; they are bright, with lots of color contrast, as in *Orange Trees.* Your eyes really bounce around. There's a lot of light coming through.

Trees are a symbol for him. He has a connection to nature. His gentleness allows things to happen and to be. When he sees a tree and he wants to draw it, the tree is kind of talking to him a little bit. He sees beauty in it, and he is seeing the essence or spirit of nature. I imagine that when he sits or stands outside with his easel and draws a landscape, without analyzing or thinking about it, this probably softens him and connects him to nature. He gets in it, and he likes to be in it and stay in it and work with it. It is a refuge. And he makes choices at his own pace. He would draw really quickly because he's excited. Then he would go back and make it sing. He's like a poet, making poetry of it. He also captures everything about it. He's so incredible in capturing different states of light. He paints and draws water really well.

There is a part of my dad—the way he senses things—that allows him to capture the essence of something in its truth and character and allows people to live there by just looking at his work. He's a master artist. That pretty much sums it up. He's mastered his way of making art. He's mastered his work ethic. He lives to make things. He doesn't harm himself through his work, which a lot of artists do. I think art is a meditation for him. It really connects him to his subject, and it probably brings his heart rate down. It has a healing effect on him; it regulates him. He paints for the peacefulness that he gets from it and the satisfaction he draws from the act of painting.

My father has given me certain gifts. In addition to music, he has given me something of a mystical nature. He is spiritual without knowing it. He has an obvious grace and moral platform that allows him to be good in the world. He opens some kind of door to other worlds.

He has also given me the gift of art making. He encouraged me. Through the tool of making art, I find all these things in myself because I am excavating my own mind, processing things.

For Kalman Aron, his son David represents family, the meaning of life, the legacy of ancestors.

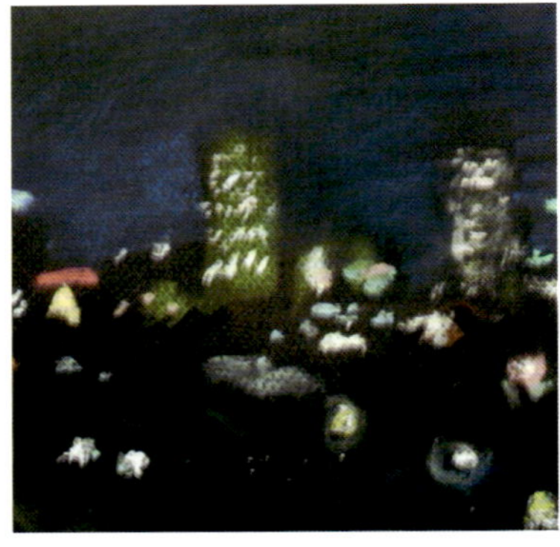

Night Lights of L.A. (detail); full image on page 98.

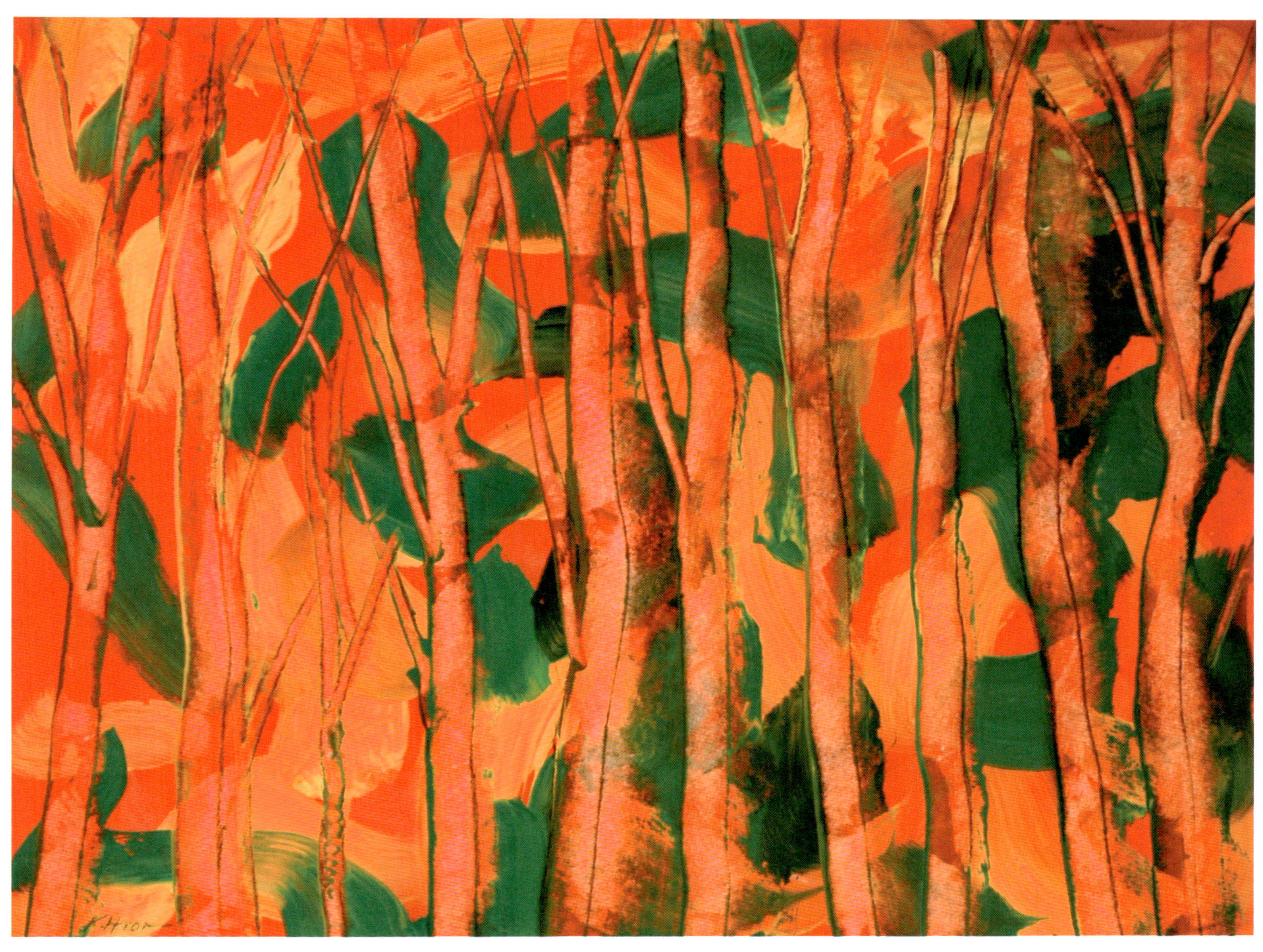

Orange Trees (early 1990s), acrylic on paper, 10½ × 14 in.

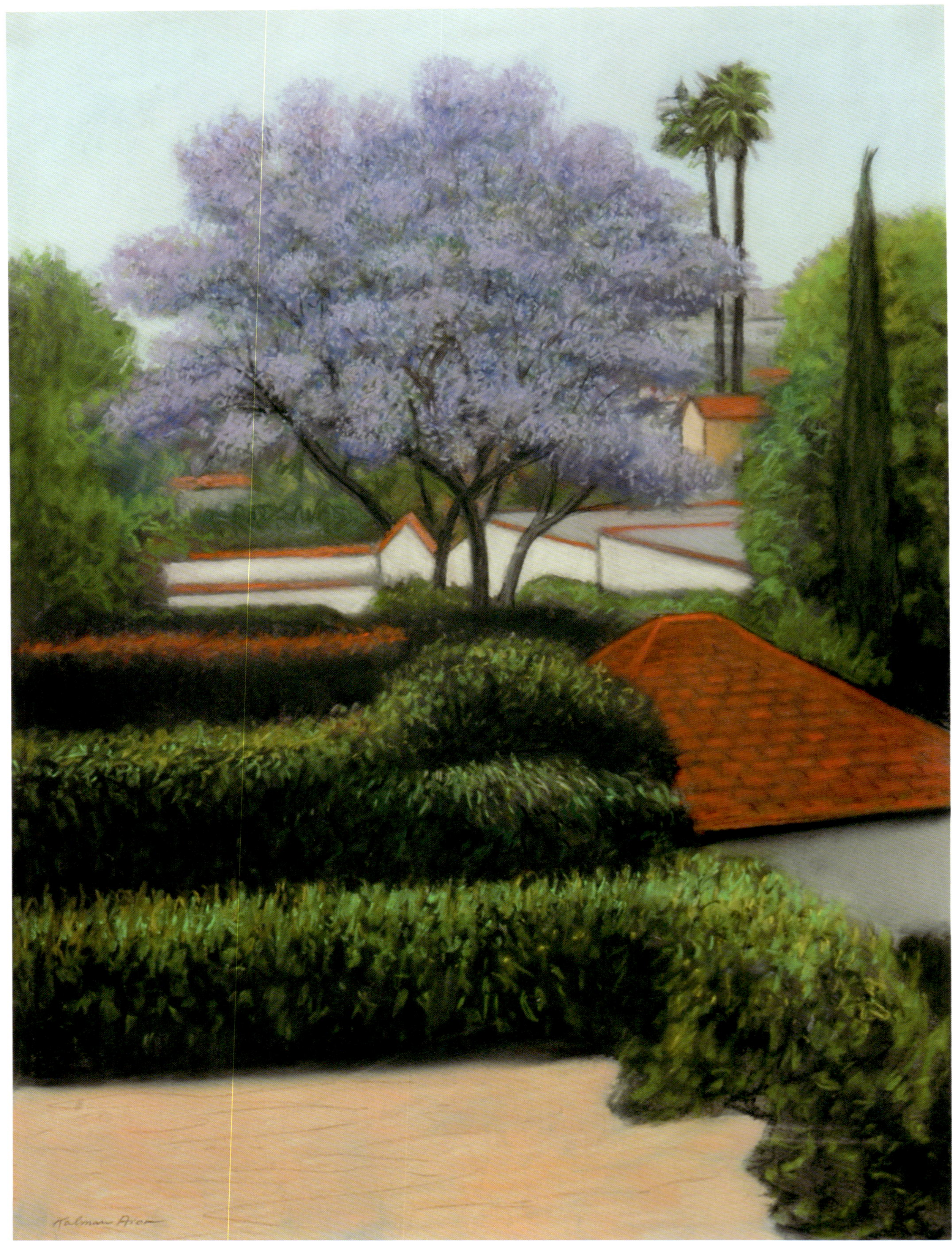

9

ILLUMINATING ALCHEMY

A Touch of Grace

He who carries his own lantern need not fear darkness.

Hasidic Proverb

The Jacaranda Tree (2005), pastel on paper, 29½ × 21¼ in.

Life is a journey. I believe each person enters the world with a unique configuration of genes, family and cultural heritage and the free will to choose how to live. Everyone experiences some joy in life, and no one escapes suffering. Loss and trauma are part of the human condition. How we respond to life's challenges shapes our personalities and realities. Individuals may remain victims of their past, or choose to remember dark experiences and proceed to heal. This process of healing is the alchemy of the soul.

By definition, alchemy is a "transforming or enchanting power." While the ancients tried to harness this power to turn lead into gold, others invoke this magic to achieve an inner transformation, heal themselves and become whole. This personal alchemy requires a journey into one's interior landscape, looking in the shadows and dark corners, shining one's light to see what is there. In this journey of discovery, we become aware of true feelings and deeply held beliefs. Much of what controls our lives and realities lies unconsciously in this inner labyrinth. Venturing into this territory requires courage, honesty and perseverance.

What are the rewards? Freedom and mastery! When we see the truth, we are free to let go of old baggage—behaviors and beliefs that no longer serve—and to make new choices. We begin to master our nature and achieve emotional neutrality about past trauma. We can remember previous sorrows and trauma without tightening up, exploding or flinching.

Kalman Aron's life exemplifies this process. He suffered extremes of human brutality. Having survived the Holocaust, he chose to explore the darkness he experienced and to process the loss of family and innocence. He did this largely unconsciously through his art for over six decades until the age of seventy-eight, when he chose to tell his story. That decision brought him face to face with the residual fear, terror, evil, hatred and rage still residing within himself.

Aron began his metamorphosis after the Holocaust when he chose to escape the Russians at Theresienstadt, to pursue his art at the Vienna Fine Arts Academy and then to leave Europe and start a new life in America. Once in Los Angeles, he continued his journey of transformation, all of which is reflected in his art.

Living Alchemy on Canvas

On canvas, Aron returned to those places of horror and during his four years in the Holocaust. Many of his paintings in the 1950s are dark and heavy, reflecting his Holocaust experience. As he worked out these complicated feelings on canvas, his view of himself and the world began to change.

The most obvious transformation appears in his self-portraits. In the early 1950s he painted a gouache of himself at Buchenwald, *Marching in the Camps*. There is no light in his eyes. He has shut down his senses, leaving only black holes for eyes to watch and a mouth to eat. Nonetheless, his face reveals a fierce determination to survive.

In his self-portrait painted in 1967 at age forty-three, Aron is no longer a skeleton; his face has filled out. He has become a man with ruddy cheeks, cautious eyes and a serious countenance. Full of sorrow, he has the vigilant look of someone who does not trust.

At age seventy Aron drew a self-portrait in charcoal. The sadness has left his eyes. Wearing his signature beret, he is a mature man with penetrating eyes—a much different visage than his drawing of himself marching in the camps.

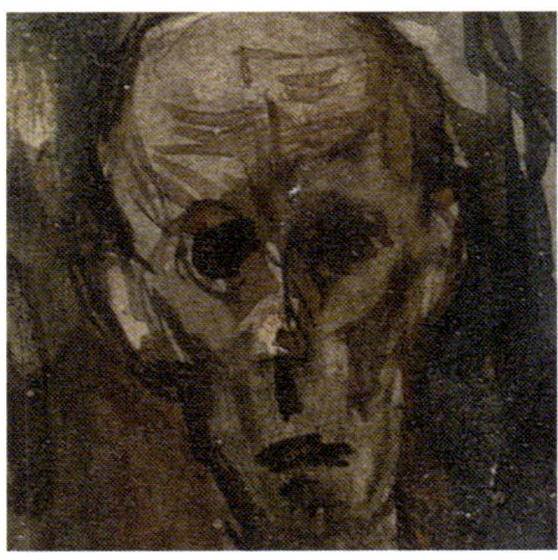

Kalman Marching in the Camp (detail); full image on page 50.

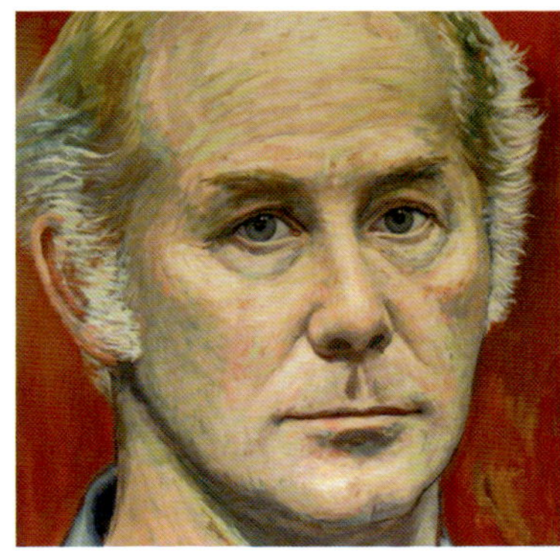

Self-Portrait (detail); full image on page 136.

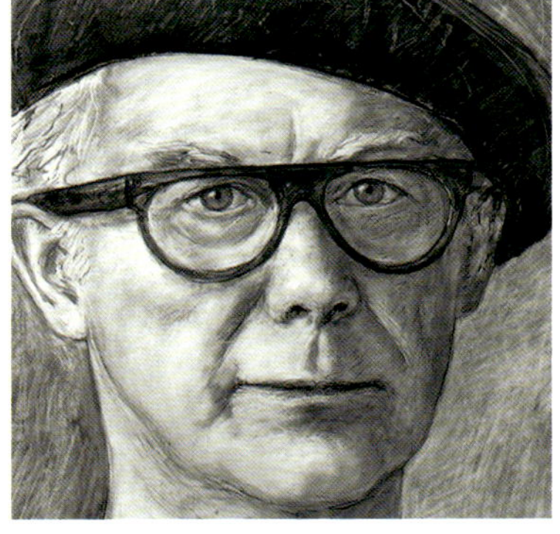

Self-Portrait (detail); full image on page 18.

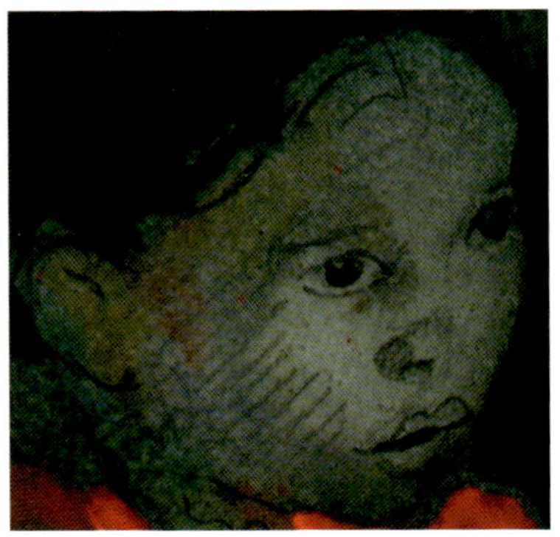

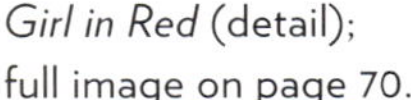

Girl in Red (detail);
full image on page 70.

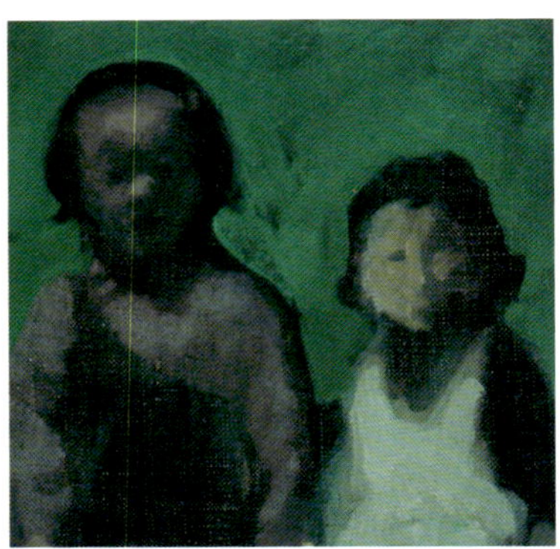

The Lost Children (detail);
full image on page 73.

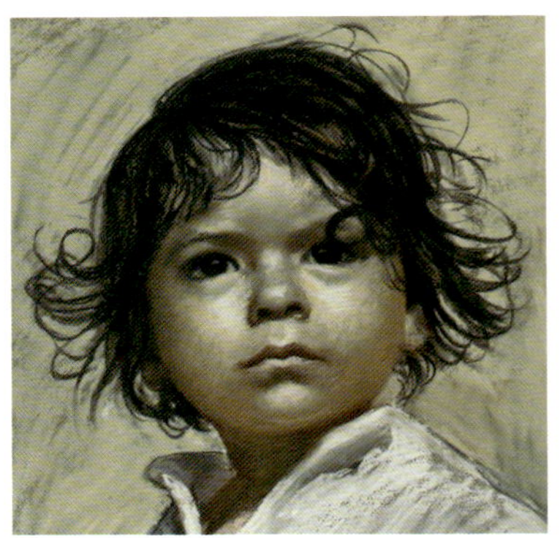

Child with Black Eyes (detail);
full image on page 8.

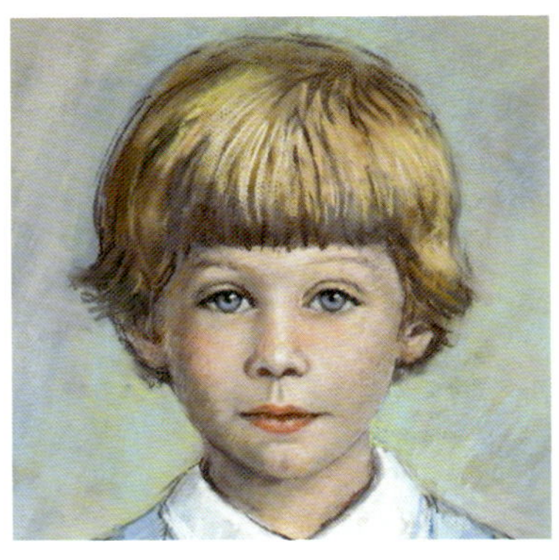

Portrait of Eric (detail);
full image on page 140.

Four details of paintings of children further illustrate this transformation. In the first two, done in the early 1950s, *Girl in Red* and *Lost Children*, Aron paints the children surrounded in darkness and shadows. There is no light in their eyes. In *Girl in Red* Aron defines the child's face by using shades of gray and black ink. Her countenance is forbidding; her look otherworldly. Alone in the darkness, she seems weary and frightened, wondering what might happen next.

He painted *Lost Children* from a drawing he made in the 1950s of two children walking in a Jewish neighborhood in Brooklyn. There is no sunlight in this painting. A shadowy fog surrounds them. They are alone. Aron gave the girl the face of an old woman, perhaps remembering how children looked during the Holocaust: not only were they lost, but they became old before their time.

These faces contrast sharply with those in *Child with Black Eyes*, painted in 1951, and *Portrait of Eric*, from 1977. In *Child with Black Eyes* the boy's countenance expresses a fierce determination to meet life's challenges. In *Portrait of Eric* the child's eyes are full of light, life and curiosity, ready to explore the world.

In the first two paintings Aron captures what happened to children who were terrorized and left alone. In the last two paintings he reconnects with the childlike qualities of curiosity, determination and exuberance for life—qualities nurtured by his parents. These four paintings provide glimpses of Aron's alchemy in integrating the simultaneous realities of darkness, shadows and light.

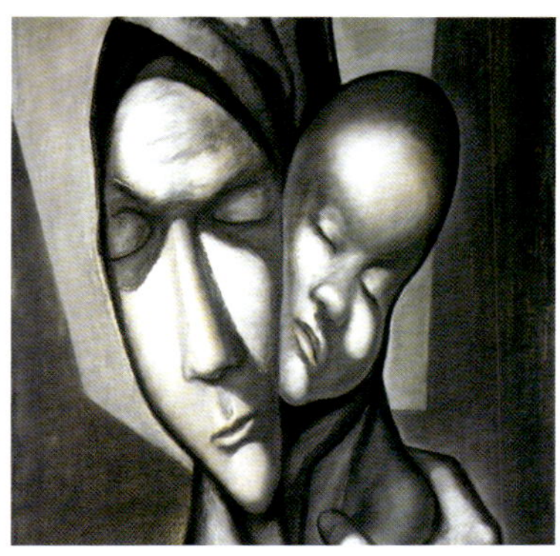

Mother and Child (detail); full image on page 85.

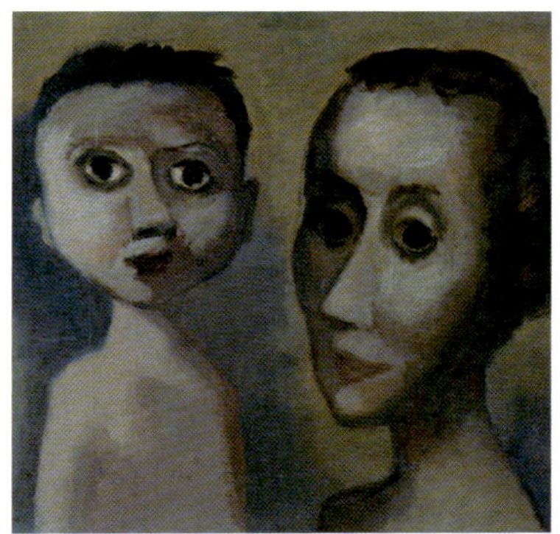

Mother and Child II (detail); full image on page 86.

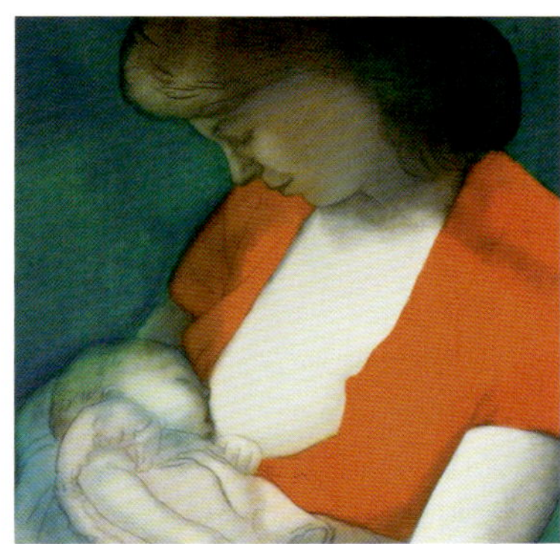

Mother Nursing Her Child (detail); full image on page 143.

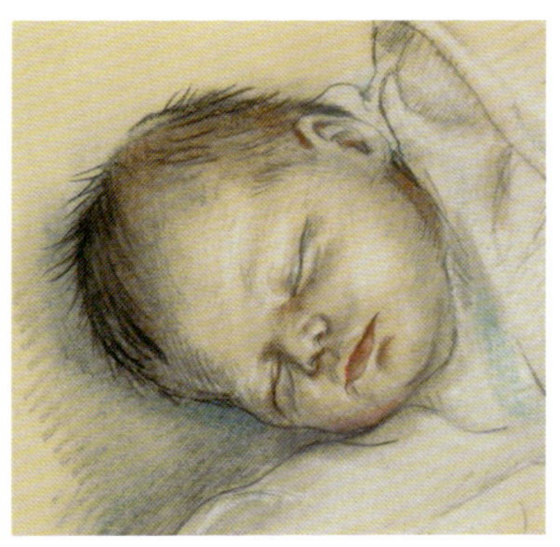

Baby David (detail); full image on page 179.

What happened to mothers and their children during the Holocaust had a profound effect on Aron. He witnessed children being torn away from their mothers and babies killed before their eyes. Once again, he dealt with these feelings on canvas. In his masterpiece, *Mother and Child,* painted in 1951, he created a distorted and warped void outside of human space and time. The mother clings to her child, bonding her to her own body. Eyes tightly shut, neither mother nor baby dares look at what is happening around them. In the small portrait *Mother and Child II,* done at the same time, Aron painted two gaunt survivors of the horror, but mother and child are no longer connected to themselves or each other. No light is left in the mother's eyes, and only a small glimmer can be found in the child's eyes.

Contrast these to what he painted thirty years later, *Mother Nursing Her Child.* With great tenderness and abundant color, Aron depicts the bond between mother and child. He captures the mystery, devotion and intimacy of the nursing mother as she gently holds her baby to her breast. His ability to paint this attests to his own inner journey in transmuting the evil he beheld. It also suggests that he recaptured a certain intimacy within himself, one linked to the woman who raised him, his mother, Sonia. He brought a child into the world, and recorded David's early life in drawings. In *Baby David* he gently captures him resting, using soft pastels on paper.

The alchemical changes within Aron's interior landscape dramatically affected what he saw in nature. This transformation can be seen in a comparison of two landscapes from the 1950s with two painted in the 1980s.

What caught Aron's eye in his early years in Los Angeles were old, run-down houses on Bunker Hill. In the charcoal drawing *Old House on Bunker Hill,* Aron draws a haunted-looking Victorian house in shades of black and gray. Standing alone, it is reminiscent of the wooden structures in Aron's old world in Riga.

Painting his new neighborhood in *Hills in Silver Lake,* he shifts the prism through which he sees the world. He draws this neighborhood in black and white—still no color. Nor do people or animals inhabit this world. Nonetheless, this landscape is quite different from *Old House on Bunker Hill.* It has more clarity and contrast. Nature reappears in the California shrubs and trees around the buildings and on top of the hill. There is a different quality of light in this pristine rendering. Aron is slowly coming back to life.

Thirty years later, Aron's landscapes explode with life, color and texture. In *Balcony View from My Studio* he boldly paints his neighborhood full of movement, light and contrasting colors. The sky is alive as the clouds touch the top of the Hollywood Hills. The red Spanish tile roofs contrast with a range of greens found in the surrounding trees and bushes. Aron's view of his surroundings has clearly changed. This painting reveals the light, warmth and comfort he recaptured in himself.

The intriguing *Night Lights of L.A.* contains mystery. Aron peers into the night sky and explores the light within the darkness. His experience taught him that light, darkness and shadows are companions in man as well as in nature. They define both. Further, humans and nature mirror each other. "As within, so without," as the ancients said. Aron arrived at this knowledge intuitively and unconsciously.

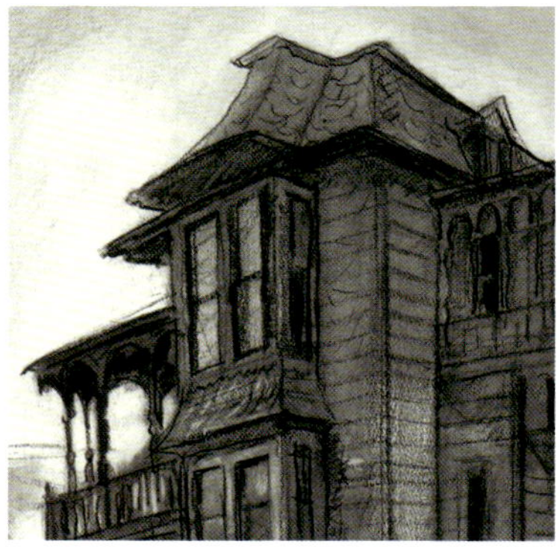

Old House on Bunker Hill (detail); full image on page 76.

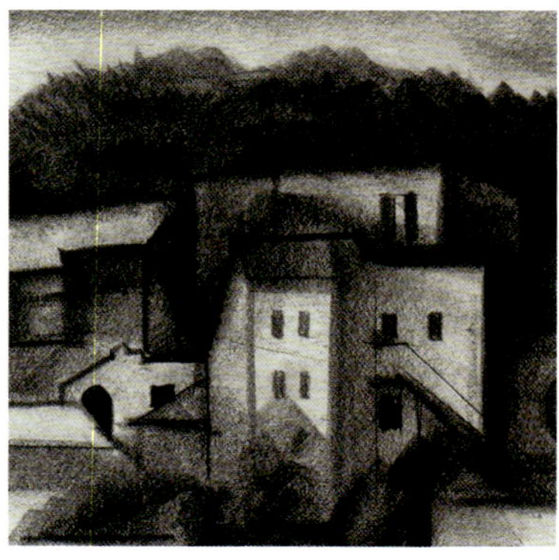

Silver Lake (detail); full image on page 80.

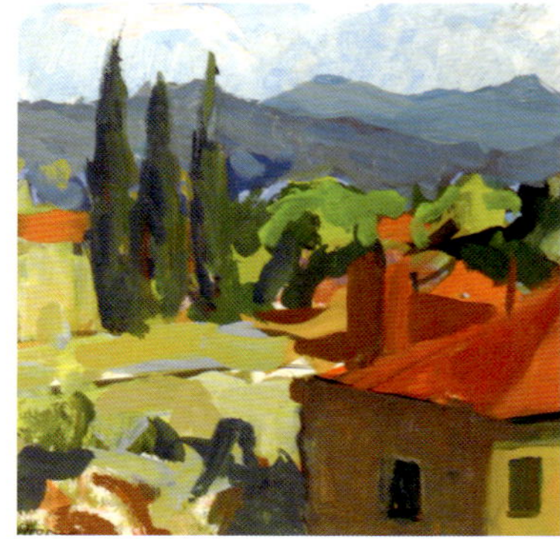

Balcony View from My Studio (detail); full image on page 97.

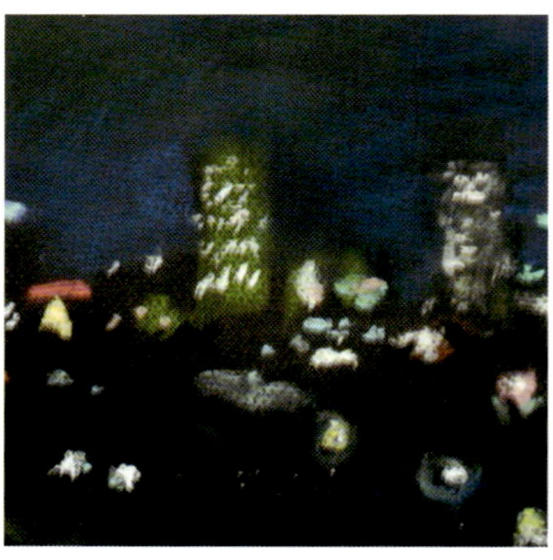

Night Lights of L.A. (detail); full image on page 98.

A Decision: To Remember

Remembering involves pain and leads to freedom.

When Aron arrived in Los Angeles, he buried his past to move forward in his new life and country. His art became his therapy and salvation. On canvas he explored the complex emotions and questions he carried inside. One can see how much he processed and changed by comparing his early art to his paintings in the 1980s. But alchemy is a lifelong process. How much trauma does the body still hold? At age seventy-eight Aron decided to go deeper. He decided to remember and tell his story.

This decision required courage. Aron survived the Holocaust in part by learning to be invisible. To be seen meant death. Decades later, as he and I worked together, he experienced an ongoing internal war between two conflicting voices. One voice said, "Do not tell our story. Paint, but remain invisible. If you are seen, you will be killed." The other voice said, "Go ahead; it is time." At some point in everyone's life, the pain of burying the past may become greater than the pain of remembering. Perhaps Aron reached that point.

In researching his story I continually opened windows and triggered memories of his past. In the beginning I spent eighteen hours interviewing him, asking about his family, childhood and experience in the Holocaust, about his art before and after the war. I interviewed his family and friends. In the archives of the United States Holocaust Memorial Museum in Washington, I looked for evidence of his experience in the Riga ghetto and seven concentration camps. I called him, asking questions to help me find information in the museum. I met him regularly in California to show him what I had found: photos of his neighborhood synagogue—the Great Choral Synagogue—burning, the Riga ghetto, the clothing factory where he worked, and photos of the camps Kaiserwald, Stutthof, Buchenwald and Theresienstadt.

One of the first documents I found was a mimeographed report published in Prague, which listed the prisoners liberated by the Russians on May 8, 1945, at Theresienstadt. There was his name, "ARON KALMAN, * 14. 9. 1924—Riga" in bold print, a historical document confirming that yes, the man named Kalman Aron, who was born in Riga on September 14, 1924, was freed on May 8, 1945. I also found a map of the Riga ghetto and asked him to mark the street where he lived for two and a half years. I discussed books by other Latvian survivors and asked, Did you know him? Did you know her? Were you together in the ghetto or the camps? Do you realize you are one of only 1,000 Latvian Jews to survive? Andrew Ezergailis in his book *The Holocaust in Latvia, 1941–1944*, estimates that 70,000 to 75,000 Jews lived in Latvia when the Germans invaded in 1941. Only 1,000 survived.

ARDITTI MAURICE, * 13. 1. 1923 — Paris.
ARJE SCHMUL JOSEF, * 1. 5. 1920 — Łódz.
ARKUSZ MOTEL, * 10. 7. 1918 — Dialoszice.
ARMUTH TIBOR, * 12. 3. 1910 — Györ.
ARON KALMAN, * 14. 9. 1924 — Riga.
ARON LILLY, * 26. 3. 1925 — Teke.
ARON RIKSA, * 18. 2. 1924 — Halmı.
ARON WOLF, * 13. 4. 1927 — Recklinghausen.
ARONOWITZ ALEXANDER, * 24. 9. 1913 — Łódź.
ARONSOHN JOSUA, * 28. 8. 1910 — Salonique.
AROUH ABRAHAM, * 7. 8. 1913 — Budapest.

Kalman Aron's name appears in the official volume *Terezin Ghetto*, published by the Czech Republic's Repatriation Protection Department, Ministry of Labor and Social Welfare (Prague, 1945).

I went to Europe to walk the streets of Riga, visit the ghetto and see the remains of the burned synagogue. I found the empty lot where his home once stood, overlooking the Daugava River. On his 80th birthday I called him from Riga. I had just visited the Bikernieki Forest, where his father most likely was killed in July 1941, and I had spent the morning at the killing field at Rumbula, where the Germans executed his mother along with 25,000 other Riga Jews in two *Aktions* in November and December 1941. I described my experience at both killing sites and explained that I wanted to place a memorial stone honoring his parents with their names at a recently built memorial at Rumbula. He agreed.

I found all three camps in Latvia. An apartment sits on the grounds of the transit camp, Kaiserwald, on the outskirts of Riga. The work camps in the Baltic forest where Aron spent a year have returned to pasture and forest. He wanted to know the name of the commandant at Poperwahlen, the man for whom he drew a miniature portrait of his parents that went in his ring. I told him about Gustav Sorge, called "Iron Gustav," the commandant of Dundaga who led "his children" on the march to the sea as the Russians were nearing Latvia. Aron recalled his failed attempt to escape as he neared the ship that would take him to his next camp, Stutthof. I could not find out what happened to his young love, Kori Brown, the Hungarian woman at Poperwahlen.

I traced Aron's steps across Europe to Stutthof, Buchenwald, Rehmsdorf and Theresienstadt. In Stutthof I sat before a gas oven and wondered how Aron felt being reunited with his brother briefly in 1944, only to be separated again for life. At Buchenwald I walked down to the Little Camp, where Aron had slept on the ground. I found the transit paper marking his arrival there on August 16, 1944. I showed Kalman the transit paper, and he recalled the arrival of a famous Latvian surgeon who died as as a prisoner in Buchenwald.

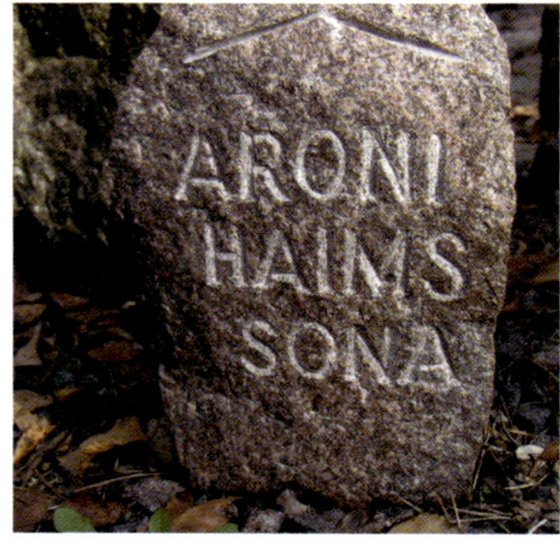

A stone placed by the author bears the names of Kalman's parents, Chaim and Sonia Aron (in a Latvian iteration) at the site of the Rumbula Massacre.

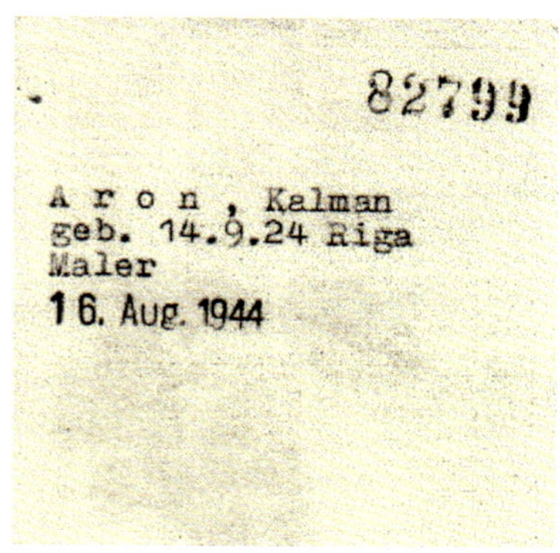

82799

Aron, Kalman
geb. 14.9.24 Riga
Maler
16. Aug. 1944

A transit paper issued at Buchenwald records data for Kalman Aron.

At Rehmsdorf I met a man who at age sixteen had been part of the Hitler Youth paramilitary organization. He watched the prisoners leave the camp before dawn, then return after sunset after working all day in the Brabag synthetic gasoline factory. Now he maintains a small historical memorial to honor the prisoners. He walked me to the barracks, where just outside stands the small home of a woman who placed pieces of bread on her windowsill for the passing prisoners each day.

Kalman's body tightened as he recalled being buried alive in a hill of dirt from a bomb. He remembered his friend's body being blown apart. As he told me the story, he turned his head aside, as though he might avoid seeing what had happened. He learned not to make friends in the camps. Losing them was too likely, and too painful.

One of his most powerful reactions came when he remembered the arrival of his father's cousin and son at Rehmsdorf. They were starving. His father's cousin reached down to the ground to pick up a dead bird to eat. In relating the event, Aron became quiet, visibly shaken. He could not finish. A day later he continued: As he watched his relative put the bird to his mouth, he yelled out, "Stop!" But it was too late. The cousin ate it and died.

I learned the exact dates and route of the train and forced march from Rehmsdorf when the Germans moved the prisoners away from the advancing Allies. Beaten as they were put into the cattle cars, they then stood for several days and nights with no food or water while the Germans repaired the bombed-out tracks. Once on the move, the train was bombed again. Aron and the remaining prisoners had to leave the train and march over fifty-two miles in four days to Theresienstadt. I told him that he was one of only seventy-five prisoners from the original group of 2,775 from Rehmsdorf to survive to liberation day. When I shared this, Aron remembered the panic and confusion at the time:

What now? Where to? Are we being taken to be gassed? Or shot? How close are the Allied troops? One more day. I must survive one more day. If I run, where can I hide?

He recalled the typhus epidemic at Theresienstadt and thought it a miracle that he and his friend Zaltzy did not succumb. He remembered being separated from the other prisoners, along with five other Latvians and Lithuanians, when the Russians entered the camp. Taken to the forest and held up at gunpoint, he thought he would be shot. Instead, the Russian stole the Red Cross packages he had just been given.

So many memories.

I kept probing, bringing up what I was learning. Aron's body reacted. Anticipating our first interview, he got pneumonia. After our conversations, he had nightmares or woke with a racing heart, having trouble breathing. There were many trips to the hospital. What he experienced was physical, held in the marrow of the body. The body both resists remembering and purges memories as the heart heals.

A particularly poignant reaction occurred when I presented the first draft of this book to Aron. His body became rigid, and his head tilted away from the manuscript as I handed it to him. He put it on the table and lay his hand on the cover. He was visibly nervous. He asked some questions. He wanted to be sure it was accurate. Leaving it on his table, he said, "Give me a week to read it."

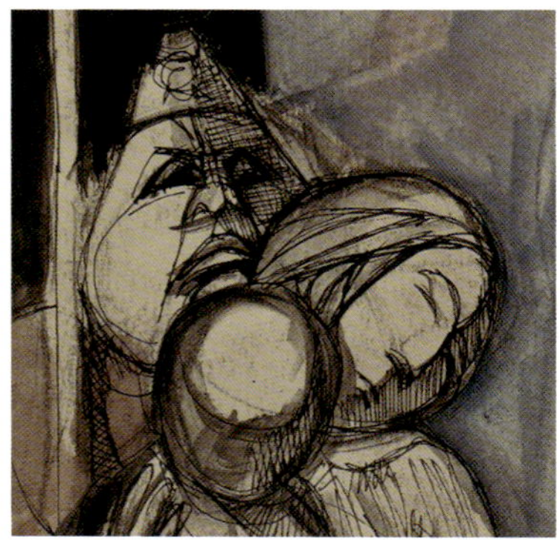

Memory (detail);
full image on page 43.

I returned to his apartment after he finished reading it. He looked at me with his piercing blue eyes and said, "I am overwhelmed. I don't know how an American girl could possibly understand what a European man went through. You have done it."

Throughout this process I have made more than twenty trips to California to interview him, show him materials and select paintings for the book. I have called him regularly with questions as I researched, traveled his path across Europe, wrote and edited the book. I have shared what I have learned at Holocaust museums in America and Europe. I told him I placed the names of his father, mother and uncle in the Hall of Names at Yad Vashem in Jerusalem.

During each step in the process, I have sat in meditation to gain insight and guidance about his life and art. My own healing journey and practice with others have informed this process profoundly. I have held a vision of placing memories and healing tools before him. What he embraces is entirely up to him. I understand how challenging it is for the body, mind and heart to remember. Only Aron knows how much he dares remember and at what pace. I trust his instinct.

Benefits of Remembering

The path of remembering offers great gifts. It allows mastery of one's emotions and behaviors. A step at a time, it enables the body, heart and mind to heal. Peace and freedom are the rewards.

Aron has seized a number of new opportunities. In 1994 an oral historian taped an interview with Aron on film for the Survivors of the Shoah Visual History Foundation archives. Toward the end she asked, "What didn't you tell us?" In this filmed interview, his voice wavers as he responds about one regret in his life: "I don't know. The problem of being single, divorced and not having a family. Not having anybody has been a problem. My son lives in New York. I live here. I'm alone, although I have a lot of friends."

A decade later, Aron took a leap of faith again. When I called him from Riga in 2004 to report on my progress, he had a surprise for me. He had met a woman at a local pharmacy the previous winter. Her name is Miriam Sandoval. Delighted, I had hoped the process of remembering would open his heart. "I was getting cough medicine," he remembered. "It was a cold night and she passed by with a wonderful smile. I asked her name. She told me 'Miriam.' I said 'Your name should be Sunshine.' After a brief conversation I asked for her phone number, and I called her one hour later. I was very interested in her optimistic outlook. We started dating."

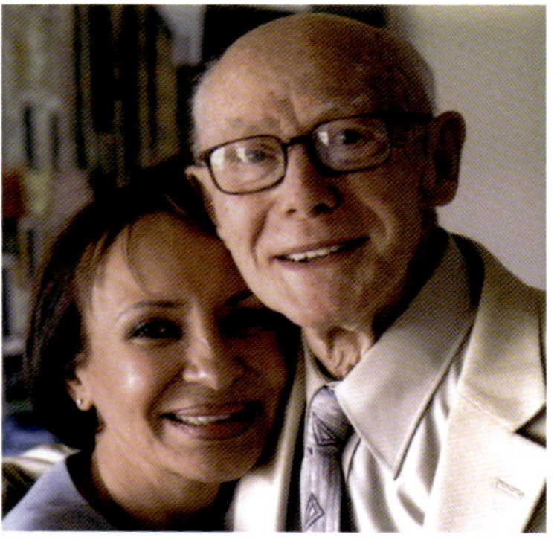

Kalman Aron and his wife Miriam Sandoval shortly after their wedding in 2005.

His son David said at the time, "My dad's gone from eighty to eighteen. I've never seen him like this. Things are happening. He and Miriam definitely love each other a lot. She loves his sense of humor; they're laughing and joking the whole time. On a day-to-day basis they give each other a lot of joy. Miriam is twenty-seven years younger than my dad. She comes from a large, close Catholic family in Venezuela. They are all well educated. Education is very important to her family." Miriam has a master's degree in business; her two daughters, who live in Los Angeles, both graduated from UCLA.

In the spring of 2005 Aron and Miriam attended David's wedding atop a hill on a farm in the Catskill Mountains. Five months later Kalman married Miriam Sandoval in a simple ceremony in Los Angeles. "She's a wonderful partner. I love her. I love being with her and waking up to her beautiful smile," he says. "She makes my day."

Studying their wedding photograph, I see light, hope and a willingness to open his heart, to try one more time. I can hear him say:

I've lived a long life. I can see far into the distance.

I can't fool myself. I hope that Miriam and I will bring happiness to each other. This is my last chance.

Life has not been easy. I have given up a lot for my art.

I have no real regrets. I just know how fragile life and love are.

Portrait of Miriam (2006), oil on canvas, 40 × 30 in.

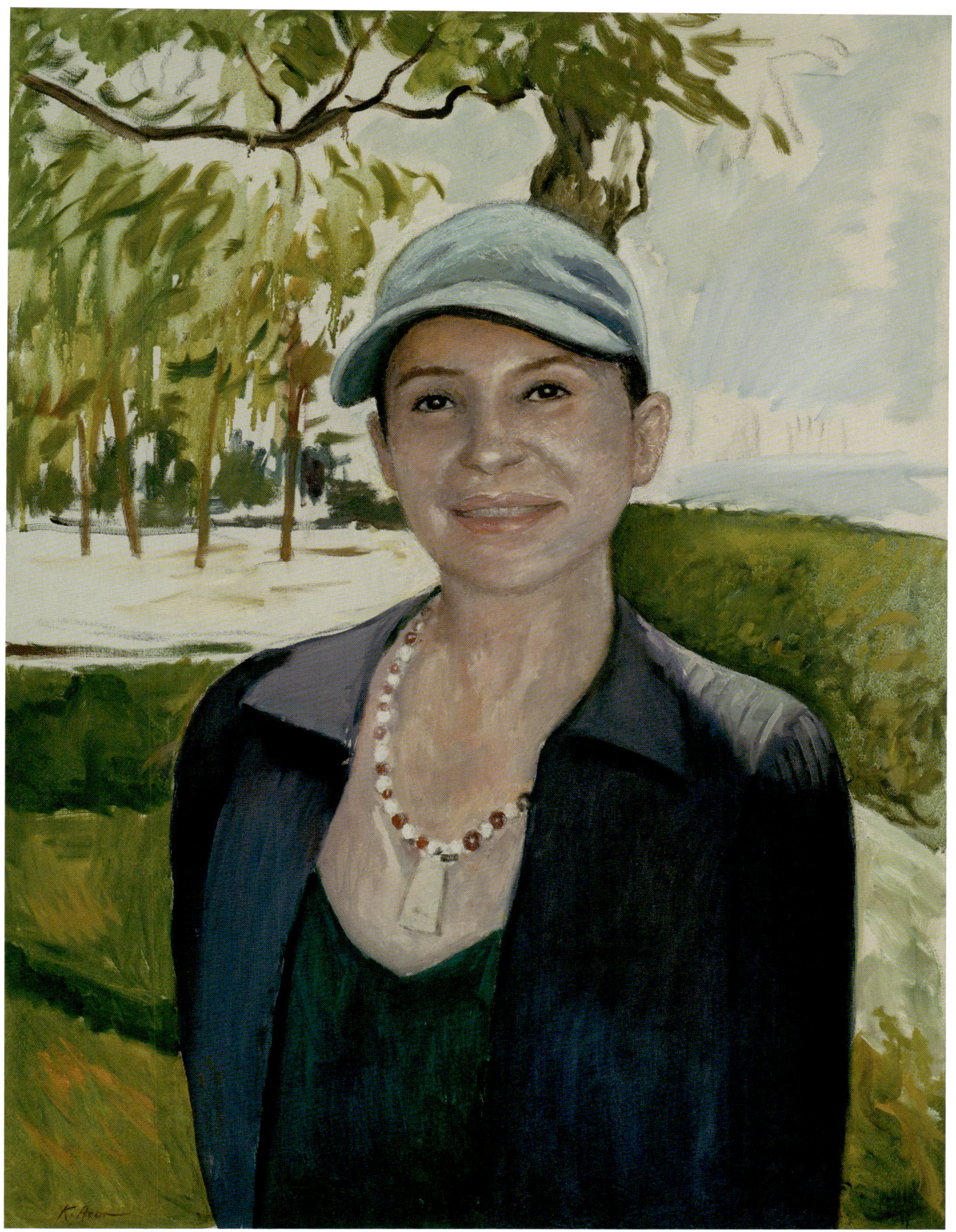

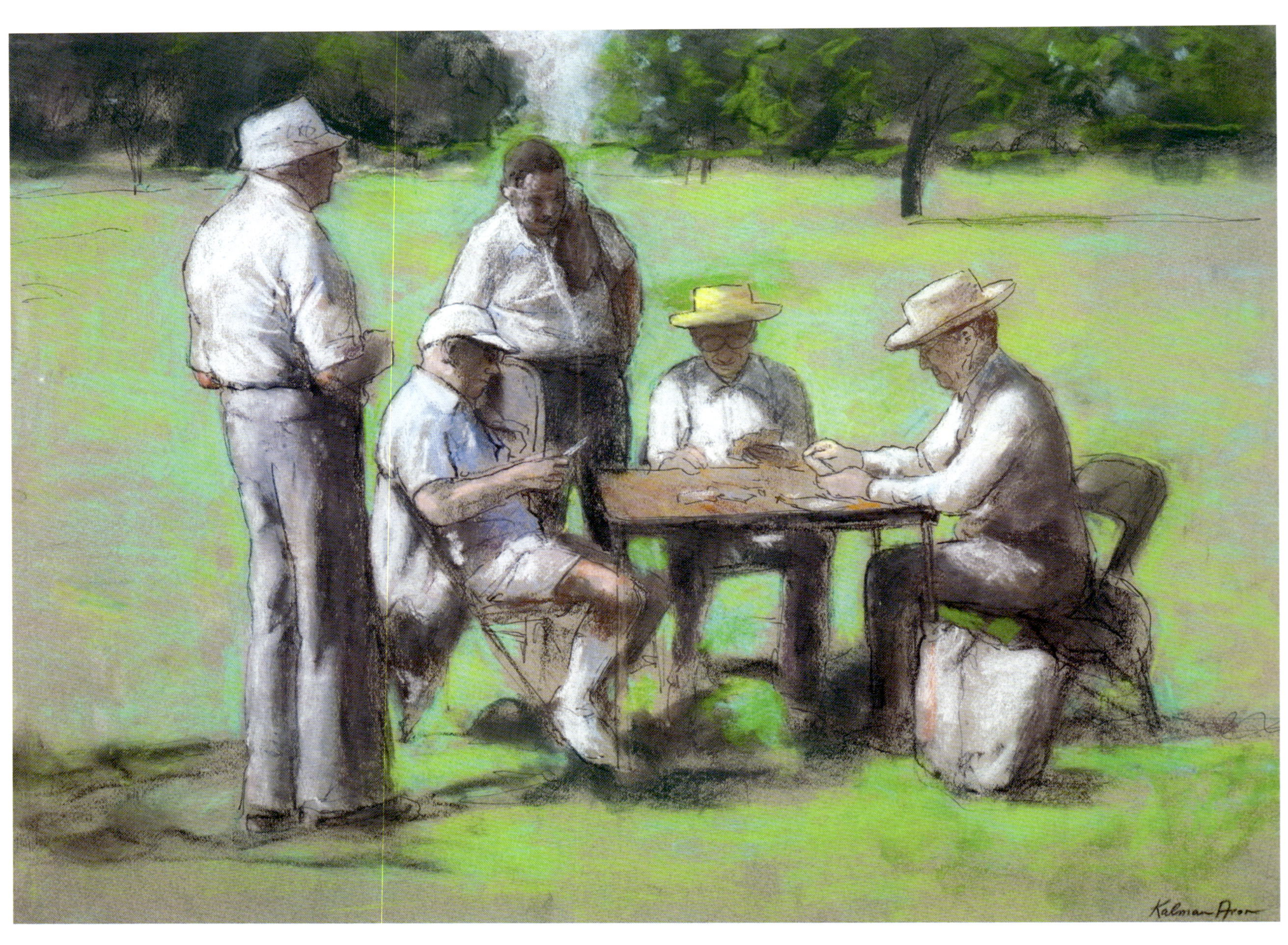

Men Playing Cards in Roxbury Park (2004), pastel on paper, 20¼ × 28½ in.

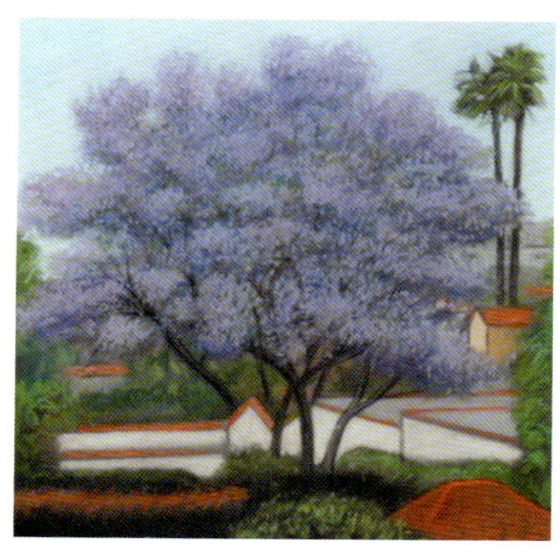

The Jacaranda Tree (detail); full image on page 192.

New Freedom in Aron's Art

Aron's decision to remember led to changes to his art. In 2005 he painted a view off his balcony in *The Jacaranda Tree*. Every city has its distinct smells, plants and architecture. In this painting he captures the quintessential qualities of his adopted home: the brilliant jacaranda tree in full bloom, towering over the familiar Spanish stucco walls and red-tiled roofs, surrounded by neatly trimmed hedges. Aron reaffirms his connection to nature and celebrates its power and beauty. The balance expressed in the landscape of homes, greenery and sky reflects a gentle harmony he has created in himself. Nature embraces those who notice.

In *Men Playing Cards in Roxbury Park* (2004), Aron returned to his neighborhood park to paint men gathered in the afternoon sun, playing cards. This drawing feels effortless. Once again he outlines the men in black. He uses a rich field of lime green grass and places a yellow hat on the head of the center card player. While the men are concentrating on their cards to decide their next play, they are comfortably dressed, enjoying each other's company. Aron celebrates this gathering of older men, playing together, participating in life.

This painting shows Aron's evolution. There is a different quality of light in this pastel compared with his earlier paintings of men playing games together. These men are relaxed, not brooding. Nor are they penetrating the meaning of life. They are simply living it.

Since 2005 Aron has painted a series of small pastels from his balcony that capture downtown Los Angeles at dawn and midday. He continues to explore the power, mystery and beauty in the cycles of day and night.

In *Morning Light in L.A.* Aron captures the moment when night turns to day. The rising sun shines a warm, pale lavender–peach light, gently illuminating the silhouette of the city's downtown buildings. Much in the foreground is still in darkness, although the sun's rays begin to reach the top of nearby trees and building roofs.

In *L.A. in Late Morning* he paints his view with a strong lavender-blue sky and white-blue clouds. He captures the details in the tiled roof and uses distinct strokes to define the trees. The downtown buildings seem distant, apart from this verdant land. There is a suggestion of mystery, one cannot see into all the spaces, even though it is daytime.

There is a mystical quality in *Morning Light* and a crisp depth in *L.A. in Late Morning*. Intuitively, Aron is playing with the dance of light and dark, the seen and unseen, the knowable and the unknown. In his ninth decade he understands that life is a mystery which can never be fully explained or understood; but it may be lived, one day at a time, with a deep connection to the beauty of mother earth.

Morning Light in L.A. (2007), pastel on paper, 11 × 15½ in.

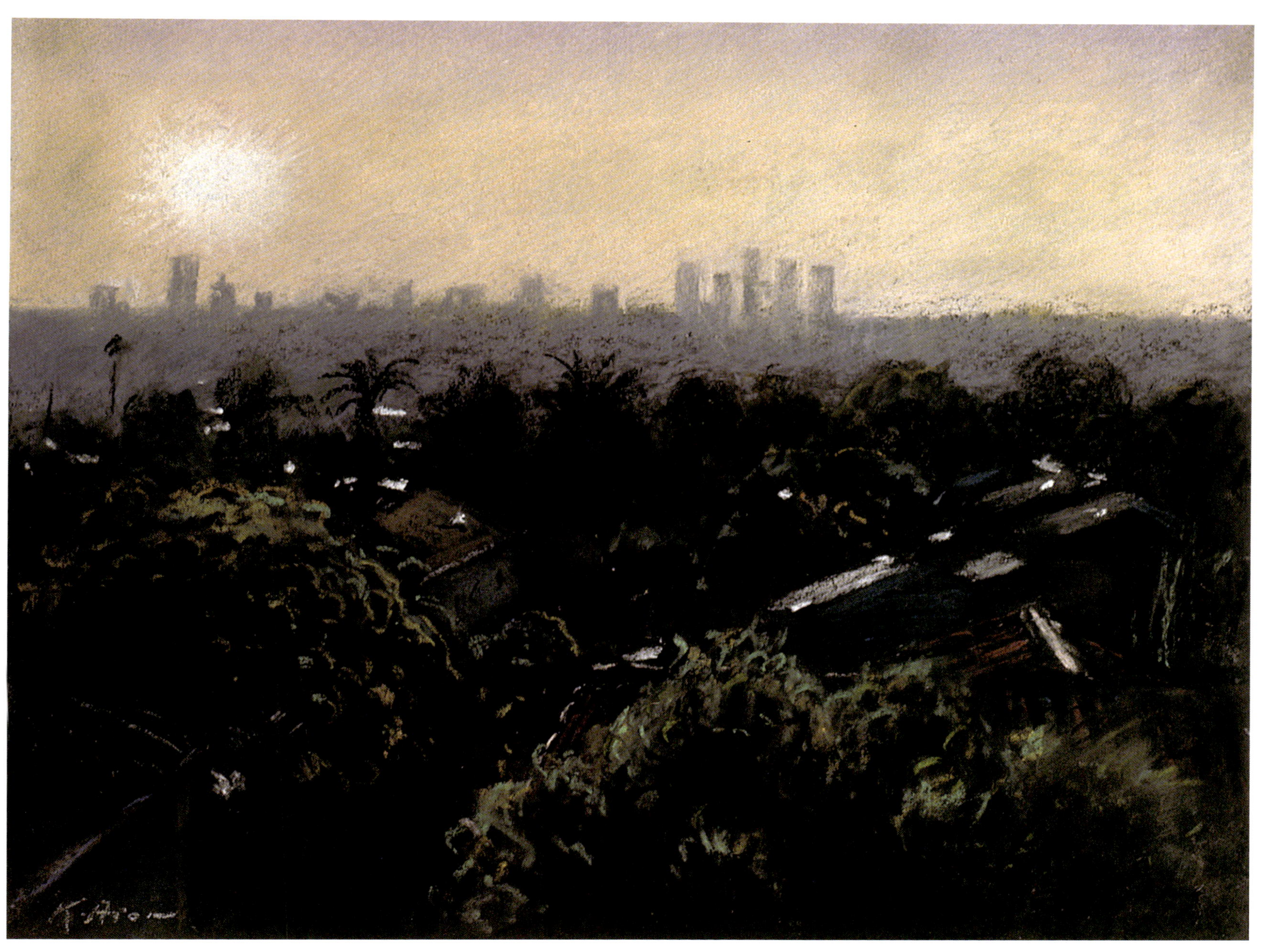

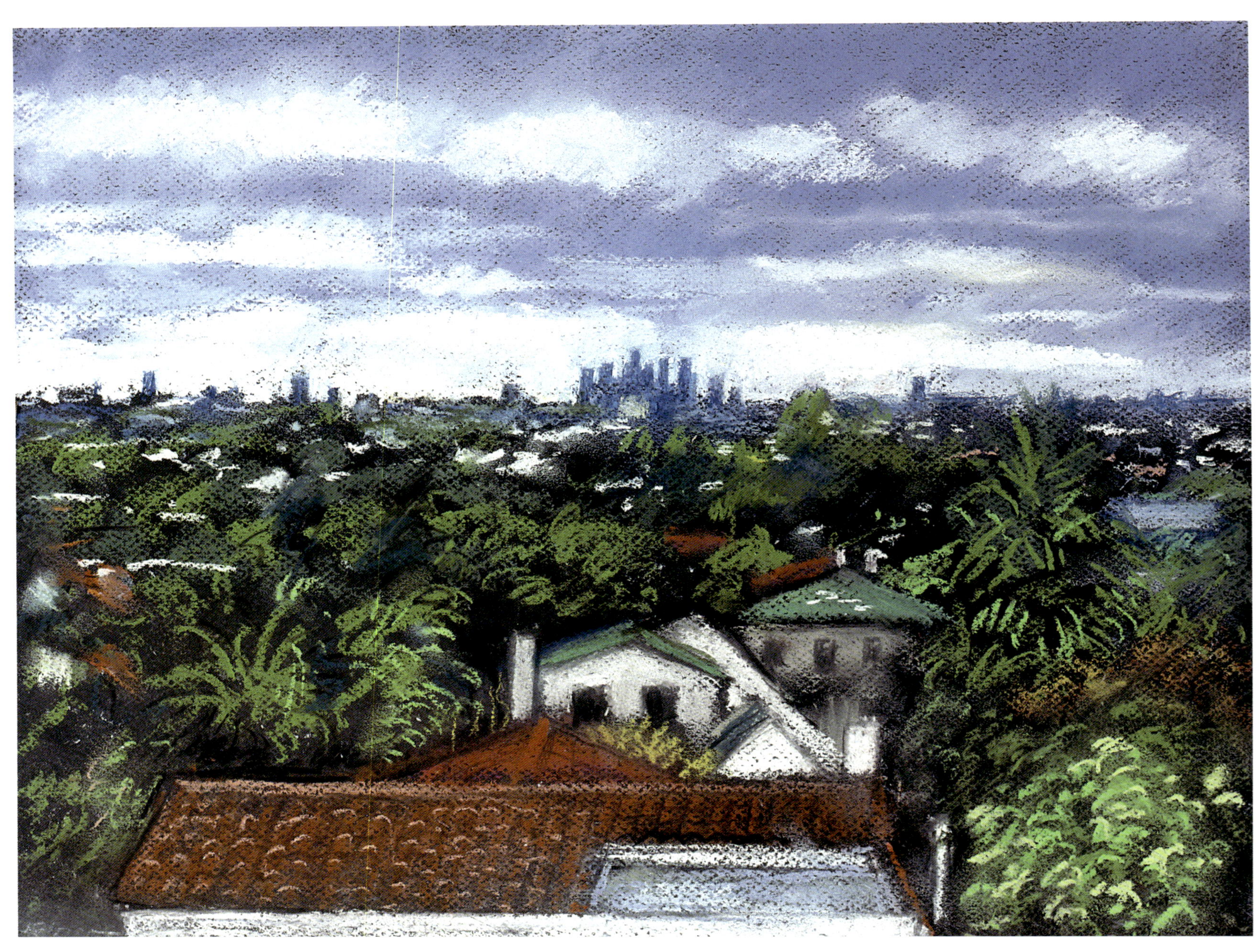

L.A. in Late Morning (2007), pastel on paper, 12 × 15½ in.

Into the Sunlight

For Aron the benefits of telling his story have been incalculable. He confronted the fear, fury and evil he experienced decades before. He married one more time. He recaptured freedom and joy in his painting. Then one day he made another big decision that symbolizes his new freedom. For the first time, he allowed some of his Holocaust paintings to be exhibited publicly in a one-man show.

Aron's Holocaust decision equating invisibility with life shaped his career in powerful ways. Successful as an artist, he nonetheless chose to keep his circle small. He passed up multiple opportunities to show in cities such as New York, Washington, D.C., Munich and Vienna. He never promoted himself. He had many successful exhibitions and gallery shows but he never sought a formal agent to promote and market his art. He also turned down opportunities to show his Holocaust paintings in group shows. He was not ready.

Mother and Child (detail); full image on page 85.

With the writing of this book, Aron made a different choice when asked. An art consultant, Richard Almada, approached him about a solo exhibit for the opening of the new Tolerance Education Center, founded by a Holocaust survivor, Earl Greif, in Rancho Mirage in California's Coachella Valley. The center wanted to honor Aron and showcase his masterpiece *Mother and Child*, along with eleven other pastels and oils. After keeping *Mother and Child* in his studio for almost sixty years, he decided to exhibit it.

Mother and Child's journey was not complete. After being on exhibit in the Tolerance Education Center for nine months in 2010, it moved back to Los Angeles to hang permanently in the stunning new building of the Los Angeles Museum of the Holocaust in Pan Pacific Park. Just inside the entrance the pastel hangs on a tall wall, seeming to have been painted precisely for that location. It shares the same palette as the wall, and the angles in the painting reflect those in the space. Aron joined other Holocaust survivors at the October 2010 opening of the new museum building. He was deeply moved to see it in its new home. He always said that if he ever let go of the painting, it would have to hang in a perfect place. So it does.

His decision to show this painting in the world is a direct result of his telling his story. He no longer needs to hold everything tightly. He can let things go. Aron is living with a new freedom.

Agents of Change

Much can be learned from Aron's personal alchemy. He entered the world with invaluable gifts. His parents' love and support of his talent provided a firm foundation. His art gave him passion and purpose in life: he was determined to paint and to see the world. He was blessed with a keen intelligence, a curious mind and solid integrity. He carried a powerful voice of survival within.

Beginning with these gifts, Aron made significant choices. To survive in the camps, he risked his life by drawing guards to get an extra piece of bread. He made split-second decisions that kept him alive time and time again. He never gave up hope. And yes, he learned to be invisible while he watched the guards intently.

Upon liberation, he escaped the Russians and accepted the chance opportunity to study at the Academy of Fine Arts in Vienna. He decided to leave Europe, marry Trude Schneider and seek a new life together in Los Angeles. His new home was significant in his transformation. Full of sunshine and warmth, Los Angeles is the antithesis of the cold, icy climate in Riga where he grew up. Los Angeles is an open society with few boundaries or confining walls. It is fertile ground for artists, and it has been a sanctuary where Aron could explore the loss of his innocence and process the evil he had experienced.

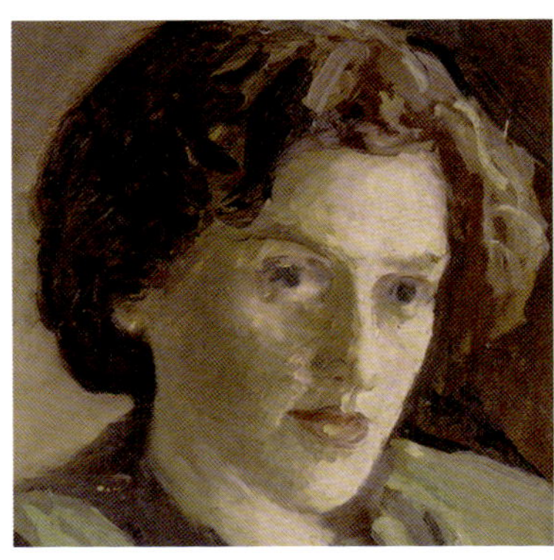

Portrait of Gertrude Schneider (detail); full image on page 65.

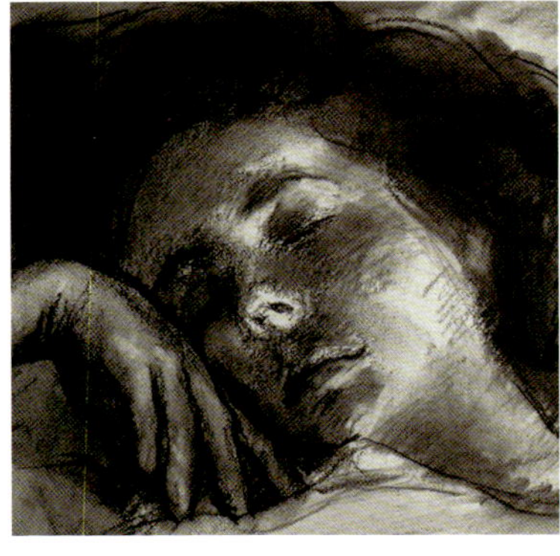

Suzanne (detail); full image on page 120.

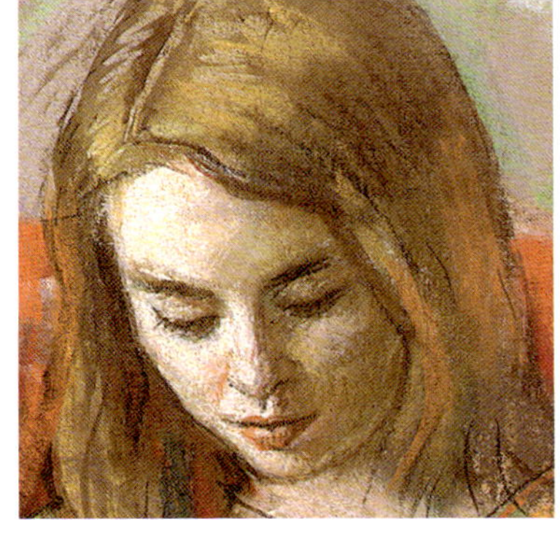

Tanis Reading (detail); full image on page 168.

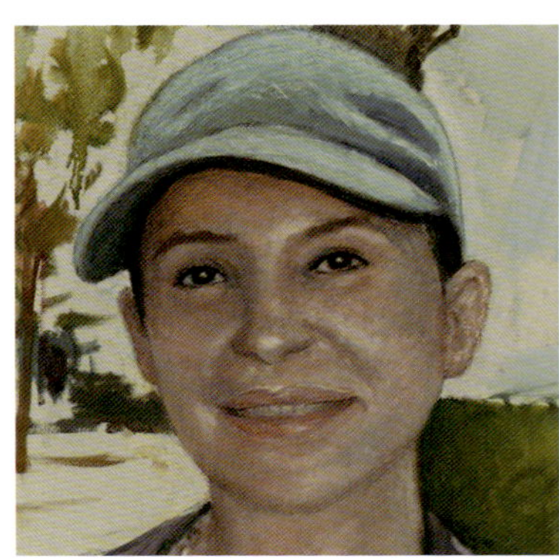

Portrait of Miriam (detail); full image on page 205.

Throughout his career Aron chose independence and freedom to paint as he wished. Settled in a job in Los Angeles, when offered a raise Aron chose to quit and paint full time. He told his wife he would earn money selling his paintings, and he did. Following a successful gallery show, he consistently resisted the owner's call to paint the same material for the next show.

Nature sustained him. As his son David noticed, Aron maintains a special conversation with nature. It has nourished him his whole life and remains a mirror of Aron's interior landscape.

A charming man, Aron has enjoyed a circle of interesting friends. Conversant about politics and world events, he meets people easily. He has an upbeat attitude about life and an obvious passion for painting. His friends enjoy his art and his company.

His marriages have been a critical part of his transformation as well. Trude shared his loss of family, appreciated his integrity and artistic talent and accompanied him to America to create a new life. Suzanne saw a debonair, artistic giant who stood up to her father. She gave him love and a human touch. Tanis enjoyed their intellectual repartee and gave Aron his son, David. Today Miriam offers him companionship and the hope of happiness. Each has provided human connection.

Aron also made a choice not to be bitter. Nietzsche wrote, "Whoever fights monsters should see to it that in the process he does not become a monster." There has never been any danger that Aron would become an evil man. He has a fundamental goodness and powerful integrity. Nonetheless, hatred and rage are natural human responses to what happened to him. Further, when a person experiences evil, the body absorbs and encapsulates it to prevent damaging oneself or others. Although buried, the energies of hatred, rage and evil are present and take up space in the body. Over the years Aron metabolized this evil as he painted his feelings on canvas. Deciding to tell his story allows him to release whatever residual rage, hatred and evil lie unconsciously in his body. This process lightens his body and frees him to choose love, safety or trust as replacements.

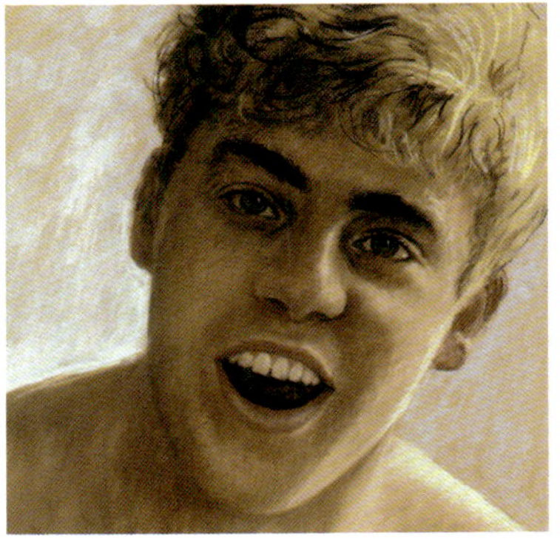

David as a Teenager (detail); full image on page 180.

The Meaning of Kalman Aron's Life

As I have written this book, I have been asked many times, "How is this different from other Holocaust histories?" I responded, "This is not only a Holocaust memoir." The Holocaust was the defining crucible that forged Kalman Aron's life and influenced his art. But this book is about how he responded to the Holocaust and recaptured the light, texture and spirit of his own life, one painting at a time. His is a universal story of human courage and personal alchemy that applies to people everywhere. Everyone suffers trauma, loss and betrayal. The circumstances and degree differ from person to person, but no one escapes. Further, the healing process is fundamentally the same for all, whether a person was abused as a child, maimed in a war or witnessed genocide.

I know this from my own experience. I was abused as a child, then made my way as an adult until I could no longer ignore the old facts nor contain the memory. I began a healing journey to become aware. Like Kalman, I had to remember what happened and explore the sorrow, rage and loss. Then I became free to release vows and beliefs I had adopted at the time of trauma and walk out of the prison I had created to survive.

Because Kalman suffered in the extreme, much can be learned from his journey. His choices illustrate the fruits of remembering, and his body of art provides a visual map of the journey from darkness to light. It is a companion for anyone who chooses to remember and heal. There are no shortcuts here. We accompany him through each stage of his personal alchemy.

Kalman's example is also an invitation. Life creates for all of us circumstances that trigger our painful history. If we choose not to remember, life will continue to present situations that resonate the past, that ask us to remember. Left unconscious, traumatic memories determine our behavior in spite of our conscious desire to change. Hence unresolved trauma hobbles us, weighs us down. But we always have a choice. We may ignore the past, or we may remember, integrate and heal. When we choose to make the journey through trauma to acceptance—as Aron has done—we light the way for each other.

We are never alone on this journey. Kalman shared some of what happened with his family and friends. Now he is relating his whole story to a wider audience with this book. It is critical to have a companion on a journey back in time, whether it is a friend, spiritual counselor, religious adviser, or psychological therapist. As we recall the trauma with a trusted companion, it begins to lose its power, and a sense of safety develops. This process takes time, sometimes a lifetime. It is always accompanied by grace and magic.

Living Alchemy: A Touch of Grace

Grace may be a strange word to use in referring to this man. I have never discussed it with him, but I see it throughout his life. One does not have to be religious to experience grace. It comes in moments of magic to help us manifest our desires and dreams. It is a state of being. Grace was present in his boyhood home. He found it in the camps when he got quiet so no one would see him. It was present as he chose art school in Vienna, a new life in Los Angeles. It is present in the humility he learned in the camps. It is the state he occupies when he paints. In a mysterious way, grace has touched his life and helped him walk with courage and freedom upon this earth in the light of the sun.

What a gift, his life. What a revelation of truth and beauty, his art.

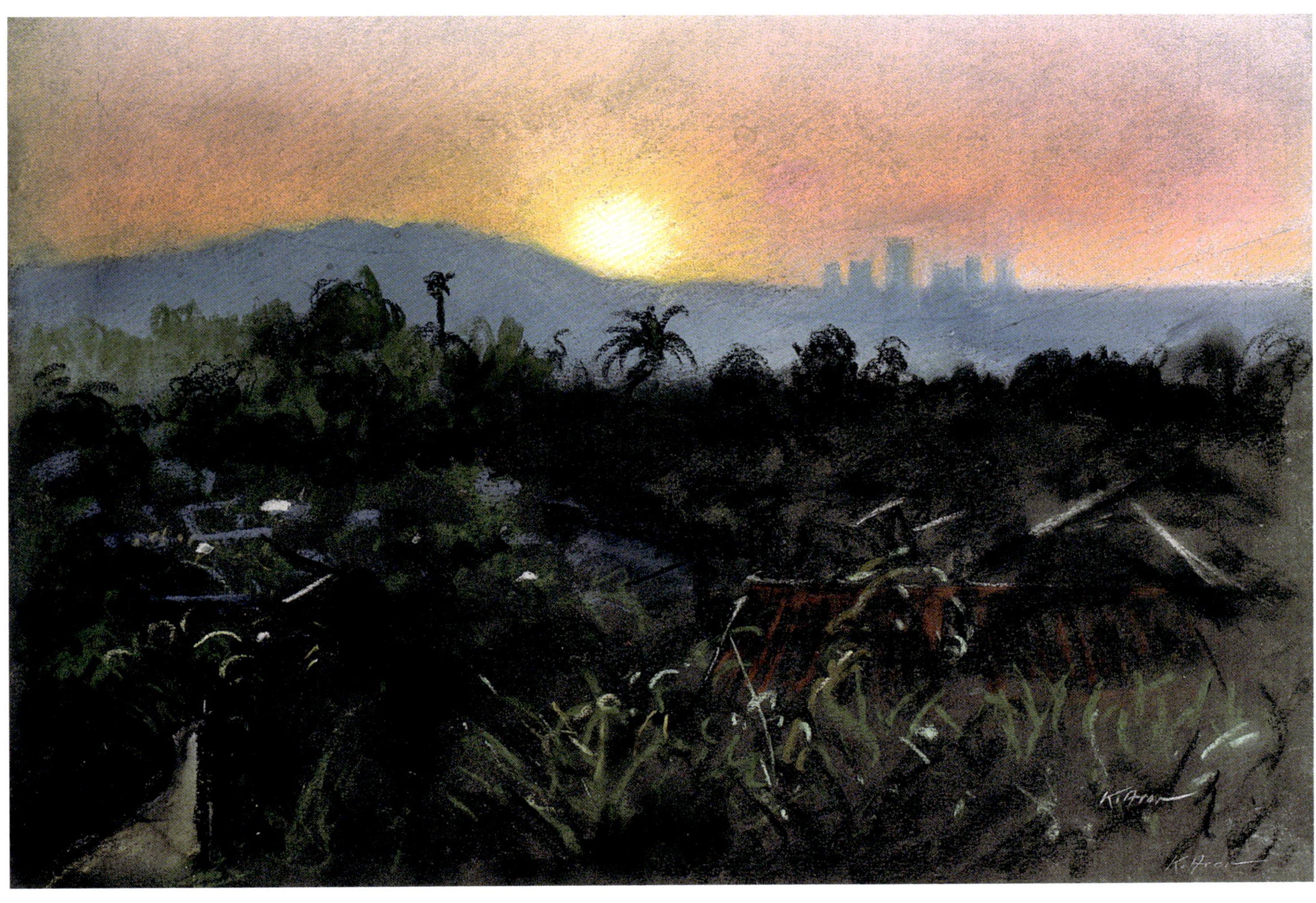

Morning Light (2007), pastel on paper, 12 × 16 in.

Acknowledgments

Writing *Into the Light: The Healing Art of Kalman Aron* has been an extraordinary privilege. I thank Kalman for asking me to write his story and for trusting me to relate his life within a larger narrative of healing. I thank him for cooperating fully in our endless conversations; for sharing his art, memorabilia and papers; and for introducing me to his circle.

With joy and appreciation, I thank Kalman's family and friends for their generous support and many contributions of memories and insights: his wife, Miriam Sandoval; his son, David Aron; his former wives, Trude Shiner and Tanis Furst; and his friend and patron, Lou Lenart. I also honor his parents, Sonia and Chaim Aron, and his brother, Henech Aron.

The Shoah Foundation is justly celebrated for recording, collecting and preserving information about the Nazi Holocaust through interviews with survivors and witnesses. I gratefully acknowledge the USC Shoah Foundation Institute for Visual History and Education, at University of Southern California, for allowing me to use the testimony of interviewee Kalman Aron.

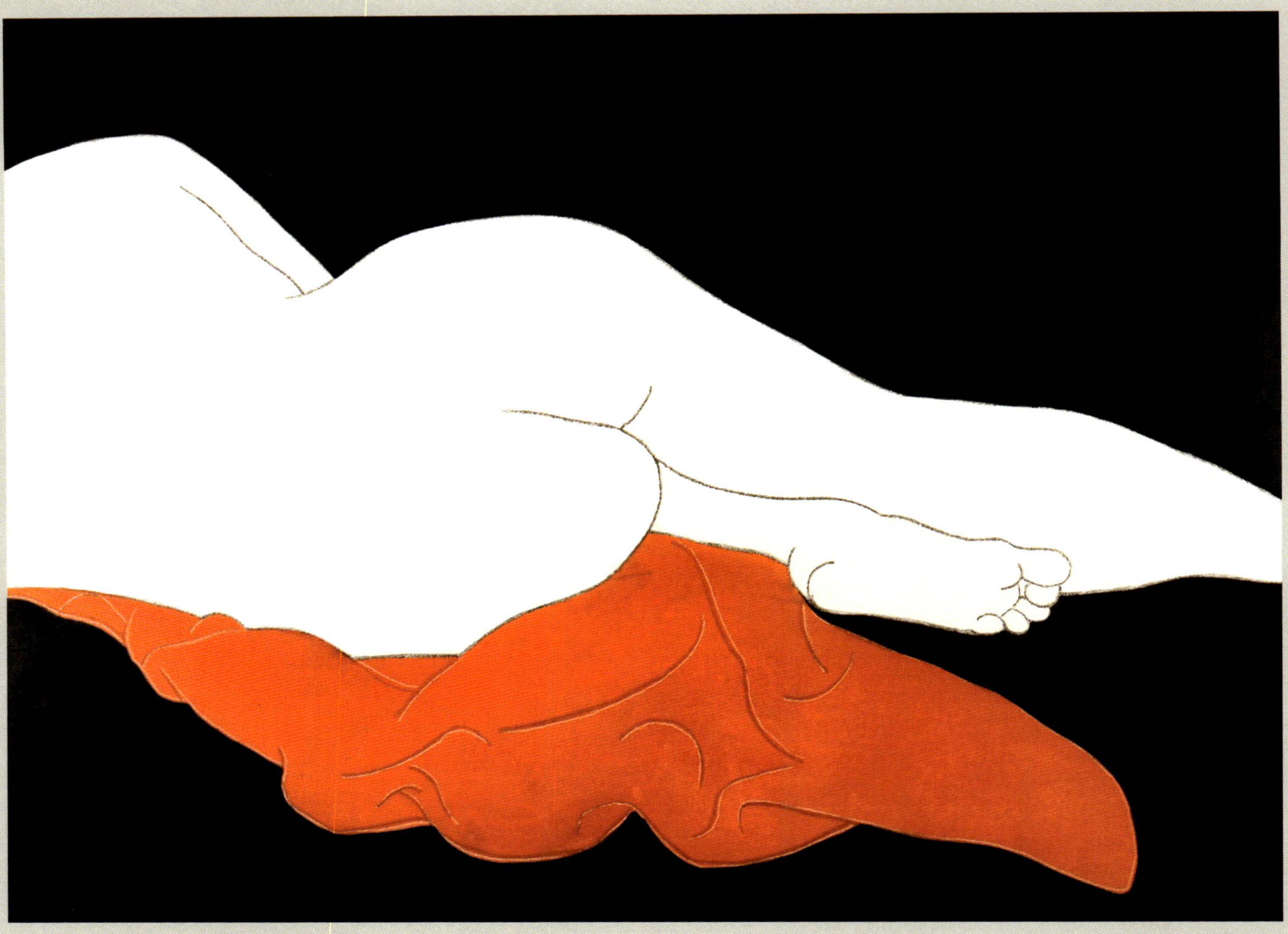

Nude with Red Drape (late 1960s), oil on canvas, 36 × 48 in.

To reiterate this volume's dedication, I thank my husband of forty-two years, John Benjamin Magee, for his generous love and support. He has given me the freedom to pursue my dreams, and he has shown great patience and understanding during the near-decade that this project has been a focal point of my life.

This book would not have been written but for my parents, Richard and Marichu Beilby, and their first daughter, Nonnie, whose brief life and jet-black eyes brought a unique artist into our home a lifetime ago. I thank my sister, Elena, and her husband, Bill Hermanson, for their unflagging interest, moral support and good advice. I thank my nephew, Eric Hermanson, for his help with video, recording and technical matters.

My editor and publisher Philip Kopper has played a monumental role. Starting with my original manuscript, he wisely commented, cautioned and cajoled, encouraging me to reshape the story and present it more clearly, poetically and forcefully. He engaged the brilliant graphic designer Robert Wiser to develop a sensitive and dynamic visual plan which integrated art and narrative into this beautiful volume. The copyediting by Duke Johns was meticulous. I thank you—bookmakers all—for your dynamic and sensitive work. I also thank Anne Bei of Hard Press Editions, Dan Farrell of Hudson Hills Press, and their associates Liz Riviere and Kit Latham.

I especially thank two dear friends, the media producers Michal Carr and Al Hillmann, for their technical assistance, guidance and advice from the very start of this project. I further thank their colleague, Tom Bell, who advised me about the interview process and handled all my video and audio recordings. Finally, I thank those who transcribed the interview recordings: Michelle Wright, Patti Pancoe, Ingeborg Wagner Kolodney and Michael Reyz.

I am also deeply grateful to my friend photographer-author Stephen R. Brown and his assistant Jessica Warren for making the first version of the book and its website and for ongoing helpful and practical advice. I thank five masters of a special art—record/archival photography—for making photographs of Kalman Aron's paintings: Dub Rogers, Lindsay George, Kate Carr, Brandon Webster and Gregory R. Staley. And I thank Athena Angelos for her excellent archival photo research.

I have had the privilege of meeting five other Latvian Holocaust survivors, three in Latvia—Marger Vestermanis, Aleksandrs Bergmanis and Abrams "Max" Kit—and two in America, Jack Ratz and Yakob Basner. Each took time to share their stories and answer my many questions. I honor and thank each of you.

In doing the research for this book, I traveled widely in Europe and Israel, and I encountered many people who provided variously nuggets of information, logistical help, timely introductions and other guidance. In this regard, I am grateful to the individuals I met: in Latvia, my wonderful guide Elena Spungina and her husband, Boris Spungin, Kalman Freizus, Edith Bloch, Erik Prokopovich, Daiga Freimute, Gita Umanoska and Aina Antane; in Germany, Daniel Gaede, Lothar Czossek, Ronald Hirte, Claudia Schumann and my dear friend, Natalie Wasserman; in the Czech Republic, Eva Medricka and Milan Adamovsky; in Sweden, Johan Wallin, Anna Furst and her mother; in Poland, Michal Rucki, Jerzy Malenczyk .and Waclaw Wojciechowski; and in Israel, Yoav and Edna Gal, Liron Peleg Hadomi, Ido Heruty, Noha Khatieb, Anat Meiri, John L. Peterson, and Niv Goldberg and Jacqueline Benatar at Yad Vashem.

I thank Dr. Andrew Ezergailis, the retired Professor of History at Ithaca College, for his generosity in answering all of my questions. His definitive work, *The Holocaust in Latvia: 1941–1944*, was invaluable in giving me the broad context and detailed understanding of Nazi actions throughout the war.

In California, I thank my dear friends Lynn Schenk and C. Hugh Friedman for their inspiring and sustaining help. I thank former Governor Gray Davis for his help in moving forward. I thank the leaders of the Los Angeles Museum of the Holocaust (LAMH)—founder Jona Goldrich, Chairman Randy Schoenberg and Executive Director Mark Rothman—for giving Kalman's *Mother and Child* its permanent home and for establishing the Kalman Aron Project. Others who have supported the project include: the Stanley and Joyce Black Foundation, Beverly and William McKee, Lynne and William Nelson, Marlene and Marshall Grossman, Vivienne and Nathan Hochman, Ellen and Barry Direnfeld, Stacey and Michael Sherman, Peter and Diane Gray. I thank Rabbi Marvin Heir and Rabbi Meyer H. May, respectively the dean and executive director of the Simon Wiesenthal Center and the Museum of Tolerance in Los Angeles.

At the US Holocaust Memorial Museum in Washington, DC, I thank the director Sara J. Bloomfield, Michael Abramowitz and Michlean Amir. I thank Judah Gribetz, a trustee of the Museum of Jewish Heritage in New York City.

I am grateful for all I have learned from my spiritual teachers: Gina Simpson, Master Chang, De Fano, Raymon Grace, my daughter Elizabeth Perez, and my granddaughter Natalia Semenova.

In addition, for numerous acts, ideas, prods and inspirations too varied to mention, I also thank: Joan Abrahamson, Richard Almada, Lisa Bartolomei, Shannon Best, Allida Black, Sharon Bronte, Susie Tompkins Buell, Marvin Chester, Carole A. Crumley, Keith Fleer, Chris Furst, Orly Halevy, Eric Herzl, Nancy Jacobson, Marcia Josephy, Cheryl Kane, Mary Kopper, Jay Lavely, Ann Lewis, Ricki Lieberman, Ann McClellan, Lissa Muscatine, Susan Ness, Ilse Nusbaum, Mary Patsel, Leila Perez, George (Robbie) S. Robinson, Ph.D, Jane Scott, Claire Simmons, Alan Singer, Ann Stock, Richard S. Taffet, Cynthia Wilcox, and George S. Wills.

In listing those who have helped I regret any omissions as I hasten to meet my last manuscript deadline before publication.

Finally, I thank the spirit of the book for emerging, and I wish it well on its journey into the world. May it help heal those who have suffered and in so doing free their children.

Washington, DC

Index of Art

Neighbor Seated (1951–52), oil on board, 22 × 28 in., p. 83

Night Club (1957), compressed charcoal, 22 × 17 in., p. 91

Night Lights of L.A. (1980s), pastel on paper, 21 × 29 in., p. 98

Non-Objective I (2007), acrylic on paper, 14 × 10½ in., p. 107 (left)

Non-Objective II (2009), oil on board, 15 × 13 in., p. 107 (right)

Non-Objective III (2010), pastel and black ink, 10½ × 14 in., p. 109 (bottom)

Nude with Red Drape (late 1960s), oil on canvas, 36 × 48 in., p. 216

Oak Tree in the Poconos (1970s), pastel on paper, 22 × 30 in., p. 22 (bottom)

Observation in Echo Park (1970s), oil on canvas, 36 × 48 in., p. 156 (bottom)

Old House on Bunker Hill (1950s), charcoal on paper, 19¼ × 25½, p. 76

Orange Trees (early 1990s), acrylic on paper, 10½ × 14 in., p. 191

Portrait of Elena (1951), pastel on paper, 21 × 17½ in., p. 16

Portrait of Elizabeth (1987), pastel on paper, 23 × 19¼ in., p. 139

Portrait of Eric (1977), pastel on paper, 25¾ × 20 in., p. 140

Portrait of Gertrude Schneider (1949), oil, 29½ × 24 in., p. 65

Portrait of Henry Miller (late 1960s), oil on canvas, 40 × 36 in., p. 129

Portrait of Jaffa (1966), pastel on paper, 46½ × 34½ in., p. 171

Portrait of Laura (1977), pastel on paper, 25¾ × 20 in., p. 141

Portrait of Maestro André Previn (1988), pastel on paper, 48 × 36 in., p. 131

Portrait of Miriam (2006), oil on canvas, 40 × 30 in., p. 205

Portrait of Mr. Bachrach (1965), pastel on paper, 38 × 28 in., p. 130

Portrait of Nonnie (1951), pastel on paper, 16 × 13 in., p. 12

Portrait of President Ronald Reagan (1980), pastel on paper, p. 126

Portrait of Susan (1951), pastel on paper, 21 × 17½ in., p. 15

Profile of David (1971), charcoal on paper, 14 × 10¾ in., p. 182

Profile of Elizabeth (1987), pastel on paper, 22 × 17½ in., p. 17

Profiles (late 1960s), black ink on paper, 11 × 14 in., p. 25

Rabbi Jacob Sonderling (late 1950s–early 1960s), charcoal on paper, 40 × 30 in., p. 93

Reagan Sketch (1980), pastel on paper, 14 × 12 in, p. 125

Rooftops Off My Balcony (1980s), pastel on paper, 12½ × 29½ in., p. 6

Searching for Answers (1950), compressed charcoal, 8 × 15½ in., p. 84 (top)

Self-Portrait (1954), charcoal pencil, 31 × 21 in., p. 89

Self-Portrait (mid 1960s), sepia stick on white paper, 24 × 18 in., p. 2

Self-Portrait (1967), oil on canvas, 48 × 36 in., p. 136

Self-Portrait (late 1960s–early 1970s), ink on paper, 14 × 11 in., p. 220

Self-Portrait (1994), charcoal on foam core, 40 × 30 in., p. 18

Silver Lake (1952), compressed charcoal on paper, 18 × 24 in., p. 80

Sketch for Mother and Child (1951), oil on paper, 21 × 12 in., p. 84 (bottom)

Sleeping Next to the Rock (1951), gouache on paper, 3½ × 5 in., p. 86 (bottom)

Small Boat in the San Jacinto Mountains (1990), pastel on paper, 30 × 21½ in., p. 99

Study of a Woman (1975), oil on canvas, 48 × 36 in., p. 148

Suzanne (1962), charcoal on paper, 21 × 29½ in., p. 120

Suzanne Reading (1963), charcoal pencil, 14 × 10½ in., p. 150

Tanis Reading (1968), pastel on paper, 40 × 30 in., p. 168

The Thinker (early 1970s), oil on paper, 13½ × 10½ in., p. 160

Three Children Playing (late 1950s), pastel on paper, 20¾ × 29 in., p. 74

Tractor in a Field (1970s), pastel on paper, 21½ × 29½ in., p. 22 (top)

Trees I (2003), acrylic on paper, 18 × 23½ in., p. 108

Two Children (1952), ink on paper, 8½ × 4½ in., p. 36

Two Men Seated (early 1970s), oil on paper, 10½ × 13½ in., p. 159

View of Laguna Cove (1980s), oil on canvas, 36 × 24 in., p. 66

White Flowers (2000s), acrylic on paper, 14 × 11 in., p. 106 (left)

Winter in Uppsala (mid 1970s), oil on canvas, 36 × 48 in., p. 94

Woman in Black (early 1980s), oil on canvas, 30 × 40 in., p. 167

Woman in Blue (1970s or 80s), oil on paper, 14 × 11 in., p. 122

Woman in Repose (early 1980s), oil on canvas, 40 × 36 in., p. 166

Woman Looking Out the Window (1970s), oil on projection screen, 54 × 34 in., p. 151

Woman Seated (1959), charcoal pencil, 40 × 30 in., p. 141

Young Woman (1980s), oil on canvas, 48 × 24 in., p. 177

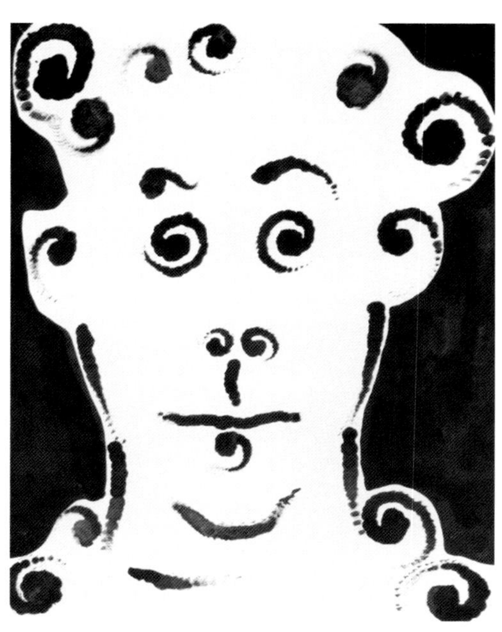

INTO THE LIGHT: THE HEALING ART OF KALMAN ARON was designed by Robert L. Wiser in Silver Spring, Maryland. The book is composed in *Chronicle* and *Verlag*, both created by the Hoefler & Frere-Jones digital type foundry in New York. *Chronicle* is a transitional serif type face, inspired by the work of Scottish type-founders Alexander Wilson and William Miller of the eighteenth century. Scotch-style typefaces have been popular among book printers in the United States, beginning with the types of Binny & Ronaldson in 1796 and continuing with W. A. Dwiggins's *Caledonia* and Matthew Carter's *Miller* in the twentieth century. *Verlag* is a modernist sans-serif type face, inspired by the Art Deco designs of architect Frank Lloyd Wright for the Guggenheim Museum in New York in the late 1950s. It shares an affinity for rationalist geometric design with Paul Renner's *Futura* of 1929 and R. Hunter Middleton's *Tempo* of 1930.